VICTIMOLOGY

Legal, Psychological, and Social Perspectives

Second Edition

Harvey Wallace

California State University, Fresno

PEARSON

Boston • New York • San Francisco
Mexico City • Montreal • Toronto • London • Madrid • Munich • Paris
Hong Kong • Singapore • Tokyo • Cape Town • Sydney

Series Editor: Dave Repetto
Series Editorial Assistant: Jack Cashman
Senior Marketing Manager: Kelly May
Production Editor: Won McIntosh
Editorial Production Service: Stratford
Composition Buyer: Linda Cox
Manufacturing Buyer: Megan Cochran
Cover Administrator: Joel Gendron

For related titles and support materials, visit our online catalog at www.ablongman.com.

Between the time website information is gathered and then published, it is not unusual for some sites to have closed. Also, the transcription of URLs can result in typographical errors. The publisher would appreciate notification where these errors occur so that they may be corrected in subsequent editions.

Library of Congress Cataloging-in-Publication Data

Wallace, Harvey.
    Victimology: legal, psychological, and social perspectives/Harvey Wallace.—2nd ed.
       p. cm.
    Includes index.
    ISBN 0-205-48625-8 (alk. paper)
  1. Victims of crimes—United States.   2. Victims of crimes—Legal status, laws, etc.—United States.   3. Criminal justice, Administration of—United States.   I. Title.
HV6250.3.U5W35 2006
362.880973—dc22

                                                                                2006031159

Printed in the United States of America

10 9 8 7 6 5 4 3 2   11 10 09 08 07

In Memoriam Randa F. Wallace, my partner and wife 1946–2003

CONTENTS

Responses to Victimization

Special Types of Victims

Victims' Rights

PREFACE

The study of victimology is in its infancy. However, the plight of victims of crime has been discussed for centuries. In our early history, victims were an integral part of the criminal process. We then moved away from that model and the state became the representative of the victim. Finally, we are again moving toward acknowledging the rights of victims of crime. This shift has caused scholars to reexamine the victim–offender relationship in more detail.

Victimology as a discipline is an outgrowth of law, sociology, psychology, and criminology and as such has its distractors as well as its advocates. It will continue to grow and take on more substance with the passage of years. Any attempt to list those topics that are critical to the study of victimology is bound to generate controversy. Most texts on the market today include sections dealing with family violence issues. That may be because we have more information regarding the victim–offender interaction in these areas or because many scholars believe these are critical issues in the study of victimology. I have included a number of these same topics in this text. I drew upon my previous text, *Family Violence: Legal, Medical, and Social Perspectives,* as a source of information. Based on comments from professors using that text, I updated and changed the material when appropriate to reflect the victim's perspective.

I have also attempted to take a global perspective on the study of victimology and have divided the text into four major areas: the Introduction section includes the traditional theories regarding victimology, the measurement of crime, and both the civil and criminal processes. I included the civil process because it is an important aspect of the victim–offender interaction. I have also included a brief discussion of the juvenile system, because more attention is being focused on youth violence. The second section, Responses to Victimization, includes two relatively new topics: the consequences of victimization and empowering victims. Several excellent texts already deal with the physical and mental consequences of crime; however, very few discuss the financial impact of crime. Chapter 6, "Empowering Victims," deals with issues that confront victim services providers as well as victims who are trying to change the system. The third section, Special Types of Victims, discusses traditional subjects such as homicide victims and family violence victims, and includes a discussion of special victims such as the disabled, those subjected to hate crimes, and gay and lesbian victims. The final section, Victims' Rights, includes civil remedies available to victims of crime.

This is not to say that I have covered all these topics adequately. I have attempted to present an overview of some complex and controversial subjects and to supply the reader with resources in the form of references and reading that allow for more in-depth study and research of these areas. Omission of some topics, such as robbery, burglary, kidnapping, and others, does not mean they are unimportant. Victims of these crimes would argue that they have suffered just as much as other victims. Space limitations, however, preclude discussion of every crime and its implications for victims. The crimes that are discussed, along with the broader topics such as the consequences of victimization and victims' rights, can be generalized to varying degrees to apply to all victims.

Just as we are becoming more interested in the study of family violence, so are increasingly more universities offering classes on victim issues. These classes will become more popular as students, the general public, and the various professionals who deal with victims become aware of their availability. It is a young discipline that continues to grow, and it is exciting to be present to watch that growth.

I would like to express my appreciation to a number of individuals for their support, guidance, and advice during the time it has taken to complete this project. First and foremost, I would like to thank my editor, Karen Hanson, executive editor at Allyn & Bacon, who provided support for this project. I would also like to thank Donna Simons of Allyn & Bacon and Carol Lallier, who assisted in the preparation and copyediting of the manuscript. Christine Edmunds, Anne Seymour, Ellen Alexander, Skip Sigmon, Trudy Gregorie, Janice Lord, Dan Eddy, Dean G. Kilpatrick, Ph.D., Jane Burnley, Ph.D., and other friends associated with various victim organizations provided their advice and guidance regarding a number of issues. Mario Gaboury, University of New Haven, and Steve Walker, Kansas Community College provided me with invaluable suggestions and corrections that helped improve this text. Finally, I express appreciation to my family for their support during this time.

This revision has taken more time and effort than I originally envisioned. My editors at Allyn & Bacon have been pillars of support in allowing me the leeway to make modifications and have granted me a number of extensions to finish this product. I am eternally grateful to David Repetto and Jennifer Jacobsen.

So many friends, colleagues, and students have helped me with this revision, I cannot begin to name them all. Some have been there to offer words of encouragement and support: Tom Dull, Otto Schweizer, and Arthur Wint are those good friends. Many professionals, colleagues, and academics have offered advice or suggested changes that have resulted in a better product: Thomas Underwood for his suggestions about discussing more theories and Steve Walker for his update on the history of victimology are just two of those professionals. Of special note is John Dussich, who made substantial suggestions regarding the text. John went through every page and updated or corrected the first edition. I have incorporated many of these changes into this edition. Most importantly, there have been a number of students who have helped me in a variety of ways. Many graduate students, including Lindsey Fausett and Stephanie Fratto, were of great assistance in gathering various research materials for this text. Shiho Yamamoto, another graduate student, was also of invaluable assistance. She conducted much of the early research and was always there to assist in any manner. Finally, the many students who used this text in my classes and other classes across the nation have contributed to its content with suggestions, questions, and comments.

Harvey Wallace

1

INTRODUCTION AND HISTORY
OF VICTIMOLOGY

Chapter Outline

Learning Objectives

After reading this chapter, you should be able to:

- Distinguish between criminology and victimology
- Discuss how laws have affected victims
- Understand social forces that have impacted on the development of victimology
- Distinguish between the various victimology theories

Introduction

Although victimology as an academic discipline is a relatively new concept in the United States, the victims' movement continues to gain strength and momentum across the country.[1] States continue to enact laws giving victims of crime more opportunities to participate in the criminal justice system. Therefore, those individuals who work or interact with victims need to understand the legal, psychological, and social aspects of victimology.

Currently, few academic institutions offer courses of study in victimology. However, some universities offer courses that examine various aspects of the

---

FOCUS: Critical Dates in the History of Victimology

1750 B.C.—Code of Hammurabi adopted	1787—U.S. Constitution created
1200 B.C.—Mosaic Code established	1965—First victims' rights law passed
450 B.C.—Twelve Tables written	1976—Birth of NOVA
529 A.D. Roman Empire—Justinian Code drafted	1979—World Society of Victimology created
1066 A.D.—Norman Conquest of England	1985—United Nations Declaration
Middle Ages—Development of common law	1996—U.S. constitutional amendment proposed
1215—Magna Carta signed	

victim–offender relationship. These courses are typically found in sociology, criminal justice, social work, criminology, and psychology. Victimology is a discipline that combines theoretical research with practical experience. Although there is some interaction between these two groups or approaches, there is still much to learn from the combination.

Criminology is the science upon which victimology is founded. Criminology itself is a relatively new discipline and there are those who argue that it is not a true academic discipline or science, but rather a subspecialty of sociology.[2] However, there is an abundance of current literature and research to support the proposition that criminology is a science.

In 1947 Edwin H. Sutherland, an eminent criminologist, set forth the following definition:

> *Criminology is the body of knowledge regarding crime as a social phenomenon. It includes within its scope the process of making laws, of breaking laws. . . . The objective of criminology is the development of a body of general and verified principles and of other types of knowledge regarding this process of law, crime, treatment or prevention.*[3]

Criminology is the study of crime as a social phenomenon. Scholars have looked at several aspects of criminology and several have presented definitions of victimology which will be examined in detail later in this chapter. For purposes of clarity, however, the following definition of victimology is offered: *victimology* is the study of the victim, the offender, and society. This definition can encompass both the research or scientific aspects of the discipline as well as the practical aspects of providing services to victims of crime. This combined definition allows for a wide-ranging examination of various issues affecting victims of crime.

A complete and accurate understanding of the concepts inherent in victimology can only be attained by a review of the development of law, its history, and its philosophy. Modern criminal law is the result of an evolutionary process in the development of law that has attempted to deal with deviant behavior in society.

The Development of Laws

Primitive law was a system of rules used by preliterate societies to govern the tribe, clan, or other gathering of individuals. These rules or regulations represent the foundation upon which the modern legal system is built. Primitive laws usually contained three characteristics: (1) acts that injured others were considered private wrongs; (2) the injured party was entitled to take action against the wrongdoer; and (3) this action usually amounted to in-kind retaliation. These types of laws encouraged blood feuds and revenge as the preferred methods of making the victim whole.

As society continued to evolve, we learned the art of reading and writing. One result of this evolution was the development of written codes of conduct. An example of an early written code was the Code of Ur-Nammu, which dates back to the twenty-first century B.C. Many of these codes treated certain wrongs, such as theft or assault, as private wrongs with the injured party being the victim.[4]

The Code of Hammurabi

The Code of Hammurabi is considered one of the first known attempts to establish a written code of conduct. King Hammurabi ruled Babylon at approximately 2000 B.C. He was the sixth king of the First Dynasty of Babylonia and ruled for nearly fifty-five years. Babylon during that period was a commercial center for most of the known and civilized world. Because Babylon's fortune lay in trade and other business ventures, the Code of Hammurabi provided a basis for order and certainty. The code established rules regarding theft, sexual relationships, and interpersonal violence, and it was intended to replace blood feuds with a system sanctioned by the state.[5]

The Code of Hammurabi was divided into five sections:

1. A penal or code of laws
2. A manual of instruction for judges, police officers, and witnesses
3. A handbook of rights and duties of husbands, wives, and children
4. A set of regulations establishing wages and prices
5. A code of ethics for merchants, doctors, and officials[6]

The code established certain obligations and objectives for the citizens of Babylon to follow. These included:

1. An assertion of the power of the state. This was the beginning of state-administered punishment. Under the code, the blood feuds that had occurred previously between private citizens were barred.
2. Protection of the weaker from the stronger. Widows were to be protected from those who might exploit them, elder parents were to be protected from sons who would disown them, and lesser officials from higher ones.
3. Restoration of equity between the offender and the victim. The victim was to be made as whole as possible and in turn forgave vengeance against the offender.

Of noteworthy importance in the code was its concern for the rights of victims.[7] In reality, this code may have been the first "victim rights statute" in history. However, it was relatively short lived. Victims were again to be neglected in society's rush to punish the offender with the result that victims' rights would not resurface again until the mid-nineteenth century.[8]

Other Early Codes and Laws

The Mosaic Code, which is based on the assumption that God entered into a contract or covenant with the tribes of Israel, had a long-lasting impact on our collective consciousness. According to legend, Moses returned from a mountaintop carrying the Ten Commandments, which were inscribed on two stone tablets. These commandments subsequently became the foundation of Judeo-Christian morality.

The Mosaic Code also became the basis for many of the laws in our modern society: The prohibition against murder, perjury, and theft were all present in the Mosaic Code thousands of years before the founding of the United States.[9]

Another important milestone in the development of American law was early Roman law. Roman law was derived from the Twelve Tables, which were written around 450 B.C. These laws had existed for centuries as unwritten law and applied only to the ruling patrician class of citizens. A protest by the plebeian class who were the workers and artisans of Rome caused commerce to come to a standstill. These workers wanted the law to apply to all citizens of Rome.[10] As a result, the laws were inscribed on twelve wooden tablets and prominently displayed in the forum for all to see and follow. These tables were a collection of basic rules relating to the conduct of family and religious and economic life.

In the middle of the first century, England was conquered by Roman legions. Roman law, customs, and language were forced on the English people during the next three centuries of Roman rule.

In 529 A.D., Emperor Justinian I codified the Roman laws into a set of writings. The Justinian Code, as these writings became known, distinguished between two major types of laws: public laws and private laws. Public laws dealt with the organization and administration of the Republic. Private laws addressed issues such as contracts, possessions and other property rights; the legal status of various persons such as slaves, husbands, and wives; and injuries to citizens. It contained elements of both our civil and criminal law and influenced Western legal theory into the Middle Ages.

Prior to the Norman Conquest of 1066, the legal system in England was very decentralized. There was little written law except for crimes against society. As a society, we had forgotten or moved away from the teaching of the Code of Hammurabi, and crimes during this period were again viewed as personal wrongs.

When an offense was committed, compensation was paid to the victim or to the victim's family. If the perpetrator failed to make payments, the victim's family could seek revenge, usually ending in a blood feud. For the most part during this period, criminal law was designed to provide equity to what was considered a private dispute.

The Norman Conquest under William the Conqueror established royal administrators who rode circuit and rendered justice. These royal judges would use local custom and rules of conduct as a guide in rendering their judgment. This system known as *stare decisis* (Latin for the phrase "to stand by the decided law") would have far-reaching effects on modern American criminal law.

The next major development in the history of law was the acknowledgment of the existence of common law. Early English common law forms the basis for much of our present-day legal system.[11] Common law is a traditional body of unwritten legal precedents created by court decisions throughout the Middle Ages in England. During this period, when cases were heard, judges would start their deliberations from past decisions that were as closely related as possible to the case under consideration. In the eleventh century, King Edward the Confessor proclaimed that common law was the law of the land, and subsequently court decisions were recorded and made available to lawyers who could then use them to plead their case. This concept is one of the most important aspects of today's modern American law.

Modern Codes and Laws

The Magna Carta of England and the U.S. Constitution both stand as great documents and great moments in the history of American law. The Magna Carta was signed on June 15, 1215, and was later interpreted to grant basic liberties for all British citizens. The U.S. Constitution established certain individual rights, defined the power of the federal government, and limited punishment for violation of laws.

American law combines both common law and written statutes. Statutory laws are enacted by state legislatures and Congress and are the major source of American criminal law today. These laws are usually compiled in various codes and are subject to revision by the legislatures.

An offshoot of written law, *administrative law* is made up of rules and regulations adopted by governmental agencies at the federal, state, and local levels. Many governmental agencies are invested with the power to pass regulations that prohibit certain types of conduct. Some of these regulations provide for fines rather than imprisonment of the offender.

In 1787, the U.S. Constitution was adopted. Constitutional law is another source of American criminal law. The Constitution does not define new crimes (the only crime defined in the Constitution is treason); rather it sets limits on other laws as they apply to individuals. An example of this principle is the U.S. Supreme Court ruling that flag burning, which was proscribed as criminal conduct by a state statute, is protected under the First Amendment right of freedom of expression.

Social Forces

A number of forces in the past several decades have contributed to the development of victims' rights. The major contributing forces have been the feminist movement, the development of civil rights laws, and a growing conservatism regarding crime.[12]

The Feminist Movement

The feminist movement alerted us to centuries of discrimination and violence directed against women. By speaking out, feminists forced us to realize that women were victims not only of violent crime on the streets of cities, but also of sexual harassment within the work environment and family violence within the home. Although men may also become victims of crime and violence, the types of crimes suffered by women are distinct from those suffered by men.

Many of these crimes, although sexual in nature, are in fact nothing more than aggressive assaults that have little to do with sex. Sexual assaults are in reality a way for the perpetrator to control, dominate, and humiliate the victim.

Three works by feminist authors and researchers set the stage for the beginning of our awareness of the sexual victimization of women. Millett's *Sexual Politics*, Griffin's article "Rape: The All American Crime," and Brownmiller's *Against Our Will* each raised our consciousness regarding the domination of women by men.[13]

Sexual Politics examines the concept of patriarchy, which Millett claims is a social and political system utilized by men to control women. She argues that patriarchy is a feature of all past and present societies and exists across cultures and socioeconomic systems today. Millett concludes that power and coercion are central features of patriarchy and are used to control women's sexuality.

Griffin's short article, "Rape, The All American Crime," contains numerous themes. One important theme concerns the nature of the crime of rape. She argues that rape is not a sexual act but rather a violent, political act. Griffin concludes that the threat of rape is used as a method of social control and affects all women.

Brownmiller discusses the history of rape. She asserts that rape is an act used by men to maintain their dominance over women through the use of force. She expands on both Millett's and Griffin's work and concludes that the threat of rape creates a climate of fear. It is this fear that acts as a form of social control that benefits men.

Kelly, in her book *Surviving Sexual Violence*, reviewed these early feminist approaches to sexual abuse and concluded that sexual violence is based on three concepts: power, sexuality, and social control.[14]

Power in the feminist analysis is not police or political power; rather power is defined in terms of a relationship that structures the interactions between men and women. Power therefore is not a property right, but a personal force that establishes male control and dominance over women. This power is multifaceted and thus quite complex. It not only is present in interpersonal relationships but also extends to society's social structure and beliefs.

Sexuality has two aspects: first, male control of women's sexuality is a key factor in women's oppression; and second, sexuality is defined by men's experiences that legitimatize the use of force or coercion in intimate relationships. There is some conflict among feminists regarding the issue of sexuality and whether it has the same significance for women in all cultures.

Social control is the outcome of power and sexuality. The mere threat of sexual violence may result in women developing strategies for self-protection that will limit their mobility, work, or advancement. The reality of sexual violence not only impacts women in intimate and work relationships but also spills over into a previously thought safe environment: the campus setting. Many colleges and universities now provide "escort services" for women who attend evening classes. This measure speaks volumes for the fear that exists in all areas of our lives.

These and other feminists laid the foundation that allows us to more fully understand the concept of sexual violence and women. The first concrete effort by feminist groups in the United States to help women who were victims of crime was the establishment of rape crisis centers in Berkeley, California, and Washington D.C., in 1972. These centers have spread rapidly and are now an integral part of the criminal justice system. In 1976, the federal government established a comprehensive research program, the National Center for the Prevention and Control of Rape, within the Department of Health, Education, and Welfare (this agency is now called Health and Human Services).

The feminist movement not only attacked society's perceptions regarding victims of sexual assault but also focused its efforts on educating the public regarding domestic violence. It is important to note that at the same time battered women's shelters were being established, there was a growing awareness that victims of crime, as a class of citizens, were being treated unfairly by the criminal justice system. This awareness coincided with changes within the judicial system.

Development of Civil Rights Laws

During the 1960s and 1970s, a series of U.S. Supreme Court decisions established certain principles regarding the constitutional rights of individuals. These decisions were in the areas of both criminal procedure and civil rights. The Supreme Court established constitutional safeguards for those accused of crime. By interpreting the Constitution as applying to each and every individual, the court required that society afford those accused of crime certain procedural and substantive rights. These rights embraced the entire spectrum of liberties, including freedom from unreasonable search and seizures, the right to an attorney, and fundamental fairness during a criminal trial. By adopting a philosophy that individuals carried with them certain inalienable rights, the court was poised to expand this concept in the area of civil rights.

The Supreme Court acted to enforce both statutory and constitutional provisions during the 1960s and 1970s in the area of civil rights. These decisions allowed a black man to attend a previously all-white university, maintained that police officers could be held liable for use of excessive force, and required that all persons be treated equally under the law. As a result of these and other decisions, cases such as *Thurman v. City of Torrington*[15] (discussed in Chapter 16) were decided in favor of victims of family violence.

Conservatism Regarding Crime

Another factor that contributed to the awareness of the plight of victims arose as a result of a change in attitude in America. In the 1980s and 1990s, society became more conservative and concerned about crime in general. This law and order movement was a result of citizens becoming more fearful of violent crime and of many groups consequently calling for more stringent punishment of those who violate the law. In addition, the victims' rights movement was gaining momentum. Imprisoning offenders was viewed as a way of vindicating victims of crime. Victim organizations began lobbying for changes in the criminal justice system.

These changes were aimed at making the system more victim oriented. The rights of victims of family violence began to grow and expand as our society became more aware of this type of violence.

These forces focused an awareness on the plight and the dilemma of victims of crime.[16] As a result, victims began to realize that they could have an effect on sentencing in criminal cases and could pursue civil litigation to recover for damages they suffered as a result of the perpetrator's actions.

Victimology Theories

As with any new profession, many of victimology's early thinkers proposed theories or concepts that, on further study, were revealed as incorrect. However, by examining these early efforts we can better understand the growth and present status of victimology. From its inception in the 1940s to the present day, victimology, like family violence, has been an interdisciplinary approach to violence and its effect on victims.

Mendelsohn's Theory of Victimization

Benjamin Mendelsohn was a practicing attorney. In the course of preparing a case for trial, he would conduct in-depth interviews of victims, witnesses, and bystanders.[17] He would use a questionnaire that was couched in simple language and contained more than three hundred questions concerning the branches of criminology and associated sciences. The questionnaire was given to the accused and all others who had knowledge of the crime. In 1963, on the basis of these studies, Mendelsohn came to the conclusion that there was usually a strong interpersonal relationship between the offender and the victim. In an effort to clarify these relationships further, he developed a typology of victims and their contribution to the criminal act.[18] This classification ranged from the completely innocent victim to the imaginary victim. Mendelsohn classified victims into six distinct categories:

1. *The Completely Innocent Victim.* This victim may be a child or a completely unconscious person.
2. *The Victim with Minor Guilt.* This victim might be a woman who induces a miscarriage and dies as a result.
3. *The Victim Who Is as Guilty as the Offender.* Those who assist others in committing crimes fall within this classification.
4. *The Victim More Guilty Than the Offender.* These are persons who provoke others to commit a crime.
5. *The Most Guilty Victim.* This occurs when the perpetrator (victim) acts aggressively and is killed by another person who is acting in self-defense.
6. *The Imaginary Victim.* These are persons suffering from mental disorders such as paranoia who believe they are victims.

Many scholars credit Mendelsohn with coining the term victimology, and still others consider him the father of victimology.[19] His typology was one of the first attempts to focus on victims of crimes rather than to simply examine the perpetrator. However, Mendelsohn was only one of two early scholars who explored the relationship between victims and offenders. The other noted early researcher in victimology was Hans von Hentig.

von Hentig's Theory of Victimization

In 1948, in an early classical text, *The Criminal and His Victim*, von Hentig explored the relationship between the "doer" or criminal and the "sufferer" or victim.[20] Von Hentig also established a typology of victims.[21] This classification was based on psychological, social, and biological factors. Von Hentig established three broad classes of victims: the general classes of victims, the psychological types of victims, and the activating sufferer. His classification identified victims by examining various risk factors. The typology includes:

- The General Classes of Victims

    1. *The Young.* They are weak and the most likely to be a victim of an attack. Youth is the most dangerous period of life.[22]
    2. *The Female.* The female sex is another form of weakness recognized by the law, because numerous rules of law embody the legal fiction of a weaker (female) and stronger (male) sex.[23]
    3. *The Old.* The elder generation holds most positions of accumulated wealth and wealth-giving power, and at the same time is physically weak and mentally feeble.[24]
    4. *The Mentally Defective.* The feeble-minded, the insane, the drug addict, and the alcoholic form another large class of victims.[25]
    5. *Immigrants, Minorities, and Dull Normals.* Immigration means more than a change in country. It causes a temporary feeling of helplessness in vital human relations. The inexperienced, poor, and sometimes dull immigrant, minority, or other are easy prey to all kinds of swindlers.[26]

- The Psychological Types of Victims

    6. *The Depressed.* These victims may suffer from a disturbance of the instinct of self-preservation. Without such an instinct, the individual may be easily overwhelmed or surprised by dangers or enemies.[27]
    7. *The Acquisitive.* This type of person makes an excellent victim. The excessive desire for gain eclipses intelligence, business experience, and inner impediments.[28]
    8. *The Wanton.* Often a sensual or wanton disposition requires other concurrent factors to become activated. Loneliness, alcohol, and certain critical phases are "process-accelerators" of this type of victim.[29]

9. *The Lonesome and the Heartbroken.* Loneliness causes critical mental facilities to be weakened. These individuals become easy prey for criminals.[30] The heartbroken victims are dazed by their loss and therefore become easy targets for a variety of "death rackets" that might, for example, charge a widow an outlandish fee for a picture of her late husband to be included in his biography.[31]

10. *The Tormentor.* This victim becomes a perpetrator. This is the psychotic father who may abuse the wife and children for a number of years until one of the children grows up and under extreme provocation kills him.[32]

11. *The Blocked, Exempted, and Fighting.* The blocked victim is so enmeshed in such a losing situation that defensive moves become impossible. This is a self-imposed form of helplessness and an ideal condition for a victim from the point of view of the criminal.[33]

- The Activating Sufferer

12. *The Activating Sufferer.* This occurs when the victim is transformed into a perpetrator. A number of factors operate as activators on the victim: certain predispositions, age, alcohol, and loss of self-confidence.[34]

Von Hentig theorized that a large percentage of victims, because of their acts or behavior, were responsible for their victimization.[35] This concept has since been repudiated by modern studies that have more closely examined and defined the relationship between the victim and the offender.

Schafer's Functional Responsibility

In 1968, using von Hentig's approach, a third scholar was also instrumental in establishing another classification of victims. Stephen Schafer examined both Mendelsohn's and von Hentig's work in his text, *The Victim and His Criminal*, and attempted to classify victims on a basis of responsibility instead of risk factors.[36] Schafer believed that the study of the criminal–victim relationship indicated an increasing recognition that the criminal justice system must consider the dynamics of crime and treat both criminals and victims.

Schafer went on to state that "the study of criminal–victim relationships emphasizes the need to recognize the role and responsibility of the victim, who is not simply the cause of, and reason for, the criminal procedure, but has a major part to play in the search for an objective criminal justice [system] and a functional solution to the crime problem."[37] He stated that responsibility is not an isolated factor in society; rather it is an instrument of social control used at all times by all societies to maintain themselves.[38] Schafer believed responsibility was a critical issue in the problem of crime.

According to Schafer, crime was not only an individual act but also a social phenomenon. He believed that not all crimes simply "happen" to be committed, but that victims often contribute to crime by their acts of negligence, precipitative actions, or provocations. Schafer concluded that the functional role of a victim is to do nothing to provoke others from attempting to injure him and at the same time to actively prevent such attempts. In other words, this is the victim's functional responsibility.[39]

Wolfgang's Study of Homicide

From 1948 to 1952 in Philadelphia, Marvin E. Wolfgang conducted the first major study of victim precipitation.[40] He focused on homicides, studying both the victim and the offender as separate entities and as "mutual participants in the homicide."[41] Wolfgang evaluated 588 homicides and found that 26 percent (150) of all the homicides studied in Philadelphia involved situations in which the victim was a direct positive precipitator in the crime—the first to use force during the acts leading to the homicide.[42] Wolfgang's study and other theories of homicide are addressed in Chapter 7.

Karmen's Theory of Victimology

Scholars have continued to expand their scope of inquiry and explore other aspects of the victim's role in society. Karmen discusses the development of victimology and points out that those who study this relatively new discipline have three main areas of concentration:

1. Victimologists study the reasons (if any) for why or how the victim entered a dangerous situation. This approach does not attempt to fix blame on the victim; rather it examines the dynamics that resulted in the victim being in the risky situation.
2. Victimology evaluates how police, prosecutors, courts, and related agencies interact with the victim. How was the victim treated at each stage in the criminal justice system?
3. Victimologists evaluate the effectiveness of efforts to reimburse victims for their losses and meet the victim's personal and emotional needs.[43]

Karmen correctly points out that victimologists view the dynamics of the victim's role in society from a multidisciplinary perspective. There is still debate among scholars, however, regarding the correct or predominate role for the victimologist. Similar to the development and study of criminology, a number of different perspectives regarding victimology have also developed throughout the years.

Other Theories of Crime, Victimology, and Victimization

A number of more recent theories regarding victimology and victimization have emerged. Starting in the late 1970s, researchers began to examine victims and victimization from different perspectives and to also examine lifestyles and activities of potential victims. Many of the theories that developed from such research seek to examine the convergence of time, offenders, lack of guardians, and victims as the cause of victimization. Others look at society as a major factor in crime and victimization. This section briefly examines some of these newer victimology and victimization theories.

Lifestyle Theory

Hindelang and his colleagues examined exposure and guardianship as they relate to victimization. They call this theory the lifestyle approach to victimization, which argues that the likelihood of becoming a victim depends on an individual's lifestyle. In other words, various changes in everyday life and lifestyles are assumed to present a criminal opportunity by enhancing exposure and proximity of victims or targets to motivated offenders.[44]

Using the principle of homogamy, Hindelang argues that people are more likely to be victimized the more often they come into contact with groups that contain a larger share of potential offenders. For example, young persons are more likely than older persons to be victimized, since the young are more likely to come into contact with other youths who are disproportionately involved in crime or violence.

Routine Activities Approach

One of the more popular criminology theories dealing with crime trends and victimization was advanced by Cohen and Felson.[45] They argue that a "routine activities approach" should be used in analyzing crime trends and victimization. Routine activities are recurrent, prevalent activities that provide for basic population and individual needs. Routine activities may occur at home, in the workplace, or in other settings.

These researchers examined the circumstances surrounding a crime by looking at the convergence of space, time, motivated offenders, suitable victims or targets, and absence of capable guardians. Criminal violations are treated as routine activities that will occur when a set of circumstances converge. Cohen and Felson emphasized that the lack or absence of any of the three factors (offender, victim, guardian) would probably prevent any criminal activity.

The Opportunity Model of Victimization

Cohen and several other associates later combined the lifestyle and routine activities theories to explain why income, race, and age affect the likelihood of victimization.[46] This approach examines five factors: exposure, guardianship, proximity, attractiveness of targets, and definitions of specific crimes. According to this theory, exposure and guardianship, which are aspects of the lifestyle theory, are not sufficient to establish a formal theory of victimization.

The opportunity theory links dimensions of social inequity to criminal victimization. It involves exposure to potential offenders; proximity between where victims or targets reside and where potential offenders are found; guardianship, which involves the effectiveness of persons or objects in preventing crime; target attractiveness, which is the desirability of persons or property to potential offenders; and definition of certain crimes, which establishes the difficulty in committing certain acts. For example, thefts are easier to commit than burglaries.

It is significant that Cohen does not blame persons for being victims. Rather, he and his associates approach the study of crime and victimization from the perspective that a number of factors cause crime, not just the victim.

Critical Victimology

Mawby and Walklate have proposed a view of victimology that they call critical victimology.[47] They define critical victimology as "an attempt to examine the wider social context in which some versions of victimology have become more dominant than others and also to understand how those versions of victimology are interwoven with questions of policy response and service delivery to victims of crime." They question why certain actions are defined as criminal and others are not. These scholars rightfully point out that many "crimes" committed by wealthy or powerful individuals or even by nations are not considered crimes. For example, genocide has occurred and is occurring in some countries, yet we do very little about it. Rape as a weapon of war has been reported in several countries. Abuse of power by those in control is very seldom mentioned as a crime in the media or other sources.

Victim Blaming

One of the most controversial areas of victimology has been and continues to be the concept known as victim blaming, victim responsibility, or victim perception. As discussed earlier in this chapter, some of the world's most prominent victimologists established classifications that included victims as a cause of criminal act. Mendelsohn, von Hentig, Schafer, and Wolfgang all classified victims as having some form of causation in the commission of the crime.

The concept of victim perception was first used by Wolfgang in his study of homicide victims and later by Amir in one of the first studies of rape.[48] Wolfgang's interpretation dealt with situations in which the victim was a direct participator in the crime, while Amir's focused on the offender's perception of the victim's willingness to participate in the sexual act.

Wolfgang's study of homicide involved examination of homicide records in Philadelphia from 1948 to 1952. He reviewed these files and found that one out of four victims initially used force against their perpetrators. He also found that many of the victims were acquainted with the perpetrator. Amir was a student of Wolfgang, and in fact, Wolfgang wrote the introduction to Amir's text, *Patterns in Forcible Rape*. It is therefore hardly surprising that Amir would follow the same reasoning as his mentor, Wolfgang, when he analyzed the dynamics of rape.

Psychologist William Ryan has the distinction of coining the phrase "blaming the victim."[49] In his book, *Blaming the Victim*,[50] Ryan argues that the concept of victim blaming arose in the American middle class. This group of people is aware of the benefits they have and that others do not share these entitlements. This awareness creates a need to reconcile their status with others who are not as fortunate. One way to accomplish this is to accept the fact of violence and crime but blame the victim for letting it happen. This approach, argues Ryan, does not directly threaten the middle class and allows them to propose changes in society to address victimization. For example, poverty is caused under this victim-blaming approach because poor people share cultural values that make them poor and not because of any structural flaws that cause inequities in the distribution of income. The solution to poverty, according to Ryan, is to educate the poor people so their values become more like those of the middle class.

The process of victim blaming has severe consequences for both the victim and society. For example, if the victim feels or perceives that he or she will be blamed or condemned by other members of society, the victim may not file a report of the crime. He or she may believe that the social cost of reporting the crime is too high a price to pay. Victims of certain crimes may also believe that reporting offense may subject them to further victimization at the hands of the perpetrator. This is particularly true for crimes such as family violence, including incest, sexual assault by an acquaintance or relative, spousal abuse, and elder abuse. This failure or reluctance to report victimization is not confined to individuals. Corporations or other companies may feel pressure not to report crimes so as to avoid bad publicity and a possible drop in their stock prices. Our society suffers severe consequences when crimes are not reported, investigated, and prosecuted.

There is also a great deal of controversy surrounding the media's role in victim blaming—a debate that promises to be eternal. The media argue that they must represent the general public, and the public has a right to know all the facts surrounding any incident. Such facts may include the identity of the victim of any crime, including sexual assault. Victim advocates argue that exposing the identity of sexual assault victims increases the chances of their being revictimized. Some papers will not print the identity of sexual assault victims, while others may actually print their names or allow information to be broadcast or printed that will lead to their identification. As in so many areas of victimology, we are making progress, but we have a long way to go.

There are a number of other problems with victim blaming. First, some victim blaming assumes that some victims share certain physical or psychological characteristics that cause them to be victimized. Others assume there is some sort of continuum that ranges from the totally innocent victim to the completely guilty victim.

American society is concerned with the rights of those who are accused of crimes. The first ten Amendments to the United States Constitution focus on individual liberties and attempt to insure that government does not infringe upon these individual rights. However, the rights of victims of crime are not mentioned in these amendments. Kelly and Enez describe the evolution of the crime victim role as one moving from an eye-for-an-eye, in which victims were expected to deal with their perpetrator directly, to a system in which the king dispensed justice, and finally to its modern-day form in which the People of the state or federal government are the "victims" and the real victim is relegated to that of a witness.[51]

One prominent victimologist, Emilio C. Viano, has suggested that the victimization of individuals is better understood if we shift away from analyzing what they did, where they were, and how they reacted to the incident to looking at the cultural, social, and economic factors that support a view allowing for victim blaming. He argues that sexism, racism, and ageism are not always acknowledged to exist, and some would rather deny the existence of these forces and continue to blame the victim. He concludes that changing the focus of the inquiry will lead to a different understanding of what causes certain individuals or groups in society to be victimized.[52]

The movement away from victim blaming to victim protection is a relatively new process. We must continue to educate the professionals in the field as well as the general public about the dynamics of victimization in order to move away from this backward and harmful process of victim blaming.

The Rise of the Victims' Rights Movement

As the various social forces were developing, a series of events took place that began to raise the consciousness of the victims themselves regarding their impact on the criminal justice system.

The Beginning of the Movement

During the late 1960s, victims of crime began volunteering to serve within various victim assistance programs. As these crime victims continued to speak out, states and the federal government reacted by establishing commissions to study crime and its consequences.

There were two federal responses to crime victimization during this period. One was the establishment of the National Crime Survey, which is discussed in more detail in Chapter 2. The second major action on the part of the federal government was the establishment of the Law Enforcement Assistance Administration (LEAA). This agency provided funds to law enforcement agencies for a variety of purposes including the establishment of victim-witness programs.[53] LEAA's role in fundraising is discussed in Chapter 6.

In 1974, the LEAA called a meeting in Florida of various victim advocates to discuss methods of increasing victims' rights. One consequence of this meeting was the formation of the National Organization for Victim Assistance (NOVA) in 1976. NOVA is considered by many to be one of the leading victim rights organizations in the world.

Gains and Losses

During the late 1970s and early 1980s, the movement foundered. Lack of funding by the federal government caused many community-based victim organizations and service providers to cease operations. Additionally, within the movement issues such as professionalism and training caused increasing divisiveness. The movement began to separate into specialized groups that focused on specific issues. Several sexual assault and domestic violence organizations, such as the National Coalition Against Sexual Assault, were established to address the specific needs of those victims.[54]

Although there was tension between various service providers because of diminishing funding and disagreement regarding specific goals, there was also progress in other areas of the victims' movement during this time period. Parents of Murdered Children (POMC) was founded by Robert and Charlotte Hullinger in 1978, and Mothers Against Drunk Driving (MADD) was founded by Candy Lightner in 1980. Both of these organizations continue to have an impact on victims' rights and the victims' movement. Additionally, Congress passed a federal Victims' Bill of Rights. By 1990, two-thirds of the states had enacted similar types of laws protecting victims.

In what may become one of the most critical dates in the history of victim rights, on June 25, 1996, President Clinton proposed a Victims' Rights Constitutional Amendment to the U.S. Constitution. In a speech made in the Rose Garden announcing the Victims' Rights Constitutional Amendment, President Clinton stated:

> *Having carefully studied all of the alternatives, I am now convinced that the only way to fully safeguard the rights of victims in America is to amend our Constitution and guarantee these basic rights—to be told about public court proceedings and to attend them; to make a statement to the court about bail, about sentencing, about accepting a plea if the victim is present, to be told about parole hearings to attend and to speak; notice when the defendant or convict escapes or is released, restitution from the defendant, reasonable protection from the defendant and notice of these rights.*[55]

The Victims' Rights Constitutional Amendment faces a long and complex process before it becomes law. It must be approved by Congress and then adopted by three-quarters of the states to become part of the Constitution. It is not something that will happen in a few weeks or months and there are those who already claim that the proposed amendment is too detailed and should be made broader. No matter what the outcome, the simple fact that such an amendment has actually been proposed is a significant acknowledgment of the plight of victims of crime.

Increased Public Awareness

During 1982 through 1986, victims' organizations began to use the media to increase public awareness of crime victim issues. President Ronald Reagan, and Congress, responded to this heightened awareness with actions that would eventually have long-term consequences for the victims' movement. In 1982, President Reagan appointed a Task Force on Victims of Crime. This task force published a report that has since become a foundational platform for victims' rights.[56] The

---

Victims' Rights Constitutional Amendment

Section 1. To ensure that the victim is treated with fairness, dignity, and respect, from the occurrence of a crime of violence and other crimes as may be defined by law pursuant to section two of this article, and throughout the criminal, military, and juvenile justice process, as a matter of fundamental rights to liberty, justice and due process, the victim shall have the following rights: to be informed of and given the opportunity to be present at every proceeding in which those rights are extended to the accused or convicted offender; to be heard at any proceeding involving sentencing, including the right to object to a previously negotiated plea, or to a release from custody; to be informed of any release or escape; and to a speedy trial, a final conclusion free from unreasonable delay, full restitution from the convicted offender, reasonable measures to protect the victim from violence or intimidation by the accused or convicted offender, and notice of the victim's rights.

Section 2. The several States, with respect to a proceeding in a State forum, and the Congress with respect to a proceeding in a United States forum, shall have the power to implement further the rights established in this article by appropriate legislation.

Source: OVC, U.S. Department of Justice, Washington, D.C., 1996.

Office for Victims of Crime (OVC) was created in the Department of Justice to implement the task force's recommendations.

In 1984, another key event took place when Congress passed the Victims of Crime Act (VOCA).[57] This act established the OVC in the Office of Justice Programs, Department of Justice. OVC provides grants to states for programs with direct services for victims of all crimes. VOCA also established the Crime Victims Fund to provide money to local victim assistance programs and state victim compensation programs. The fund receives money from federal criminal fines, penalties, and bond forfeitures. VOCA's operation is further examined in Chapter 16.

Increased Professionalism

From 1984 to the present, the victims' movement has been characterized by an increase in the professionalism of the victims service advocates and providers. In previous times, the victims' movement was heightened by strong dynamic leaders with vision and determination. At present, the movement has expanded beyond the ability of any one person being able to influence its direction. It is now a national movement with a tremendous influence on local, state, and national politics.

Universities are expanding their victim-related courses. Various victim oganizations are offering increased training opportunities, and in 1995, the U.S. Department of Justice sponsored the first National Victim Assistance Academy in Washington, D.C. This academy was repeated in 1996 and 1997 using distance learning technology to link other universities in a joint academic effort.

The public awareness of victim issues continues to grow, and victim advocates have become an acknowledged force in modern politics. Victim services providers are realizing that their profession requires training that is multidisciplinary in nature. There is a growing awareness that to be accepted by other professionals requires continuing education, certifications, or other acknowledged credentials. This increased professionalism should translate into more sophisticated interventions and a faster rate of progress within the victims' movement.

Additional Laws

Increased professionalism also means increased knowledge and insight into the problems of victims. In 1994, Congress enacted the Violent Crime Control and Law Enforcement Act. Title IV of that law is entitled the Violence Against Women Act (VAWA). Congress mandated that various professions form partnerships and work together to respond to all forms of violence against women.

The attorney general is required to make a report to Congress annually on the grants that are awarded under the act and ensure that research examining violence against women is encouraged. The report must include the number of grants, funds distributed, and other statistical information. Additionally, the report must assess the effectiveness of any programs which are funded under VAWA.

The act provides funding for a variety of research-based studies. It also requires that federal agencies engage in research regarding violence against women. For example, the National Institute of Justice is mandated to conduct four important projects: (1) the development of a research agenda that will address violence with particular emphasis on underserved populations; (2) the assessment of establishing state databases to record the number of sexual and domestic violence incidents; (3) a study to determine how abusive partners obtain addresses of their victims; and (4) the examination with other agencies of the battered woman syndrome.[58]

Summary

The history of victimology is in many ways the history of our world. As long as there has been crime, there have been victims who have suffered. Early law viewed crime as a personal act that required response by the victim or the victim's family. The Code of Hammurabi, although harsh and violent, recognized victims as injured parties and may have been the first victims' rights law. Other codes and laws evolved throughout history to shape our modern concept of justice.

A number of social forces affected the development of victimology. The feminist movement raised our awareness of the plight of women. The civil rights movement resulted in a number of laws being passed which afforded individuals certain rights. As crime increased, our society became increasingly conservative and became more aware of the trauma suffered by victims of crime.

Theories regarding victimization have undergone a subtle but encouraging change. We have moved from the victim being the cause of the crime to studying how crime occurs and how persons are selected as victims. These newer theories include lifestyle theory, the routine activity approach, and opportunities model of victimization. It is a major accomplishment within victimology that we are developing our own theories as they relate to victimization.

The victims' rights movement began as a small group of volunteers who themselves were crime victims and who had been victimized a second time as a result of their involvement with the criminal justice system. This small group of volunteers has grown and become a powerful force in America that continues to expand and change the way we view victimology.

Key Terms

Criminology is the study of crime as a social phenomenon.

Victimology is the study of the victim, the offender, and society.

Primitive law was a system of rules in preliterate societies.

Stare decisis means to stand by the decided law.

Administrative law is made up of rules and regulations adopted by governmental agencies at the federal, state, and local levels.

Discussion Questions

1. Explain why some authorities call the Hammurabi Code the first victims' rights law.

2. What was the most significant event in the development of law that has affected the victims' movement?

3. Is the feminist movement still important to the victims' movement? Why?

4. Compare and contrast von Hentig's and Mendelsohn's theories of victimology.

5. Why is Schafer's theory of functional responsibility important?

6. Wolfgang studied homicide; how does this relate to the study of victimology?

7. Discuss the other theories of victimology.

8. Has the victims' movement reached its full potential? Name three specific goals that the movement should strive for in the next ten years.

Suggested Readings

G. B. Vold & T. J. Bernard, *Theoretical Criminology*, 3rd ed. (Oxford University Press, New York) 1986.

Sir Henry Summer Maine, *Ancient Law*, 10th ed. (John Murray, London) 1905.

S. Schafer, *The Victim and His Criminal*, (Random House, New York) 1968.

Masters & Roberson, *Inside Criminology*, (Prentice-Hall, Englewood Cliffs, N.J.) 1985.

I. Drapkin & E. Viano, Eds., *Victimology: A New Focus*, vol. 2 (D.C. Heath, Lexington, Mass.) 1974.

S. A. Cook, *The Laws of Moses and the Code of Hammurabi*, (Adam and Charles Black, London) 1903.

S. T. Reed, *Criminal Justice*, 3rd ed. (Macmillan Publishing Company, New York) 1993.

A. Karmen, *Crime Victims: An Introduction to Victimology,* 2nd ed. (Wadsworth, Belmont, Calif.) 1995.

L. Kelly, *Surviving Sexual Violence,* (University of Minnesota Press, Minneapolis, Minn.) 1988.

N. A. Weiner & M. E. Wolfgang, Eds., *Pathways to Criminal Violence,* (Sage, Newbury Park, Calif.) 1989.

Emilio C. Viano, *Victim/Witness Services: A Review of the Model,* (GPO, Washington, D.C.) 1979.

President's Task Force on Victims of Crime, (Final Report, GPO, Washington, D.C.) December 1982.

J. M. Sqazi & J. McDevitt, *Victimology: A Study of Crime Victims and Their Roles* (Prentice Hall, Englewood Cliffs, N.J.) 2002.

A. Karmen, *Crime Victims: An Introduction to Victimology* (Wadsworth Publishing, Belmont, Calif.) 2006.

L. J. Moriarty, *Controversies in Victimology* (Anderson Publishing, Cincinnati, Ohio) 2003.

Endnotes

1. California State University at Fresno was the first academic institution in the United States to offer a B.S. in criminology with a victimology option.
2. For an excellent discussion of criminology as a science, see G. B. Vold and T. J. Bernard, *Theoretical Criminology,* 3rd ed. (Oxford University Press, New York) 1986.
3. Edwin H. Sutherland, *Principles of Criminology,* 4th ed. (Lippincott, Philadelphia) 1947.
4. Sir Henry Summer Maine, *Ancient Law,* 10th ed. (John Murray, London) 1905.
5. S. Schafer, *The Victim and His Criminal,* (Random House, New York) 1968.
6. Masters & Roberson, *Inside Criminology,* (Prentice-Hall, Englewood Cliffs, N.J.) 1985.
7. H. Gordon, *Hammurabi's Code: Quaint or Forward Looking,* (Rinehart, New York) 1957.
8. G. O. Mueller & H. H. A. Cooper, "Society and the Victim: Alternative Responses," in I. Drapkin & E. Viano, Eds., *Victimology: A New Focus,* vol. 2 (D. C. Heath, Lexington, Mass.) 1974, pp. 85–102.
9. S. A. Cook, *The Laws of Moses and the Code of Hammurabi,* (Adam and Charles Black, London) 1903.
10. O. W. Mueller, "Tort, Crime and the Primitive," 43 *Journal of Criminal Law, Criminology, and Police Science,* 303, 1955.
11. S. T. Reed, *Criminal Justice,* 3rd ed. (Macmillan Publishing Company, New York) 1993.
12. A. Karmen, *Crime Victims: An Introduction to Victimology,* 2nd ed. (Brooks/Cole, Pacific Grove, Calif.) 1985.
13. K. Millett, *Sexual Politics,* (Abacus, London) 1972, S. Griffin, "Rape: The All American Crime, "*Ramparts* 10(3), pp. 26–35, 1971, and S. Brownmiller, *Against Our Will: Men, Women and Rape,* (Penguin Books, New York) 1975.
14. L. Kelly, *Surviving Sexual Violence,* (University of Minnesota Press, Minneapolis, Minn.) 1988.
15. 595 F. Supp. 1521 (Conn. 1984).
16. G. D. Gottfredson, "The Experiences of Violent and Serious Victimization," in N. A. Weiner & M. E. Wolfgang, Eds., *Pathways to Criminal Violence,* (Sage, Newbury Park, Calif.) 1989, pp. 202–234.
17. B. Mendelsohn, "The Origin and Doctrine of Victimology," 3 *Excerpta Criminologica,* June 1963, pp. 239–244.
18. S. Schafer, *The Victim and His Criminal,* (Random House, New York) 1968.
19. B. Mendelsohn, "Rape in Criminology," *Giustizia Penale,* 1940.
20. Hans von Hentig, *The Criminal and His Victim,* (first published by Schocken Books, New York 1979, republished by Yale University Press 1984) (Hereafter *The Criminal and His Victim*).
21. Some scholars have subdivided von Hentig's original typology (probably for ease of understanding). See, for example, Doerner and Lab, *Victimology,* (West Publishing, St. Paul, Minn. 1994) where the authors list thirteen classifications. They arrive at this number by listing immigrants, minorities, and dull normals as separate categories instead of one subdivision as von Hentig did.

22. *The Criminal and His Victim*, p. 404.
23. Id. at p. 406.
24. Id. at p. 410.
25. Id. at p. 411.
26. Id. at p. 415.
27. Id. at p. 420.
28. Id. at p. 422.
29. Id. at p. 427.
30. Id. at p. 428.
31. Id. at p. 431.
32. Id. at p. 431.
33. *The Criminal and His Victim*, p. 433.
34. Id. at p. 445.
35. H. von Hentig, *The Criminal and His Victim*, (Yale University Press, New Haven, Conn.) 1948.
36. S. Schafer, *The Victim and His Criminal*, (Random House, New York) 1968.
37. Id. at p. 5.
38. Id. at p. 139.
39. Id. at p. 152.
40. M. E. Wolfgang, *Patterns of Criminal Homicide*, (University of Pennsylvania Press, Philadelphia, Penn.) 1958.
41. M. E. Wolfgang, *Analytical Categories for Research in Victimization*, (Kriminologische Wegzeichen, Munich, Germany) 1967, p. 17.
42. Id. at pp. 24, 72.
43. Andrew Karmen, *Crime Victims, An Introduction to Victimology*, 2nd ed. (Brooks/Cole, Pacific Grove, Calif.) 1995.
44. M. Hindelang, M. Gottfredson, & J. Garofalo, *Victims of Xpersonal Crime: An Empirical Foundation for a Theory of Xpersonal Victimization*, Ballinger, Cambridge, Mass. (1978).
45. Lawrence E. Cohen & Marcus Felson, "Social Change and Crime Rate Trends: A Routine Activity Approach," *American Sociological Review* 588 (1979).
46. Lawrence E. Cohen, James R. Kluegel, & Kenneth C. Land, "Social Inequality and

Xpredatory Criminal Victimization: An Exposition and Test of a Formal Theory," *American Sociological Review* 505 (1981).
47. R. I. Mawby & S. Walklate, *Critical Victimology, International Perspectives*, p. 21, Sage, Thousand Oaks, Calif. (1994).
48. M. Amir, *Patterns in Forcible Rape*, University of Chicago Press, Chicago (1971).
49. L. W. Kennedy & V. F. Sacco, *Crime Victims in Context*, Roxbury Publishing, Los Angeles, (1998).
50. W. Ryan, *Blaming the Victim*, Vintage Books, New York (1976).
51. R. C. Davis, A. J. Lurigio, & W. G. Skogan (Eds.), *Victims of Crime* 2nd ed., p. 232, Sage, Thousand Oaks, Calif. (1997).
52. E. C. Viano, "Victimology Today: Major Issues in Research and Public Policy," in E. C. Viano (Ed.), *Crime and Its Victims: International Research and Public Policy Issues*, pp. 3–14, Hemisphere, New York (1989).
53. Emilio C. Viano, *Victim/Witness Services: A Review of the Model*, (GPO, Washington, D.C.) 1979.
54. M. Largen, "Grassroots Centers and National Task Forces: A Herstory of the Anti-Rape Movement," 32 *Aegis*, Autumn 1981, pp. 46–52.
55. "Remarks by the President at Announcement of Victims Constitutional Amendment," *Press Release*, The White House, Office of the Press Secretary. Washington, D.C. June 25, 1996, p. 2.
56. *President's Task Force on Victims of Crime*, (Final Report, GPO, Washington, D.C.) December 1982.
57. Victims of Crime Act of 1984, 42 U.S.C. Section 10601 (1984).
58. Jeremy Travis, "Violence Against Women: Reflections on NIJ's Research Agenda," *National Institute of Justice Journal*, February 1996.

2

MEASUREMENT OF CRIME AND ITS EFFECTS

Chapter Outline

Official Reports
  Uniform Crime Reports
  National Incident-Based Reporting System
  National Crime Victimization Survey
  A Comparison of the Uniform Crime Reports and the National Crime Victimization Survey
  National Assessment Program

Other Reports
  National Family Violence Surveys
  Other Sources of Data on Violence
  Other Types of Crime Research

Summary

Key Terms

Discussion Questions

Suggested Readings

Learning Objectives

After reading this chapter, you should be able to:

- Explain the differences between the various types of official reports
- Distinguish between the other types of reports that provide information regarding the commission of crimes

- Understand the advantages and disadvantages of each of the various mechanisms that are used to measure crime

Official Reports

There are many different types of official reports which are compiled by private or public agencies in the form of statistical data. These provide a much needed resource for further research into the extent of crime and victimization. Those most commonly relied on are reports by local law enforcement agencies, the Uniform Crime Reports (UCR), and the National Crime Victimization Surveys (NCVS).

Uniform Crime Reports

During the 1920s, the International Association of Chiefs of Police (IACP) formed the Commission on Uniform Crime Reports to develop a uniform system of reporting criminal statistics. The committee evaluated various crimes based on their seriousness, frequency of occurrence, commonality across the nation, and likelihood of being reported to the police. In 1929, the committee finished its study and recommended a plan for crime reporting that became the foundation of the UCR program.

The Extent of Crime

In 2003, Americans twelve years and older experienced approximately 24.2 million violent and property victimizations. The crime rate has stabilized, and violent and property crimes remain at the lowest level since the inception of the National Crime Victimization Surveys. Following are some category-specific statistics:

- **Fatal crimes.** These crimes, which include murders and nonnegligent manslaughters, claimed 16,503 victims in 2003. Approximately 90 percent of these victims were adults. The victims and perpetrators knew each other in 77.6 percent of the cases.
- **Forcible rapes.** There were 93,433 reported cases of forcible rape in 2003, a decline from 95,235 reported in 2002.

- **Robbery.** There were 413,402 robberies in 2003. Firearms were the weapon of choice when a weapon was used during the robbery.
- **Thefts.** In 2003, there were more than 7 million larceny-thefts in the nation, costing victims approximately $4.9 billion in losses. The month of July had the highest rate of thefts over the last three years. Thefts from motor vehicles accounted for the largest number of thefts.
- **Drunk driving.** There were 17,013 alcohol-related fatalities in 2003, representing an average of one alcohol-related death every thirty-one minutes.

Source: *Criminal Victimization, 2003*, Bureau of Justice Statistics, U.S. Department of Justice (September 2004); *Uniform Crime Reports 2003*, Federal Bureau of Investigation, U.S. Department of Justice; and *2003 Traffic Safety Facts*, National Center for Statistics and Analysis, Washington D.C.

Seven crimes were chosen to serve as an index for determining fluctuations in the overall rate of crime. These seven offenses became known as the "crime index" and included the following crimes: murder and manslaughter, forcible rape, robbery, aggravated assault, burglary, larceny-theft, and motor vehicle theft. In 1979, Congress mandated that an eighth crime, arson, be added to the index. During the study phase of the project, members recognized that differences in state criminal codes would cause the same act to be reported in various methods and categories. To avoid this problem, they made no distinction between felony and misdemeanor crimes and established a standardized set of definitions to allow law enforcement agencies to submit data without regard for local statutes. In 1930, Congress enacted federal law that authorized the attorney general to gather crime information.[1] The attorney general designated the FBI as the national clearinghouse for all data, and since that time data based on this system have been obtained from the nation's law enforcement agencies.

The *Uniform Crime Reports (UCR)* program is a nationwide statistical computation involving over sixteen hundred city, county, and state law enforcement agencies who voluntarily provide data on reported crimes. During 1993, law enforcement agencies in the UCR program represented over 245 million inhabitants or approximately 95 percent of the total population of the United States. The program is administrated by the Federal Bureau of Investigation which issues assessments on the nature and type of crime. The program's primary objective is to generate a set of reliable criminal statistics for use in law enforcement administration, operation, and management.[2]

The Federal Bureau of Investigation is tasked with administering the UCR program and issues periodic reports addressing the nature and type of crime in the United States. Although the UCR's primary objective is the issuance of reliable statistics for use by law enforcement agencies, it has also become an important social indicator of deviance in our society.

The UCR prepares an annual crime index. This index is composed of selected offenses used to gauge changes in the overall rate of crime reported to law enforcement agencies. The crime index is composed of those specific crimes previously discussed. Therefore, the index is a combination of violent and property crimes. In 1993, for example, 14 percent of the index offenses were violent crimes and 86 percent were property crimes.

The UCR is an annual report that includes the number of crimes reported by citizens to local police departments, and the number of arrests made by law enforcement agencies in a given year. This information is of somewhat limited value, because the data are based on instances of violence that are classified as criminal and are reported to the local law enforcement agencies. Many serious acts of violence are not reported to the police and therefore do not become part of the UCR.

A number of factors influence the reporting or non-reporting of crimes to local law enforcement. The Bureau of Justice Statistics reports that the most common reason victims give for reporting crimes to the police is to prevent further crimes from being committed against them by the same offender.[3] For both household crimes and other theft-related crimes, the most common reason given by victims in reporting the offenses is to assist in the recovery of the property.

Violent crimes are the most likely to be reported to the police. Household crimes are the next highest reported form of crime. Personal thefts are the least likely crimes to be reported to the police.

The most common reason given for not reporting violent crimes to the police is that the crime was considered by the victim to be a private or personal matter. The second most common reason for not reporting violent crimes is that the offender was unsuccessful in his attempt to commit the crime. The most common reason for not reporting household crime or other theft-related crime is that the object was recovered.

Victims gave different reasons for not reporting crimes to the police when the offender was a stranger instead of an acquaintance. Victims of crimes committed by strangers gave the following reasons for not reporting:

- The offender was unsuccessful.
- The victim considered the police inefficient.
- The victim felt the police did not want to be bothered.
- It was not important enough to the victim to report the crime.

Victims of crimes committed by acquaintances gave the following reasons for not reporting:

- The victim considered the crime a private or personal matter.
- The victim had reported the crime to another official.

The Hate Crime Statistics Act was passed by Congress in 1990 and mandates that a database of crimes motivated by religion, ethnic, racial, or sexual orientation be collected. On January 1, 1991, the UCR program distributed guidelines for reporting hate crimes, and the first report was published in 1992. Participation in reporting hate crimes continues to grow and as of 1993, 6840 law enforcement agencies representing 56 percent of the U.S. population were reporting hate crime data.

With the exception of the hate crime category as noted, the UCR remained virtually unchanged for fifty years. Eventually, various law enforcement agencies began to call for an evaluation and redesign of the program. Because the UCR only lists crimes that are reported to it, this presents a serious problem as not all police agencies report crimes to the FBI and the Department of Justice. Because the UCR relies on law enforcement agencies to voluntarily report crimes, there is the possibility of underreporting by some agencies based on political reasons.[4] The UCR generally provides only tabular summaries of crime and does not provide crime analysts with more meaningful information. Additionally, the method of counting crimes causes problems. For example, only the most serious crime is reported. If a person is robbed and his car stolen, police agencies are instructed to report only the robbery. Finally, some crimes, such as white-collar crime, are excluded from the UCR system. After several years of study, the FBI began to institute various modifications to the UCR program. These changes established a new, more effective crime reporting system.

National Incident-Based Reporting System

The National Incident-Based Reporting System (NIBRS) collects data on each single incident and arrest within forty-six crime categories. Incident, victim, property, offender, and arrestee information is gathered for each offense known to the agency. Data comes from local, state, and federal automated records systems. The goal of the system is to modernize crime reporting information by collecting data presently maintained in law enforcement records. While the UCR does not distinguish between attempted and completed crimes, the NIBRS does collect and maintain that data. Importantly from a victimology perspective is that is it able to record rapes of both males and females. This is a critical improvement over the UCR, which does not distinguish between genders in reporting rapes. The Bureau of Justice Statistics conducted a study comparing the differences in reporting between the UCR and the NIBRS and found the average differences between the two reports to be small—less than 2 percent.

Local law enforcement agencies continue to join the NIBRS. In 1991, there were 269 agencies covering a population of 4.1 million persons. By 1996, the NIBRS participation had increased to 1,082 agencies covering a population of 14.8 million. The enhanced UCR program is a by-product of modern law enforcement records systems that have the capability to store and collate information regarding criminal offenses.[5]

National Crime Victimization Survey

The *National Crime Victimization Survey (NCVS)* is a nationwide sample of interviews of citizens regarding victimization. It attempts to correct the problems of non-reporting inherent in the UCR. The report was originally entitled the National Crime Survey (NCS) but was renamed to more clearly reflect its emphasis on the measurement of victimizations experienced by citizens. The NCVS began in 1973 and collects detailed information about certain criminal offenses, both attempted and completed, that concern the general public and law enforcement (see Figure 2.1). These offenses include the frequency and nature of rape, robbery, assault, household burglary, personal and household theft, and motor vehicle theft.[6] The NCVS does not measure homicide or commercial crime.

A single crime may have more than one victim; for example, a bank robbery may involve several bank tellers. A victimization, the basic measure of the occurrence of crime, is a specific criminal act because it affects a specific victim. The number of victimizations, however, is determined by the number of victims of each specific criminal act.

OMB No. 1121-0111: Approval Expires December 31, 1987

NOTICE — Your report to the Census Bureau is **confidential** by law (U.S. Code 42, Sections 3789g and 3735). All identifiable information will be used only by persons engaged in and for the purposes of the survey, and may not be disclosed or released to others for any purpose.

FORM NCS-1 and NCS-2
(4-10-88)

U.S. DEPARTMENT OF COMMERCE
BUREAU OF THE CENSUS

ACTING AS COLLECTING AGENT FOR THE
BUREAU OF JUSTICE STATISTICS
U.S. DEPARTMENT OF JUSTICE

NATIONAL CRIME SURVEY

NCS-1 BASIC SCREEN QUESTIONNAIRE

NCS-2 CRIME INCIDENT REPORT

PGM 2

Sample   Control number
PSU | Segment | CK. | Serial | HH No.

J ___

NCS 1 and 2

ITEMS FILLED AT START OF INTERVIEW

1. **Interviewer identification**
   201   Code | Name

2. **Unit Status**
   202   1 ☐ Unit in sample the previous enumeration period — *Fill 3*
   2 ☐ Unit in sample first time this period — *SKIP to 4*

3. **Household Status** — Mark first box that applies
   203   1 ☐ Same household <u>interviewed</u> the previous enumeration
   2 ☐ Replacement household since the previous enumeration
   3 ☐ Noninterview the previous enumeration
   4 ☐ Other — *Specify* ⌐

4. **Line number of household respondent**
   204   _____ Go to page 2

TRANSCRIPTION ITEMS FROM CONTROL CARD

5. **Special Place type code**
   205   _____

6. **Tenure**
   206   1 ☐ Owned or being bought   2 ☐ Rented for cash   3 ☐ No cash rent

7. **Land Use**
   207   1 ☐ Urban   2 ☐ Rural

8. **Farm Sales**
   208   x ☐ Item blank   1 ☐ $1,000 or more   2 ☐ Less than $1,000

9. **Type of living quarters**
   Housing unit
   209   1 ☐ House, apartment, flat
   2 ☐ HU in nontransient hotel, motel, etc.
   3 ☐ HU permanent in transient hotel, motel, etc.
   4 ☐ HU in rooming house
   5 ☐ Mobile home or trailer with no permanent room added
   6 ☐ Mobile home or trailer with one or more permanent rooms added
   7 ☐ HU not specified above — *Describe* ⌐

   OTHER unit
   8 ☐ Quarters not HU in rooming or boarding house
   9 ☐ Unit not permanent in transient hotel, motel, etc.
   10 ☐ Unoccupied site for mobile home, trailer, or tent
   11 ☐ Student quarters in college dormitory
   12 ☐ OTHER unit not specified above - *Describe* ⌐

   Use of telephone
10a. **Location of phone** — Mark first box that applies.
   210   1 ☐ Phone in unit . . . .
   2 ☐ Phone in common area (hallway, etc.) . . . .
   3 ☐ Phone in another unit (neighbor, friend, etc.) . .   } *Fill 10b*
   4 ☐ Work/office phone . . . . .
   5 ☐ No phone — *SKIP to 11a*

10b. **Is phone interview acceptable?**
   211   1 ☐ Yes   2 ☐ No   3 ☐ Refused to give number

TRANS. ITEMS FROM CONTROL CARD — Cont.

11a. **Number of housing units in structure**
   212   1 ☐ 1 - *SKIP to 12*   4 ☐ 4   7 ☐ Mobile home or trailer - *SKIP to 12*
   2 ☐ 2   5 ☐ 5-9
   3 ☐ 3   6 ☐ 10 +   8 ☐ Only OTHER units

11b. **Direct outside access**
   213   1 ☐ Yes   3 ☐ Don't know
   2 ☐ No   x ☐ Item blank

12. **Family income**
   214   1 ☐ (a) Less than $5,000   8 ☐ (h) 20,000-24,999
   2 ☐ (b) $5,000- 7,499   9 ☐ (i) 25,000-29,999
   3 ☐ (c) 7,500- 9,999   10 ☐ (j) 30,000-34,999
   4 ☐ (d) 10,000-12,499   11 ☐ (k) 35,000-39,999
   5 ☐ (e) 12,500-14,999   12 ☐ (l) 40,000-49,999
   6 ☐ (f) 15,000-17,499   13 ☐ (m) 50,000-74,999
   7 ☐ (g) 17,500-19,999   14 ☐ (n) 75,000 and over

PGM 3   **ITEMS FILLED AFTER INTERVIEW**

13. **Proxy information** — Fill for all proxy interviews

a. Proxy interview obtained for Line No.	b. Proxy respondent		c. Reason (Enter code)
	Name	Line No.	
301 ___		302	303
304 ___		305	306
307 ___		308	309
310 ___		311	312

Codes for Item 13c
1 — 12 – 13 years old and parent refused permission for self interview
2 — Physically/mentally unable to answer } *FILL INTER-COMM*
3 — TA and won't return before closeout }

14. **Type Z noninterview**

a. Interview not obtained for Line No.	b. Reason (Enter code)	Codes for item 14b
313	314	1 - Never available . . .
315	316	2 - Refused . . . . } *FILL INTER-COMM*
317	318	3 - Physically/mentally unable to answer — no proxy available
319	320	4 - TA and no proxy available . . . .
		5 - Other . . . .
		6 - Office use only

▶ Complete 17 – 28 for each Line No. in 14a.

15a. **Household members 12 years of age and OVER**
   321   _____ Total number

15b. **Household members UNDER 12 years of age**
   322   _____ Total number
   0 ☐ None

16. **Crime Incident Reports filled**
   323   _____ Total number — *Fill BOUNDING INFORMATION*
   0 ☐ None

Notes

FIGURE 2.1   National Crime Victimization Survey Questionnaire

PERSONAL CHARACTERISTICS

17. **NAME** (of household respondent)	18. **Type of interview** PGM 4	19. **Line** **No.**
Last	401	402
First	1 ☐ Per. — Self-respondent 2 ☐ Tel. — Self-respondent 3 ☐ Per. — Proxy ⎱ *Fill 13 on* 4 ☐ Tel. — Proxy ⎰ *cover page* 5 ☐ Noninterview - *Fill 19-28 and 14 on cover page*	Line No.

20. **Relationship to reference person**	21. **Age last birthday**	22a. **Marital status THIS survey period**	22b. **Marital status LAST survey period**	23. **Sex**	24. **Armed Forces member**	25. **Education — highest grade**	26. **Education —complete that year?**	27. **Race**	28. **Hispanic origin**
403 1 ☐ Reference person 2 ☐ Husband 3 ☐ Wife 4 ☐ Own child 5 ☐ Parent 6 ☐ Brother/Sister 7 ☐ Other relative 8 ☐ Non-relative	404 ___ Age	405 1 ☐ Married 2 ☐ Widowed 3 ☐ Divorced 4 ☐ Separated 5 ☐ Never married	406 1 ☐ Married 2 ☐ Widowed 3 ☐ Divorced 4 ☐ Separated 5 ☐ Never married 6 ☐ Not inter-viewed last survey period	407 1 ☐ M 2 ☐ F	408 1 ☐ Yes 2 ☐ No	409 ___ Grade	410 1 ☐ Yes 2 ☐ No	411 1 ☐ White 2 ☐ Black 3 ☐ Amer. Indian, Aleut, Eskimo 4 ☐ Asian, Pacific Islander 5 ☐ Other	412 1 ☐ Yes 2 ☐ No

PGM 5

29. Date of interview

501 ☐☐ ☐☐ ☐☐
  Month   Day   Year

30. Before we get to the crime questions, I have some questions that are helpful in studying where and why crimes occur.

How long have you lived at this address?

Enter number of months OR number of years. If more than 11 months, enter number of years and leave months blank.

502 _____ Months (1-11) — *SKIP to 31*

OR

503 _____ Years (Round to nearest whole year) — *Fill Check Item A*

CHECK ITEM A   How many years are entered in 30?
☐ 5 years or more — *SKIP to Check Item B*
☐ 1-5 years — *SKIP to 32*

31. How many people 12 years of age or older were living in your previous household, including you?

504 _____ Number of people 12 +

32. Altogether, how many times have you moved in the last 5 years, that is, since_____, 19_____?
                           (Mo. of Int.)   *(5 yrs. ago)*

505 _____ Number of times

CHECK ITEM B   Is the respondent 16 years or older?
☐ Yes — Ask 33
☐ No — *SKIP to 35a*

33. Did you work at a job or business LAST WEEK?
(Do not include volunteer work or work around the house)

INTERVIEWER — *If farm or business operator in the household, ask about unpaid work.*

506   1 ☐ Yes — *SKIP to 35a*
      2 ☐ No

34a. Did you work at a job or business DURING THE LAST 6 MONTHS?

507   1 ☐ Yes — *Ask 34b*
      2 ☐ No — *SKIP to 35a*

34b. Did that job/work last 2 consecutive weeks or more?

508   1 ☐ Yes
      2 ☐ No

35a. Does anyone in this household operate a business from this address?

509   1 ☐ Yes — *Ask 35b*
      2 ☐ No — *SKIP to 36*

35b. PERSONAL — *Fill by observation.*
TELEPHONE — *Ask.*

Is there a sign on the premises or some other indication to the general public that a business is operated from this address?

510   1 ☐ Yes
      2 ☐ No

Notes

Page 2

FORM NCS-1 (4-10-86)

FIGURE 2.1   (Continued)

Continued

HOUSEHOLD SCREEN QUESTIONS

36. Now I'd like to ask some questions about crime. They refer only to the last 6 months — between _____ 1, 19___ and _____, 19___. During the last 6 months, did anyone break into or somehow illegally get into your (apartment/home), garage, or another building on your property?
☐ Yes — How many times?
☐ No

37. (Other than the incident(s) just mentioned) Did you find a door jimmied, a lock forced, or any other signs of an ATTEMPTED break in?
☐ Yes — How many times?
☐ No

38. Was anything at all stolen that is kept outside your home, or happened to be left out, such as a bicycle, a garden hose, or lawn furniture? (other than any incidents already mentioned)
☐ Yes — How many times?
☐ No

39. Did anyone take something belonging to you or to any member of this household, from a place where you or they were temporarily staying, such as a friend's or relative's home, a hotel or motel, or a vacation home?
☐ Yes — How many times?
☐ No

40. What was the TOTAL number of motor vehicles (cars, trucks, motorcycles, etc.) owned by you or any other member of this household during the last 6 months? Include those you no longer own.
511
0 ☐ None — SKIP to 43
1 ☐ 1
2 ☐ 2
3 ☐ 3
4 ☐ 4 or more

41. Did anyone steal, TRY to steal, or use (it/any of them) without permission?
☐ Yes — How many times?
☐ No

42. Did anyone steal, or TRY to steal parts attached to (it/any of them), such as a battery, hubcaps, tape-deck, etc.?
☐ Yes — How many times?
☐ No

INDIVIDUAL SCREEN QUESTIONS

43. The following questions refer only to things that happened to YOU during the last 6 months — between _____ 1, 19___ and _____, 19___. Did you have your (pocket picked/ purse snatched)?
☐ Yes — How many times?
☐ No

44. Did anyone take something (else) directly from you by using force, such as by a stickup, mugging or threat?
☐ Yes — How many times?
☐ No

45. Did anyone TRY to rob you by using force or threatening to harm you? (other than any incidents already mentioned)
☐ Yes — How many times?
☐ No

46. Did anyone beat you up, attack you or hit you with something, such as a rock or bottle? (other than any incidents already mentioned)
☐ Yes — How many times?
☐ No

47. Were you knifed, shot at, or attacked with some other weapon by anyone at all? (other than any incidents already mentioned)
☐ Yes — How many times?
☐ No

48. Did anyone THREATEN to beat you up or THREATEN you with a knife, gun, or some other weapon, NOT including telephone threats? (other than any incidents already mentioned)
☐ Yes — How many times?
☐ No

49. Did anyone TRY to attack you in some other way? (other than any incidents already mentioned)
☐ Yes — How many times?
☐ No

50. During the last 6 months, did anyone steal things that belonged to you from inside ANY car or truck, such as packages or clothing?
☐ Yes — How many times?
☐ No

51. Was anything stolen from you while you were away from home, for instance at work, in a theater or restaurant, or while traveling?
☐ Yes — How many times?
☐ No

52. (Other than any incidents you've already mentioned) was anything (else) at all stolen from you during the last 6 months?
☐ Yes — How many times?
☐ No

53. Did you find any evidence that someone ATTEMPTED to steal something that belonged to you? (other than any incidents already mentioned)
☐ Yes — How many times?
☐ No

54. Did you call the police during the last 6 months to report something that happened to YOU which you thought was a crime? (Do not count any calls made to the police concerning the incidents you have just told me about.)
512
☐ No — SKIP to 55
☐ Yes — What happened?

CHECK ITEM C Look at 54. Was HHLD member 12 + attacked or threatened, or was something stolen or an attempt made to steal something that belonged to him/her?
☐ Yes — How many times?
☐ No

55. Did anything happen to YOU during the last 6 months which you thought was a crime, but did NOT report to the police? (other than any incidents already mentioned)
513
☐ No — SKIP to Check Item E
☐ Yes — What happened?

CHECK ITEM D Look at 55. Was HHLD member 12 + attacked or threatened, or was something stolen or an attempt made to steal something that belonged to him/her?
☐ Yes — How many times?
☐ No

CHECK ITEM E Who besides the respondent was present when screen questions were asked? (If telephone interview, mark box 1 only.)
514
1 ☐ Telephone interview — Go to Check Item F
Personal interview — Mark all that apply.
2 ☐ No one besides respondent present
3 ☐ Respondent's spouse
4 ☐ HHLD member(s) 12 +, not spouse
5 ☐ HHLD member(s) under 12
6 ☐ Nonhousehold member(s)
7 ☐ Someone was present — Can't say who
8 ☐ Don't know if someone else present

CHECK ITEM F If self-response interview, SKIP to Check Item G
Did the person for whom this interview was taken help the proxy respondent answer any screen questions?
515
1 ☐ Yes
2 ☐ No
3 ☐ Person for whom interview taken not present

CHECK ITEM G Do any of the screen questions contain any entries for "How many times?"
☐ Yes — Fill Crime Incident Reports.
☐ No — Interview next HHLD member. End interview if last respondent.

FORM NCS-1 (4-10-86)

FIGURE 2.1   (Continued)

NCVS is an annual survey of citizens that is collected by the U.S. Bureau of Census in cooperation with the Bureau of Justice Statistics of the U.S. Department of Justice. Census Bureau personnel conduct interviews with all household members over the age of twelve. These households stay in the sample for three years and are interviewed every six months. The total sample size of this survey is approximately 66,000 households with 101,000 individuals.[7]

The NCVS provides data regarding the victims of crime, including age, sex, race, ethnicity, marital status, income, and educational level, as well as information about the offender. Questions covering the victim's experience with the justice system, details regarding any self-protective measures used by the victims, and possible substance abuse by offenders are included in the survey. There are periodic supplemental questionnaires that address specific issues such as school crime.

However, the NCVS suffers from problems that mitigate its validity, such as respondents underreporting or overreporting crimes. The NCVS is based on an extensive scientific sample of American households. Therefore every crime measure presented in the NCVS report is an estimate based on results of the sample. Because it is only an estimate, it will have a sampling variation or margin of error associated with each sample. Additionally, it is only an estimate of criminal activity and does not mean that the crime actually occurred.

Each method of collecting data on violence presents a different perspective and has its own validity problems. What is certain is that violence occurs on all social and economic levels in our nation. Its toll on victims is severe and long lasting. No matter which statistic or sample one uses, all agree further research is necessary. Other researchers have gathered data regarding specific forms of violence.

In 1989, the NCVS was redesigned, and after a careful evaluation, it was implemented in 1993. The NCVS was redesigned because of criticism of the survey's capacity to gather information about certain crimes, including sexual assaults and domestic violence. New questions were added to accommodate heightened interest in certain types of victimizations. These changes have substantially improved the reporting of many types of personal and household crimes.[8]

According to the NCVS, violent crimes have shown a steady decline since 1994, reaching, in 2003, the lowest level ever recorded. Property crimes declined until 2002 and stabilized in 2003. Persons from age twelve to twenty-four suffered violent victimizations at higher rates than individuals of all other ages. When comparing whites, blacks, and persons of all other races, blacks had the highest rate of violent victimization. Excluding rape and sexual assault crimes, males were victimized at a higher rate than females.[9]

A Comparison of the Uniform Crime Reports and the National Crime Victimization Survey

The U.S. Department of Justice administers both the UCR and the NCVS. These programs provide valuable information about various aspects of the United States' crime problems. The UCR and the NCVS serve different purposes and use different methods to measure crime. Because of these approaches, the information they produce provides a comprehensive picture of the crime problem in the United States.

The NCVS was designed to complement the UCR, and each program therefore has similarities. Both programs examine rape, robbery, assault, burglary, theft, and motor vehicle theft. Rape, robbery, theft, and motor vehicle theft are defined in the same way in both programs. However, the UCR only measures rape against women, while the NCVS measures rape against both sexes.

The UCR's primary mission is to produce a reliable set of criminal justice statistics for law enforcement administration, operation, and management. The NCVS was established to provide previously unreported data about crime, victims, and offenders. The UCR measures crime reported to law enforcement agencies, while the NCVS includes both reported crime and unreported crime.

The programs define some crimes differently. For example, the UCR defines burglary as the unlawful entry or attempted entry of a structure to commit a felony or theft. The NCVS does not want victims to try to determine the intent of the offenders, so it defines burglary as the entry or attempted entry of residence by a person who had no right to be there.

For certain property crimes, the UCR measures these crimes per capita (number of crimes per 100,000 persons), while the NCVS measures these crime per household (number of crimes per 1,000 households). Because the number of households may not grow at the same rate as the total population, any growth or decline of these crimes may not be similar.[10]

National Assessment Program

The National Institute of Justice conducts the *National Assessment Program (NAP)* survey approximately every three years that seeks to determine the needs and problems of state and local criminal justice agencies. Although not technically a measurement of crime, it identifies the day-to-day issues affecting professionals in the criminal justice system. It therefore provides a valuable insight into concerns that are raised by the professional whose job it is to fight crime.

The 1994 NAP survey contacted over 2500 directors of criminal justice agencies including police chiefs and sheriffs, prosecutors, judges, probation and parole agency directors, commissioners of corrections, state court administrators, prison wardens, and other criminal justice professionals. The samples covered all fifty states and the District of Columbia. Both urban (populations greater than 250,000) and rural (populations of 50,000 to 250,000) counties were included in the survey. Respondents were asked a variety of questions dealing with workload problems, staffing, and operations and procedures.

The results of the survey indicate a great concern about the impact that violence, drugs, firearms, and troubled youth are having on society and an overburdened criminal justice system. Overall, the survey indicates that cases involving violence caused problems with agencies' workloads. Police chiefs and sheriffs indicated that domestic violence was primary among crimes of violence, causing them increased workload problems. Prosecutors ranked child abuse and domestic violence as significantly increasing their workload.[11] In the opinion of police chiefs

Uniform Crime Reports (UCR) and the National Crime Survey (NCS) Are the Main Sources of National Crime Statistics

How do UCR and NCS compare?

	Uniform Crime Reports	National Crime Survey
Offenses measured	Homicide Rape Robbery (personal and commercial) Assault (aggravated) Burglary (commercial and household) Larceny (commercial and household) Motor vehicle theft Arson	Rape Robbery (personal) Assault (aggravated and simple) Household burglary Larceny (personal and household) Motor vehicle theft
Scope	Crimes reported to the police in most jurisdictions; considerable flexibility in developing small-area data	Crimes both reported and not reported to police; all data are available for a few large geographic areas
Collection method	Police department reports to FBI or to centralized State agencies that then report to FBI	Survey interviews; periodically measures the total number of crimes committed by asking a national sample of 49,000 households encompassing 101,000 persons age twelve and over about their experiences as victims of crime during a specified period.
Kinds of information	In addition to offense courts, provides information on crime clearances, persons arrested, persons charged, law enforcement officers killed and assaulted, and characteristics of homicide victims	Provides details about victims (such as age, race, sex, education, income, and whether the victim and offender were related to each other) and about crimes (such as time and place of occurrence, whether or not reported to police, use of weapons, occurrence of injury, and economic consequences)
Sponsor	Department of Justice Federal Bureau of Investigation	Department of Justice Bureau of Justice Statistics

Source: *Report to the Nation on Crime and Justice*, 2nd ed. Bureau of Justice Statistics, U.S. Department of Justice, Washington, D.C., March 1988, p. 11.

and sheriffs, programs that prevent young people from obtaining guns is one of their greatest needs. In essence, it appears that law enforcement views the problem of juvenile crime in large part as a result of firearms.

Interest in community policing continues to grow. Although the controversy around the effectiveness of community policing still exists, most law enforcement officials express a desire to implement all or portions of a community policing program in their jurisdiction. This approach recognizes the importance of involving the community in addressing the crime problem.

The program points out that we continue as a nation to become more culturally diverse. Law enforcement officials acknowledge this trend in a variety of ways. Sheriffs and police chiefs state that they are aware of the need to respond to culturally diverse populations in the wake of changing national demographics.

These findings will assist policymakers in establishing research priorities for the near future. Professionals in the field have the same concerns that researchers and citizens display—the need for an end to violence in our society. These official reports provide insight into the problem, but they do not offer any concrete solutions.

Other Reports

National Family Violence Surveys

Two of the most comprehensive studies of family violence were carried out by Murray Straus and Richard J. Gelles in 1975 and 1985.[12] Both surveys involved interviews with a nationally representative sample of 2143 respondents in 1975 and 6014 respondents in 1985. The results of these landmark surveys continue to provide information and data for study in the area of family violence. They are continually cited as authority in numerous texts, articles, and research projects.

In both surveys, violence was defined as an act carried out with the intention, or perceived intention, of causing physical pain or injury to another person. Acts of violence that had a high probability of causing injury were included even if injury did not occur as a result. Violence was measured by using the Conflict Tactics Scale (CTS). This tool was developed at the University of New Hampshire in 1971 and is still used in many studies of family violence. The CTS measures three variables: (1) use of rational discussion and agreement, (2) use of verbal and nonverbal expressions of hostility, and (3) use of physical force or violence. Respondents were asked how many times within the last year they used certain responses that fell within one of the three classifications when they had a disagreement or were angry with family members.

Both studies were judged to be reliable because of the sampling procedure, the large number of respondents, and the validity of the conflict tactics scale as a measuring instrument. The studies surveyed families from all fifty states and assessed several different relationships: parent to child, child to parent, wife to husband, husband to wife, and sibling interactions. Interviews were conducted by trained investigators and lasted approximately one hour in the 1975 study and thirty minutes in the 1985 survey.

A comparison of the results of these studies indicated that physical child abuse declined from 1975 to 1985. Straus points out that there are several explanations for such a result. First is the increased awareness of child abuse from 1975 to 1985. During that ten-year period, child abuse became a common media topic. This knowledge, on the part of the respondents, may have lessened the likelihood of their reporting such acts of violence. Second, different data collection techniques were used in the two surveys: the 1975 data was obtained via the telephone, and the 1985 results were collected by means of personal interviews. Finally, there may have actually been a decline in child abuse incidents from 1975 to 1985. Even if the last explanation is correct, as Straus points out, this still translates into the fact that one of every thirty-three children, three to seven years old and living with their parents, are victims of child abuse.

Other Sources of Data on Violence

Clinical studies are another source of information regarding violence. These studies are carried out by practitioners in the field—medical professionals, psychiatrists, psychologists, and counselors—all of whom use samples gathered from actual cases of family violence. These researchers collect information from hospitals, clinics, and therapy sessions. Clinical studies normally have small sample sizes and therefore caution must be used when drawing any conclusions. However, these studies provide valuable data on the nature of abuse and assist in evaluating the different types of interventions utilized in family violence as well as pointing out areas for further research.

Women are not the only victims of violent crime. Researchers and professionals have attempted to study violent crime from a variety of perspectives including both the offender's and the victim's. In 1989, Weiner conducted a review of the major research dealing with individual violent crime.[13] He reviewed over forty major studies conducted by scholars between 1978 and 1987. He concluded that the further an offender advances into the sequence of violent crime, the greater the risk that the offender will continue his violent behavior.[14]

There are also other violent acts that have only recently become criminalized. Stalking is the crime of the nineties.[15] It is a newly emerging area of criminal law that is being studied by several experts in the field of human behavior. Zona and his associates are using the files of the Threat Management Unit of the Los Angeles Police Department in an effort to study stalkers.[16] Meloy has published several articles and texts that examine the nature and extent of stalkers and violence.

Other Types of Crime Research

Violent crime receives most of the publicity in our society; however, it is only one of many crimes suffered by citizens. Property crime, fraud, and white-collar crime take a tremendous toll on their victims. There is a number of reasons for this lack of attention regarding nonviolent crime: the victims' movement initially focused on serious violent crime, a lack of understanding regarding the psychological and financial consequences of property or economic crimes, and a traditional underreporting of the nature and extent of this type of crime.

Sutherland's classic definition of white-collar crime is one way of viewing this offense. He defined white-collar crime as an offense committed by a person of respectability and high social status in the course of his occupation.[17] The FBI on the other hand, defines white-collar crime as those illegal acts characterized by deceit, concealment, violation of trust, and nondependence on the application or threat of physical force or violence. They are committed to obtain money, property, or services; or to avoid the payment or loss of money, property, or services; or to secure personal or business advantage.[18] Both of these definitions deal with economic crimes, or crimes that have the gathering of assets from the victim as their objective.

Several prominent researchers have called for more information about economic crime.[19] Understanding the nature and extent of economic crime is necessary if we are to attempt to respond to its consequences. One of the most common forms of economic crime is fraud. A nationwide survey of fraud revealed that a sizable portion of the adult population in the United States is affected.[20] Fraud was defined as a deliberate intent, targeted against individuals, to deceive for the purpose of illegal financial gain.[21] Included in this definition were various forms of telemarketing frauds, frauds involving consumer goods and services, deceptive financial advice, and insurance scams.

The survey used a random sample of the adult population of the United States. The respondents were asked about twenty-one types of fraud plus a catch-all category and were asked if they had ever been victimized or if an attempt had been made to victimize them. Fraud crosses all sociological barriers and victimization occurs in all ages, genders, races, or incomes.

More than half of those surveyed indicated that they experienced victimization, or an attempted victimization at some time in their past. Approximately one in every three respondents were potential victims of fraud within the year preceding the survey. The attempt to defraud these victims was successful 50 percent of the time.

Economic crime is a serious form of victimization that is often overlooked by those tasked with, or interested in, studying the effects of crime on individuals. The consequences of fraud will be addressed in more detail later in this text. At this stage, it is important to acknowledge that there are other forms of victimization than violence-related crimes.

Summary

It is important in the study of any discipline to know how to measure the variables that affect that discipline. Because of a number of factors, which are discussed in more detail later in this text, the measurement of crime can never be completely accurate.

Official reports are those measurements of crime conducted by federal agencies. The most well-known official report is the Uniform Crime Report. This report, prepared annually by the FBI, acts as a barometer of our society. Because of several inherent shortcomings in the UCR, the National Crime Victimization Survey was developed. This survey relies on self-reporting in an attempt to determine a more accurate accounting of the nature and extent of crimes in our society.

Other reports include the National Family Violence Survey and a variety of other sources of information regarding acts of violence. Researchers are paying significant attention to economic crimes and their effects on victims. Recent studies indicate that economic crimes, such as fraud, are widespread and occur at all socioeconomic levels within our society.

We continue to modify our measurement tools in the hopes of perfecting a valid and true method of measuring crime. Understanding the nature and extent of criminal victimization is only the beginning in understanding the process of victimization itself. However, it is a critical phase in the study of victimology and one that all professionals in the field should understand.

Key Terms

Uniform Crime Reports (UCR) program is a nationwide statistical computation involving over 1600 cities, counties, and state law enforcement agencies who voluntarily provide data on reported crimes.

National Crime Victimization Survey (NCVS) is a nationwide sample of interviews of citizens regarding victimization.

National Assessment Program (NAP) seeks to determine the needs and problems of state and local criminal justice agencies.

Discussion Questions

1. Explain the problems in using the UCR. If you were in charge of preparing it, what changes would you suggest to make it more reliable?

2. How would you improve the NCVS?

3. How does the NAP information benefit victim service professionals?

4. The National Family Violence Surveys were conducted over ten years ago. Why are data from the surveys still important?

5. Compare and contrast the other types of crime research. Can you think of another method to collect information about crime and victims?

Suggested Readings

M. A. Straus, R. J. Gelles & S. K. Steinmetz, *Behind Closed Doors: Violence in the American Family*, (Anchor/Doubleday, New York) 1980.

M. A. Straus, "Is Violence Toward Children Increasing? A Comparison of the 1975 and 1985 National Survey Rates," R. J. Gelles, ed., *Family Violence*, (Sage, Newbury Park, Calif.) 1987.

D. G. Kilpatrick, C. N. Edmunds & A. K. Seymour, *Rape in America: A Report to the Nation*, (National Victim Center, Arlington, Va.) 1992.

D. E. H. Russell, *Sexual Exploitation*, (Sage, Beverly Hills, Calif.) 1984.

N. A. Weiner and M. E. Wolfgang, eds. *Violent Crime, Violent Criminals*, (Sage, Newbury Park, Calif.) 1989.

E. H. Sutherland, *White Collar Crime, The Uncut Version*, (Yale University Press, New Haven, Conn.) 1983.

Report of the Attorney General, *National Practices for the Investigation and Prosecution of White*

Collar Crime, U.S. Department of Justice, (Office of the Attorney General, Washington, D.C.) 1990.

Geis, Gilbert & R. A. Stotland, *White Collar Crime: Theory and Research,* (Sage, Newbury Park, Calif.) 1980.

Endnotes

1. 28 USC 534 (1930).
2. "Crime in the United States, 1994," *Uniform Crime Reports,* (Superintendent of Documents, Washington, D.C.) 1994.
3. Bureau of Justice Statistics, *Criminal Victimization in the United States, 1992,* (U.S. Department of Justice, Washington, D.C.) 1994, p. 100.
4. M. E. Milakovich & Kurt Weis, "Politics and the Measure of Success in the War on Crime," 21 *Crime and Delinquency,* 1–10 (January 1975).
5. Ramona R. Santala, "Effects of NIBRS on Crime Statistics," *Special Report, Bureau of Justice Statistics,* U.S. Department of Justice, Washington, D.C. (July 2000).
6. The UCR states that the NCVS started in 1973. See "Crime in the United States, 1994," *Uniform Crime Reports,* (Superintendent of Documents, Washington, D.C.) 1994.
7. The UCR presents a different estimate of households than the NCVS. See "Crime in the United States, 1994," *Uniform Crime Reports,* (Superintendent of Documents, Washington, D.C.) 1994.
8. Wesley G. Skogan, "A Review: The National Crime Survey Redesign," vol. 54 *The Public Opinion Quarterly,* No. 2 (Summer 1990), pp. 256–272.
9. Online: www.opj.usdoj.gov/bjs/glance/ciort.htm.
10. Michael R. Rand and Callie M. Rennison, "True Crime Stories? Accounting for Differences in Our National Crime Indicators," vol. 15 *Chance,* No. 1, p. 47 (2002).
11. Tom McEwen, "National Assessment Program: 1994 Survey Results," *Research in Brief,* National Institute of Justice, (May 1995) p. 2.
12. See M. A. Straus, R. J. Gelles & S. K. Steinmetz, *Behind Closed Doors: Violence in the*

American Family, (Anchor/Doubleday, New York 1980) for an in-depth discussion of the 1975 survey; and M. A. Straus, "Is Violence Toward Children Increasing? A Comparison of the 1975 and 1985 National Survey Rates," R. J. Gelles, ed., *Family Violence,* (Sage, Newbury Park, Calif. 1987) for an analysis of the 1985 survey.
13. Neil Alan Weiner, "Violent Criminal Careers and 'Violent Career Criminals,'" *Violent Crime, Violent Criminals,* N. A. Weiner and M. E. Wolfgang, eds. (Sage, Newbury Park, Calif.) 1989.
14. Id. at p. 127.
15. See for example, H. Wallace, "Stalkers, The Constitution's and Victims' Remedies," vol. 10/1 ABA *Criminal Justice,* 16 (Spring 1995).
16. Michael A. Zona, et al., "A Comparative Study of Erotomonic and Obsessional Subjects in a Forensic Sample," 38 *Journal of Forensic Science,* 894 (July 1993).
17. E. H. Sutherland, *White Collar Crime, The Uncut Version,* (Yale University Press, New Haven, Conn.) 1983.
18. Report of the Attorney Gerneral, *National Practices for the Investigation and Prosecution of White Collar Crime,* U.S. Department of Justice, (Office of the Attorney General, Washington, D.C.) 1990.
19. Geis, Gilbert & R. A. Stotland, *White Collar Crime: Theory and Research,* (Sage, Newbury Park, Calif.) 1980.
20. Much of the material presented in this section dealing with fraud comes from Richard Titus, Fred Heinzelmann & John M. Boyle, "The Anatomy of Fraud: Report of a Nationwide Survey," Research in Action, *National Institute of Justice Journal,* 28 (August 1995).
21. Id.

3

THE CRIMINAL JUSTICE SYSTEM AND VICTIMS

Chapter Outline

Deliberation and Verdict
Sentencing

Summary

Key Terms

Discussion Questions

Suggested Readings

Learning Objectives

After reading this chapter, you should be able to:

- Understand the principle of federalism and how it affected the structure of our court system
- Discuss how the dual system of state and federal courts functions
- Describe the characteristics of the American court system
- Discuss how the juvenile court system functions
- Understand the roles and responsibilities of each party in the criminal justice system
- Describe the various steps in the criminal justice process
- Explain the differences between the various types of pleas a defendant may enter

The Criminal Court System[1]

Introduction

Understanding the role and functions of the various court systems in the United States provides professionals with a solid foundation for understanding the dynamics of the law. It is a complex aspect of our legal system that can be confusing and frustrating to victims when they are first exposed to it. Understanding the rationale behind its present-day structure may help victims understand more clearly the manner in which laws operate and interact.

To comprehend the role of federal and state law, it is essential to have a firm grasp of the principles of how the American criminal justice system functions. For a victim of crime, it is the most confusing, frustrating, and complex environment to navigate. This section will provide a brief overview of the criminal court system in the United States.

The court system in the United States is based on the principle of federalism. The first Congress established a federal court system, and the individual states were permitted to continue their own judicial structure. There was general agreement among our nation's founders that individual states needed to retain significant autonomy from federal control. Under this concept of federalism, the United States developed as a loose confederation of semi-independent states having their own courts, with the federal court system acting in a very limited manner. In the early history of our nation, most cases were tried in state courts. It was only later that the federal government and the federal judiciary began to exercise jurisdiction over crimes and civil matters. *Jurisdiction* in this context simply means the ability of the court to enforce laws and punish individuals who violate those laws.

As a result of this historical evolution, a dual system of state and federal courts exists today. Therefore, federal and state courts may have concurrent jurisdiction over specific crimes. For example, a person who robs a bank may be tried and convicted in state court for robbery, then tried and convicted in federal court for the federal offense of robbery of a federally chartered savings institution.

Another characteristic of the American court system is that it performs its duties with little or no supervision. A Supreme Court justice does not exercise supervision over lower court judges in the same way that a government supervisor or manager exercises control over employees. The U.S. Supreme Court and the various state supreme courts exercise supervision only in the sense that they hear appellate cases from lower courts and establish certain procedures for these courts.

A third feature of the U.S. court system is one of specialization and occurs primarily at the state and local level. In many states, courts of limited jurisdiction hear misdemeanor cases. Other state courts of general jurisdiction try felonies. Still other courts may be designated as juvenile courts and hear only matters involving juveniles. This process also occurs in certain civil courts that hear only family law matters, probate matters, or civil cases involving damages. At the federal level, there are courts such as bankruptcy that hear only cases dealing with specific matters.

The fourth characteristic of the American court system is its geographic organization. State and federal courts are organized into geographic areas. In many jurisdictions these are called judicial districts and contain various levels of courts. For example, on the federal level, the Ninth Circuit Court of Appeals has district (trial) courts that hear matters within certain specific boundaries; and an appellate court that hears all appeals from cases within that area. Several studies have been conducted regarding the differences in sentences for the same type of crime in geographically distinct courts. For example, in Iowa the average sentence for motor vehicle theft is forty-seven months whereas the average sentence for the same offense in New York is fourteen months.[2] This and similar discrepancies may reflect different social values and attitudes within specific geographic areas.

State Court System

Historically, each of the thirteen original states had its own unique court structure. This independence continued after the American Revolution and resulted in widespread differences among the various states, some of which still exist today. Because each state adopted its own system of courts, the consequence was a poorly planned and confusing judicial structure. Several reform movements have attempted to streamline and modernize this system. These reforms have resulted in many of the state court systems adopting a three-tier judicial system.

Many state courts are now divided into three levels:

- Trial courts
- Appellate courts
- State supreme courts

Trial Courts

Trial courts are courts where criminal cases start and finish. The trial court conducts an entire series of acts that culminate in either the defendant's release or sentencing. State trial courts can be further divided into courts of limited or special jurisdiction and courts of general jurisdiction. The nature and type of case determines which court will have jurisdiction.

Courts that only hear and decide certain limited legal issues are courts of *limited jurisdiction*. These courts hear and decide issues such as traffic tickets or set bail for criminal defendants. Typically, these courts hear certain types of minor civil or criminal cases. There are approximately 13,000 local courts in the United States. They are called county, magistrate, justice, or municipal courts. Judges in these courts may be either appointed or elected. In many jurisdictions these are part-time positions and the incumbent may have another job or position in addition to serving as a judge. However, simply because they handle minor civil and criminal matters does not negate the fact that these courts perform important duties. Often, the only contact the average citizen will have with the judicial system occurs at this level.

In addition, courts of limited jurisdiction may hear certain types of specialized matters such as probate of wills and estates, divorces, child custody matters, and juvenile hearings. These types of courts may be local courts or, depending on the state, courts of general jurisdiction that are designated by statute to hear and decide specific types of cases. For example, in California, a superior court is considered a court of general jurisdiction; however, certain superior courts are designated to hear only juvenile matters, thereby becoming a court of limited jurisdiction when sitting as a juvenile court.

Courts of *general jurisdiction* are granted authority to hear and decide all issues that are brought before them. These courts normally hear all major civil or criminal cases. They are also known by a variety of names, such as superior courts, circuit courts, district courts, or courts of common pleas. Because they are courts of general jurisdiction, they have authority to decide issues that occur anywhere within the state. Some larger jurisdictions such as Los Angeles or New York may have hundreds of courts of general jurisdiction within the city limits. These courts also hear the most serious forms of criminal matters including death penalty cases.

Courts of general jurisdiction traditionally have the power to order individuals to do, or refrain from doing, certain acts. These courts may issue injunctions that prohibit persons from performing certain acts, or they may require individuals to do certain functions or duties. This authority is derived from the equity power that resides in courts of general jurisdiction.

Equity is the concept that justice is administered according to fairness, as contrasted with the strict rules of law. In early English common law, such separate courts of equity were known as courts of Chancery. These early courts were not concerned with technical legal issues; rather they focused on rendering decisions or orders that were fair or equitable. In modern times the power of these courts has been merged with courts of general jurisdiction, allowing them to rule on matters that require fairness as well as the strict application of the law. The power to issue temporary restraining orders (TROs) in spousal abuse cases comes from the equitable powers of the court.

Appellate jurisdiction is reserved for courts that hear appeals from both limited and general jurisdiction courts. These courts do not hold trials or hear evidence. They decide matters of law and issue formal written decisions or "opinions." There are two classes of appellate courts: intermediate, or courts of appeals and final, or supreme courts.

Courts of Appeals

The intermediate appellate courts are known as courts of appeals. Approximately half the states have designated intermediate appellate courts. These courts may be divided into judicial districts and will hear all appeals within their jurisdiction. They will hear and decide all issues of law that are raised on appeal in both civil and criminal cases. Because these courts deal strictly with legal or equitable issues, there is no jury to decide factual disputes. These courts accept the facts as determined by the trial courts. Intermediate appellate courts have the authority to reverse the decision of the lower courts, and to send the matter back with instructions to retry the case in accordance with their opinion. They may also uphold the decision of the lower court. In either situation, the party who loses the appeal at this level may file an appeal with the next higher appellate court.

Supreme Courts

Final appellate courts are the highest state appellate courts. They may be known as supreme courts or courts of last resort. There may be five, seven, or nine justices sitting on this court depending on the state. Final appellate courts have jurisdiction to hear and decide issues dealing with all matters decided by lower courts, including ruling on state constitutional or statutory issues. Their decision is binding on all other courts within the state. Once this court has decided an issue, the only appeal left is to file in the federal court system.

Federal Court System

Whereas state courts have their origin in historical accident and custom, federal courts were created by the U.S. Constitution. Section 1 of Article 3 established the federal court system with the words providing for "one Supreme Court, and . . . such inferior Courts as the Congress may from time to time ordain and establish." From this beginning, Congress has engaged in a series of acts that has resulted in today's federal court system. The Judiciary Act of 1789 created the U.S. Supreme Court and established district courts and circuit courts of appeals.

Federal District Courts

Federal district courts are the lowest level of the federal court system. These courts have original jurisdiction over all cases involving a violation of federal statutes. District courts handle thousands of criminal cases per year.

Federal Circuit Courts

Federal circuit courts of appeals are the intermediate appellate level courts within the federal system. These courts are called circuit courts because the federal system is divided into eleven circuits. A Twelfth Circuit Court of Appeals serves the Washington, D.C., area. These courts hear all criminal appeals from the district courts and habeas corpus appeals from state court convictions. These appeals are usually heard by panels of three appellate court judges rather than by all the judges of each circuit.

U.S. Supreme Court

The United States Supreme Court is the highest court in the land. It has the capacity for judicial review of all lower court decisions, as well as state and federal statutes. By exercising this power the Supreme Court determines what laws and lower court decisions conform to the mandates set forth in the U.S. Constitution. The concept of judicial review was first referred to by Alexander Hamilton in the *Federalist Papers*, in which he described the Supreme Court as ensuring that the will of the people will be supreme over the will of the legislature.[3] This concept was firmly and finally established in our system when the Supreme Court asserted its power of judicial review in the 1803 case of *Marbury v. Madison*.[4]

Although it is primarily an appellate court, the Supreme Court has original jurisdiction in the following cases: cases between the United States and a state; cases between states; cases involving foreign ambassadors, ministers, and consuls; and cases between a state and a citizen of another state or country.

The Court hears appeals from lower courts including the various state supreme courts. If four justices of the U.S. Supreme Court vote to hear a case, the court will issue a *Writ of Certiorari*—an order sent to a lower court requiring the records of the case to be sent to the Supreme Court for review. The Court meets on the first Monday of October and usually remains in session until June. The Court may review any case it deems worthy but in actuality hears very few of the cases filed. Of approximately 5,000 appeals each year, the Court agrees to review less than 200; however, it may not issue an opinion on each case.

Juvenile Court System

Because of the significant increase in importance of juvenile crime in our society, an overview of juvenile courts within the state and federal court system is warranted. Although there are some differences, both federal and state systems were initially founded on the concept of rehabilitating young offenders. Additionally, both systems wanted to shield juveniles from public scrutiny; therefore, each contained provisions for keeping matters confidential.

The Federal Court Juvenile System

When Congress addressed the issue of juvenile offenders it established two alternatives for their prosecution:

- The juvenile can waive personal rights to be treated as a juvenile; or
- The juvenile can have the matter treated as a civil proceeding called *juvenile adjudication*.

If the court finds that the juvenile committed the offense, that individual faces a series of federal sanctions including incarceration. There is a federal preference for state prosecution of juveniles, because there is no separate federal juvenile court judge or juvenile detention system. If adjudicated to be a delinquent, the juvenile is placed in a state juvenile facility. The federal government contracts with states for this service.

Until the passage of the Crime Control Act of 1990, the federal government prosecuted only juveniles who committed crimes on federal reservations, where the states had no jurisdiction. The Crime Control Act added two other categories of juveniles who fall under federal juvenile court jurisdiction: juveniles who commit felony crimes of violence and juveniles involved in certain drug felonies. Similar to most state court systems, federal law allows for the transfer or certification of a juvenile to "adult status." This procedure allows juveniles to be tried as adults in either the state or the federal court system.

Under federal law, juveniles are those persons under twenty-one who commit a federal offense before their eighteenth birthday. A federal judge acts as the federal equivalent of the state juvenile court judge. The proceedings are confidential with no member of the public or press in attendance. Federal jurisdiction in juvenile matters is established when:

- The state does not have jurisdiction;
- The state does not have programs or services available for juveniles; or
- The offense charged is a violent felony or drug offense and there is a substantial federal interest in the case.

A juvenile proceeding is initiated by the filing of an "information." In most cases, the U.S. attorney must file a certification stating there are grounds for federal jurisdiction. The hearing in federal court is very similar to a court trial.

The State Court Juvenile System

The present-day American state court system of dealing with children involved in crimes began in 1899 when the state of Illinois passed the Illinois Juvenile Court

Act. It was at that time that the juvenile court system as we know it today came into existence.[5] This statute separated the juvenile court system from the adult criminal system. It labeled minors who violated the law as "delinquents" rather than criminals, and required that juvenile court judges determine what "is in the best interests of the minor" in rendering their decision.

The juvenile court system is guided by five basic principles:

1. The state is the ultimate parent of all children within its jurisdiction, the doctrine of *parens patrea*.
2. Children are worth saving and the state should utilize nonpunitive measures to do so.
3. Children should be nurtured and not stigmatized by the court process.
4. Each child is different and justice should be tailored to meet individual needs and requirements.
5. The use of noncriminal sanctions is necessary to give primary consideration to the needs of the child.[6]

It is important to note that each state determines its own jurisdictional age of minors who are handled by its juvenile system. Most involve children who are under eighteen years of age. A few states use higher ages, up to twenty-one. Three states cover children up to fifteen years of age and adjudicate sixteen-year-olds in adult criminal courts.

Although these principles were originally adopted for delinquents or minors who committed criminal acts, they have been broadly applied to proceedings involving children who are victims of abuse. This aspect of the juvenile court system is examined in the next chapter.

Understanding the criminal court system is only the beginning of appreciating the complexity of the American criminal justice system. Professionals working in this area must also understand the parties involved in the criminal justice system. The different parties that comprise our system are reviewed in the following sections.

The Parties

Seven parties are involved in the criminal justice process: the victim, the perpetrator, law enforcement, the prosecutor, the defense attorney, the courts, and the correctional system. Each of these parties or organizations has different goals and needs. Not all emotions or objectives are the same for all the parties. It is obvious, for example, that the prosecutor and defense attorney will have different perspectives on the outcome of the trial. Those who work in this area must be familiar with the various responsibilities of each of these parties and be able to explain their functions to those who are involved in the criminal justice system.

The Victim

The victim of any crime is often the forgotten party in the criminal justice system. For many years, victims were perceived as simply another witness to the crime. The prevailing attitude was that the real victim was the "People of the State" in which the crime was committed. Families of murder victims could not obtain information regarding the case and were often ignored by overworked and understaffed criminal justice personnel. Within the last twenty years, this attitude has begun to change as we become more aware of the needs and desires of crime victims.

Professionals dealing with crime victims must understand that they may be suffering emotional and/or physical trauma as a result of the offense.[7] Care must be taken to ensure that victims understand how the process works and what their rights are. It is also important to realize that individuals other than the original victim may have an interest in the process. These parties include the victim's family and friends, and in some situations the victim's employer. All appropriate parties should be notified of every significant event within the criminal justice process. Victim services providers must also respect and protect the victim's right to privacy if that is the victim's desire.

Victims of crime will normally have a number of questions and concerns regarding the court system and their involvement in it. One frustrating aspect of this process is that victims often perceive that the defendant has more rights and faster access to the courts than they do. Other chapters of this text examine in detail the rights of victims of crime during the criminal justice process.

The Perpetrator

The perpetrator of a crime is guaranteed certain rights within our form of government. Many aspects of the criminal procedure process are controlled by the U.S. Constitution, specifically the Bill of Rights (the original ten amendments to the Constitution). These federal constitutional protections concerning individual rights are, for the most part, binding on state courts.[8]

These rights attach to the perpetrator early in the criminal procedure process, and violation of these rights may result in the case being dismissed. For example, if the perpetrator confesses to the crime of murder, and that confession is obtained in violation of the person's constitutional rights, it may be suppressed.[9] If the confession is the only link connecting the defendant to the crime, the case may have to be dismissed. When these types of incidents occur, it is difficult for the victim to understand why the defendant goes free when there has been a confession. If this happens, professionals working with victims must attempt to offer other alternatives such as availability of filing civil lawsuits against the perpetrator.

Law Enforcement

One law enforcement role in the criminal process is to apprehend the perpetrator.[10] Although this may seem to be a simple concept, understanding the organization and function of law enforcement agencies in the United States can be an exercise in frustration. American law enforcement activities take place on three independent levels: federal, state, and local. There is little uniformity among these entities. Additionally, each of these agencies may enforce different criminal laws based on different jurisdictional authority. For example, the U.S. Customs Service may arrest individuals who violate federal laws regarding the importation of goods into the United States, the state highway patrol may be tasked with enforcing traffic laws on highways and streets, and the local police department may be engaged in tracking down a serial rapist.

To confuse the issue further, there is another emerging form of law enforcement activity in the United States whose activities are expanding. Private protective services have been defined as "those self-employed individuals and privately funded business entities and organizations providing security-related services to specific clientele for a fee . . . in order to protect their persons, private property, or interests from various hazards."[11] Normally these firms are employed by corporate clients to protect private interests. They act as private citizens and may make arrests for violations of crimes committed in their presence.

The Prosecutor

The prosecuting attorney is a familiar individual in the criminal justice process. The office of the prosecuting attorney is known by a variety of names including district attorney, county attorney, commonwealth attorney, and, at the federal level, the U.S. attorney. The prosecutor plays a critical role in the criminal process for a variety of reasons. That person is the go-between for law enforcement and the courts and decides what type of charges to file, whether to plea bargain a particular case, and how to present the case to the court or jury.

One hotly debated issue surrounding the prosecutor's function concerns plea bargaining.[12] From a criminal justice perspective, a plea bargain serves several purposes: a defendant may receive the opportunity to plead guilty to a lesser charge that will reduce the time spent in jail or prison; or the prosecutor may have a weak case and a plea bargain may ensure that the defendant is convicted of something rather than walking free after an acquittal. Also, from the judge's perspective, a plea bargain eliminates one more case.[13] A plea bargain may also benefit a victim in several ways: a plea to a lesser offense eliminates the requirement that the victim relive the crime by testifying in court and, similar to the prosecutor's position, a plea bargain guarantees that the defendant is convicted of some crime. Conversely, many victims resent plea bargains because they believe that a jury should decide the case and that if the perpetrator is guilty, he or she should be punished to the maximum extent allowed by the law.

Another controversial aspect of plea bargaining is that some prosecutors fail to notify the victim of their intent to reduce or dismiss some of the charges in exchange for a plea of guilty. There are victims who have found out about the plea bargain at the time the prosecutor called to inquire about the status of the case. If plea bargaining is to occur, the preferred method is to fully involve the victim in the decision-making process. If the victim is adamantly opposed to the reduction or dismissal of charges, the prosecutor should seriously consider not going forward with the plea bargain.

The prosecuting attorney is the representative of the people of the state or of the United States. This person is not the crime victim's personal attorney. This aspect of our criminal justice system is very troubling to many victims. However, a prosecutor who is sensitive to the needs and concerns of victims of crime can help reduce these concerns and many of the other traumas suffered by these individuals.

The Defense Attorney

The defense attorney represents the rights and interests of the perpetrator. Unlike the prosecutor who is concerned with justice and fairness, the defense attorney's obligation as established by the American Bar Association's General Standards of Conduct is to use all available courage, devotion, and skills to protect the rights of the accused. Many defense attorneys interpret this obligation as requiring that they do everything possible to obtain an acquittal even if they know that the defendant in fact committed the offense.

The Sixth Amendment to the U.S. Constitution requires that those who are accused of crimes have a right to be represented by an attorney. The Supreme Court in the landmark case of *Gideon v. Wainwright* established the principle that all defendants have a right to counsel in all felony cases even if they could not afford to hire their own attorney.[14] The court extended this concept to misdemeanor cases in *Argersinger v. Hamilin* holding that absent a waiver no person may be imprisoned for any offense, either misdemeanor or felony, unless represented by an attorney.[15]

There are basically four types of defense attorneys: public defenders, contract defense services, assigned defense counsel, and private defense counsel. Public defenders are hired and paid for by the government and are appointed to represent those persons charged with crimes who cannot afford to hire an attorney for representation. Many counties have public defender's offices that are staffed by very able, aggressive attorneys. However, there are instances when, for a variety of reasons, the public defender's office has a conflict of interest in a case. For example, this may occur if there were two defendants in one case. In this situation, the court may appoint an attorney from the contract defense services to represent one of the two defendants. Contract defense services are normally composed of a group of attorneys who have entered into an agreement with the county to represent indigent defendants for a specified amount of money.

Assigned defense counsel exist in the majority of the counties in the United States.[16] Many of these counties are small and cannot afford the cost of maintaining a public defender's office. Under the assigned defense counsel format, the court maintains a list of attorneys who are willing to be appointed to represent indigent criminal defendants. When a defendant appears in court, the judge appoints the next attorney on the list to represent the perpetrator.

The last form of defense attorney is the private defense counsel. These attorneys usually represent those defendants who are capable of paying for their services. Well-known examples of private defense counsel include attorneys such as Johnny Cochran, F. Lee Bailey, and Alan Dershowitz of the "Dream Team" who represented O. J. Simpson.

Not only do perpetrators have a right to an attorney, the courts have held that the attorney must be competent.[17] Although the Constitution requires competent counsel who will vigorously defend the perpetrator, there is no requirement or right to have an attorney who will knowingly present perjured testimony. In *Nix v. Whiteside*, the defense attorney, upon learning that his client was going to take the stand and commit perjury, informed the client that he could not permit such testimony and if the client insisted on going forward and giving this testimony, the attorney would disclose the perjury and withdraw from the case. The perpetrator testified and did not commit perjury; however, he did file an appeal claiming ineffective counsel. The court disagreed holding that attorneys who follow their state's rules of professional (ethical) conduct do not violate the Sixth Amendment right to counsel.[18]

The Courts

Both the structure and organization of the court system were explained earlier in this chapter. Here it is only necessary to explain that the courts play a critical role in the criminal justice process. They bring an impartiality and formality to the system that provides it with balance, and hopefully justice.

The Correctional System

One of the least discussed entities in the criminal justice process is the correctional system. Victims' involvement with perpetrators does not end at the conviction and sentencing phase. Many victims must appear each year and offer evidence as to why a certain perpetrator should not be released from custody. Therefore, it is necessary for any professional involved with victims to understand the role and responsibilities of the various correctional institutions.

There are two basic types of penal facilities: jails and prisons. *Jails* are operated by local agencies such as cities or counties. Jails are used for pretrial detention, holding after sentencing, and for incarceration of those persons who are not being sentenced to prison. Normally these are individuals who have been convicted of misdemeanors and will serve up to one year of imprisonment. Some jurisdictions are experimenting with jail "boot camps" where the inmates undergo rigorous mental and physical training during their incarceration. *Prisons* are administrated by states or the federal government and are reserved for the more serious offenders. There are various types of prisons that range from minimum security institutions to those that house the most violent predators in society.

There are three types of persons involved in the corrections field: probation officers, parole officers, and correctional officers. Probation is a distinctly American institution. It began with John Augustus, who in 1841 asked a Boston judge to permit him to sponsor an offender. The court agreed to his request and the perpetrator was sentenced to Augustus's custody instead of jail. (Augustus is considered the father of probation.) *Probation* is a conditional release of the offender after he or she has been found guilty. It is traditionally used on misdemeanor or other low-level crimes. It allows the perpetrator to remain free so long as that person meets certain conditions. Probation officers are those persons employed by the local jurisdictions to supervise these offenders. Many different forms of probation services are offered in the United States, and there is a continuing debate on which one is the most effective.

Parole is the conditional release of an inmate back into the community from a prison or other form of correctional institution. Many jurisdictions allow for the parole of offenders, which normally occurs after a board or commission has made a determination that the prisoner would benefit from early release. Many victims who appear at these hearings and oppose the release of those predators have been sexually assaulted themselves or had their loved ones killed. These hearings are held every year in many jurisdictions with the result that the victim must relive the crime annually in an attempt to keep the perpetrator incarcerated.

Correctional officers are those persons who are hired to maintain security in jails or prisons. Many of these positions require only a high school education and a clean criminal background. Some states are beginning to impose more educational requirements on applicants and several states have upgraded their training for correctional officers.

The court system and the parties involved are only a small part of the entire criminal justice system. Victim advocates must also be familiar with the criminal justice process. The next section examines the various steps in this system.

Criminal Justice Procedures

A criminal proceeding involves many steps. *Adjudication* includes all the formal and informal decisions and steps within the criminal proceeding process. It is important to remember that in criminal cases, the government has the burden of proof. At each stage in the proceedings, the accused is afforded certain rights that are guaranteed by both federal and state constitutions. These constitutional protections have shaped the way in which our criminal process functions. From the first encounter to the execution of an inmate, certain constitutional protections mandate that law enforcement officers and those representing the government carry out their duties in certain ways. These constitutional mandates have resulted in a complex series of hearings and/or actions that must occur during any criminal proceeding. The examination of this process starts with the first formal court activity, that is, those pretrial activities associated with bringing an accused into the system.

Pretrial Activities

Pretrial activities include a variety of acts including the arrest, the booking, and the filing of a complaint. An *arrest* is taking a suspect into custody in a manner prescribed by law. An arrest usually occurs in one of two ways: when a warrant of arrest has been issued by a magistrate, or when an officer has probable cause to believe that the suspect has committed a crime. Arrest usually involves transporting the suspect to jail so charges regarding the offense can be filed. In misdemeanor or infraction cases, instead of taking the suspect to jail, the officer may simply issue a citation to the suspect. A *citation* is an order to appear before a judge at a later time. An example of a citation is a traffic ticket issued by an officer to a person who violates the vehicle code laws.

When the officer transports the offender to the local police station, the booking process begins. *Booking* involves entering the suspect's name, offense, and other information into the police records. The suspect is also fingerprinted and photographed at this time. The suspect is usually allowed to make a phone call during this process. For certain types of offenses, a bail schedule is established and made available at the police department. If the suspect can pay the amount listed on the bail schedule, he or she is freed and ordered to report to a judge at a predetermined time. In more serious cases, the suspect is taken before a judge for a bail hearing. This type of hearing is discussed in more detail later in this chapter.

In many jurisdictions, pretrial activities include filing a complaint by the local prosecutor's office. However, prior to filing the complaint, the prosecutor reviews the facts of the case and decides what charge to file. This process takes place with both felonies and misdemeanors.

The First Appearance

Once the suspect is in custody, the suspect (who is now called the defendant) must be brought before a judge without unnecessary delay. In *County of Riverside v. McLaughlin* the Supreme Court held that defendants must be brought before a judge within forty-eight hours.[19] The court further held that weekends and holidays could not be excluded from the forty-eight-hour rule, and in some cases delays of less than two days may still be considered unreasonable.

At this first hearing the defendant is informed of the charges and of his or her right to counsel. If the defendant is indigent, the judge begins the process of appointing an attorney for him or her. It is during this first appearance that bail is set.

Historically, the right to bail was considered so important that the drafters of the U.S. Constitution included it in the Bill of Rights. The Eighth Amendment states that excessive bail shall not be required; however, this does not mean that all defendants have a right to bail for all crimes. The right to bail requires that the judge consider the defendant's individualized circumstances in setting bail.[20] These factors include the nature and circumstances of the offense, the weight of evidence against the defendant, the financial ability of the defendant to pay the bail, and the character of the defendant.

In recent years, the defendant's dangerousness has also come under scrutiny in establishing bail. Preventive detention allows the court to deny bail based on a finding that the defendant may commit further crimes if released. The most elaborate preventive detention scheme in existence is found in the Federal Bail Reform Act of 1984, which makes the safety of any other person, or the community, a relevant consideration in setting bail.[21] This aspect of bail is especially important in family violence situations, and every effort must be made by professionals who work in this field to gather all pertinent information and forward it to the prosecutor in a timely manner so that it can be presented to the judge during the bail hearing.

Preliminary Hearing or Grand Jury Hearing

In felony cases, the next step is the preliminary hearing or grand jury hearing. The preliminary hearing is similar to the first appearance in that it occurs before a judge of a lower or municipal court. The purpose of the preliminary hearing is for the judge to make an impartial determination of whether there is probable cause to believe a crime has been committed and that the defendant committed it. The defendant is present during this hearing and is represented by counsel who has the right to cross- examine any witnesses that are called to testify by the prosecutor. At the end of the presentation of evidence, the judge must determine if there is sufficient evidence to "bind over" or forward the case to the superior court for further proceedings and/or trial.

The grand jury hearing is conducted in secret. The grand jurors are citizens selected to serve for one year. They decide by majority vote whether to issue an indictment. The prosecuting attorney presents the evidence, and neither the defendant nor the defendant's attorney is present. If the grand jury finds there is sufficient evidence, it files a "true bill" with the superior court. A true bill is an indictment charging the defendant with the crime or crimes.

The Constitution does not require that states use a grand jury.[22] In about one-half of the states, a grand jury indictment is used for at least some of the felony cases. Grand juries are used in federal courts and in those states that mandate the use of grand juries. In many states, if the prosecutor has a sensitive case such as one dealing with a young child who has been molested, that prosecutor may decide to use a grand jury even if not mandated to do so by state statute. If a grand jury indictment is not used, the preliminary hearing is held and any information is filed by the prosecutor with the trial court. Similar to an indictment, the information sets forth all charges against the defendant.

Arraignment

Once the indictment or information is filed, the defendant is brought before the court and *arraigned*. In this hearing the charges are formally read and the defendant is asked to enter a plea. This is not a trial, and other than reading the charges, the court does not examine any of the evidence against the defendant at this time.

It is during this hearing that the defendant may enter one of three basic pleas: guilty, not guilty, or nolo contendere. In a guilty plea, the defendant admits to committing the offenses charged. If the defendant is entering a guilty plea, the court will normally inquire if he or she understands the nature and consequences of the plea and if the plea is being entered voluntarily. Many courts will read all the consequences of a plea into the record to prevent appeals by the defendant at a later time.

A not-guilty plea requires that the matter be set for trial and mandates that the prosecutor prove every element of the crimes charged and prove that the defendant committed the crime. Once the defendant enters a not-guilty plea, the judge will then inform him of his right to a court or jury trial and set the case for further proceedings. Another form of not-guilty plea that may be entered at the arraignment is not guilty by reason of insanity. This type of plea is used when the defense attorney has reason to believe that her client may not be responsible for his actions as a result of a mental disorder or disease.

Nolo contendere pleas literally mean "no contest." The defendant is not contesting the charges. In essence, it is a guilty plea and carries the same criminal sanctions as a guilty plea but, significantly for victims, it cannot be used in any subsequent civil action to establish liability against the defendant.

Jury Selection

The right to a jury trial is one of our most fundamental constitutional guarantees. The use of twelve jurors in criminal cases is common, but not constitutionally mandated. It is more an historical tradition than a legal requirement. In *Williams v. Florida*, the U.S. Supreme Court held that the individual states may decide how many jurors should hear a noncapital criminal case, and as long as the number is large enough to ensure a cross section of the community, it will be considered constitutionally sound.[23]

Prospective jurors are selected based on the various states' legislative schemes. Many states use a combination of property tax roles, Department of Motor Vehicles listings, and voter registration records. When these jurors report for duty, a panel is sent to the courtroom for further selection. Twelve jurors are initially called to take their seats in the jury box and the voir dire examination of prospective jurors begins. *Voir dire* means to "seek the truth." While this process may vary by jurisdiction, it normally involves the judge questioning jurors about details in their past or about present beliefs that might uncover possible bias or prejudice. Once the judge has finished with the questioning, the defense attorney and the prosecutor each have an opportunity to question jurors. Either side may challenge a juror for cause, meaning that the juror has disclosed something that will not allow him or her to be fair during the trial. Once all the challenges for cause are finished, each side may use what is called peremptory challenges to remove other prospective jurors from the panel. A *peremptory challenge* does not require an explanation and is used by either side to excuse a prospective juror without stating the reason for the dismissal. There are a limited number of peremptory challenges available, and once they are exhausted, or the prosecutor or defense attorney is satisfied with the panel, the remaining jurors will sit as the jury.

Opening Statement

The opening statement is the first opportunity for the attorneys to tell the jury about the detailed facts in the case. Many trial lawyers believe that the opening statement is like the table of contents of a book. It points out the important facts and acts as a guide for the jury. Opening statements may be brief summaries or detailed accounts of the crime. The nature and scope of the opening statement depend on the preferences of the attorney who is presenting. Opening statements are not evidence; rather they are the attorney's beliefs of what evidence will be introduced during the trial. The prosecutor is allowed to make the first opening statement. The defense may make a statement at that time or wait until the prosecution has rested and make the opening statement prior to putting on any defense evidence.

Case-in-Chief

Once the opening statements have been made, the prosecution presents its evidence dealing with the guilt of the defendant. It is during this phase that the victim of the crime will be called to testify. The prosecution must prove each element of every crime and that the defendant committed those crimes.

After a witness has testified, the defense has the right to cross-examine. After the defense has finished with its cross- examination, the prosecution has a right to question the witness again on matters raised on cross-examination. This is called *redirect examination*. After the prosecution finishes with redirect, the defense may engage in recross examination. As anyone who watched the O. J. Simpson trial observed, this process can take hours or even days. Once all witnesses for the prosecution have testified and all physical evidence has been admitted by the judge, the prosecution rests it case.

The Defendant's Evidence

It is at this time that the defense must decide what, if any, evidence it will present. The defense does not have to call any witnesses. It can rely on the presumption of innocence and argue to the jury that the prosecution has failed to meet its burden. There have been a number of cases in which the defense has elected to not call any witnesses, and the trial then moves to the next step. In the event the defense elects to put on any evidence, it will follow the same process previously described.

Once the defense has finished presenting its evidence, the prosecution has the opportunity to present rebuttal evidence. The defense is then entitled to surrebuttal and it alternates back and forth until both sides are finished. When both sides have finished presenting their evidence, the trial moves on to what many attorneys consider to be the most dramatic stage.

Closing Argument

Closing argument is the final opportunity for the attorneys to address the jury. The prosecution presents its closing argument followed by the defense argument. The prosecution has the right to a final summation after the defense argument because it bears the burden of proof in criminal cases.

Closing arguments are not evidence, rather they are the attorney's attempt to persuade the jury to accept the position regarding the guilt or innocence of the defendant. Many attorneys believe that oral argument is more an art than an science. Clarence Darrow was the defense attorney in the famous case dealing with Darwin's theory of evolution, the Scopes Trial. Darrow is considered by many legal scholars and practitioners to be one of the most outstanding trial attorneys in the history of the United States, and his final summations are required readings for many young trial attorneys.

Deliberation and Verdict

Once both sides have rested, the judge reads the instructions to the jury. These instructions are the law that the jury must follow in its deliberations. The jury then retires to a jury room and selects one member to be the foreperson. The jury will then review all the evidence and reach a verdict regarding whether the defendant is guilty of the crimes charged. In the event the jury cannot reach a verdict, it informs the judge. This is called a "hung jury" and the judge may declare a mistrial. If the jury reaches a verdict, it notifies the judge and all parties reassemble in the courtroom. The judge's clerk reads the verdict. If found not guilty, the defendant is free to go. In the event the defendant is found guilty of all or some of the charges, the next step in the criminal process begins.

Sentencing

A review of our history demonstrates that various views and beliefs regarding punishment have evolved over time.[24] At one point in ancient Rome, punishment was viewed as a right of the victim's family. Eventually, we began to accept the concept of the sovereign as the dispenser of justice and punishment.

The four basic purposes for sentencing are: deterrence, rehabilitation, retribution, and incapacitation. *Deterrence* involves the concept that criminal sanctions, such as imprisonment, deter the public and convince them that they should not commit crimes. *Rehabilitation* focuses on reducing the offender's criminal propensities by counseling, therapy, and vocational training while incarcerated. *Retribution* is based on the biblical theme of "an eye for an eye, a tooth for a tooth." K. G. Armstrong has argued that retribution is not based on vengeance but rather is the lawful act of the state to protect its members from further injury.[25] Another theory regarding retribution involves the concept of "just desserts." This rationale for punishment is based on Von Hirsh's classic work, *Doing Justice*, in which he argues that those who commit crimes deserve to be punished.[26] *Incapacitation* removes offenders from society by keeping them incarcerated. The "Three Strikes and You're Out" law is an example of incapacitation of offenders.

Before imposing a sentence, the court usually receives a presentence report. This report is generally prepared by the probation department and normally begins with a recitation of the crime. It then presents the prosecution's version of the case followed by the defendant's version. It may present information about the background of the offender, including the parents and siblings, marital history, education, health, financial condition, and previous employment. The report also includes the nature and extent of previous criminal activities and discusses the victim's desires and needs. It makes a recommendation regarding what the probation department considers to be the most appropriate sentence for this particular defendant.

Once the presentencing report is complete, the defendant is returned to court for sentencing. At this time, the prosecution has an opportunity to argue for whatever sentence it feels is appropriate. The defense can also present any evidence it chooses to convince the judge to sentence the offender according to its desires. In many jurisdictions, victims have a right to appear and tell the judge of their own wishes and how the crime has impacted on their lives. This victim impact statement is addressed in more detail later in this text.

Summary

Understanding the criminal justice system is a critical aspect in the study of victimology. Many people are victimized or feel victimized for a second time when they become involved in the judicial process. Long delays, complex procedures, and technical arguments by both prosecutors and defense attorneys can lead to a renewed feeling of helplessness on the part of a victim who only wants to see justice carried out.

The American criminal court system is a combination of historical accident and thoughtful planning by our founding fathers. Criminal courts function at both the federal and state level. The nature of the crime may determine where the offender is prosecuted.

Concern regarding the increasing role of juveniles in the commission of crime has led to a renewed interest in the juvenile justice system. This system operates out of the general public's view most of the time because of the fundamental principle of confidentially. This concept was instituted to protect the identity of the juvenile offender and thereby avoid stigmatizing the offender as a criminal. It was believed that this would assist in the juvenile's rehabilitation; however, this concept has recently come under a great deal of criticism.

Each party in the criminal justice system has a distinct role to play, which makes it adversarial in nature. Understanding the roles and responsibilities of each party is a necessary aspect of the duties of any victim services provider.

In many instances, criminal justice procedures are based on constitutional protections set forth in the Bill of Rights and in other amendments to the Constitution. The process can be very confusing to the victim who often must navigate it alone. Because conviction of crime may result in restricting the freedom of the accused, the criminal is afforded a number of rights. These rights may cause the victims of crime much frustration and anger.

It is important to remember that the criminal justice system is only a small part of the entire spectrum of victimology; however, this process is critically important to any victim. Professionals in this area must maintain the proper perspective when dealing with all parties involved in the criminal justice system.

Key Terms

Jurisdiction means the ability of the court to enforce laws and punish individuals who violate those laws.

Trial courts are courts where criminal cases start and finish.

Limited jurisdiction courts are those that hear and decide only certain limited legal issues.

General jurisdiction courts are granted authority to hear and decide all issues that are brought before them.

Equity is the concept that justice is administered according to fairness, as contrasted with the strict rules of law.

Writ of certiorari is an order sent to a lower court requiring the records of the case to be sent the Supreme Court for review.

Jails are operated by local agencies such as cities or counties. Jails are used for pretrial detention, holding after sentencing, and incarceration of those persons who are not being sentenced to prison.

Prisons are administrated by states or the federal government and are for the more serious offenders.

Probation is a conditional release of the offender after having been found guilty. It is traditionally used on misdemeanor or other low-level crimes. It allows the perpetrator to remain free so long as that person meets certain conditions.

Parole is the conditional release of an inmate back into the community from a prison or other form of correctional institution.

Correctional officers are those persons who are hired to maintain security in jails or prisons.

Adjudication includes all the formal and informal decisions and steps within the criminal proceeding process.

Arrest is taking a suspect into custody in a manner prescribed by law.

Citation is an order to appear before a judge at a later time.

Booking involves entering the suspect's name, offense, and other information into the police records.

Nolo contendere pleas literally mean "no contest." The defendant is not contesting the charges. In essence, it is a guilty plea and carries the same criminal sanctions as a guilty plea but, significantly for victims, it cannot be used in any subsequent civil action to establish liability against the defendant.

Voir dire means to "seek the truth." While this process may vary by jurisdiction, it normally involves questioning jurors about details in their past or about present beliefs that might uncover possible bias or prejudice.

Peremptory challenge does not require explanation and is used by either side to excuse a prospective juror without stating the reason for the dismissal.

Deterrence involves the concept that criminal sanctions, such as imprisonment, deter the public and convince them that they should not commit crimes.

Rehabilitation focuses on reducing the offender's criminal propensities by counseling, therapy, and vocational training while the criminal is incarcerated.

Retribution is based on the biblical theme of "an eye for an eye, a tooth for a tooth."

Incapacitation removes offenders from society by keeping them incarcerated.

Discussion Questions

1. Why is it important for victim services providers to understand the criminal justice system? Doesn't anyone who watches television already have a basic understanding of how courts work?

2. Should we continue to have separate state and federal courts? Wouldn't one unified court system make more sense and be more efficient?

3. Should we treat juveniles as adults once they commit a violent crime? What crimes would apply, and how old would the minor have to be to be tried as an adult?

4. Should the victim have the same constitutional rights as the defendant?

5. Should victims have the right to veto any proposed plea bargain? Why? Why not?

6. Should all child sex abuse cases go to the grand jury?

7. Which justification for punishment is the most popular in today's climate of violent crime? Is it the most effective use of our resources?

Suggested Readings

American Bar Association, *Law and the Courts: A Handbook about United States Law and Court Procedures*, (American Bar Association, Chicago) 1987.

Territo, Halsted, & T. Bromley, *Crime and Justice in America: A Human Perspective*, (West Publishing Company, St. Paul, Minn.) 1992.

Siegal, L. & T. Senna, Juvenile Justice, (West Publishing Company, St. Paul, Minn.) 1994.

D. W. Neubauer, *America's Courts and the Criminal Justice System* (Wadsworth Publishing, Belmont, Calif.) 2004.

F. Adler, *Criminology and the Criminal Justice System*, 6th ed. (McGraw-Hill, Columbus, Ohio) 2006.

Endnotes

1. This section has been adapted from the author's previous work published in the *National Victim Assistance Academy Text* (1995), which was supported by Grant No. 95-MU-GX-K002 awarded by the Office for Victims of Crimes, Office of Justice Programs, U.S. Department of Justice.

2. Robert Pursley, *Introduction to Criminal Justice*, 6th ed. (MacMillan Publishing Company, New York) 1994.

3. *The Supreme Court of the United States.* (Government Printing Office, Washington, D.C.)

4. 1 Cranch 137 (1803).

5. S. Fox, *Modern Juvenile Justice: Cases and Materials*, (West Publishing Company, St. Paul, Minn.) 1972.

6. R. Cadwell, "The Juvenile Court: Its Development and Some Major Problems." *Juvenile Delinquency: A Book of Readings.* (John Wiley & Sons, New York) 1996, p. 358.

7. M. Randell & L. Haskell, "Sexual Violence in Women's Lives," 1/1 *Violence against Women*, 6 (1995).

8. The Fifth Amendment's right to grand jury indictment and the Eight Amendment's right regarding excessive bail have not been applied to the states. See *Hurtado v. California*, 110 U.S. 516 (1884).

9. If the confession was obtained by coercion, it may not be admitted even for impeachment purposes. See *Mincey v. Arizona*, 437 U.S. 385 (1978).

10. H. Wallace, C. Roberson & C. Steckler, *Fundamentals of Police Administration*, (Prentice-Hall, Englewood Cliffs, N.J.) 1994.

11. *Private Security: Report of the Task Force on Private Security*, (U.S. Government Printing Office, Washington, D.C.) 1976, p. 4.

12. See H. Wallace & C. Roberson, *Principles of Criminal Law*, (Longman, White Plains, N.Y.) 1996.

13. See P. W. Lewis & K.D. Peoples, *The Supreme Court and the Criminal Process*, (W.B. Saunders, Philadelphia) 1978, p. 974–975.

14. 372 U.S. 335 (1963).

15. 407 U.S. 25 (1972). See also *Scott v. Illinois*, 440 U.S. 367 (1979) where the U.S. Supreme Court held that the right to counsel only applies when imprisonment is actually imposed rather than merely authorized by statute.

16. Bureau of Justice Statistics Bulletin, *Criminal Defense Systems* (U.S. Department of Justice, Washington, D.C.) August 1984, p. 6.

17. *Strickland v. Washington*, 466 U.S. 668 (1984).

18. 475 U.S. 157 (1986).

19. 500 U.S. 44 (1991).

20. *Stack v. Boyle*, 342 U.S. 1 (1951).

21. 18 U.S.C. Section 3141 et seq. (1984).

22. *Hurtado v. California*, 110 U.S. 516 (1884).

23. 399 U.S. 78 (1970). However, in *Ballew v. Georgia*, 435 U.S. 223 (1978) the court held a five-person jury was a violation of the Fifth Amendment. More recently, a statute authorizing a vote of five of six jurors was struck down in *Burch v. Louisiana* 441 U.S. 130 (1970).

24. For more information on the various aspects of sentencing, see H. Wallace & C. Roberson, *Principles of Criminal Law.*

25. K. G. Armstrong, "The Retributionist Hits Back," 70 *Mind*, 471 (1969).

26. Andrew von Hirsh, *Doing Justice*, (Hill and Wang, New York) 1976.

4

THE CIVIL JUSTICE SYSTEM AND VICTIMS

Chapter Outline

Learning Objectives

After reading this chapter, you should be able to:

- Explain the basic differences between a criminal and a civil trial
- Understand the concepts of negligence and intentional torts
- Describe the various stages of a civil trial
- Discuss the phases of a juvenile dependency hearing

Civil Procedures

Introduction

The preceding chapter discussed various aspects of the criminal justice system and its effect on victims. This chapter briefly explores the second aspect of the legal system to impact victims: the civil law system. A criminal action punishes a person for committing a public wrong, whereas a civil action punishes a person for committing a private wrong or injury.[1] Civil law includes all actions that are not deemed criminal in nature.[2] Understanding the civil law system is important to those studying victimology because many victims of crime turn to civil law in an effort to obtain redress for injuries not compensated by the criminal law system.[3]

Victims file civil actions against their perpetrators for various reasons. One reason may be that they do not believe they received appropriate satisfaction as a result of any criminal proceedings. The defendant may have been acquitted or convicted of a lesser charge than the victim believes is proper. Victims may also feel mistreated by the criminal justice system and have a desire to be in control of the proceedings instead of being treated as merely a witness in a case. They may also want to receive more compensation for injuries than is available in the criminal justice system.

Civil law includes a wide variety of subjects including the following:

- *Torts:* Injury that does not involve a contract.
- *Contracts:* Violation of an agreement.
- *Property:* Disputes relating to real or personal property.
- *Estates:* Issues relating to inheritance and probate.
- *Family:* Issues regarding marriage, children, and divorce.
- *Civil rights:* Injury to another in violation of certain statutory rights.

Some of these common legal concepts that affect victims are examined in more detail in other chapters. When a victim suffers a civil injury, it is necessary to begin the civil process. This process starts with an examination of whether the courts have jurisdiction over the parties and the cause of action. The next section examines the concept of jurisdiction.

Jurisdiction

Jurisdiction is the ability of a court to hear and decide issues of law and fact. If a court does not have jurisdiction, it is without power to act. Courts must have jurisdiction over both the parties and the subject matter of the complaint.[4]

Jurisdiction over the parties or personal jurisdiction requires that the court be able to bring the party before it. Personal jurisdiction is of two types: in personam and in rem. *In personam* personal jurisdiction refers to the court's powers to bind the parties to the court's judgment. *In rem* personal jurisdiction is one that involves property that is located in the state where the court is located, and in which the parties have their dispute. Jurisdiction of the person is normally obtained by serving upon the individual a copy of the complaint. This process is discussed later in this section.

Jurisdiction of the subject matter requires that the court have authority to hear and decide the issue of law involved in the dispute. For example, some courts require that a minimum level of damages be requested before the matter can be heard in their court.[5] Other courts hear only certain types of matters and cannot rule on any issues. For example, probate courts cannot hear family law issues and vice versa.

Due process is a constitutional mandate that requires fairness in judicial proceedings. Occasionally one raises a question as to whether a person or organization that does not live or is headquartered in a state can be forced to appear in that state and defend a lawsuit which has been filed there. The doctrine of due process may prevent the out-of-state defendant from having to appear and defend lawsuits unless the defendant has some sort of minimum contacts in the state. This doctrine is based on the concept that it would be unfair to require a person or business to travel to a state and defend a lawsuit where that defendant has had no other contact with that state. In the leading case of *International Shoe Co. v. State of Washington*, the U.S. Supreme Court held that certain activities engaged in by a corporation in a state will allow it to be sued in that state.[6] These activities must involve some minimum contacts in the forum state of such character that being forced to defend a suit in that state would not offend traditional notions of fair play and substantial justice.

The concept of venue is closely associated with jurisdiction but is a separate and distinct aspect of civil litigation. Lawsuits must be filed in the proper location. Venue statutes determine the geographic districts in which the case can be heard. Once the question of jurisdiction and venue is determined, the plaintiff can evaluate the possibility of filing a complaint for damages.

Filing a Complaint

Filing a complaint is the first concrete step in the civil process. Unlike the criminal law process in which the prosecutor determines the nature and type of charges to file, the victim and the victim's attorney have complete control over the causes of action that are filed against the perpetrator. Additionally, as mentioned previously, the victim as the plaintiff has control over the location where the complaint is filed.

The *complaint* is a written document, called a *pleading*, that contains three essential components: (1) it establishes the subject matter jurisdiction, (2) it sets forth facts constituting various causes of action, and (3) it asks for certain types of relief (see Figure 4.1). Causes of action are legal theories that, if proved, entitle the plaintiff to recover for any injuries suffered. Many victims will allege alternative, and sometimes conflicting, causes of actions in the complaint and after discovery dismiss those that cannot be proved.

A variety of relief is available in civil proceedings. The first and most common form of relief is monetary damage. Monetary damages may be either compensatory or punitive in nature. *Compensatory damages* are awarded to plaintiffs to make them whole financially for any injuries they suffered as a result of the defendant's

---

UNITED STATES DISTRICT COURT FOR THE CENTRAL DISTRICT
OF CALIFORNIA

Judy Jones
v.   No. _____
Dan Defendant   Civil Action

COMPLAINT

Plaintiff Judy Jones complains against Dan Defendant as follows:

1. Jurisdiction in this case is based on diversity of citizenship and the amount in controversy. Plaintiff is a citizen of the State of California and defendant is a citizen of the State of Oregon. The amount in controversy exceeds, exclusive of interests and costs, the sum of fifty thousand ($50,000) dollars.

2. On September 30, 1996, at approximately 10:00 P.M., plaintiff Judy Jones (Jones) was standing near the intersection of First Street and Thomas Road in Fresno, California. Defendant Dan Defendant (Defendant) was driving a vehicle eastbound on Thomas Road at that intersection.

3. Defendant intentionally fired a handgun at Jones which resulted in a bullet entering Jones's left arm.

4. As a direct and proximate result of Defendant's actions, Jones suffered injuries to her arm and shoulder and other body parts, received other physical injuries, suffered physical and mental pain and suffering, incurred medical expenses and lost income in the future.

WHEREFORE, plaintiff Judy Jones demands judgment against defendant Dan Defendant for the sum of $1,000,000 with interest and costs.

Dated:

_____
John Smith
Attorney for Plaintiff

FIGURE 4.1   Sample Complaint

actions. ***Punitive damages*** are awarded to punish the defendant and to send a message to other similarly situated persons that if they commit the same or similar type of action they could face a similar fate.

Other forms of relief available in civil courts are *injunctions,* or orders that prohibit a person from doing certain acts. This form of relief is possible because of the courts equity power. This power authorizes the court to issue orders preventing injustice or wrongs from occurring. This power resides with the court, and juries do not decide issues of equity.

These orders are issued by judges after they receive evidence regarding the facts surrounding the necessity for the issuance of an injunction. A specific form of injunction, the temporary restraining order (TRO) or protective order is used in domestic violence or stalking cases and is discussed in more detail in Chapter 16, which examines constitutional and civil rights of victims.

The complaint is filed in a court that has jurisdiction over the parties and the subject matter. For example, a case dealing with the commission of intentional torts on federal land would be filed in federal court, because only that court has jurisdiction. The same acts if committed elsewhere would be filed in state court.

The complaint lists the parties and is known by the name of the plaintiff and the defendant. For example, if Laura Leonard was suing John Jones for striking her, the lawsuit would be entitled *Leonard v. Jones.* After identifying the parties and stating that the court has jurisdiction, the complaint sets forth the various causes of actions and asks for relief. This relief is contained in what is known as the *prayer.* The prayer sometimes asks for a specific amount of money or may include language stating "damages according to proof." This allows the plaintiff extra time to fully assess the nature and extent of any damages.

The complaint is usually filed by the plaintiff's attorney. All courts require parties filing a lawsuit to pay a filing fee. Depending on the jurisdiction, this can range from a nominal fee in small claims courts to several hundreds of dollars in superior courts. Once the complaint is filed, the defendant must be served with a copy. Normally, the plaintiff pays the county to serve the complaint using deputy sheriffs. Sometimes, private process servers are used to serve defendants that are hard to contact or who are evading service of the complaint. There are several other methods of serving the defendant including using registered mail, posting a copy of the complaint on the defendant's property, or publishing the complaint in a newspaper. It is not necessary that the defendant have actual notice of the complaint so long as the method of service is likely to provide notice.[7] Once the defendant is served with a copy of the complaint or has received notice of the lawsuit, a response is required within thirty days or a default judgment may be entered for the plaintiff. A default judgment is an order granting the plaintiff the relief asked for in the complaint. Because of the drastic nature of default judgments, most defendants respond to complaints.

Filing a Response

Once the defendant is served with a copy of the complaint there are a number of alternative responses available. The defendant may file any of the following responses: an answer with or without affirmative defenses, a demurrer, a motion to strike, or a cross-complaint or counterclaim. Each response has a definite purpose and is commonly used in many civil cases.

Answer

The defendant may file a response that is known as an *answer*, which is a response to the complaint, and may admit or deny the allegations. Answers are pleadings and may contain detailed responses or be a general denial of everything contained in the complaint. An answer, like the complaint, is filed with the court and served on the plaintiff.

Affirmative Defenses

The defendant may assert *affirmative defenses*, which are certain defenses that, if proved, negate any legal responsibility for the injuries suffered by the plaintiff. Affirmative defenses include such common theories as accord and satisfaction, assumption of the risk, contributory negligence, duress, estoppel, fraud, illegality, laches, license, statute of frauds, statute of limitations, and any other matter constituting an avoidance. The affirmative defenses are usually listed at the end of the answer before the prayer.

Demurrer

A *demurrer* is a response that in essence admits all the allegations of the complaint as true but goes on to state that even if they are true the plaintiff has not pled any theories that would allow for recovery of damages.[8] The demurrer is filed instead of the answer because if the court grants the demurrer the case is over. Most courts allow the plaintiff to amend the complaint to overcome the defects raised in the demurrer.

Motion to Strike

A motion to strike is a response that requests the court to strike out certain language in the complaint. Motions to strike are often used in conjunction with demurrers in an attempt to get the case dismissed.

Cross-Complaint or Counterclaim

If the defendant answers the complaint, but claims that another party caused the plaintiff's injuries, the defendant may file a lawsuit against that party at the time the answer is filed. This lawsuit, which is made a part of the original action, is known as a cross-complaint or counterclaim. The defendant may also file a cross-complaint or counterclaim against the plaintiff alleging that the plaintiff injured the defendant.

Once the initial pleadings have been filed, the lawsuit moves into the pretrial stage. In some jurisdictions this occurs very quickly because of a court procedure known as fast-tracking of civil cases. In other jurisdictions, the case can take several years before anything further occurs.

Pretrial Activities

Pretrial activities include a wide range of legal maneuvers designed to clarify the issues and/or reach settlement regarding liability. Much of the criticism aimed at the legal profession has centered around some of the activities that occur during this stage of a civil lawsuit.[9] Pretrial activities include filing motions, discovery, and settlement conferences.

Motions

There are a number of motions that may be filed during the pretrial stage of a civil case. The most important motion is called a *summary judgment*. This motion can be used to dismiss the entire case or strike portions of the complaint. A summary judgment motion is a pleading that alleges there is no triable issue of fact established by the pleadings or discovery and therefore the undisputed portions of the case should be dismissed. If these portions are essential to the plaintiff's case, this motion may result in dismissal of the entire complaint.

For instance, if the plaintiff is alleging that he was battered by the defendant and during discovery it is established that the plaintiff and the defendant both agree that the incident occurred during a sporting event, the defendant could file a summary judgment motion which would be granted by the court. The court would hold that when one is injured during a sporting event or game, no cause of action for battery is available because the law presumes the injured party consented to the actions of the other person while they were on the playing field. Conversely, if the plaintiff alleges that the defendant struck him after the game was over and the defendant contends the injury occurred during the game, there is a triable issue of fact for the jury to decide (when and how the injury occurred), and the summary judgment motion will not be granted.

Discovery

The discovery process in civil lawsuits can be both time consuming and expensive. *Discovery* is the legal term that includes a number of devices that allow each party to learn the facts and theories that the other side is claiming will allow them to prevail. Both the plaintiff and defendant engage in discovery during the pretrial period. In fact, a television drama showing a civil attorney being surprised during trial is a myth and has little basis in modern courtroom procedures. It is more the exception than the rule that surprises occur in civil cases. By the time a case goes to trial, attorneys representing each side know exactly what each witness will testify and what the theories of recovery or defense are.

There are a number of discovery techniques used in civil cases. The more complex cases use all, or most, of these discovery tools. They include depositions, interrogatories, and requests for production of documents. Each of these discovery techniques has specific goals and purposes.

Depositions. *Depositions* are formal, out-of- court procedures in which one party questions others regarding the facts surrounding the case. The questioning occurs under oath and is recorded by a court reporter. Either the plaintiff or the defendant may conduct a deposition and both parties are usually deposed by the other. Witnesses, experts, and other persons that may have information regarding the lawsuit may be deposed. The rules of evidence are relaxed during depositions and the parties are allowed to ask questions that may lead to other information. Once a party has given its deposition, if they change the statement during trial, the deposition may be introduced to impeach the party's credibility.[10]

Interrogatories.   *Interrogatories* are written inquiries to the other side asking specific questions. Interrogatories may ask for a party to state the theory behind a cause of action and all the facts supporting that theory. Interrogatories may also ask parties to admit or deny certain specific issues.

Production of Documents.   In many cases, one party will ask the other to produce all the records surrounding the occurrence that is the basis for the lawsuit. Some defendants are reluctant to produce these records absent a court order. A motion to produce can be enforced by the court and if the party fails to bring or send all the records to the other party, a court may order sanctions.

Conferences

Once the discovery phase of the civil action is complete, many jurisdictions require the parties to meet and discuss the possibility of settling the case or narrowing the issues.[11] This conference may result in the parties entering into agreements or stipulations about issues that are not in conflict such as the date of events, who took which pictures, and other items that move the trial along without undue time being spent on mundane matters.

Often, the parties will enter into serious settlement discussions at these pretrial conferences.[12] After the discovery phase ends, the attorneys representing each side and the settlement judge have a fairly accurate idea of how the trial is going to go and what the probable outcome will be. The judge, as a disinterested third party, may facilitate these discussions by separating the parties and talking to each one individually. The judge may make recommendations regarding the value of the case and discuss the credibility of certain witnesses. Some judges will move back and forth between the two parties, communicating offers and counter-offers until the parties agree to settle. Many attorneys believe a good settlement judge can dispose of most, if not all, civil lawsuits. In the event the case cannot be settled, the next phase is the trial.

Trial

The trial of a civil case is conducted in much the same manner as a criminal case. The jury selection, including the voir dire, is very similar to a criminal case. Opening statements are conducted with the plaintiff's attorney going first, followed by the defendant's attorney. The plaintiff's attorney presents that side's evidence and then the defendant presents evidence if desired. Closing arguments and rebuttal follow the same pattern as a criminal case, the jury receives its instructions, and then retires to deliberate.

However, there are some significant differences between a criminal trial and a civil trial. These differences include constitutional issues, the burden of proof, and the number of jurors who must agree on a verdict. The Fifth Amendment prohibition against self-incrimination does not apply and therefore the plaintiff may call the defendant to the stand to testify during the plaintiff's case-in-chief. As indicated earlier in this text, civil cases only require a preponderance of the evidence whereas criminal cases require proof beyond a reasonable doubt. Finally, in civil cases, only nine of twelve jurors must agree for a verdict to be reached. In criminal cases, the great majority of states require a unanimous verdict.

Verdict

Unlike a criminal case in which the jury renders a verdict of guilty or not guilty, civil cases may require juries to evaluate complex facts and legal theories. Some cases require juries to apportion fault among the parties. For example, juries may be asked to determine if the plaintiff contributed to his or her own injuries. In these cases, the jury may return a verdict finding the defendant 80 percent at fault and the plaintiff 20 percent at fault. If the jury determined that the plaintiff suffered injuries in the amount of $100,000, the award based on this division of fault would then be reduced by 20 percent leaving the plaintiff with a final award of damages in the amount of $80,000.

In complex civil cases, judges may use what is known as a special verdict form. Instead of simply ruling for either the plaintiff or the defendant, the jury is given a series of questions regarding factual issues. Based on its response, the judge determines the outcome of the case.

Judgment

There is no sentence in a civil case. If the jury finds for the defendant, the case is over. However, if the jury returns a verdict for the plaintiff, the court must enter a judgment. Once a judgment is recorded, the plaintiff can request the sheriff or marshall to execute the judgment and seize and sell most of the defendant's real and personal property to pay the amount listed in the judgment. However, many persons are judgment-proof in that they have very little if any assets that can be used to pay the judgment. Others, such as O. J. Simpson, have assets such as pensions that cannot be attached. When this situation occurs, plaintiffs must look at other options for recovery. These alternatives are discussed in more detail in the sections dealing with victims' rights.

Juvenile Court Dependency Procedures[13]

The previous chapter discussed juvenile courts and those minors classified as either delinquents or status offenders. This section discusses dependent children, as these proceedings are normally considered civil rather than criminal in nature. Dependent children are defined as those children who are in need of state intervention because of abuse or neglect by their caretakers.

Although the procedure is basically the same for delinquents and dependent minors, the juvenile court process dealing with children who are victims of abuse or neglect is of particular importance to professionals who work in the criminal justice field. This process is normally initiated by filing a petition with the court. A petition is a formal pleading that alleges that the parents or custodians endangered the health or welfare of the child. The petition may allege neglect or physical, emotional, or sexual abuse of the child, and it gives the juvenile court the authority to act.

Detention Hearing

Once the petition is filed, many jurisdictions hold a show cause or detention hearing. This hearing is usually conducted within twenty-four to forty-eight hours after filing the petition or the emergency removal of the child. The *detention hearing* requires child protective services or police to produce evidence justifying the emergency removal of the child or to present evidence that would allow the court to order the removal of the child if the child is still in the custody of the parents. The parents may also admit or deny the allegations contained in the petition at this hearing.

If they admit the allegations, the court orders child protective services to conduct an investigation to determine where the child should be placed as a result of the admissions by the parents. If the parents deny the allegations, the court sets a date for an adjudicatory or jurisdictional hearing. Pending this hearing, the court may order the child temporarily placed in a living arrangement outside the home.

Adjudicatory or Jurisdictional Hearing

An *adjudicatory* or *jurisdictional hearing* is used to determine if there is sufficient evidence to determine that the allegations in the petition are true. At the conclusion of this hearing, the court will render its decision. If the petition is upheld, the court sets a date for a dispositional hearing. If the petition is not upheld, the child is returned to the parents and the case is dismissed.

During the adjudicatory hearing, the state presents evidence to support its claim that the child has been abused. This may take the form of having the child testify to the incident, or experts employed by the state may render their opinion regarding the facts surrounding the case. The state is represented by a juvenile prosecutor, state's advocate, county counsel, or other governmental attorney. The parents have a right to cross-examine witnesses and present any evidence they desire in rebuttal to the state's evidence. At the end of the hearing, both parties may present arguments in favor of their position. The burden of proof to uphold the petition is the same as for a civil case. In civil trials, the plaintiff has the burden of proving the case by a preponderance of the evidence. This is normally defined as slightly more than 50 percent. A criminal case requires proof beyond a reasonable doubt. This is not proof beyond all doubt, because all things are subject to some doubt, but it is proof beyond a reasonable doubt to a moral certainty that all the material facts did occur.

In juvenile dependency cases, to remove the child from the custody of the parents, some jurisdictions require proof by clear and convincing evidence. This is more than a preponderance of the evidence but less than beyond a reasonable doubt.[14]

The Dispositional Hearing

Once the adjudicatory or jurisdictional hearing is concluded, the next hearing to occur is the *dispositional hearing*. This hearing is to determine where the child should be placed. The court will decide whether the child should be immediately returned to the parents or placed in an out-of-home environment for a specific time. The guiding principle in this hearing is "the best interests of the child." If the court orders the child placed outside the home, it may schedule periodic reviews to determine if or when the child will be reunited with the parents. Typically, a specific plan regarding placement is established and monitored.

From the beginning of the intervention process until the final dispositional hearing and beyond, every party in the action has certain rights. The parents and the child each have distinct rights which must be observed and protected. These rights include:

- Notice
- An opportunity to be heard and to present evidence
- The right to confront and cross-examine witnesses
- Effective representation by an attorney

In a dependency hearing, the rights of a child include appointing an attorney who will speak on behalf of the child. This attorney must represent what is believed to be in the best interests of the child regardless of what CPS or the parents' advocate believes is appropriate. In some jurisdictions this is a government-funded attorney; in others, it is a private attorney appointed by the court to represent the child. Depending on the case, the attorney may side with the parents and argue for return of the child to their care, or the attorney may take the position that it is in the best interests of the child to be removed from the custody of the parents. Even if the child is removed temporarily from the custody of the parents, the child has a right to reunification efforts after a reasonable time.

Many jurisdictions additionally engage court-appointed special advocates (CASAs), or similarly trained (typically nonattorney) individuals. The role of these child advocates is to present to the court an independent analysis of what is best for the child. This is particularly important; as the child's legal representative, the court-appointed lawyer must forward the child's wishes when an objective view would be to the contrary. For example, the lawyer may decide to vigorously advocate a juvenile's wish to return home, when an independent child advocate may determine that this is not actually in the child's best interest.

During dependency hearings, parents have a right to notice of the hearing, an opportunity to be present at that hearing, and to be represented by an attorney. They may present any evidence they desire to rebut the charges. If the child is removed from their custody, they have the right in most jurisdictions to a reunification plan that will allow them to regain custody of the child once they have finished treatment or counseling.

Juvenile courts that hear dependency cases oftentimes face a conflict: protection of the child versus the trauma of removing a child from the parents. Courts will normally err on the side of removing the child if there is any substantial evidence to support the allegations that the child is in danger. The juvenile court dependency process is a civil action that must always stay focused on the best interests of the child.

Restorative Justice

Introduction

More and more researchers are suggesting an alternative to the traditional criminal sanctions imposed on perpetrators by the state. These scholars are examining the concept of restorative justice as a new vision for dealing with both offenders and victims.[15] The topic of restorative justice is included in a discussion of the civil justice system because it is more similar to that philosophy than the current philosophy of criminal sanctions.

Some believe the United States is the most punitive nation in the Western world and that this country outstrips all other nations in prison-building programs. A common refrain in almost all elections is that one's opponent is too soft on crime. Therefore, American politicians must be tough on crime to get elected. This political stance has resulted in harsher criminal sanctions in an effort to stop or deter future criminal activity.

The general public is frightened of crime and its consequences. The media feed this fear by showing drive-by shootings and all the grisly details on television daily. Americans are demanding a stop to this violence. At the same time, the public is asking that victims of crime be included in the process. Society is not only interested in including victims in the process, the public wants to make them whole emotionally and financially. This section deals with some methods of making victims whole financially by using the civil justice system. Restorative justice is also a method of healing victims.

Restorative justice promotes maximum involvement of the victim, the offender, and the community in the justice process and presents a clear alternative to sanctions based on retribution and punishment.[16] Restorative justice is based on three principles: (1) all parties (offender, victim, and the community) should be included in the response to crime; (2) government and local communities' actions should complement each other; and (3) accountability is based on the offender's understanding of the harm that has been inflicted.

The restorative justice philosophy gives meaning to sanctions such as restitution and community service. Without an understanding of the restorative justice philosophy these sanctions appear to be simply bureaucratic and punitive in nature. Restorative justice also links different programs such as restitution, community services, and victim–offender mediation together with the goal of accomplishing its mission.

Function of a Restorative Justice Program

There are three roles in any restorative justice program: accountability, competency, and community protection. No single role or principle is more important than another. Each role is intertwined with the others in an effort to present a balanced approach to justice.[17]

The accountability role or principle holds that when a crime occurs, a debt incurs and justice requires that every effort be made by the offender to restore any losses suffered by the victim. Accountability requires that offenders become aware of the harmful consequences of their action and make every effort to make amends to the victim and the community. The competency development role or principle requires that offenders leave the criminal justice system more capable of participation in society than when they entered the system. Competency involves work experience, active learning, and opportunities for offenders to develop productive skills. The community protection role or principle holds that the public has a right to a safe environment and the criminal justice system should use a progressive response system to ensure offender control in the community. Community-based control and surveillance can channel the offender's energy into productive activities during nonschool or nonworking hours.

Restorative justice programs focus on repairing the harm inflicted on the victim and the community using a process of negotiation, mediation, victim empowerment, and reparation. Restorative justice believes that victims are central to the process of resolving a crime and offers direct involvement of the participants in the process. One common strategy used in restorative justice programs is victim–offender mediation.

Victim–Offender Mediation

Victim–offender mediation (VOM) has its roots in the Victim–Offender Reconciliation Program (VORP) started in Canada in the mid-1970s.[18] The purposes of the original VORP project were to provide an alternative method of dealing with crime, to allow the victim and offender to mutually agree on restitution, to use third parties to facilitate reconciliation, and to resolve the conflict caused by crime.[19]

Increasing numbers of crime victims are choosing to meet face to face with their perpetrator. In these meetings, the victim can let the offender know how the crime affected his or her life and possibly receive from the offender answers to lingering questions the victim may have. Additionally, this form of mediation allows the victim to be directly involved in holding offenders accountable for the harm they caused.

There are more than three hundred VOM programs in various communities across the United States.[20] These programs are different from traditional mediation program in that there is no "dispute" for the parties to resolve. One of the parties in VOM is an offender, and guilt has already been established. These programs focus on dialogue with emphasis on the victim's needs, offender accountability, and some restoration of losses. Victims who meet with their offenders appear to be more satisfied with the justice system response to their cases than do victims of similar crimes who go through the traditional court process. The four most common offenses referred to VOM in order of frequency are vandalism, minor assaults, theft, and burglary. Almost half (45 percent) of the VOM programs work exclusively with juvenile offenders. The satisfaction with VOM appears to be high, and it should be evaluated as an alternative to the traditional sanctions imposed by courts.

Summary

The civil system is an important aspect of the study of victimology. Often, victims do not feel that they received justice in the criminal justice system. Victims become plaintiffs and engage in civil lawsuits for a variety of reasons. These victims turn to the civil system in an effort to obtain redress for injuries suffered that could not be addressed in the criminal justice process. They may also believe that the defendant did not receive just punishment in the criminal justice system. Civil lawsuits allow victims to control the proceedings—something they are denied in criminal actions. They hire their own attorney and have the right to participate in all phases of the lawsuit. They sit at the counsel table during the trial, and they can direct the proceedings by ordering or asking their attorney to carry out certain acts in certain ways.

The juvenile justice system provides civil remedies for children who are abused or neglected. The system is based on the premise of doing whatever is in the best interest of the child. The dependency process is very powerful, and children can be removed from the care and custody of their parents if the court finds they are in danger.

The civil law process is complex, time consuming, and expensive. It can also be frustrating to victims of crime. Professionals must exercise care before advising any victim to pursue civil remedies. The consequences and benefits of filing a civil lawsuit should be fully explained, and victims must make this decision with their head, not their emotions.

More victims are turning to the use of restorative justice programs in an effort to deal with the consequences of crime. For the most part, these programs deal with nonviolent crimes. These programs appear to fulfill a need for some victims.

Key Terms

Jurisdiction is the ability of a court to hear and decide issues of law and fact.

In personam jurisdiction refers to the court's powers to bind the parties to the court's judgment.

In rem jurisdiction is one that involves property that is located in the state where the court is located and in which the parties have their dispute.

Due process is a constitutional mandate that requires fairness in judicial proceedings.

Complaint is a written document, called a *pleading*, that contains three essential components: (1) it establishes the subject matter jurisdiction, (2) it sets forth facts constituting various causes of action, and (3) it asks for certain types of relief.

Compensatory damages are awarded to the plaintiff to make them whole financially for any injuries they suffered as a result of the defendant's actions.

Punitive damages are awarded to punish the defendant and to send a message to other similarly situated persons that if they commit the same or similar type of action, they could face a similar fate.

Answer is a response to the complaint and may admit or deny the allegations.

Affirmative defenses are certain defenses that, if proved, negate any legal responsibility for the injuries suffered by the plaintiff.

Demurrer is a response that in essence admits all the allegations of the complaint as true but goes on to state that even if they are true, the plaintiff has not pled any theories that would allow for recovery of damages.

Depositions are formal, out-of-court procedures in which one party questions others regarding the facts surrounding the case.

Interrogatories are written inquiries to the other side asking specific questions.

Detention hearing requires child protective services or police to produce evidence justifying the emergency removal of the child or to present evidence that would allow the court to order the removal of the child if the child is still in the custody of the parents.

Adjudicatory or *jurisdictional hearing* is used to determine if there is sufficient evidence to determine that the allegations in the petition are true.

Dispositional hearing is to determine where the child should be placed.

Discussion Questions

1. List all the reasons victims may desire to sue perpetrators. Which reason is the most important?

2. Why should victim services providers understand the civil justice system?

3. Compare and contrast the criminal justice procedures and the civil justice procedures. List those areas that empower victims.

4. Why are juvenile court dependency procedures important for victims to understand?

5. If you could change one thing about the civil justice system that would help victims, what would it be?

Suggested Readings

H. J. Berman & W. R. Greiner, *The Nature and Functions of Law*, 4th ed. (Foundation Press, Mineola, N.Y.) 1980.

R. Grutman & B. Thomas, *Lawyers and Thieves*, (Simon and Schuster, New York) 1990.

G. C. Hazard, Jr. & M. Taruffo, *American Civil Procedure: An Introduction,* (Yale University Press, New Haven, Conn.) 1993.

M. S. Umbreit, *Victim Meets Offender: The Impact of Restorative Justice and Mediation* (Willow Tree Press, Inc., Monsey, N.Y.) 1994.

R. Cranston, *How Law Works: The Machinery and Impact of Civil Justice* (Oxford University Press, New York) 2006.

Endnotes

1. See *Leatherman v. Tarrant County Narcotics Intelligence & Coordination Unit,* 113 S. Ct. 1160 (1993).

2. Linda S. Mullenix, "The Influence of History on Procedure: Volumes of Logic, Scant Pages of History," 50 *Ohio Law Journal,* 803 (1989).

3. F. Carrington & G. Nicholson, "Victims' Rights: An Idea Whose Time Has Come— Five Years Later: The Maturing of an Idea," 17 *Pepperdine L. Rev.,* 1 (1987).

4. Lawrence W. Moore, "Federal Jurisdiction and Procedure," 41 *Loyola Law Review,* 469 (Fall 1995).

5. See *DeAguilar v. Boeing Co.,* 47 F.3d 1404 (5th Cir. 1995) for a discussion regarding the amount in controversy requirement in federal courts.

6. 326 U.S. 310 (1945). More recently, the U.S. Supreme Court has narrowed the scope of such contacts. See *Asahi Metal Industry Co. v. Superior Court,* 480 U.S. 102 (1987) where the court held that merely placing a product in the stream of commerce is not an act that will subject a party to the forum state jurisdiction. Minimum contacts require some action directed toward the forum state.

7. H. J. Berman & W. R. Greiner, *The Nature and Functions of Law,* 4th ed. (Foundation Press, Mineola, N.Y.) 1980.

8. Mark D. Robins, "The Resurgence and Limits of the Demurrer," 27 *Suffolk University Law Review,* 637 (Fall 1993).

9. R. Grutman & B. Thomas, *Lawyers and Thieves,* (Simon and Schuster, New York) 1990.

10. Kevin A. Moore, "Simple Answers to Common Problems During Depositions," 68 *Florida Bar Journal,* 111 (June 1994).

11. G. C. Hazard, Jr. & M. Taruffo, *American Civil Procedure: An Introduction,* (Yale University Press, New Haven, Conn.) 1993.

12. William L. Adams, "Let's Make a Deal: Effective Utilization of Judicial Settlements in State and Federal Courts," 72 *Oregon Law Review,* 427 (Summer 1993).

13. Portions of this section have been adapted from the author's previous work published in the *National Victim Assistance Academy Text* (1995) which was supported by Grant No. 95-MU-GX-K002 awarded by the Office for Victims of Crimes, Office of Justice Programs, U.S. Department of Justice.

14. D. V. Otterson, "Dependency and Termination Proceedings in California—Standards of Proof," 30 *Hastings Law Journal,* 1815–1845 (1979).

15. M. S. Umbreit, *Victim Meets Offender: The Impact of Restorative Justice and Mediation* (Willow Tree Press, Inc. Monsey, New York 1994) hereinafter cited as *Victim Meets Offender.*

16. Paul McCold, "Restorative Justice: The Role of the Community," paper presented at the Academy of Criminal Justice Sciences Annual Conferences, Boston, Mass. (March 1995).

17. G. Bazemore and M. S. Umbreit, *Balanced and Restorative Justice,* (Office of Justice Programs, Washington, D.C.) October 1994.

18. *Victim Meets Offender.*

19. S. P. Hughes & A. L. Schneider, *Victim–Offender Mediation in the Juvenile Justice System,* (Office of Justice Program, Washington, D.C.) September, 1990.

20. "The Restorative Justice and Mediation Collections: Executive Summary," *OVC Bulletin,* U.S. Department of Justice, Washington, D.C. July 2000.

5

THE CONSEQUENCES OF VICTIMIZATION

Chapter Outline

Learning Objectives

After reading this chapter, you should be able to:

- Explain the types of physical injuries suffered by victims
- Understand from a nonmedical perspective the extent and nature of the various physical injuries inflicted on victims of crime
- Discuss the three stages of crisis
- List the effects on victims suffering from posttraumatic stress disorder
- Explain the symptoms of acute stress disorder
- Distinguish between posttraumatic stress disorder and long-term crisis reaction
- Understand the other types of mental consequences suffered by victims
- Explain the financial consequences of crime victimization

Physical Consequences

One obvious consequence of victimization is the physical injuries suffered by victims. These injuries are easy to observe and treat. They are also the ones we are most knowledgeable about, because the majority of us know someone who has suffered a broken arm, leg, or other injury.

Types of Injuries

There are four general classifications of physical injuries inflicted on victims during the commission of a crime. These physical traumas include immediate injuries that heal leaving no trace, injuries that leave visible scars, unknown long-term physical injuries, and long-term catastrophic injuries.

Immediate injuries include bruises, contusions, cuts, and broken bones. These injuries generally heal quickly and are not perceived as serious by most people. In fact, many of us have suffered these same types of injuries due to accidents or

---

FOCUS: Firearms and Crime

According to the National Crime Victimization Survey in 2003, 449, 150 victims of violent crimes stated they faced an offender with a firearm.

Seven per cent of the violent crimes of rape, sexual assault, robbery, aggravated assault, and simple assault involved firearms.

The Uniform Crime Reports in 2003 estimated that 67 percent of the 16,503 murders were committed with firearms.

mishaps. However, some victims face more serious consequences as a result of immediate injuries. An elderly person who suffers a broken hip during a purse snatch may have significant complications during the healing process that could lead to death. A diabetic suffering from a stab wound may take two to three times as long to heal as another person.

Injuries that leave visible scars include those that result in facial scars; loss of teeth; loss of fingers or toes; scars on the neck, arms, or legs; and loss of mobility due to incomplete healing. The injuries are not considered catastrophic in nature but can cause changes in life activities. For example, facial scarring may result in a model being unable to pursue her career.

Unknown long-term physical injuries can include a potential exposure to HIV and AIDS. These types of diseases can result in loss of life or a complete change in life activities. Other sexually transmitted diseases may occur as a result of a sexual attack, including but not limited to gonorrhea, syphilis, and the herpes simplex viruses.

Long-term catastrophic injuries include those that restrict a victim's physical movements. For example, a person struck by a drunk driver may become a paraplegic or may lose an arm or a leg. These severe injuries often result in family members having to alter their lifestyles to care for the victim, while others may result in a reduction in the life span of the victim, change in identity, and change in the quality of life.

Medical Aspects

The types of physical injuries suffered by victims of crime cover the entire spectrum of trauma, from simple bruises to deadly gunshot wounds to the head. Although victim services providers are not expected to be physicians, they should have a basic understanding of the various types of injuries that victims may suffer. The next section briefly examines the medical aspects of some of the more common traumatic injuries.[1]

Gunshot Wounds

The U.S. civilian population is the most heavily armed in history.[2] More than 850,000 civilians have been killed by bullets in this century.[3] The science of ballistics is complex, but a few basic rules will assist in understanding the nature of injuries that result from gunshot wounds. The magnitude of the injury is proportional to the amount of kinetic energy impacted by the bullet striking the victim. This kinetic energy is determined by a variety of factors including the distance between the assailant and the victim, the muzzle velocity, and the various characteristics of the bullet. At medium velocity, the missile has an explosive impact and creates a temporary passage in the tissue along its course. Bone and tissue may be fractured and torn without being directly struck by the missile. High-velocity missiles cause additional damage, including the possibility of fragmentation, which causes additional multiple trajectories and injuries. Medical personnel are interested in obtaining information regarding the type of weapon used, the distance from the assailant when the victim was shot, the suspected number of shots, the blood lost at the scene, and any type of fluids administered before arrival at the hospital.

Shotgun wounds present special types of problems. The shotgun was designed to strike a small, fast-moving target at close range. Because of the design of the pebbles inside the round, the shotgun is not an effective weapon at long range. However, when used at close range, a shotgun is extremely lethal. Shotgun wounds have been classified into three groups according to the range, the pattern of the pellets, and the depth of penetration. Type I wounds involve long range (greater than seven yards) and basically result in a penetration of subcutaneous tissue and deep fascia only. Type II wounds involve medium range (between three and four yards) and may create a large number of perforated wounds. Type III wounds involve short or point-blank range (less than three yards) and involve a massive destruction of tissue. Type III wounds are lethal in nature, carrying a mortality rate of 39 to 65 percent.

Stab Wounds

Knives are not the only instrument used in stabbings. Ice picks, pens, coat hangers, screwdrivers, broken bottles, and other sharp objects have all been used as weapons by assailants. Stab wounds usually result in lacerations or punctures. These injuries may be only a minor inconvenience or they may be life threatening, depending on the location and depth of the wound. Frequently, more than one stab wound is sustained in a violent incident. Medical personnel are interested in obtaining information regarding the type and size of the weapon, the estimated blood loss at the scene of the crime, the time of injury, and whether the victim had ingested any drugs or alcohol.

Burns

Burns are one of the most painful and devastating types of physical injuries. They are classified into superficial (first degree), partial thickness (second degree), and full thickness (third degree) according to the depth of the burned area. First-degree burns involve the epidermis tissue and may exhibit red or pink skin accompanied by hyperesthesia and tingling. The more common causes of first-degree burns are sunburn and brief contact with hot liquids. Second-degree burns involve the epidermis and dermis tissues and may exhibit red or mottled skin with blisters, considerable swelling, wet surfaces, pain, and sensitivity to cold air. The most frequent causes include scalds and flash flames. Third-degree burns involve the dermis or deeper tissues and may exhibit pale white or charred appearance with a dry surface, body fat may be exposed, and systemic symptoms include shock, hematuria, and hemolysis. The most common causes include fire, contact with hot objects, and electrical and chemical burns.

The severity of burns is based on both the extent and type of burn. The American Burn Association classifies burns as major, moderate, or minor in nature. Major burns include second-degree burns over more than 25 percent of an adult's body and 20 percent of a child's body; third-degree burns involving 10 percent of the body surface; all burns involving hands, eyes, face, ears, and feet, and all inhalation injuries and burns complicated by other injuries. Moderate burns include second-degree burns over 15 to 25 percent of an adult's body and 10 to 20 percent of a child's body and all third-degree burns of 2 to 10 percent not involving eyes, ears, face, hands, or feet. Minor burns include second-degree burns over less than 15 percent of an adult's body and less than 10 percent of a child's body and third-degree burns of 2 percent or less not involving eyes, ears, face, hands, or feet.

Trauma to the Head

A significant portion of all emergency department work involves the care of people suffering from trauma to the head. Vehicle accidents, including drunk driving incidents, account for a significant percentage of this form of injury. Other criminal acts such as muggings and batteries also constitute another important cause of head trauma. Often, people who sustain head injuries receive other associated major traumatic injuries at the same time.

One effect of trauma to the head may be the inducement of a coma. Comas may be the result of a subdural hematoma, epidural hematoma, traumatic intracerebral hemorrhage, contusion, or concussion. Defining a coma is difficult, but for the purposes here, it is an altered state that exists in a person manifesting inappropriate responses to external stimuli and who maintains eye closure throughout the stimuli.

The victim's ability to relate the course of events leading to the injury may be compromised by injury, alcohol, drugs, hysteria, or any number of factors. Medical personnel will want to know if the victim was struck on the head by the assailant and what type of object was used. Police and firefighters will be questioned about whether the victim was awake on their arrival, and any changes in consciousness between the incident and arrival at the emergency room should be noted.

Other Medical Concerns

In addition to the different types of physical injuries suffered by victims of violent crime, victims of sexual assault endure a specific trauma that results in specialized medical issues. Rape victims will undergo a particular type of examination intended to assist in the prosecution of the perpetrator. In the recent past, these medical examinations were conducted by hospital staff with little or no specialized training regarding the effects of rape on the victim. Additionally, there were times when a male police officer remained in the examination room to conduct questioning of the victim during the examination. Fortunately, there has been progression in the medical treatment of sexual assault victims, and in many jurisdictions, rape crisis counselors are available and present during this examination. They have been trained to provide support to the victim during this and other phases of the criminal justice process.

The rape victim should discuss the issue of pregnancy with hospital staff. If she was pregnant prior to the assault, the possible effects on the fetus should be discussed. If she was not pregnant, the possibility that the assailant impregnated her should be evaluated. The victim should discuss all aspects of this issue at the earliest possible time with the medical staff at the hospital or with her own physician.

The possibility of contracting a sexually transmitted disease (STD) must be evaluated. Many of these diseases can be successfully avoided if treated immediately after the assault; however, many STDs will not show up during the physical examination, so rape victims should be tested several weeks following the attack. It is therefore critical that victims discuss this possibility with medical personnel.

With the threat of AIDS and HIV so much a part of our lives today, the possibility of contracting the disease is perhaps one of the most frightening aspects of sexual assaults. Human immunodeficiency virus (HIV) causes acquired immunodeficiency syndrome (AIDS). AIDS is a disease that attacks the body's immune system, rendering the person vulnerable to infections and diseases and ultimately resulting in death. A victim may contract HIV in various ways. Victims should be tested immediately for HIV and request appropriate periodic follow-up testing. Chapter 13 discusses HIV/AIDS victimization in more detail.

Mental Consequences

Crisis

Eric Lindemann is considered by many scholars to be a leading pioneer in the study of the effects of crisis on the mental health or emotional well-being of humans.[4] Lindemann offered both a new understanding of the dynamics of crisis and a systematic approach to treating those suffering from it.[5] His study dealing with the grieving process of the survivors in the Coconut Grove fire in Boston in 1942 has become the foundation on which much of the knowledge concerning the grief process has been built. Lindemann believed that acute grief was a natural and necessary reaction to significant loss. Another scholar, Gerald Caplin, extended Lindemann's theories to include all human reactions to traumatic events and not only the grieving process as a result of loss.[6]

Individuals react differently to different situations, and what may be a crisis to one person may only be a minor annoyance to another. As a result, the term *crisis* has many valid meanings. In medicine crisis has one meaning, whereas in psychiatry the term is used in a different context. A number of scholars have defined the term *crisis*. Rather than adopt a sociological, medical, psychological, or legal definition of the term, it will be viewed from the perspective of a victim's reaction to crime. **Crisis** is therefore defined as a specific set of temporary circumstances that results in a state of upset and disequilibrium, characterized by an individual's inability to cope with a particular situation using customary methods of problem solving.[7]

Although some authorities may differ regarding the number of steps in the crisis reaction, one common analysis describes this process as involving three stages: impact, recoil, and reorganization.

The Impact Stage
The impact phase occurs immediately after the crime. Victims feel as if they are in shock. Some victims cannot eat or sleep, others may express disbelief that the

crime actually occurred. Statements such as "I can't believe this happened to me!" are common during this stage. Many victims feel exposed and vulnerable or express feelings of helplessness.

The impact phase may last for several hours to several days after the crime and is often punctuated by episodes of severe mood swings. One moment the victim may appear to be in control and the next moment exhibit disorganized and uncontrolled emotions. A crime victim is especially vulnerable at this time and susceptible to the influence of others. What may appear to be innocent statements offered by friends may be interpreted by the victim as blame for being the victim.

The Recoil Stage

During the recoil phase, victims attempt to accept or adapt to the crime and begin to reintegrate their personalities. Victims commonly experience a variety of emotions including guilt, fear, anger, self-pity, and sadness. Some victims struggle to accept the painful feelings caused by the crime; at other times they deny experiencing any of these feelings at all. Caplin explained this process as involving victims who need opportunities to rest from wrestling with their situation, but who must eventually awake and return to consideration of the problem.[8] In essence, after trying to cope with their feelings regarding the crime, victims become emotionally exhausted and put these feelings aside so that they can rest, recover, and begin the healing process. Later, they are able to examine their feelings regarding the crime with renewed emotional resources.

Many victims are in denial during this phase. This emotional detachment can be an extension of the shock of the impact phase. Such detachment allows victims to develop a gradual immunity to the feelings that would overwhelm them if they faced them all at once. Victims may believe that they must seal off any feelings in order to get on with their lives. Some victims defend against any feeling during this phase by emerging themselves in work or other projects. Other victims accomplish the same objective by becoming almost obsessional with the criminal justice system—learning about the procedures, criminal laws, parties, etcetera.

It is during this phase that victims begin to deal with their feelings about the crime. Some victims will reexamine every detail of the crime in their minds. They may want to talk about it endlessly; others will dream about the crime. As victims confront the reality of the criminal act, they may reexperience the fear. Some victims only allow themselves to feel the full intensity of emotions after the immediate threat of the crime has passed. This feeling of fear can be immobilizing. Victims must verbalize their fears and other intense emotions associated with the criminal act to begin the healing process. With time, most of the traumatic impact associated with these feelings will lessen.

Another common feeling during the recoil stage is anger toward the criminal. Victims may experience rage but be unable to vent this feeling. Some victims may spend hours thinking about revenge, especially those who have suffered from a violent attack. Victims must understand that the desire for revenge is natural and a normal part of the healing process. Many victims want to construct a reason for their victimization. These victims search for the answer to the question, "Why me?"

The Reorganization Stage

After a period of time, the recoil stage gives way to the reorganization stage. The victim moves toward a more balanced state as feelings of fear and rage diminish in intensity and he or she has energy left over to confront life's daily activities. The victim becomes more normalized as the need to deny the victimization lessens. Victims are gradually able to put their experience in perspective and commit their energies to the task of living in the present.

Victims will never forget the experience and, as indicated earlier, they will respond in a variety of ways. This discussion has focused on one reaction to victimization. Other victims may experience different feelings. Acute stress disorder is another reaction that victims of crime may experience.

Acute Stress Disorder

Acute stress disorder (ASD) is acute stress that is experienced in the immediate aftermath of a traumatic event. This is a newly categorized disorder that was first listed in the *Diagnostic and Statistical Manual of Mental Disorders*, 4th edition (DSM-IV) in 1994.[9] The characteristics of acute stress disorder are the development of anxiety, dissociative symptoms, and other manifestations that occur within one month after exposure to the traumatic event. To receive a diagnosis of ASD, the victim must have experienced, witnessed, or been confronted with an event that involved actual or threatened death, serious injury, or a threat to the physical safety of the victim or others. Additionally, the victim's response to such a condition must involve intense fear, helplessness, or horror. This diagnosis requires that the victim experience three of five PTSD dissociative symptoms during or immediately after the traumatic incident. These symptoms must persist for at least two days but last no more than thirty days. The dissociative symptoms are derealization, depersonalization, dissociative amnesia, subjective sense of numbing, and reduction in awareness of surroundings. In the event these symptoms last longer than thirty days, the victim may be suffering from posttraumatic stress disorder.

Posttraumatic Stress Disorder

Posttraumatic stress disorder was first identified when some Vietnam veterans began experiencing flashbacks of events that occurred during combat. *Posttraumatic stress disorder* is defined as the development of characteristic symptoms following a psychologically distressing event that is outside the range of usual human experience.[10] Traumatic events include, but are not limited to, military combat, violent personal assault (including rape, child sexual abuse, and child physical abuse), terrorist attack, torture, incarceration as a prisoner of war, natural or man-made disasters, severe automobile accidents, being kidnapped or taken hostage, or being diagnosed with a life-threatening illness. The characteristic symptoms require that the person experience, witness, or be confronted with an event or events that involve actual or threatened death or serious injury, or a threat to the physical integrity of self or others, and that the person's response involve intense fear, helplessness, or horror.

The symptoms that the victim may experience include reexperiencing the traumatic event, avoidance of stimuli associated with the event, numbing of general responsiveness, and increased agitation.[11]

Victims of any type of crime can experience posttraumatic stress disorder. However, several scholars have researched the effect of rape on victims.[12] Victims of rape have reported or been diagnosed as suffering from posttraumatic stress disorder. Rothbaum's study found that 94 percent of rape victims displayed classic symptoms of PTSD one week after the assault. This figure dropped to 47 percent twelve weeks after the incident.[13] Kilpatrick's study, *Rape in America*, reported that 11 percent of all women raped still suffer from PTSD, and the authors estimated that 1.3 million women in the United States are currently suffering from PTSD as a result of a rape or multiple rapes.[14]

Long-Term Crisis Reaction

Long-term crisis reaction is the name of a condition identified by the National Organization for Victim Assistance (NOVA). As discussed in Chapter 1, NOVA is considered one of the early leaders in the victims' rights movement. Organization members have responded to a number of crises throughout the world. Professionals from NOVA working with crisis victims have observed this reaction on a number of occasions. *Long-term crisis reaction* is a condition that occurs when victims do not suffer from PTSD, but may reexperience feelings of the crisis reaction when certain events trigger the recollection of the trauma in their lives.[15] The trigger event may be a number of situations, including the anniversaries of the crisis, birthdays, or holidays of loved ones lost during the trauma; significant life events such as marriage, divorces, births, and graduations; media events that broadcast similar types of incidents; and involvement in the criminal justice system.

The intensity and frequency of long-term crisis reactions usually diminish with the passage of time. As the victim develops coping mechanisms to deal with the trauma, these resources may lessen the victim's reaction to triggering events. The victim must learn to continue to function despite these reactions.

Other Mental Disorders

Victims of crime may suffer a wide variety of mental disorders as a result of their victimization. They are going through a process of attempting to regain their mental equilibrium that is off center as a result of the traumatic event. Following is a brief discussion of two common mental problems faced by victims of crime.

Depression
Depression is described as a major depressive episode lasting at least two weeks during which there is either a depressed mood or the loss of interest, or pleasure, in nearly all activities. Possible symptoms include changes in appetite or weight, sleep and psychomotor activity; decreased energy; feelings of worthlessness or guilt; difficulty thinking, concentrating, or making decisions; or recurrent thoughts of death

or suicide. The victim experiences clinically significant distress or impairment in social, occupational, or other important areas of functioning.

Substance Abuse

The essential feature of substance abuse is a maladaptive pattern of substance use leading to significant adverse consequences related to the repeated use of substances. Normally, these substances are drugs or alcohol. The victim may suffer repeated failure in fulfilling major role obligations, repeated use of substances in situations in which it is physically dangerous, legal problems related to the use of the substance, and social and interpersonal problems.

Other Effects

Different victims of the same crime suffer different reactions to that crime, and conversely, victims of different crimes may suffer similar reactions. There is no "clear bright line" that professionals can look to and determine which symptoms victims will suffer. However, researchers have attempted to establish general categories of problems suffered by victims of certain crimes. In Susman and Vittert's text, *Building a Solution: A Practical Guide for Establishing Crime Victim Service Agencies*, they listed certain crimes and typical reactions.[16] Although individual crime victims' reactions will vary depending on a number of factors, Table 5.1 summarizes these findings.

With the passage of time and other intervention techniques, the mental and emotional consequences associated with the trauma of a criminal act may lessen or be alleviated, but the victim may never be the same person as before the crime. In addition to the mental effects victims endure as a result of the crime, they also suffer fiscal consequences.

Traumatic Incident Stress

The previous sections dealt with the mental consequences to the victims of crimes or natural disasters. This section focuses on the mental consequences to those who respond to various types of victimization. Traumatic incident stress may occur during or after exposure to such traumas as catastrophic events (earthquake, fire), severely injured children or adults, dead bodies or body parts, or the loss of colleagues. Emergency response personnel, as well as untrained volunteers and others who find themselves in a "helping" role during a crisis, may experience physical, cognitive, emotional, or behavioral symptoms (or a combination of these symptoms) that result from their involvement with victims of crime or natural disasters. The Centers for Disease Control and the National Institute for Occupational Safety and Health have established a list of actions that emergency response team members can take if they believe they are being unduly affected at the scene of crime or disaster.

These on site responses include pacing themselves because the rescue or recovery efforts may continue for days or weeks. Workers need to take frequent rest breaks because many operations take place in extremely dangerous environments. Co-workers should watch out for each other. Responders should insure

TABLE 5.1   Victim Reactions to Various Crimes

Burglary	Robbery	Assault	Sexual Assault
Home is no longer a safe haven	Fear of walking alone on the streets	Anger and/or bitterness	Embarrassment
Reluctant to leave home	Relief at survival	Realization of mortality	Difficulty in describing the incident
Reluctant to stay home	Realization of mortality	Physical injury	Concern about STD/pregnancy
Express lots of "I shoulds"	Frustration at loss of personal effects	Medical bills	Bills for the medical exam
Heavy financial loss	Fear of intimidation	Time loss from work	Fear of telling family members
Sorrow at loss of sentimental items	For commercial robberies, fear of loss of job	Fear of reprisals	Fear the neighbors will find out
Disgust with destruction that occurred during the burglary		If assailant is a family member, feelings of betrayal	Fear of media publicity
Realization of isolation		If a result of a traffic incident, fear of driving	Recurring nightmares, changes in sleeping patterns, loss of appetite
Frustration with police who don't investigate thoroughly		If a result of jealousy, feeling of vulnerability	Decision to prosecute
Expense of securing home		For male victims, shame at losing a "fight"	Fear that they will have to testify about prior sexual history
			Bitterness against the offender
			Sexual dysfunction

Battered Women	Homicide—Survivor Victims	Child Victims	Elderly Victims
Decision to stay	Acceptance of death	Parents' reaction	Fear of crime
Decision to leave	Funeral arrangements	Signs of emotional distress	Acute financial loss
Financial worries	Financial problems when breadwinner is killed	Guilt	Change in lifestyle
Decision to prosecute		Parents' unconcern	Loneliness
Desire counseling for batterer and/or themselves	Delayed emotional reaction	Difficulty in describing incident	Family reactions
For separated couples, visitation offers opportunities for further attacks	Reaction of children	Fears about testifying	Reluctance to get involved in the criminal justice system
Isolation	Need for information on the criminal case	Incest—decision about family's future	
Helplessness	Media publicity	Incest—mixed reaction by mother	
Psychological dependence	Feelings of powerlessness in the criminal justice system	Reaction of other children	
Fear of recurrence	Ordeal during trial	Fear of intimidation	
Feeling of personal failure	Loneliness		
Reaction of other children	Can't stop ruminating		
	Desire for revenge		

they maintain a normal schedule and eat, drink liquids, and sleep as much as possible. Whenever possible, they should take breaks away from the scene of the crime or disaster.

Once the responders return to their regular duty station or home, they should continue to adjust to the experience. They need to reconnect in their community. They should avoid making any major life decisions immediately after returning from their response to a mass victimization. The responder's family may also be affected by the experience. Each family member needs patience, understanding, and the opportunity to communicate his or her emotions and concerns.[17]

Financial Consequences

In 1996, the National Institute of Justice released *Victim Costs and Consequences: A New Look*, an in-depth study of the costs of victimization.[18] This study raises serious questions regarding previous estimates of the costs of crime. Using the data from the Bureau of Justice Statistics and including "quality of life" or intangible losses, this study concludes that the cost of crime is higher than previously suggested. The following sections examine the results of this study.

Introduction

It is fairly easy to establish the tangible costs of crime. These costs include a number of fairly easy-to-measure items such as medical care, police services, and other items that have a specific monetary value. However, it is not as easy to value the loss of "quality of life" or intangible losses suffered by victims of crime. How much is a murder victim's life worth? What is the cost for the pain and suffering experienced by a rape victim? Additionally, costs associated with society's response to crime are difficult, if not impossible, to measure. Table 5.2 lists the major tangible, intangible, and society's costs associated with crime.

As Table 5.2 indicates, society's response to crime includes a variety of items that are not normally considered when discussing costs of crime. Measuring our actions and resulting costs based on our fear of crime is difficult. On the other hand, measuring items such as alarms for cars and homes, which are typical of the precautionary expenditures associated with protecting ourselves from criminal activity, is relatively easy. Additionally, everyone understands the costs associated with running the criminal justice system and keeping offenders incarcerated. Thus, it can be observed that society's response to crime includes both tangible and intangible costs. The costs of crime section also includes tangible and intangible losses suffered as a result of criminal acts. These costs include tangible items such as medical and mental health treatment cost. The intangible costs include quality of life and loss of companionship. Table 5.3 examines both tangible and intangible costs of crime.

Table 5.3 indicates that costs of crime show tangible and intangible losses generally exceed all tangible losses combined. By multiplying the costs of crime by the annual crime incidence, you can obtain the aggregate figures. The tangible losses

TABLE 5.2   Major Costs Associated with Crime

Cost of Crime to Victims	Cost of Society's Response to Crime
Direct property losses	Precautionary expenditures
Medical and mental health care	Fear of crime
Victim services	Criminal justice system
Lost workdays	Victim service organizations and volunteer time
Lost school days	Other noncriminal programs
Lost housework	Incarcerated offender costs
Pain and suffering/quality of life	Overdeterrence costs
Loss of affection/enjoyment	Justice costs
Death	
Legal costs associated with tort claims	
Second generation costs	

Source: Adapted from *Victim Costs and Consequences: A New Look* (U.S. Department of Justice) 1996, p. 11.

TABLE 5.3   Tangible and Intangible Costs of Crime

- The direct costs of child abuse and neglect in the United States total more than $24 billion annually. When factoring in indirect costs, the annual cost rises to more than $94 billion.
- The average monetary value of property stolen during a robbery is $1,244.
- The average loss from the misuse of a victim's personal information is $4,800.
- Telemarketing fraud has estimated losses to U.S. elderly exceeding $500 million per year.
- Many school districts report losses in excess of $250,000 because of school closings and costs of bomb search squads.

Sources: *Crime in the United States 2003*, U.S. Department of Justice, Washington D.C. (October 2004); *Identity Theft Survey Report*, Federal Trade Commission, Washington D.C. (September 2003); "Total Estimated Cost of Child Abuse and Neglect," Prevent Child Abuse America (2001); *Bomb Threats in Schools*, U.S. Department of Justice, Washington D.C. (February 2005).

amounted to $105 billion each year and the intangible losses were more than three times that amount at an annual cost of $345 billion. The next section examines the tangible costs of victimization.

Tangible Losses

Personal crime costs taxpayers, businesses, and victims approximately $105 billion per year in medical costs, lost earnings, and public programs related to victim assistance. These tangible losses do not account for the full impact of crime on victims because they ignore pain and suffering and the reduced quality of life that many victims suffer as a result of a crime. These costs are estimated at $450 billion annually. Violent crime including drunk driving and arson accounts for $426 billion of this total and property crime costs $24 billion.

The following figures put these sums into perspective to help clarify the true magnitude of the costs of crime to victims:

- Violent crime and its resulting injuries account for 3 percent of all U.S. medical spending;
- Violent crime results in wage losses equal to 1 percent of all American earnings;
- Violent crime causes 10 to 20 percent of mental health expenditures in the United States;
- Personal crime reduces the average American's quality of life by 1.8 percent.

Victims usually suffer three types of losses: (1) out-of-pocket expenses such as medical costs and property loss, (2) reduced productivity at work because of sick days, attending trial, etc., and (3) nonmonetary losses such as pain and suffering and loss of quality of life. Some of these losses are easily quantified, but even the intangible losses may be valued in dollars. Tangible losses include property damage and loss, medical care, mental health care, police and fire services, victim services, and productivity. Each of these losses are explained in the following paragraphs.

Property damage and loss includes the value of the property damaged during thze crime, or property taken and not recovered. It also includes insurance claims administration costs that arise as a result of compensating the victim under an insurance policy.

Medical care includes payments for hospital and physician care, emergency medical transportation, rehabilitation, prescriptions, allied health services, medical devices, and related insurance claim processing costs. Managed care systems are changing health care payments and are not reflected in these costs. More study is necessary in this area as medical costs adapt to changing circumstances.

Mental health care provides funding for services to crime victims by psychiatrists, psychologists, social workers, and counselors. This cost has been one of the least researched areas in crime victimization.

Police and fire services cover initial police and fire responses and follow-up investigations. The costs of other components of the criminal justice system are not included in this element. Generally speaking, police and fire costs are a relatively small portion of the cost of crime, averaging $100 per case.

Victim services costs include victim service agencies and child protective service agencies as well as foster care for maltreated children removed from their homes.

Productivity costs include lost wages, fringe benefits, housework, and lost school days suffered by victims and their families. This category includes lost productivity of coworkers and supervisors recruiting and training victims who are disabled as a result of a crime. It also includes processing costs for insurance claims and legal expenses associated with recovering productivity from drunk drivers and their insurers.

Intangible Losses

Intangible losses are hard to quantify; however, scholars have begun to place monetary values on certain aspects of a victim's quality of life. Researchers such as Ted R. Miller and others have divided intangible losses into two categories: fatal and nonfatal injuries. The monetary value for fatalities is based on the amount people routinely spend to reduce their risk of death. For example, this amount would include the cost of smoke detectors, alarm systems, and bars on house windows.

The intangible value for nonfatal injuries was established by analyzing jury verdicts for pain, suffering, fear, and loss of quality of life. As discussed in other chapters of this text, violent perpetrators rarely have sufficient funds to pay these awards, but third-party codefendants such as insurance companies or businesses that were negligent can be held liable for injuries to the victim.

M. P. Armour reviewed studies of the impact of victimization on survivors of homicide.[19] The studies included family and friends of homicide victims. Armour found that the survivors experienced a variety of mental health problems: posttraumatic stress disorder, nightmares, fear, anger, survivor guilt, and other bereavement conditions that seriously impacted their social and personal functioning.

There is no doubt that attempting to establish a monetary value on intangible aspects of victimization is a relatively recent development in the field of victimology. For example, in 1994 a Bureau of Justice Statistics publication, *The Costs of Crime to the Victim*, specifically did not examine the intangible costs of crime.[20] Because this is a new aspect of victimization, it will continue to be controversial. However, we cannot truly appreciate the consequences of crime and victimization until we begin to accept the reality of intangible costs to victims and their families. This is an area of victimology that will continue to generate more study and debate in the future.

Costs of White Collar Crime

When we think of the consequences of victimization, we typically focus on violent crime and do not automatically consider the consequences of white collar crime. This form of crime encompasses a wide variety of criminal offenses. Some of them make the front-page headlines while others are a statistic on police blotter records. This section examines some of the more common white collar crimes and their costs to the victims and society in general.

One of the better known forms of white collar crime involves organized crime, and a costly aspect of organized crime is software piracy. Software piracy is a continuing problem that involves illegal copies of software. According to the National White Collar Crime Center, a trade group that represents the world's major software manufactures, global losses in 2001 for software piracy total a staggering $11 billion dollars.[21]

Disaster Fraud

In view of disasters such as the tsunami that struck Indonesia in December 2004 and Hurricane Katrina, which devastated the north-central Gulf Coast of the United States in August 2005, it is important to understand the costs generated by disaster fraud. Disaster fraud is any activity the purpose of which is to defraud individuals or the government after a natural or man-made catastrophe. The total amount of disaster fraud costs is difficult to determine. Following a disaster, most relief agencies focus on providing victims with various forms of relief. However, property and casualty insurance fraud costs Americans an estimated $20 billion each year. For example, it estimated that the average household may pay as much as $200 to $300 extra in insurance premiums annually as a result of insurance fraud.[22]

Identity Theft

Identity theft is rapidly becoming a crime of immeasurable proportions that is causing untold injury to thousands of Americans each year. It occurs when a person knowingly transfers or uses, without legal authority, the identification

---

Perspectives on Disaster Fraud

In 2005, forty-nine people were indicted in a disaster fraud scheme that resulted in losses of thousands of dollars from the Red Cross's efforts to support Hurricane Katrina victims. At least fourteen suspects worked for a Red Cross call center located in Bakersfield, California, where they helped friends and family file false claims for aid money. The suspects are accused of stealing at least $200,000 from the fund.

The Bakersfield center was one of three Red Cross centers set up to handle callers who wished to file a claim for aid as a result of the devastation caused by Hurricane Katrina. The Red Cross contacted the FBI after an audit disclosed an usually high number of claims were being paid out in the Bakersfield area. The company that provided the employees said it didn't have time to run background checks on all of the persons it hired to work in the call centers. A Red Cross spokesperson said the organization was working to improve its anti fraud systems for the future.

Source: "49 Charged in Katrina Fraud Scam," CBS News (Fresno, California December 28, 2005); available online: www.cbsnews.com/stories/2005/12/28/national/main1167079.shtml.

FOCUS: Have You Been Contacted?

A well-known scam involves an unsolicited e-mail stating that a West African national has an unclaimed or unreported fortune in that country. The message then reports that the recipient of the e-mail was chosen as a trusted agent to help get money out of the country. All the recipient needs to do is provide bank account details. The recipient is promised a share of the fortune but is usually swindled out of large sums of money withdrawn from his or her account.

---

documentation of another person with the intent to commit, aid, or abet any unlawful activity that constitutes a felony.[23]

The Consumer Sentinel database, which is maintained by the Federal Trade Commission, estimates that in 2001 approximately 13 percent of all identity theft victims (11,012 of 86,168) reported out-of-pocket expenses totaling $12.9 million dollars. The average amount of out-of-pocket expenses reported per victim was $1,173 dollars. These costs were tangible costs and did not include intangible costs of the nature discussed earlier in this chapter. Approximately 17 percent (14,520 of 86,168) reported dollar amounts totaling $98,253,576, or an average $6,767 per victim, stolen from their financial institutions by criminals using identity theft.[24]

Another costly form of white collar crime is telemarketing fraud. It involves solicitations or campaigns to entice the purchase of goods or services or to entice charitable contributions through false representations in which telemarketing, via the mails, telephones, and the Internet, is an integral part of the effort. Many consumers do not report telemarketing fraud to law enforcement agencies as they do personal or property crime victimizations. Shame, embarrassment, disbelief, or simple unawareness that a crime has been committed may influence the nonreporting of these crimes. Congress has estimated that American consumers lose $40 billion each year—to than $1 million every hour—to telemarketing fraud.[25]

White collar crime continues to drain our society's resources and to impact each individual victim. While we have made progress in responding to and preventing this form of victimization, much work remains to be done. We are seeing more public awareness campaigns in the media, and such victimization appears to be losing the stigma it once carried. This change in viewing victims of white collar crime will allow them to come forward and report such crime with the result that we as a society may better respond to their needs.

Summary

We have known for centuries that victims of crime suffer from specific types of physical injuries as a result of their victimization. These are for the most part easy to recognize and treat. The broken arm or jaw may be repaired and hopefully the victim will regain full use of such physical faculties.

More recently, society has acknowledged that victims of crime may also suffer a wide variety of mental problems as a consequence of their victimization, including acute stress disorder, posttraumatic stress disorder, long-term crisis reaction, or other mental disorders. These reactions do not mean that the victims are insane or crazy. Rather, these are normal reactions to an abnormal event. Victim services providers and professionals who deal with victims must understand these dynamics in order to work with and assist victims of crimes.

Traumatic incident stress may be a consequence that victim services providers suffer as a result of rendering aid and support to victims of crime. In the past, we have focused on the consequences of victimization from the perspective of the victim and the victim's family. We must continue our research and study in this area. However, we must also be mindful of the consequences suffered by victim services providers and insure we care for the caretakers.

In addition to the physical and mental injuries, victims experience financial consequences of most crimes. Determining the amount of money taken from a robbery victim is relatively easy; however, it is harder to place a value on the intangible costs suffered by that victim. Recent studies have begun to address this long-overlooked aspect of crime victimization. The consequences of crime are multifaceted and, like a stone dropped in a calm pool of water, move out in ever-widening circles affecting victims, their families, and society as a whole. Professionals in the field must understand all the consequences of victimization to be able to function effectively.

Key Terms

Crisis is a specific set of temporary circumstances that result in a state of upset and disequilibrium, characterized by an individual's inability to cope with a particular situation using customary methods of problem solving.

Acute stress disorder is acute stress experienced in the immediate aftermath of a traumatic event.

Posttraumatic stress disorder is the development of characteristic symptoms following a psychologically distressing event that is outside the range of usual human experience.

Long-term crisis reaction is a condition that occurs when victims do not suffer from PTSD but may reexperience feelings of the crisis reaction when certain events trigger the recollection of the trauma in their lives.

Discussion Questions

1. What are the four stages of physical injury? How do they differ from each other?

2. Describe the various types of physical injuries that victims may suffer.

3. List and discuss the three stages of crisis. In your opinion, which stage is the most critical for the victim? Justify your answer.

4. What is acute stress disorder? How is it different from a crisis reaction?

5. Explain the symptoms of posttraumatic stress disorder.

6. Define long-term crisis reaction and explain a trigger event.

7. Compare and contrast PTSD with long-term crisis reaction.

8. List other mental effects of crime on victims. Which one, in your opinion, is the most serious? Justify your answer.

9. Should persons who commit disaster fraud be sentenced more severely than those who steal from a single victim? Why? Why not?

Suggested Readings

Albert J. Reiss, Jr. & Jeffery A. Roth, eds., *Understanding and Preventing Violence*, (National Academy Press, Washington, D.C.) 1993.

Albert R. Roberts, ed., *Crisis Intervention and Time-Limited Cognitive Treatment*, (Sage, Thousand Oaks, Calif.) 1995.

R. B. Ruback & M. P. Thompson, *Social and Psychological Consequences of Violent Victimization* (Sage, Newbury Park, Calif.) 2001.

C. P. Wing, *Crisis Intervention as Psychotherapy*, (Oxford, New York) 1978.

Gerald Caplin, *Principles of Preventive Psychiatry*, (Basic Books, New York) 1964.

Morton Bard & Dawn Sangrey, *The Crime Victim's Book*, 2nd ed. (Brunner/Mazel, New York) 1986.

Endnotes

1. Much of this information was gathered from interviewing members of the Fresno Valley Medical Center emergency room staff. Barbara Miller, RN, and Albert Velaseo, MD, were of significant assistance in providing guidance for material in this section.

2. J. D. Wright, "The Demography of Gun Control," *The Nation*, (Sept. 20, 1976), p. 241.

3. L. Adelson, "The Gun and the Sanctity of Human Life: or the Bullet as a Pathogen," *The Phasos*, (Summer 1980), p. 15.

4. Albert R. Roberts & Sophia F. Dziegielewski, "Foundation Skills and Applications of Crisis Intervention and Cognitive Therapy," in *Crisis Intervention and Time-Limited Cognitive Treatment*, Albert R. Roberts, Ed. (Sage, Thousand Oaks, Calif.) 1995.

5. E. Lindemann, "Symptomatology and Management of Acute Grief," 101 *American Journal of Psychiatry*, 141–148 (1944).

6. C. P. Wing, *Crisis Intervention as Psychotherapy*, (Oxford, New York) 1978 and Gerald Caplin, *Principles of Preventive Psychiatry*, (Basic Books, New York) 1964.

7. See Albert R. Roberts, *Crisis Intervention Handbook: Assessment, Treatment and Research*, (Wadsworth, Belmont, Calif.) 1990 and Morton Bard & Dawn Sangrey, *The Crime Victim's Book*, 2nd ed. (Brunner/Mazel, New York) 1986.

8. Caplin, *Principles of Psychiatry*, p. 46.

9. *Diagnostic and Statistical Manual of Mental Disorders*, 4th ed. (American Psychiatric Association, Washington, D.C.) 1994.

10. *Diagnostic and Statistical Manual of Mental Disorders*, 4th ed. (American Psychiatric Association, Washington, D.C.) 1994, pp. 427–429.

11. DSM-IV, pp. 427–429.

12. For an excellent discussion of the effects of rape on victims, see Bruce Taylor, "The Role of Significant Others in a Rape Victim's

Recovery: People Who Are More Likely to Be Harmful Than Helpful," paper presented at the 1996 ACJS Annual Meeting, Las Vegas, Nevada, March 1996.

13. B. O. Rothbaum, E. B. Foa, T. Murdock, D. S. Riggs & W. Walsh, "A Prospective Examination of Post-Traumatic Stress Disorder in Rape Victims," 5 *Journal of Traumatic Stress*, 455–475 (1992).

14. D. G. Kilpatrick, C. N. Edmunds & A. K. Seymour, *Rape in America: A Report to the Nation*, (National Victim Center, Arlington, Va.) 1992.

15. Marlene A. Young, "Crisis Response Teams in the Aftermath of Disasters," in *Crisis Intervention and Time-Limited Cognitive Treatment*, Albert R. Roberts, ed. (Sage, Thousand Oaks, Calif.) 1995.

16. Jarjorie Susman & Carol Holt Vittert, *Building a Solution: A Practical Guide for Establishing Crime Victim Service Agencies*, (National Council of Jewish Women, St. Louis Section) 1980.

17. Adapted from "Traumatic Incident Stress: Information for Emergency Response Workers, Centers for Disease Control and the National Institute for Occupational Safety and Health, (2005); available online: www.cdc.gov/niosh.

18. Ted R. Miller, Mark A. Cohen & Brian Wiersema, *Victim Costs and Consequences: A New Look*, National Institute of Justice, (U.S. Department of Justice, Washington, D.C.) February 1996. This section is adapted from the material presented in this study.

19. M. P. Armour, "Experiences of Convictims of Homicide: Implications for Research and Practice," -3 *Trauma, Violence, and Abuse*, 109—124 (2002).

20. Patsy A. Klaus, "The Cost of Crime to Victims," *Crime Data Brief*, (Bureau of Justice Statistics, Washington, D.C.) February 1994.

21. Jay Albanese and Melissa Parker, *Organized Crime*, National White Collar Crime Center (September 2002); available online: www.nw3c.org.

22. Shawn Hutton, *Disaster Fraud*, National White Collar Crime Center (September 2002); available online: www.nw3c.org.

23. The Identity Theft and Assumption Deterrence Act of 1998 (amending 18 U.S.C. Section 1028).

24. Ryan Brown and John Kane, *Identity Theft*, National White Collar Crime Center (September 2002); available online: www.nw3c.org.

25. Kathryn Malbon, *Telemarketing Fraud*, National White Collar Crime Center (February 2003); available online: www.nw3c.org.

6

EMPOWERING VICTIMS

Chapter Outline

Introduction

Media
  Relations with the Media
  Preparing for and Conducting the Interview

Legislation
  The Legislative Process
  Advocacy

Public Speaking
  Preparing for the Speech
  Drafting the Speech
  Some Do's and Don'ts of Public Speaking

Fundraising
  Introduction
  Types of Fundraisers

Summary

Key Terms

Discussion Questions

Suggested Readings

Learning Objectives

After reading this chapter, you should be able to:

- Distinguish between the different types of media and their objectives
- Explain the legislative process and how special interests affect the drafting of laws
- Understand how to draft a speech
- Make a presentation in public
- Understand the use of volunteers in victim services programs
- Understand the role of fundraising in victim services programs

Introduction

One common feeling experienced by victims of crime when they become involved in the criminal justice system is helplessness. Many victims want and need to do more than simply testify in a criminal trial regarding the facts of the incident. Victim services providers can assist victims in this endeavor by providing them with advice regarding the different ways that they may become involved in the system. Additionally, professionals in this field need to understand how they can work within the system to make it more responsive to the needs of the victim.

Media

The media have the ability to bring crime directly into our living rooms. It is therefore critical for victim services providers to understand how the media works and

---

FOCUS: Empowerment

Mike Reynolds—One Man's Journey

Mike Reynolds began his journey when he learned that his daughter, Kimber, had been shot and killed by an ex-felon. Mike was a professional photographer and had never been involved in politics or the victims' movement up to this point in his life. He decided one person can make a difference and set out to strengthen California's sentencing laws.

Mike Reynolds became the driving force behind the state's tough "Three Strikes and You're Out" initiative that was overwhelmingly passed by the voters. A similar law was adopted by Congress. Both statutes increased penalties for felons who committed second or third offenses or "strikes."

Although some authorities may argue that the "Three Strikes" law is reactive and imposes harsh penalties without addressing the causes of crime, it stands as a shining example of what one person can accomplish within the area of victims' rights.

how to effectively communicate with them. The media can help or hinder the victim's recovery and subsequent attitude toward life. It is therefore important that professionals develop a working relationship with the media to help bridge the gap between the media and victims.

Many victims, police officers, and criminal justice professionals view news reporters with distrust.[1] Just as the police have a mission to accomplish, so do the media. The Constitution of the United States prohibits federal and state governments from passing any law that abridges the freedom of the press. The media call this "the people's right to know." The media's attempts to inform the public occasionally conflict with a law enforcement agency's desire to keep certain information confidential. Only by understanding the media and their role in society can victims deal effectively with the media to present their side of the story.

Relations with the Media

Understanding the media must begin with a clarification of the different types of media. The victim services provider must understand that there are certain basic fundamental principles that apply to the media in general. In addition, there are distinct rules, goals, and standards that pertain to each different type of communication system.

There are three basic types of media with which criminal justice agencies interact: newspapers, radio, and television.

FOCUS: A Code of Ethics for Victim Advocates in the Media

1. Never give a reporter a victim's name and address without prior authorization from the victim.

2. Provide your clients with knowledge of their rights in the media.

3. Always inform clients that they have the right to refuse an interview.

4. When possible, accompany a victim to an interview.

5. Review with reporters, producers, and talk show hosts exactly what questions they can and cannot ask your client.

6. Reserve the right to end an interview if the client shows signs of trauma during the course of the interview.

7. Never force a client into an interview. Graciously accept the first "no" without making your client feel guilty.

8. Never provide "off the record" information about the victim; respect the victim's right to privacy at all times.

9. For victims who wish to speak to the media, obtain a signature on a media release form.

10. Discourage the participation of children in any interview or talk shows.

Source: Crime Victims and the Media, A Publication of the Victim's Rights: Opportunities for Action Series. (National Victims Center, Arlington, Va.)

Newspapers

Newspapers usually provide more in-depth coverage than the electronic media. They have the ability to print charts and graphs using statistics that allow the reader to place the current story in visual perspective. In addition, many newspapers are interested in the human aspect of the story. Newspapers may run a major story, coupled with a sidebar story that touches on another aspect of the main story. A *sidebar* story is usually an article that is placed in a column next to the main article. Many newspapers assign a reporter full time as either the police or court reporter. This reporter will know the officers, the language of the streets, and the law nearly as well as any police officer.

Different types of newspapers exist, and victim services providers need to know about the ones in their area. Some publishers print a daily newspaper and others go to press only once a week. Knowing the type of newspaper assists in understanding the time constraints or deadlines that the reporter faces. Most often when dealing with dailies, the reporter must have the information right away, whereas weeklies usually allow several days before the item must be turned in to the editor. In addition to local or regional newspapers, news or wire services such as United Press International (UPI) and Associated Press (AP) provide up-to-date coverage of local, state, national, and international events that are sent across the nation and the world on a news line.

Radio

A radio broadcast carries only the voice of the speaker, so the news broadcaster must paint a verbal picture of the situation for the listeners. Because radio reporters do not capture the scene with live pictures, many of the interviews with the victim or a victim services provider are conducted over the telephone.

There are a variety of radio formats, and anyone who has driven in a car and "surfed" the channels can vouch for the many different types of programs broadcast on the radio at any given moment. They include rock music, easy listening, classical, ethnic, educational, religious, all news, and talk shows. Each of these programs appeals to different audiences.

Many radio stations have hourly newscasts, and they can therefore update the public more effectively than can daily newspapers or nightly newscasts. In this day of visual media, an effective victim services provider should not overlook the radio as an additional source by which the public may be informed of the activities of their program.

Television

Television is the most familiar medium. It brings the action directly into our living room as it occurs. Many of us have watched hostage scenes and riots as they are happening from the comfort of our easy chairs.

There are basically three forms of television: networks, independents, and cable companies. Network television includes the major corporations such as the American Broadcasting Corporation (ABC), National Broadcasting Corporation (NBC), the Turner System, and others. Independent stations may contract with the networks for some of their shows or they may buy programs that are syndicated by private companies. Cable television combines both national and independent broadcasts and many times provides a news channel for local activities or community programming.

Television by its very nature is visual. A simple news release does not satisfy the television director, who wants and needs pictures and action: a uniformed officer speaking, a suspect being placed in a patrol vehicle, the front of a shot-up building. These graphic scenes are what television is searching for on a daily basis. In addition, television news is short and to the point. Normally, a story on the evening news is twenty to thirty seconds long. No matter how long the television reporter interviews a victim or other service provider, the final broadcast usually will run no longer than one minute.

Understanding the distinctions between the different types of media allows victims and professionals to deal with them in an effective manner. It is also important that victims understand how law enforcement agencies respond to requests for information from the media.

Some criminal justice agencies have codified the rules for these contacts by distributing a standard operating procedure (SOP) on media relations. This procedure has several advantages. First, it assures the media and the administrator of the agency that there is uniformity in dealing with the press. Second, it establishes procedures that both parties can follow. If media representatives are consulted when the document is being drafted, they will be more understanding of its purpose and will follow the procedures more readily. Lastly, the SOP informs the officer on the street how to respond to an unexpected contact with a news reporter. Understanding the process that law enforcement agencies use to release information will allow a victim services provider to interact more effectively with both the criminal justice agency and the media.

Using a public affairs officer (PAO) is becoming more common in law enforcement agencies.[2] A PAO is the department's official point of contact with the media. There are several different approaches to utilizing a PAO. One approach is to make the public affairs officer the official spokesperson for the department. All interviews are conducted by this person. While this approach may provide continuity, it is not the most effective method of dealing with either the public or the media. Any top-level administrator should be able to conduct a live interview with the media if he or she has above-average communications skills. A second approach is to establish the position as an official assignment and rotate officers through it based on their experience, intelligence, and abilities. This alternative allows the public and media to "talk" to a sworn officer. The disadvantage to this approach is that depending on the length of the assignment, the media will have to readjust to a new officer with every rotation. Victim services providers should become acquainted with the department's PAO. This affords them the opportunity to hold joint press releases in which both law enforcement and the victim's representative may present their views to the public.

Occasionally, members of the media will report information regarding private aspects of the victim's life. Some of this information is a matter of public record, whereas other sources of data may have been obtained through leaks from criminal justice agencies that have access to what is normally viewed as confidential information. News reporters are ethically bound to not reveal the identity of their sources. Just as police officers refuse to reveal the names of their confidential reliable informants, so do news reporters carefully guard the identity of their sources. Some states have "shield" laws that prevent a news reporter from being held in contempt of court for refusing to comply with a court order to reveal the name of a source. In addition, there have been numerous incidents of reporters going to jail rather than give up the identity of their sources.

Victim services providers should accept that there may be leaks to the media concerning information that the victim wishes to remain confidential. By doing so, the effective victim services provider can attempt to work out a relationship with the press to minimize the impact of such a leak. One technique is to appeal to the integrity of the reporter and inform the reporter of the consequences of releasing the story. It is fruitless to get angry at the reporter or the unnamed source. Human nature being what it is, leaks will continue for as long as there is a reporter who is willing to listen.

Members of the media are also concerned about the plight of victims of crime. Organizations such as Criminal Justice Journalists have published procedures that inform reporters about various aspects of crime and the justice system. These procedures include valuable information regarding crime victimization.[3] Criminal Justice Journalists report that crime and justice are the major subjects of American news coverage and that police and crime news rank third in the amount of space newspapers devote to it. The number-one topic is politics and government, and the number-two topic is sports. Crime news is even more prominent on television. It has been the number-one subject of new coverage for the last five years, accounting for about one fourth of all stories aired.

Journalists are responsible for providing readers, viewers, and listeners an accurate picture of crime, but they must also offer that view in context. Doing so may mean allowing the victim to comment on the consequences of the crime and how it has affected him or her as well as his or her family.

The Michigan State University School of Journalism offers the Victims and the Media Program, which educates journalists about various victim issues.[4] In "Tips on Interviewing Victims," Bonnie Bucqueroux, coordinator of the program, sets forth the following information about victims:

1. *Aim for the truth:* Many journalists try to make some stories fit a preconceived idea of what happened. It is important to accurately report what really happened, not some idealized or sensationalized version that the journalist has in his or her mind.
2. *Denial:* Understand that victims may engage in denial, and journalists must be sensitive to the perils of pushing a person to accept what has happened before he or she is ready to do so.
3. *Anger:* Many victims feel anger, which may sustain them and may also motivate them to work in the victims' movement to improve it or to make a difference.
4. *Bargaining:* Some victims may engage in "bargaining" behavior: for example, a victim may promise that if her child is returned, she will devote her life to the church.

5. *Depression:* Many victims may feel depression and appear exhausted and detached, but it is a mistake for a reporter to confuse this behavior with lack of caring.

While these symptoms and reactions are common knowledge to victim advocates, many journalists are unaware of them, and it may assist in the interviewing process if they are informed of some of the more basic reactions that victims of crime may suffer.

Bucqueroux sets forth the following guidelines for journalist to use when interviewing victims of crime:

1. Do your research before you interview the victim. Previous stories may have been inaccurate. Do not put yourself in the situation of having to interrupt a victim to get the spelling of a name.
2. Be empathic. It is respectful to acknowledge the victim's loss, but do not use phrases that might be hurtful.
3. Focus on active listening. Give the victim a chance to tell the story in his or her own way.
4. Be prepared for tears. The honest expression of grief deserves respect and not exploitation.
5. Understand the victim's guilt. Many victims blame themselves even if the blame is not justified. Be careful not to include statements by victims that indicate it was their fault. Such statements in print may have repercussions in any subsequent civil or criminal case.
6. Think twice about touching. Seeing someone in pain leads many of us to want to comfort that person with a hug or touch. You can offer nonverbal support by body gestures, but touching can be misinterpreted.
7. Consider allowing an advance reading. If possible, allow the victim to read the entire story before it is published. This is a controversial guideline among journalists.

Victim services professionals may find it helpful to inform journalists of these guidelines, provide a copy of them, or refer the journalists to the Victims and the Media Program Web site. Working with reporters instead of working against them can, in some instances, benefit the victim.

We as a society are becoming more sensitive to suicide. The Centers for Disease Control, along with several other government and non profit agencies, published a study on reporting suicides.[5] It offers tips and techniques for the media to use when interviewing surviving relatives and friends of the deceased. It raises concerns and recommends the use of certain language in reporting suicides in print and on television and radio.

Victim services providers must be aware of these and other techniques in order to assist the victim when dealing with media. While the great majority of journalists are ethical and concerned about the accuracy and effect of their story on victims, others tend toward sensationalism, and victim services providers must make independent judgments on how to approach each journalist to insure their victims not revictimized.

Effective media relations should include occasional conferences between the victim services provider and the news director of television and radio stations and the editor or publisher of the newspaper. Periodic conferences allow each party to understand the others' points of view. This relationship is especially helpful when adverse or derogatory information is disseminated about the victim. Media representatives should always attempt to contact the victim or the victim's representative for that side of the story before it is run. In the event the reporter "neglects" to reach the victim, the victim services provider should call the editor to arrange a follow-up story giving the victim's position.

Establishing an ongoing relationship with the media is a necessary function of any victim services provider. It must always be based on trust and mutual respect. Once such a relationship has been created, it will be of great benefit to all victims.

Preparing for and Conducting the Interview

Understanding the goal of the media assists the victim services provider and the victim in preparing for and conducting an interview. Most people talk with friends and colleagues on a daily basis and although this is a form of communication there is a distinct difference between this type of interaction and being interviewed by the local television station. This section examines some techniques that can facilitate a victim services provider's ability to effectively communicate in public situations. The first few times a victim services provider participates in a media interview can be frightening. When a person begins to speak and the newspaper reporter begins to take notes, or the radio or television reporter thrusts a microphone in the provider's face, it can be an overpowering experience.

Preparation before the interview can help relieve some of the anxiety. Being knowledgeable about the facts of the incident and the agency's position can enhance the communication. If photo opportunities are available, the media should know about them. One should never, never lie or distort the truth. The victim services provider's credibility is on the line.

Once the professional has reviewed the facts and has had preliminary discussions with the media, the actual interview takes place. By this time, it may seem anticlimactic. The provider should remember to speak clearly in everyday language and avoid the use of jargon.

If the victim services provider is anxious about talking to a reporter because her picture will be on the nightly news, which is seen by thousands of citizens, she should remember that this is a one-on-one conversation. The camera person only records what is being said between the professional and the reporter. On occasion a victim services provider is called on to give an interview "live" instead of having it taped, edited, and replayed at a later time. The person should approach this situation in the same manner as with a taped interview. She must be professional and must clearly communicate with the reporter, not the unseen public.

Relations with the media have traditionally been tense. By understanding their purpose and working conditions, and trying to assist them when possible, a victim services provider may become an effective spokesperson for the victim.

Legislation

One emotional issue within the victims' rights movement is the passage of the Victims' Rights Constitutional Amendment. As indicated in Chapter 1, President Clinton has proposed such an amendment. NOVA and other victims' rights organizations have made this a priority on their agendas. In the meantime, a number of other state and federal laws can be revoked, amended, or passed that will assist victims. The purpose of this section is to provide a brief summary of legislative efforts and lobbying activities in which victims and their advocates can engage. These efforts can be very satisfying and empowering to victims or they can be very frustrating, causing victims to feel like they have been victimized one more time.

The Legislative Process[6]

Victim advocates must understand how the legislature works and what is possible from a political perspective. That a proposed law may solve a problem from the victim's perspective does not mean it will be acceptable to other interest groups. We only have to turn on the evening news to hear about political gridlock at both the state and national levels to understand how politics affect our daily lives.

One of the first decisions that must be made when attempting to obtain passage of a victims' rights bill is choosing an author. The role of the author, or *sponsor*, is critical to the successful passage of the bill. The author must be committed to the proposed legislation. The legislator should have a record of supporting other victims' issues. Additionally, the potential author should not be so controversial that he or she alienates other legislative members. If the author is the chairperson of a key committee or serves in other leadership positions within the legislature, this position assists in moving the bill through the process. The reality of modern-day politics is that victim advocates will deal with the elected official's staff more often than with the actual author. It is therefore important to maintain a cordial working relationship with these staffers. Many times these staff persons will assist in identifying other cosponsors for the bill. Although obtaining an author or sponsor is critical, the addition of cosponsors, especially from both parties, indicates widespread support for any proposed legislation and dramatically improves the chances that it will become law.

The legislature has established the committee process to screen the thousands of bills that are introduced each year. Each proposed legislation is subject to review by a policy committee and if the bill involves appropriation of funds, it must also be reviewed by a fiscal committee. A major portion of the committee's time is spent holding hearings on the proposed legislation. Private citizens, victims

---

FOCUS: How a Bill Becomes a Law

A citizen, organization, special interest group, or elected official proposes potential legislation.

↓

A legislator authors the bill, often a simple, nonlegal statement of the concept.

↓

The legislative counsel drafts the bill.

↓

The drafted bill is returned to the legislator.

↓

The bill goes to the legislative desk where it is introduced, assigned a bill number, and "read" for the first time.

↓

The bill is printed.

↓

The bill is sent to the rules committee where it is assigned to a standing committee.

↓

After a certain number of days, the bill is heard in that committee.

↓

The committee acts upon the bill in one of three ways: It may pass the bill "as is," it may amend the bill, or it may hold the bill in committee. The latter course of action effectively kills the bill.

↓

If the bill involves the expenditure of state funds, it is sent to an appropriations committee.

↓

The bill is then sent to the legislative floor for a second reading.

↓

Bills that survive the second reading are again sent to the legislative floor for a third and final reading.

↓

Bills are then forwarded to the governor for signature.

↓

After signature by the governor, the bill is the law.

---

organizations, and other special interest groups may appear and testify at these hearings. The following are four key committees with which victim advocates must be familiar:

> **Rules Committee:** *Rules committees* act as housekeepers or gatekeepers and control the assignment of bills to other committees. A rules committee will normally assign bills to certain standing committees. It is an extremely powerful and important group.

> **Appropriations Committee:** An *appropriations committee* may be known by a variety of names, including *ways and means committee* or simply *finance committee.* Any bill requiring the expenditure of state funds will normally require a vote by this committee.

Standing Committee: *Standing committees* (also known as *policy committees*) consist of a group of legislators who hear testimony from interested parties. Each standing committee is responsible for a specific policy area such as criminal justice, education, or health and welfare. This committee may either pass the bill or kill it.

Select Committee: A *select committee* functions much like a standing committee except that it reports or makes recommendations to a standing committee. Sometimes bills are so complex that they need specialized hearing and select committees to serve this purpose. The select committee may propose passage of the legislation, offer amendments to the bill, or recommend that it be defeated.

Once a bill reaches a committee, victims and their advocates may testify on behalf of their bill. This is one of the most exciting aspects of the U.S. legislative process, and some would consider it to be democracy in action. It is important to coordinate the efforts of everyone who will be testifying in support of the bill. This allows for a united front to be presented to the committee members.

Individual citizens, including victims, have a right to testify at committee hearings. Many law enforcement professionals believe that the dramatic testimony from a stalking victim in front of a standing committee was a critical ingredient in the passage of the California's stalking law, which was the first one of its kind in the nation.[7] Additionally, a representative from a state or local victims organization, or coalition, should offer testimony. Whoever is selected to make the presentation should be eloquent, capable of quick thinking, and knowledgeable not only about the pending bill but also about victims' rights legislation in general.

Victim advocates should always check with the bill's sponsor prior to testifying. The author may want certain points emphasized or explained in more detail. The sponsor may want other committee members contacted before the hearing. In many jurisdictions, decisions regarding particular bills are made before the actual hearing.

The testimony should be clear and succinct. A rambling, disjointed, or boring presentation can go a long way toward killing the bill in committee. Testimony should never be read by those who are making their presentations. It should simply be discussed with the committee in a conversational tone as one would address another person. The victim services provider should know the names and districts of each committee member, and if asked a question should try to respond to that member by name and explain how the bill affects that member's district. Victims who testify should not focus on their victimization; rather they should emphasize their concern as a victim who is representing all other similarly situated actual or potential victims.

The victim advocate should write the presentation and give a copy to each member of the committee. The written document should be clear, concise, and error-free. It should be double-spaced with large (inch and one-half inch) margins. The advocate's name, the committee's name, bill number, and date should be on the upper corner of each page.

None of these suggestions ensure passage of a bill. The legislative process is complex, confusing, and at times defies logic. Because of the number of special interests that compete for a legislator's time, victim advocates must understand the principles involved in lobbying. The next section addresses this highly controversial activity.

Advocacy

Advocating for victims in the legislative arena can take many forms. One of the most common forms of advocacy is lobbying. The purpose of *lobbying* is to inform, educate, and persuade elected officials to support certain legislative goals. Lobbyists can be individuals, local groups, national corporations, or coalitions of any of these entities.

Today, political action committees, the high cost of running for reelection, high-powered lobbyists, and long-term planning have turned lobbying into a professional business. There are a number of firms located in most state capitals and in Washington, D.C., whose sole income is derived from lobbying elected officials. In some of these firms, former elected officials now represent business interests and are not reluctant to call in favors rendered during their tenure in office. However, not all lobbying involves the trading of favors or the purchasing of lunches. Many organizations and individuals strive to influence by use of information only. They rely on their expertise and reputations to carry the day with elected officials.

The Internal Revenue Service monitors nonprofit organizations to ensure that they comply with all legal requirements. An effective program should carefully observe any restraints imposed by the Internal Revenue Service regarding activities by nonprofit organizations. If lobbying becomes a substantial part of the organization's activities, it stands the chance of losing its nonprofit status.

Victim advocacy is more effective if a large number of paid or volunteer individuals work to support the legislative efforts. The following is a short list of activities that can be delegated to citizens who support this work:

Selection of a Bill Manager.   The bill manager tracks the bill and coordinates all the activities involved in presenting testimony at hearings. This person will be able to answer any questions regarding the status of the bill.

Coordinator of Support Letters.   This coordinator gathers supporters from both organizations and individuals and assists them in writing letters of support for the legislation to the appropriate elected official. These letters should be more than simple form postcards. They should indicate the organization and person and why they are supporting the bill.

Coordinator of Telephone Calls.   The coordinator of phone calls can be the same person who is coordinating support letters because the purpose is the same. Persons should call the elected officials and inform them of their name, organization, and the fact that they are supporting the bill. They will not talk directly to the legislator, but their call will be noted by the staff member handling the bill.

Press Liaison.   The press liaison is in charge of drafting press releases regarding the proposed bill and attempts to get media coverage of its progress and its impact on the field. Sometimes calling a press conference with the sponsor of the bill, victims, their organizations, and other community leaders will create an impact on undecided legislators.

It is obvious that there are no clear guidelines in the area of lobbying. A small organization may combine the above mentioned functions into one volunteer position, whereas a national organization may have paid staffers working on each activity. It is important to remember the long-range goal of serving victims and not get discouraged at defeats.

Public Speaking[8]

Most victim services providers will be called on to make presentations to the general public. It may be an informal presentation, perhaps a Neighborhood Watch meeting, or a formal presentation to the city council. Many people suffer from stage fright when speaking to groups. As with any other skill, practice makes perfect. This is not to say all of us will become dynamic and forceful speakers. Some people are better than others at appearing and communicating in public. However, by mastering certain basic and simple procedures, any victim services provider can make a creditable presentation.

Preparing for the Speech

Some of the most outgoing professionals become quivering masses of insecurity at the thought of facing a group of citizens and explaining the victim's perspective on crime. Although we may talk to other people all the time, we do so on an individual basis, not in front of a collective body. Even though public speaking can be viewed as simply talking to more than one person, the rules of communication change when we move into a group setting. Feedback may be delayed or never received or there may be physical barriers such as a nonworking microphone that prevent those in the back of the room from hearing adequately. Add to this the typical worry of making a mistake or looking unprofessional and many people dread speaking in public.

Drafting the Speech

Having to stand and present a speech to a room full of people can be an intimidating experience, and writing a speech can be an agonizing task for many victim services providers. However, a speech should be prepared differently than a term paper or an agency position paper. The following are some simple rules for speech writing:

1. *Prepare an outline of the topics to be discussed.* Start with the main objective or theme. The first thing to write is what the audience should be motivated to do as result of the speech. Keep this objective in mind while writing the rest of the speech.

2. *Draft an outline of the main points of discussion.* There should only be three or four major items on the list. If the list looks like a laundry list, consider combining some items or reconsider the desired goals of the speech.
3. *Revise the outline several times.* Then begin to add additional information to the main points. Think about each new piece of information. Does it explain the main point?
4. *Remember, we write differently than we speak.* Practice the speech by speaking it out loud. Based upon several rehearsals, the presentation may require revision.
5. *Prepare an outline and deliver the speech based on the outline.* Know the subject matter well enough beforehand to be able to refer only to the outline instead of the typewritten speech. The delivery will be more natural.
6. *When writing a speech, start at the middle or end.* The most difficult part of a speech is the opening. This should be done last.

Once the speech is written, the next step is delivery. The following section briefly examines some simple principles that can make public presentations more professional for victim services providers.

Some Do's and Don'ts of Public Speaking

There are as many rules to effective public speaking as there are dynamic speakers.[9] No one approach will work for all persons. However, there are several simple methods that are easily mastered that will allow most professionals to make a clear and meaningful presentation. The following are some rules that will assist you, as a victim services provider, in making oral presentations.

1. *Understand the topic of the speech.* What does the group expect to hear? If they want to be informed about the concept of restitution, do not deliver a speech regarding sentencing and victim impact statements.
2. *Know the audience and direct the speech to their interests and knowledge level.* Nothing is more boring than a speech full of technical jargon that the audience does not understand. Talk on their level and the reward will be an interested audience.
3. *Humor is excellent, but it can backfire.* If you are comfortable, humor can break the ice and relax the audience for the speech. However, a long, drawn out joke that does not go over with the audience leaves a bad taste with everyone.
4. *Always be on time and dress appropriately.* Common courtesy requires that you do not keep the audience waiting for your arrival. Know the exact starting time and show up a few minutes early.
5. *Do not read the speech verbatim.* We have all sat through public speeches where the speaker droned on and on reading from prepared notes.
6. *Understand how long the speech is to last and stay within that time limit.* Even if the audience is cooperative, do not prolong the speech. Remember, the group may have other business, and if you are that good, they will ask you to return.

7. *When possible, use visual aids to assist in making your points.* Nothing makes points as well as visual aids. Businesses have known this for years. We in the public sector should take the hint and use visual aids when possible.

8. *Rehearse as often as possible.* Rehearse, rehearse, rehearse. Especially during the beginning of your public speaking career.

9. *Ask for honest feedback from the person that requested the speech.* Don't simply say, "How was I?" This will lead to the standard response, "You were great." Politely press the person to offer comments on ways to make the presentation better the next time. It's amazing that, once encouraged to give feedback, many people will provide helpful suggestions on how to make a presentation more effective.

Public speaking is really more of an art than a science, but by following these rules any victim advocate can become a better public speaker. Addressing a group of citizens or elected officials requires certain techniques. These techniques can only become more refined with practice. With the passage of time and more frequent speaking experience, you may find yourself actually enjoying this aspect of victim advocacy.

Fundraising

Introduction

In this age of tightening governmental budgets, professionals in the area of victim services must be knowledgeable regarding fundraising techniques and opportunities. Some victim assistance programs are fortunate to receive a steady supply of funds that allows them to properly administer their programs. However, most victim services organizations must always be on the lookout for additional funding sources. Fundraising is more an art than a science, but any professional who works with victims should have a basic understanding of how the process works, and its pitfalls.

Many victim-related programs were originally funded by the Law Enforcement Assistance Administration. From 1974 until 1981, Congress authorized spending of funds on a variety of law enforcement–related activities. Victim assistance was included under this definition and as a result, many prosecutors' offices established such programs. In 1981, Congress ended funding for these activities and many victim assistance programs were subsequently downsized or abolished. From 1981 until 1984, victim assistance programs had to rely on other sources of funding. In 1982, President Reagan's Task Force on Victims of Crimes made a series of recommendations addressing a variety of crime victim issues. One recommendation was the passage of a federal law addressing the plight of crime victims. In 1984, Congress passed the Victims of Crime Act (VOCA) which established a federal Crime Victims Fund. This fund received federal criminal fines, penalty assessments, and forfeited bail which is used to fund local victim assistance programs and state compensation programs. The original fund was capped at $100 million, but in 1992 the cap was removed. VOCA helps pass these funds to each state which in turn provides financial assistance to a number of victim programs. As a condition of receiving these funds, each state is required to certify that it is giving priority in funding to local programs that are assisting victims of spousal abuse, sexual assault, or child abuse.

Types of Fundraisers

Although VOCA funds may provide assistance to some organizations, there are a number of other victims' groups that do not receive VOCA funding. These groups must look elsewhere for funding. There are a number of methods used to raise funds for local victims' programs. The most common fundraising activities include government and private grants, and local fundraising events.

Grants are cash donations, by either the federal or state government, or private foundations, for specific projects. During the period of 1986 through 1991, 410 foundations gave grants totaling $150.9 million to criminal justice projects. Unfortunately, less than 2 percent of all foundation grants are for criminal justice projects including victim-related programs. Taken as a whole, the nation's foundations have not gotten the word that the public considers crime a major issue.[10] Federal and state grants are normally a one-time source of funding for very specific projects. However, these governmental grants have decreased dramatically since the late 1970s.

The federal government continues to award grants each year. Some of the more common grants are awarded for research, others study "best practices" in the field, and still others provide funding to train professionals who serve in the field. A number of different governmental agencies and departments award grants. These grants vary from year to year and from agency to agency. The first step in obtaining a grant is to find out which state or federal department is awarding them. The local library is an excellent place to start the search for government funds. Victim services providers should not overlook their local elected officials. Many state and congressional staff persons have information regarding the availability of government grants. Finally, victim services providers should make contact with the local university. Many universities have offices that specialize in obtaining grants and some offer extension classes to the public on how to write a grant proposal. These universities are not only a source of information, but they also may lead to contacts which will result in joint grant writing endeavors involving faculty members and victim services providers.

Grants are handed out selectively. Most grants are very competitive and therefore victim services providers should be prepared for a series of rejections when they first attempt to obtain grants. Grant writing is a time-consuming and very technical process.

In the event that there are insufficient funds available in state or federal government for a specific program, victim services providers should consider private corporation or foundation grants. These funding opportunities are even more limited than federal grants, but they should not be overlooked. The same sources that provided information regarding federal grants can be contacted about private grants or awards.

There are disadvantages to government or private grants or awards. A victim services provider should not automatically apply for every grant that is available. Often grants contain hidden costs. They may require local objectives to be reevaluated and/or reprioritized, or impose burdensome paperwork. Some grants require matching funds that take money from other programs, and some grants build in expectations for ongoing future activities. All grants should be evaluated for any strings that are attached as well as the long-term commitments for the continued funding of the project. If possible, grants should be used for individual, one-time projects, rather than ongoing projects. Finally, those grants that require an extraordinary amount of funds in the form of matching dollars should be critically evaluated.

The final method to obtain funding involves local fundraising events. These events can be as varied as the mind of the organizer. They are not guaranteed to turn a profit and many times they take a great deal of volunteer and staff time to organize and execute. Typical fundraisers include dinners, banquets, auctions, house or garden tours, and sporting events. If the first fundraiser is a success, organizers should consider making it an annual event. Additionally, victim services providers should always consider asking local businesses to cosponsor these events. Their support may include monetary donations and many times will add visibility to the event.

Victim services providers must be knowledgeable regarding the various types of fundraising. With our constantly changing economic situation, no one source of funding is ever 100 percent safe. Victim services providers should consider having a variety of funding mechanisms available to them so that they can more effectively service their clients.

Summary

The media are not an enemy to be attacked or avoided. Certain issues require that victims be involved with the media. These might include an appeal to a kidnapper to release a victim, an assistance call to search areas where a child was last seen, or a statement to stir up public opinion regarding the release of an offender back into the community. The efficient victim services provider will become familiar with the different types of media and their specific needs.

All victim services providers need to understand the legislative process, its complexities, and its strengths and weaknesses to understand the process by which the laws that affect victims are drafted, amended, and passed.

Public speaking, like any other skill, requires practice and the knowledge that speeches are most effective when tailored to the different types of audiences. An effective victim services provider can enhance a program by knowing how to present that information to members of the community.

Fundraising is a necessary activity of most victim programs. Various types of funds are available to these programs; however, the competition for this money is fierce. Often, the best way to become proficient in this area is to work with people who already have established a successful track record of raising money. By watching and learning their techniques, victim services providers can adapt those techniques to their individual programs.

Key Terms

Sidebar story is usually an article placed in a column next to the main article.

Rules committees act as housekeepers or gatekeepers and control the assignment of bills to other committees.

Appropriations committee may be known by a variety of names including *ways and means committee* or simply *finance committee.*

Standing committees (also known as *policy committees*) consist of a group of legislators who hear testimony from interested parties. Each standing committee is responsible for a specific policy area such as criminal justice, education, or health and welfare.

Select committee function much like standing committees except that they report or make recommendations to a standing committee.

Lobbying is to inform, educate, and persuade elected officials to support certain legislative goals.

Grants are cash donations, by either the federal or state government or private foundations, for specific projects.

Discussion Questions

1. Is there any occasion that you can think of when a victim services provider should become a "source" for a news reporter?

2. What is the most important hearing in the legislative process?

3. Should victim advocates compromise on amendments to their bills? What if failure to compromise means that the bill will be killed in a committee?

4. What is the most difficult aspect of public speaking?

5. What makes one speaker more dynamic than another? List specific characteristics that you believe are essential to effective public speaking.

6. How would you secure a steady form of money for a victims' program?

Suggested Readings

H. Wallace, C. Robinson, & C. Steckler, Written and Interpersonal Communication Methods for Law Enforcement, (Prentice Hall, N.Y.) 1997.

B. Wurman, *Information Anxiety*, (Bantam Books, New York) 1990.

Endnotes

1. Some of this mistrust is based on law enforcement's perception of how the media report crime; see, Steven M. Chermak, "Body Count News: How Crime Is Presented in the News Media," 11/4 Justice Quarterly, 561 (December 1994).
2. See Craig A. Sullivan, "Police Public Relations," Law and Order, 94 (October 1993), for a discussion of how one agency interacts with the media.
3. See for example, Ted Gest, Covering Crime and Justice; available online: www.justice-journalism.org/crimeguide/intro.html.
4. Bonnie Bucqueroux, "Tips on Interviewing Victims: The Anniversary Story," University of Michigan School of Journalism, Victims and the Media Program (no date); available online: http://victims.jrn.msu.edu/public/articles/anniv.html.
5. *Reporting on Suicide: Recommendations for the Media*, Centers of Disease Control, et al.; available online: www.afsp.org/education/recommendations/5/1.htm.
6. The material in this section and the diagram are based on the author's discussions with leaders of several victims' rights organizations that monitor legislation in California. The actual format and process may differ slightly in other jurisdictions.
7. Presentation by Lt. John Lane, LAPD Threat Management Unit, (Threat Assessment Conference, Los Angeles, Calif.) July 1995.
8. This section has been adapted from Wallace, Robinson, & Steckler, Written and Interpersonal Communication Methods for Law Enforcement, (Prentice Hall, New York) 1997.
9. For an excellent discussion of public speaking, see Steven N. Bowman, "The Practical Local Government Manager," Public Administration, 22–23 (December 1991).
10. See Ordway P. Burden, "Big-Game Hunting: Foundations' CJ Bucks Are a Rare Quarry," Law Enforcement News, 9 (April 30, 1991).

7

HOMICIDE VICTIMS

Chapter Outline

Introduction
    Nature and Extent of the Problem
    Theories, Types, and Characteristics of Homicide
    Drinking, Driving, and Homicide

Responding to Special Needs
    Family Relationships
    Mental and Emotional Responses
    Notification

Summary

Key Terms

Discussion Questions

Suggested Readings

Learning Objectives

After reading this chapter, you should be able to:

- Know who are the survivors of homicide victims
- Describe the extent of homicide in the United States
- Describe the typical homicide victim
- Understand the different types of homicides
- Understand the dynamics involved in the death of a family member

- Explain the mental and emotional consequences suffered by homicide survivors
- Understand how death notification adds to the trauma suffered by homicide victims

Introduction

Criminal acts take many forms and shapes. However, one particular crime has a drastic and long-lasting impact on society. Homicide not only affects the immediate victim whose life is cut short but also has a lifelong impact on the victim's family and friends. Tens of thousands of survivors of homicide victims suffer shock, grief, and an overwhelming sense of helplessness at the loss of a loved one, friend, or acquaintance. *Survivors of homicide victims* are those individuals who had special ties of kinship with the person murdered and who were thus victimized not only by the loss of someone close to them but also by the horrific circumstances of that untimely death.[1] Because of the special nature of homicide, it is included as a separate chapter in this text.

Nature and Extent of the Problem

In November 2004, the Department of Justice issued an update on homicide trends in the United States.[2] The FBI defines *murder* is the willful (nonnegligent) killing of one human being by another. This definition does not include deaths caused by negligence, suicide, or accident, nor does it include justifiable homicide or attempted homicides. This analysis indicates that after a sharp increase in homicides in the late 1980s, the rate fell dramatically after 1991. Since 1999, the homicide rate has remained stable, with approximately 5.6 per 100,000 persons. In 2003, the number of persons murdered was 16,420. The homicide rate increased in the Northwest by 5.1 percent, in the South by 2.8 percent, and in the West by 1.8 percent. In the Midwest, the number of homicides declined by 4.7 percent.[3]

Homicide is of interest to researchers not only because of its severity but also because many professionals believe it is a fairly accurate indicator of violent crime in general. Victimologists study it because of the severe impact it has on the survivors.

The dramatic rise in homicides during the late 1980s was attributed to the rise in gun violence by teens and young adults. Males were most often both the victims and the perpetrators of homicide. They were ten times more likely than females to commit murder. Young adults between ages 18 and 24 have the highest rates for committing homicide. Most of the perpetrators of infanticides (victims under age five) were a parent. When information about the victim—offender relationship was available, approximately 76 percent of the offenders were known by the victim. There has been a decline in homicides of intimates, especially in the killing of males.

Homicides by firearm may happen during the commission of other crimes, such as robbery and burglary. Of all the homicides from 1993 to 1997, 69 percent were committed with firearms. Sixty percent of the offenders who used a firearm to commit murder were under the age of 25. A profile of the victims of firearm homicide indicates that 28 percent were killed because of an argument, 19 percent were killed during the commission of a crime, and 7 percent were killed because of juvenile gang violence.[4]

In its annual report, Crime in the United States, 2004, the FBI reported there were 16,503 criminal homicides in 2003. This figure represented an increase over previous years from 1999 to the present. The Annual Crime Clock indicated that there was one murder every 31.8 minutes in the United States.[5]

Theories, Types, and Characteristics of Homicide

As indicated in Chapter 1, Wolfgang conducted the first major study of victim precipitation.[6] He focused on homicides and studied both the victim and the offender as separate entities and as "mutual participants in the homicide."[7] Wolfgang found that 26 percent of all homicides studied in Philadelphia involved situations in which the victim was the first to use force during the acts leading to the homicide.[8]

Wolfgang identified several factors that he associated with victim participation in homicides: (1) the victim and perpetrator usually had some sort of prior relationship—spouse, family members, or close acquaintances; (2) the events leading up to the homicide started as a small disagreement that escalated into a burst of anger that resulted in a killing; and (3) alcohol was used or consumed by many of the victims prior to the incident.[9]

Spousal homicide involves the killing of one's legally married partner. This definition does not require that the parties be cohabitating at the time of the killing;

FOCUS: Murderers

Do You Know a Killer When You See One?

Wouldn't life be simpler and safer if all murderers resembled large, ugly, and deformed Neanderthals? Unfortunately, this is not the case even though our fears may conjure up such images. In reality, a murderer may be a middle-aged man who is a Boy Scout leader and church congregation president. Such was the life style of the infamous "BTK" serial killer, Dennis Rader. BTK stands for Bind, Torture, and Kill, which is what Rader did to his ten victims over a thirty-year period before he was caught in 2005 and sentenced to ten consecutive life terms. Kansas, where the crimes occurred, did not have the death penalty during the time of Rader's killings.

Statistical facts drawn from arrest records indicate the following regarding murderers:

Age:	50% were 25 to 49 years old
Sex:	88% males
	12% females
Race:	46% white
Relationship:	50% acquaintance
	17% family
	20% stranger
	12% unknown
Weapon preferred:	64% firearm

Source: Snyder, H., T. Finnegan, Y. Wan, & W. Kang. (2002). "Easy Access to the FBI's Supplementary Homicide Reports: 1980–2000." Available online: http://ojjdp.ncjrs.org/ojstatbb/ezashr/asp/profile.asp.

however, it does preclude same-sex living arrangements or situations. This is not to diminish the seriousness of those killings that occur in a homosexual relationship; rather it is an acknowledgment that there is very little information or statistics dealing with this type of violence.

Segall and Wilson conducted an eight-year study involving spousal homicides and established certain characteristics associated with these types of cases.[10] Most of the homicides in this study occurred in major urban locations and involved single-victim–offender killings. Spousal homicide victims tended to be older than other homicide victims. Spousal homicide victims were typically female in contrast to male victims in most other homicides.

In a classic study of family violence, David Finkelhor established characteristics that can lead to spousal homicide.[11] According to Finkelhor, the presence of these characteristics in family violence situations can also lead to homicide. These factors include power differentials between the parties, perceived powerlessness on the part of the abused, and ambiguity regarding acceptable discipline and punishment.

One type of homicide that is most difficult to understand is *parricide*, which is the killing of one's parents. The trials of the Menendez brothers brought the specter of children killing their parents into our living rooms via television. Recent statistics indicate that 1.97 percent of all murder victims in the United States were killed by their children.[12] Parricide usually does not occur as a result of a single episode; rather it is a manifestation of a culmination of unresolved conflicts.

Heide researched adolescents who killed their parents and found certain characteristics to be present in these events.[13] There was a history of family violence, the adolescent's attempt to get help or escape from the situation failed, the children experienced isolation, and the family situation became increasing desperate immediately prior to the killings. The youths felt helpless in coping with their stressful situations and ultimately experienced a loss of control. Most of the murderers had no prior criminal history; however, they did have easy access to guns. Recognizing and intervening in family violence situations may prevent parricide, a particularly devastating form of murder.

Considered particularly violent are mass murderers, and until the relatively recent emergence and research into the serial killers, they were considered society's most dangerous of predators. *Mass murderers* are those who kill several people at one time in the same location. One of the most famous mass murderers is James O. Huberty, who is believed to have committed the worst one-day massacre in the United States. Huberty was an unemployed security guard who told friends that he would kill others if he could not find a job and support his family. On July 18, 1984, he walked into a McDonald's restaurant in San Ysidro, California, and opened fire, killing twenty-one persons and wounding another twenty. In 1989, a deranged welder named Patrick Edward Purdy entered a Stockton, California, schoolyard armed with an AK-47 assault rifle and began a killing rampage that ended with five dead children and thirty wounded victims. The Stockton School Yard Massacre is another chilling example of mass murder.

A variation on the mass murderer is the spree murderer. A *spree killer* kills several persons at two or more locations with very little if any time break between the killings. Some experts would call the former Eagle Scout leader and college honor student Charles Whitman a spree killer. In 1966, Whitman murdered his wife and mother, and then armed with a variety of weapons and ammunition, climbed to the top of a tower at the University of Texas. Whitman continued his killing spree and as a result sixteen persons died and another thirty were wounded before the police shot and killed him. He subsequently became known as the Texas Tower Killer.

One of the most deadly and fearsome murderers is the serial killer. With the chilling film *The Silence of the Lambs,* our collective consciousness was raised to acknowledge that killers similar to Hannibal the Cannibal exist and, indeed, may have sat next to us on a bus, train, or plane. The serial killer is the night stalker of murders. Although debate continues over a comprehensive definition, most authorities agree that a ***serial murderer*** is one who kills several persons over a period of time that can range from weeks to years.[14]

One of the best-known and notorious of serial murderers is Jack the Ripper, who killed several women in London over a period of time during the 1800s. He was never caught and the crimes were never solved, although speculation continues as to his identity, and theories and articles are still written about his grievous acts. Other well-known serial murderers are the Green River Killer, who is believed to have killed over fifty female hitchhikers, transients, and prostitutes near the Seattle area; the "Witch," Sarah Aldrete, who sacrificed victims to provide an aura of protection for members of a Mexican drug smuggling ring; Dorothea Puente, who poisoned renters at her boardinghouse and then cashed their social security checks; and the infamous Hillside Strangler in Los Angeles.

In 2005, the BTK (Bind, Torture, and Kill) Killer saga was a topic of morbid discussion across the nation. Dennis Rader, who called himself the BTK Killer, admitted to killing ten people over a thirty-year period. Rader was a former Cub Scout leader, regular church member, and local ordinance enforcement officer in Wichita Kansas. His killing spree started in 1974 and stopped in the late 1970s. He would send letters to the media naming himself the BTK Killer and asking how many more he had to kill before he received national notice. He also included clues to his identity in several letters. In 1979, he stopped communicating and remained silent for twenty years. Then he sent another letter discussing an unsolved 1986 killing. On the basis of DNA evidence, the police arrested Rader. After his arrest, he called himself a monster and was sentenced to ten consecutive life terms.

In an effort to understand crime and criminals, researchers create typologies, or classifications based on certain characteristics. By studying these characteristics, scholars, researchers, law enforcement officials, and others hope to understand why particular individuals commit certain types of crimes. Several noteworthy typologies of serial murderers have been developed. Holmes and DeBurger identified four types of serial killers:[15]

> *Visionary type:* These serial killers murder in response to commands or directions from a voice or vision. Many of these killers suffer from some form of psychosis.
>
> *Mission-oriented type:* These serial killers believe their mission or goal in life is to rid society of certain types of people, such as prostitutes.

Hedonistic type: These serial killers are perhaps the most chilling of the lot in that they seek thrills during the murder. Many of these killers become sexually involved with their victims either prior to or after killing them. They may also engage in sexual mutilation of their victims.

Power/control-oriented type: These serial killers seek power over their victims. They report enjoyment from watching their victims plead, beg, and cower before them.

Eric Hickey has conducted several studies on serial killers and is considered a nationally recognized expert in this area. In an early work, he classified serial killers into three distinct groups based on mobility:[16]

Traveling serial killers: These serial killers often travel to different locations seeking victims to kill.

Local serial killers: This type of serial killer stays in one area and conducts crimes in this location.

Serial killers who never leave their home or place of employment: These serial killers lure their victims into their residence or place of employment, and the killing takes place within these areas.

The study of serial killers continues today, and more typologies are certain to emerge as knowledge of the psychology of these killers and profiling techniques become more sophisticated. Those professionals who study this type of behavior admit that there is both a repulsion and attraction inherent in their research; however, the suffering of the survivors of these types of homicides must not be allowed to recede into the background.

Although these crimes are committed by only a marginal percentage of society, the number of their victims is not insignificant. Hickey pointed out that between 1975 and 1988, thirty-four female and sixty-nine male serial killers were responsible for a minimum of 1,483 deaths and a maximum of 2,161 deaths![17] The toll in human tragedy and the resulting trauma visited on the survivors requires extraordinary skill and compassion on the part of today's victim services providers.

Drinking, Driving, and Homicide

Many vehicular homicides happen as a result of a person drinking and then getting behind the wheel of a car. This behavior used to be called "drunk driving," and although most people still use this term as a shorthand way of describing a behavior, it is not considered a legal term. A person does not have to be drunk to be convicted under most "driving under the influence" laws. These laws simply require that the driver's ability to operate a motor vehicle be impaired. In fact, many statutes define "under the influence" in a variety of ways. One example states that the defendant is under the influence if it can be proved that the alcohol, or alcohol and drugs, have affected the nervous system, brain, or muscles to the

FOCUS: Mothers Against Drunk Driving

In November 1979, five-month-old Laura Lamb was riding in a carseat next to her mother as they drove to the store. They were hit head-on by a drunk driver going in excess of 120 miles per hour. The perpetrator had no driver's license, no insurance, and thirty-seven previous traffic violations including three prior drunk driving arrests. Laura became one of America's youngest quadriplegics.

In May 1980, thirteen-year-old Cari Lightner was walking to a church carnival with her friend when she was hit and killed by a man who had been out of jail for only two days for another hit-and-run drunk driving crash.

As a result of these incidents, in 1980 Mothers Against Drunk Driving (MADD) was formed. Since then, thousands of volunteers and other victims have joined this organization in its fight against death on the highway. MADD has become one of the most notable victim organizations in the nation with chapters in every state.

degree so as to impair, to an appreciable degree, the ability to operate a motor vehicle in a manner like that of an ordinary, prudent, and cautious person in full possession of his faculties using reasonable care and under like circumstances.

In 1983, in an effort to address drinking and driving, some states began raising the minimum drinking age to twenty-one. By 1989, all states had twenty-one as the minimum age that a person could drink. Additionally, a majority of the states adopted laws that require administrative sanctions for all persons, who when asked, refuse to take a test measuring the presence and concentration of alcohol. Many of these states now permit the law enforcement officer on the scene to immediately confiscate the driver's license of a person arrested for driving under the influence (DUI) who refuse such tests.[18]

Unfortunately, despite increased penalties at the state and federal level, the death on our roadways continues. According to the National Highway Traffic Safety Administration, 16,694 people were killed in alcohol-related crashes: almost one death every half hour. These alcohol-related fatalities constitute approximately 39 percent of the 42,636 total traffic deaths in 2004.

Blood alcohol level is a legal and medical term that is expressed in milligrams of alcohol per milliliters of blood. This level has been translated into the ability or fitness to operate a motor vehicle based on several broad categories, or zones of impairment. Tables 7.1 and 7.2 indicate the blood alcohol level of an individual who has consumed an alcoholic beverage. The data in Table 7.1 is based on weight and amount of alcohol consumed; Table 7.2 indicates the effects on the individual based upon the blood alcohol level.

Some states have enacted presumptions that shift the burden of proving this element. If the driver of the vehicle has tested for a certain blood alcohol level and it can be shown that this level existed during the operation of the vehicle, the offender must prove he was not under the influence. This level varies from state to state, but many statutes establish the range with the 0.08 to 0.10 blood alcohol level as a presumptive indication that the defendant was under the influence of alcohol and/or drugs at the time of the operation of the motor vehicle.

TABLE 7.1   Blood Alcohol Level and Impairment

Two Drinks	Four Drinks			Six Drinks			Eight Drinks			Ten Drinks		
Hours Spent Drinking	Body Weight 120 150 180			Body Weight 120 150 180			Body Weight 120 150 180			Body Weight 120 150 180		
1 hour	0.05	0.04	0.03	0.11	0.09	0.07	0.16	0.13	0.11	0.21	0.17	0.14
2 hours	0.02	0.01	—	0.08	0.05	0.04	0.14	0.10	0.08	0.20	0.15	0.12
3 hours	—	—	—	0.06	0.04	0.02	0.12	0.08	0.06	0.18	0.13	0.10
4 hours	—	—	—	0.05	0.02	0.01	0.11	0.07	0.04	0.17	0.12	0.09

TABLE 7.2   Blood Alcohol Level and Behavioral Effects

Present Blood Alcohol Level	Behavioral Effects
0.02	Pleasant feelings including a sense of warmth and well-being
0.04	Relaxed, energetic, and happy; flushed skin and slight impairment of motor skills
0.06	Lightheadness, giddiness, lowered inhibitions, impaired of judgment
0.08	Definite muscle coordination impairment, slowed reaction time, heavy pulse and slow breathing; numbness in cheeks, lips, and extremities may occur
0.10	Clear deterioration of coordination and reaction time, staggering and slurring of speech, judgment and memory further affected
0.20	Increased depression of motor and sensory skills, pronounced slurred speech, double vision, difficulty in standing and walking
0.30	Stuporous and confused; individuals may lose consciousness
0.40	Unconscious, skin is sweaty and clammy, circulation and respiration is depressed
0.50	Near death or dead

Homicide in any form has a devastating effect. Family members, friends, and others within the community are left in a state of shock as a result. The next section briefly examines the impact of homicide on the survivors.

Responding to Special Needs

Family Relationships

Grief, sorrow, and emotional pain are the hallmarks of suffering experienced by the homicide victim's surviving relatives, friends, and acquaintances. The level of grief that is experienced can generally be measured by the intensity of the relationship that existed between the survivor and the victim before death. The following section will briefly examine several relationships within a family unit and how those relationships are affected by the homicide of one of its members.

The murder a child is one of the least expected incidents in life.[19] In the normal order of things, parents expect to die before their children. Parents serve as protectors, healers, and givers of life. These duties or obligations can, in turn, promote a sense of guilt in the parents of a murdered child, even if the child was an adult when the murder occurred.

This is, in part, due to the amount of time parents invest in planning for their child's future. They want their child to accomplish more and hopefully transcend their own circumstances. Many parents link their own immortality to their child, hoping and believing that they themselves will continue to live on in some form, even after their own death. Therefore, the grief suffered over the loss of a child is increased by the perception of the loss of the parents' own immortality.

Today many families are intermixed, or "blended," with stepparents and stepchildren as a result of second or even third marriages. Because many stepparents love their stepchildren as much as their own natural children, they may also suffer guilt at the loss of the child and their grief should not be ignored by victim services providers.

Also, parents not only must deal with their own sorrow or grief but at the same time attempt to comfort any other siblings and/or relatives who are feeling the pain of loss. Some parents may idealize the deceased child, bestowing on the victim qualities that are longed for rather than real, thereby magnifying the grief.

The murder of a spouse affects the surviving husband or wife in a variety of ways. The reaction to the death of a spouse depends on the nature and quality of the relationship prior to the homicide. If there was discord, anger, or bitterness in the marriage, the survivor may feel intense guilt at not trying harder to make the relationship better while the deceased was alive. If the relationship was a loving, close, supportive one, the loss may be overwhelming to the survivor.

The age of the surviving spouse also plays a critical role in the grief process. In some instances, older survivors do not recover as quickly and easily as their younger counterparts. They may be displaced from their home either because they can no longer care for themselves alone or because their financial situation has changed as the result of the loss of one income or pension. The surviving spouse, no matter what age, may also experience feelings of anger and bitterness at being left with responsibilities he or she now has to face alone. These responsibilities may include raising children as a single parent, attempting to make ends meet financially, or caring for relatives of the deceased spouse.

The murder of a parent may leave young children worrying about their own life and stability.[20] They may see the death as a form of desertion by the parent. They may also blame the parent and question why the parent didn't fight back. Children will certainly feel an overwhelming sense of loss and abandonment that can affect them for the rest of their lives. Older children may feel guilt because they did not pay enough attention to their parent prior to the murder, or they may blame themselves if the parent–child relationship was strained prior to death.

Murder of a sibling may leave the other brothers and sisters neglected by the professional caregivers. Many agencies concentrate on assisting the parents of murdered children and occasionally overlook the fact that the other children are suffering as a result of the loss of a cherished brother or sister. Siblings may also experience extreme guilt that they are left alive and their brother or sister is dead. They may experience anger at the parents' preoccupation with the dead sibling. They may feel vulnerable and experience anxiety at being left alone. They may wonder if they also will be murdered.

If the siblings are young, this may be their first encounter with death and they may not understand why their brother or sister will not be coming home. Additionally, the victim may also have been the surviving siblings' best friend, playmate, and confidant. This loss can leave them feeling isolated and alone and increase their sense of sorrow and grief.

Although many families share emotional responses to the death of a family member and appear to be mutually supportive of one another, victim services providers must be aware of the special needs of each one of them and respond accordingly. The loss of a loved one is traumatic and long-lasting. In the event that the perpetrator was a family member, the grief and suffering endured by the survivors can be immeasurable.

Mental and Emotional Responses

Chapter 5 examined the consequences of victimization; however, homicide by its very nature is a unique type of crime that presents special needs and responses. Parents of Murdered Children, Inc., has examined a number of mental and emotional problem areas for survivors of homicide.[21]

There are *unexpected financial consequences.* Funeral, medical expenses, and psychiatric care for family members are all unanticipated expenses. These are serious consequences that contribute to the continuing distress that survivors of homicide suffer.

As discussed in previous chapters, *the criminal justice system* adds to the stress suffered by survivors of homicide. These survivors must learn to cope with body bags, crime scene pictures, autopsies, and other stressors inherent in a homicide trial. One of the most comforting acts a victim services provider can do in assisting the survivor of a homicide is obtain information from the participants within the criminal justice system regarding the facts surrounding the killing.

Survivors of homicide often report that there is *an impact on their ability to function at their job or work.* Motivation may be altered, and what was considered important at work before the homicide is no longer viewed as critical. Some survivors may experience emotional outbreaks of crying or shouting during work, and having to apologize for these outbreaks at a later time contributes to their stress. Other survivors use work as an excuse or an escape to avoid working through their grief.

It is not uncommon for marriages to break up when a child of that marriage is murdered. Each partner grieves and may blame the other for the loss. They may also find it painful to be with their partner because of the memories evoked by that person. Some parents are unable to help each other, because their grief is so terrible that they cannot help themselves.

Children within the family of survivors of homicide also are affected by the killing. Children who actually witness the murder suffer a special mental and emotional upheaval, discussed in more detail later in this section. However, children who don't witness the murder are also impacted. If the murdered victim was a child, the other children in the family may be ignored by the parents as they attempt to deal with their own grief. The children sense the parents' suffering and simply withdraw into themselves. Additionally, children suffer the same psychological reactions as other survivors of homicide.

Many survivors report that their *religious faith has been weakened* as a result of homicide. Some express anger and frustration or question their deity regarding the reason for the death of their loved one. Others seek answers from unorthodox sources such as spiritual advisors and those who claim to talk to the dead.

Homicide survivors are often subjected to the *scrutiny of an insensitive press.* The quest for news may cause members of the media to televise a survivor's anguish on the evening news. Survivors may be subjected to views of the crime scene or other painful memories during the homicide trial as the press attempts to re-create the killing for its audience.

Finally, survivors of homicide may be *revictimized by professionals within the criminal justice system.* Many survivors report that some professionals do not fully understand the impact of a death by homicide on the remaining members of the family. This is an area that victim services providers can contribute to by continuing to educate professionals regarding the effect of crime on victims.

As indicated, children who witness homicide suffer a terrible experience.[22] Many of them suffer posttraumatic stress disorder. Children who witness killings must many times perform other tasks associated with homicides such as calling 9-1-1, trying to assist the dying victim, telling police what occurred, and testifying in court. These additional tasks can present intense conflicts or dilemmas for children. They may blame themselves for not protecting the victim or not responding to the killing in other more acceptable ways. Depending on the age of the child and the circumstances surrounding the homicide, witnessing a murder can have long-range serious mental health consequences for the child.

In some situations, a child who could also have been killed is spared for no apparent reason. This can create both terror and extraordinary guilt. Any witnesses, but especially children, may be afraid that the killer will retaliate against them at another time. This is especially true if a child witnesses a continuing history of spousal abuse against the mother that finally ends in her death. The child may then endow the perpetrator with imagined superhuman powers and feel extremely threatened that the offender will return to kill him.

Survivors of sudden death sometimes have unusual experiences. Mothers Against Drunk Driving is only one organization studying this phenomenon.[23] Mystical experiences, as they are known, can take a variety of forms both before and after death. These experiences include premonitions of death, visitations from loved ones at the time of death or shortly following, unusual dreams or nighttime visitations, or the presence of the loved one sensed through sound, smell, touch, or taste.

Professionals who work with survivors of homicide victims should not discount these experiences. When the issue of mystical experiences is raised in support groups around the country, more than half of those in attendance indicate that they have experienced some sort of unusual episode. The vast majority of those surveyed indicate that the experience was both positive and concrete.[24] These were not ghostly sightings; rather they involved explicit, physical incidents with the loved one. Mystical experiences occur across all socioeconomic, race, and gender lines. Because mystical experiences appear to be common and comforting to survivors of homicide victims, it is important to normalize the experience and allow the survivors the opportunity to express their feelings.

Notification

One of the most traumatic moments in a survivor's life is receiving notification of their loved one's death.[25] The notification by itself is a devastating event, but it can become even more traumatic if it is carried out in an insensitive manner.[26] Some authorities believe that death notification should be given by a uniformed officer because that person is generally perceived by most citizens as an authority figure. However, some communities are training crisis intervention workers. These are usually members of the local victim assistance staff. These persons accompany the officer on the notification call. This procedure allows for a notification team that can work together to ease the pain of the survivor.

Whoever makes the notification call should have as much information regarding the death as possible. The team should be able to tell the survivor what happened, when it occurred, how the victim died, and the source used to identify the victim. The notification team should never, if at all possible, make a death notification by telephone. The team should never take personal items with them on the call—these items will only add to the suffering of the victim. However, at a later time, the victim services provider should offer to retrieve and return all property of the deceased.

When making a call, the notification team should ask to enter the home and indicate that they have important medical information but would rather talk inside the house. Once inside the home, the team should ensure that they are talking to the appropriate relative. If a child has been murdered, the team should ask to speak to both parents at the same time if at all possible. A team member should ask the survivors to take a seat and then sit down next to them. The message should be clear, direct, and simple. For example, the team may tell the parents, "I have some very bad news for you. Your son, John, was shot during an armed robbery, he died immediately." They should not use terms such as "expired" or "passed on," as they can confuse the message and leave room for doubt or false hope.

Members of the notification team should not be shocked by a variety of responses their news might elicit from the survivors. The survivors may cry, faint, laugh, or simply withdraw. The notification team should attempt to focus on the immediate needs of the survivors and help them get in touch with close relatives or friends if they want assistance. As indicated elsewhere in this chapter, one of the most important aspects of the notification process is furnishing all available information to the survivors. This simple detail may alleviate some of the suffering and allow them to understand exactly how and why the death occurred. This process is one of the hardest duties a victim services provider will have to perform. Notification is not something that gets easier with the passage of time, but it can provide survivors with the information they need to begin the healing process.

Summary

Homicide forever affects the lives of the survivors. It is a serious crime that has long-term effects for anyone close to the victim including family, friends, neighbors, and possibly even the community where the victim lived.

There are a number of different types of homicide including, but not limited to, spousal homicide, mass murder, serial murder, and vehicular homicide. Any murder represents a special problem for the victim services provider who becomes involved. These individuals should be as knowledgeable as possible regarding the different types of homicide and their effects on the survivors.

Murder affects the whole family. When a child is murdered, the effect on the parents and remaining siblings can be devastating. Professionals should ensure that in their desire to provide assistance to the parents, they do not overlook the siblings or other family members who may also be suffering shock, despair, and tremendous loss.

Just as professionals should take the lead in training law enforcement agencies regarding cultural sensitivity, so should they ensure that death notification procedures do not traumatize the survivor. Law enforcement personnel should consider including victim services providers on all notification calls. This allows for immediate contact with the survivor and provides the professional with the opportunity to coordinate details and activities with the survivor from the very beginning of the process. This technique may help some survivors to begin the grieving process.

Key Terms

Survivors of homicide victims are those individuals who had special ties of kinship with the person murdered, and who were, thereafter, victimized not only by the loss of someone close to them but also by the horrific circumstances of that untimely death.

Murder is the willful (nonnegligent) killing of one human being by another.

Spousal homicide involves the killing of one's legally married partner.

Parricide is the killings of one's parent.

Mass murderers are those who kill several people at one time in the same location.

Spree killer kills several persons at two or more locations with very little if any time break between the killings.

Serial murderer is one who kills several persons over a period of time which can range from weeks to years.

Discussion Questions

1. Is homicide on the rise in your community? What can your local elected officials do to solve this problem?

2. What type of homicide is the most dangerous? Justify your answer from a law enforcement perspective, a victim services provider's perspective, and a prosecutor's point of view.

3. Who suffers the most when a family member is killed? Parents, children, siblings, or others?

4. How would you notify parents that their child has been murdered? Would the notification process be any different if the child was the perpetrator in a crime and was killed by the intended victim during a shootout?

Suggested Readings

M. E. Wolfgang, *Patterns of Criminal Homicide,* (University of Pennsylvania Press, Philadelphia, Penn.) 1958.

A. Y. Wilson (ed.), *Homicide: The Victim–Offender Connection,* (Anderson, Cincinnati) 1993.

D. Finkelhor, R. J. Gelles, G. T. Hotaling & M. A. Strauss (eds.), *The Dark Side of Families: Current Family Violence Research,* (Sage, Beverly Hills, Calif.) 1983.

Eric W. Hickey, *Serial Murderers and Their Victims,* 3rd ed., (Wadsworth, Belmont, Calif.) 2002.

R. M. Holmes & J. DeBurger, *Serial Murder,* (Sage, Newbury Park, Calif.) 1988.

T. A. Rando, *Parental Loss of a Child,* (Research Press Company, Champaign, Ill.) 1986.

E. Furmann, *A Child's Parent Dies,* (Yale University Press, New Haven, Conn.) 1974.

Lula M. Redmond, *Surviving When Someone You Love Was Murdered,* (Consultation and Education Services, Inc., Clearwater, Florida) 1989.

R. J. Meadows, *Understanding Violence and Victimization,* 4th ed. (Prentice Hall, Englewood Cliffs, N. J.) 2004.

Endnotes

1. "Survivors of Homicide Victims," 2/3 *NOVA Network Information Bulletin,* 1 (Washington, D.C.), October 1985.

2. James Alan Fox, "Homicide Trends in the United States: 2002 Update," *Crime Data Brief,* Bureau of Justice Statistics, U.S. Department of Justice, Washington, D.C. (November 2004).

3. Shannan Catalano, "Criminal Victimization, 2003," *National Crime Victimization Survey,* Bureau of Justice Statistics, U.S. Department of Justice, Washington, D.C. (September 2004).

4. Marianne W. Zawitz and Kevin J. Strom, "Firearm Injury and Death from Crime, 1993–1997," *Selected Findings,* Bureau of Justice Statistics, U.S. Department of Justice, Washington, D.C. (October 2000).

5. As the Uniform Crime Reports indicates, the Crime Clock should be viewed with caution. It indicates an annualized frequency of occurrence and should not be taken to imply a regularity in the commission of crime.

6. M. E. Wolfgang, *Patterns of Criminal Homicide,* (University of Pennsylvania Press, Philadelphia, Penn.) 1958.

7. M. E. Wolfgang, *Analytical Categories for Research in Victimization,* (Kriminologische Wegzeichen, Munich, Germany) 1967, p. 17.

8. Id at 24, 72.

9. Wolfgang, *Patterns in Homicide,* 265.

10. W. Segall & A. Y. Wilson, "Who Is at Greatest Risk in Homicides?: A Comparison of Victimization Rates by Geographic Region." in A. Y. Wilson (ed.), *Homicide: The Victim–Offender Connection,* (Anderson, Cincinnati) 1993.

11. D. Finkelhor, R. J. Gelles, G. T. Hotaling & M. A. Strauss (eds.), *The Dark Side of Families: Current Family Violence Research,* (Sage, Beverly Hills. Calif.) 1983.

12. J. M. Dawson & P. A. Langan, *Murder in Families,* Bureau of Justice Statistics, (Department of Justice, Washington, D.C.) 1994.

13. Kathleen Heide, "Adolescent Parricide Offenders: Synthesis, Illustration and Future Directions," in A. Y. Wilson (ed.), *Homicide: The Victim-Offender Connection,* (Anderson, Cincinnati) 1993.

14. See Eric W. Hickey, *Serial Murderers and Their Victims,* (Brooks/Cole Publishing Company, Pacific Grove, Calif.) 1991, p. 8.

15. R. M. Holmes & J. DeBurger, *Serial Murder,* (Sage, Newbury Park, Calif.) 1988, pp. 55–60.

16. E. Hickey, "The Female Serial Murder," 2 *Journal of Police and Criminal Psychology,* 72–81 (October 1986).

17. Hickey, *Serial Murders and Their Victims,* 18–19.

18. Robyn L. Cohen, "Drunk Driving," Bureau of Justice Statistics, (U.S. Department of Justice, Washington, D.C.) September 1992.

19. T. A. Rando, *Parental Loss of a Child,* (Research Press Company, Champaign, Ill.) 1986.

20. E. Furmann, *A Child's Parent Dies,* (Yale University Press, New Haven, Conn.) 1974.

21. "Additional Problems of Survivors of a Homicide," *Report on Families of Homicide Victims Project* (Parents of Murdered Children, Inc., Victim Service Agency, New York) 1989.

22. This section is based on information provided by the Family Bereavement Center, 1441 St. Antoine Street, Detroit, Mich.

23. Stephanie Frogge, "Mystical Experiences," Paper presented at 1995 NOVA Conference, Maui, Hawaii (August 1995).

24. Id.

25. For an excellent in-depth discussion of this process, see "Survivors of Homicide Victims," 2/3 *NOVA Network Information Bulletin,* (October 1985).

26. Lula M. Redmond, *Surviving When Someone You Love Was Murdered,* (Consultation and Education Services, Inc., Clearwater, Florida) 1989.

8

FEMALES AS VICTIMS

Chapter Outline

Sexual Assault
  Definition
  Theories of Sexual Violence
  Rape Typologies
  Extent of the Problem

Stranger Rape
  Definitions
  Legal Aspects
  Victim Selection

Acquaintance Rape
  Introduction
  Definition

Marital Rape
  Historical Perspective
  Factors Contributing to Marital Rape

Stalking

Sexual Harassment
  Introduction
  Definitions

Summary

Key Terms

Discussion Questions

Suggested Readings

Learning Objectives

After reading this chapter, you should be able to:

- Understand the various theories regarding sexual violence
- Distinguish between the various types of rape typologies
- Explain the historical resistance to acknowledging the existence of acquaintance and marital rape
- Recognize a hostile working environment

Sexual Assault

Definition

Exactly what do the terms *rape, marital rape, acquaintance rape,* and *sexual violence* mean? Should we define sexual violence strictly from a legal perspective, a medical view, a psychological view, or a combination of these views? Each discipline has valid reasons for defining sexual violence in a certain manner.

The use of aggression and violence against women has existed since the beginning of recorded history. Sexual violence against women traditionally has been viewed as stranger rape—a violent, forceful sexual assault on a woman. Only recently have we recognized other forms of sexual violence. We now acknowledge that spouses may be raped, and acquaintance rape has become a common term in our vocabulary. In addition, there are other forms of sexual violence that are more subtle but just as damaging—sexual harassment and sexual discrimination are still rampant in the United States. To define sexual violence by any one of these acts is to do injustice to the whole concept that women are equal to men. A legal definition of sexual violence focuses on certain conduct that is prohibited and strictly defined. A medical definition views sexual violence as injury to the body. A psychological

---

FOCUS: Some Startling Facts About Rape in 2004

- Most rapes and sexual assaults against females were not reported to the police.
- The National College Women Sexual Victimization Study (NCWSV), a National Institute of Justice– and Bureau of Justice–funded telephone survey of 4,446 women attending two- or four-year colleges, found victimization rates for completed and attempted rapes at 35.3 per 1,000 college women during the academic year 1996–1997. For both completed and attempted rapes, the victims knew their offenders in nine out of ten incidents.
- In 2002, the rate of rape was 0.4 per 1,000 persons age 12 or older. This was a 60 percent drop of the rate of rape in 1993.

Sources: *Rape and Sexual Assault: Reporting to Police and Medical Attention 1992–2000,* Bureau of Justice Statistics, Washington, D.C. (August 2002); *Criminal Victimization, 2002,* Bureau of Justice Statistics, Washington, D.C. (August 2003); *National Victim Assistance Text,* U.S. Department of Justice, Washington, D.C. (2003).

evaluation of sexual violence examines the effect on the mind and emotions of the victim. Each of these approaches has certain strengths and weaknesses.

Sexual violence can take the form of a single act or a long and protracted series of incidents. It can also involve aggression and/or discrimination against women. For purposes of this discussion, *sexual violence* is any intentional act or omission that results in physical, emotional, or financial injury to a woman. The phrase "financial injury" is included to cover sexual harassment situations in which women have been terminated from employment for refusing to engage in sexual acts with their supervisors. Sexual violence does not include the termination of a romantic relationship. The ritual of courting, dating, and marriage in America commonly results in one person being hurt or heartbroken when the relationship terminates. Although this may not be appropriate, it does not rise to the level of sexual violence. Although some may argue that this definition is too comprehensive, to narrow it would be to exclude certain types of acts that result in harm to women.

Theories of Sexual Violence

As with other forms of violence, a number of theories regarding this form of aggression exist, but the exact cause of sexual violence is undetermined. No single factor can be highlighted as the cause of rape. Just as there are many forms of sexual violence, so are there a multitude of theories on the cause or causes of sexual aggression toward women. Some of the more common theories on the causes of rape include the following: sexual motivation, socialization, machoism, biological factors, psychological forces, and our culture of violence.

Sexual Motivation.   Most current research dismisses the sexual motivation theory of rape. It is not viewed as a sexual act, rather as an act of violence, aggression, and power by the male.

Socialization.   The socialization concept holds that in our society young boys are taught to be aggressive, forceful, tough, and a winner in any sport or activity. This socialization creates aggressors and can spill over into the sexual area where men are taught to sexually conquer as many women as possible. This aggressive attitude encourages, if not gives consent, for men to engage in rape.[1]

Machoism.   The machoism theory holds that men who believe in male machoism will be more aggressive toward women. Machoism is a set of beliefs that include a view of women as objects simply to be added to a numerical list of sexual conquests. These conquests may include the act of rape.[2]

Biological Factors.   The view of biological factors argues that rape is a male instinctive reaction, which is a drive to perpetuate the species. Symons believes that men still have a genetic holdover that impels them to have sex with as many women as possible and he argues that rape is closely linked to sexuality and violence.[3]

Psychological Forces.   The theory of psychological forces holds that men rape because they suffer from some sort of personality disorder or mental illness. Studies have attempted to define the dynamics of convicted sex offenders and determine exactly what type of people rape and what mental condition causes them to rape. To date, there is no conclusive profile of a rapist.

Culture of Violence.   The culture of violence theory states that our society is a violent environment which encourages some men to use violence to obtain sex. The use of violence and aggression is expected, and these individuals view women as legitimate targets of sexual aggression. These men believe that women want to be dominated and overpowered by an aggressive male.[4]

Rape Typologies

Although there are many causes of rape and sexual violence, past studies have failed to define clearly or predict who will rape. Researchers have now developed different typologies of rapists in an effort to streamline and to define this type of personality. One authority states there are over fifty different types of rapists.[5]

Groth and his associates conducted a study in Massachusetts of 133 convicted rapists and 92 victims. This classic study, Rape: Power, Anger and Sexuality, established that issues of power, anger, and sexuality are important concepts in understanding the various types of rape. Additionally, this was one of the first research efforts to recognize that rape is a crime of violence and not a sexual act.[6] Groth and his associates classified rape types into two major categories: power and anger.

Power rapes involve the offender seeking power and control over his victim by use of force or threats. The sexual assault is evidence of conquest and domination. The perpetrator will plan and fantasize about the rape believing that the victim will respond to his advances after initially resisting. Power rapes may be further classified as power-assertive rapes or power-reassurance rapes. The power-assertive rapist views the assault as an expression of his virility, mastery, and dominance. The power-reassurance rapist, on the other hand, commits rapes to resolve doubts about his masculinity and sexual adequacy.

Anger rapes involve the expression of anger, rage, contempt, or hatred toward the victim. The objective of this type of rapist is to vent his rage on the victim and retaliate for rejections or perceived wrongs he has suffered in the past by other women. Anger rapes may be categorized as anger-retaliation or anger-excitation rapes. In anger-retaliation rapes, the rape is an expression of hostility and rage toward women. Anger-excitation rape occurs as a result of the offender's desire to obtain pleasure, thrills, and arousal secondary to the suffering of the victim during the assault.

Two years after their initial publication, Groth and Birnbaum established a more refined version of the original typology. In *Men Who Rape,* they established three categories of rapists and determined three types of rape offenses: anger rapes, power rapes, and sadism rapes.[7]

The anger and power rapes are very similar to those in the earlier study, and the sadistic rapist is obsessed with ritual during the rape. He may tie up his victim, torture her, or humiliate her and may become intensely excited during the act. This type of rape is very traumatic, and Groth found that victims of this type of rape needed long-term psychiatric counseling.

Sexual violence will continue to be researched and perhaps one day rapists will be identified by a series of tests or events. However, until that time, sexual violence continues to be a serious problem that must be evaluated and treated.

Extent of the Problem

How many women are raped each year? Exactly what is involved in the act of rape? Is sexual assault the same as rape? Should we determine if a woman has been raped once in a lifetime or just attempt to determine how many rapes occur each year? These are legitimate questions that surface when the study and research of sexual violence is undertaken. Determining the exact nature and extent of sexual violence is a complex and difficult process.

One major problem in the area of women and sexual violence is the lack of agreement among scholars, researchers, and professionals on definitions and research methodology. Depending on which article, paper, or text one reads, the estimates regarding the incident of rape will vary. This disparity has caused problems and confusion within the professions ever since the study of women and violence began. There are a number of reasons for the different figures and definitions within this area of family violence. The following is a summary of some of the more common problems encountered when this phenomenon is studied.

Definitional Issues.   Some scholars use the term *rape*, others use *sexual assault*, and still others define each of the foregoing terms differently. For example, one researcher may define rape as vaginal intercourse accomplished by use of force or fear whereas other researchers may define rape as vaginal, oral, or rectal intercourse accomplished by force or fear. The simple addition of two terms changes the entire results of any study.

Professional Issues.   Various professionals approach rape from different perspectives. Attorneys view rape in a certain legalistic way, physicians treat it as a medical problem, and psychologists approach it from a mental health point of view.

Gathering of Information.   Problems in the screening techniques, formation of questions, context of questioning, and issues of confidentiality all impact on the validity and type of response which the researcher will receive.[8]

Koss compiled many of the various studies on rape and her work illustrates the different approaches various researchers have used when attempting to determine the incidence of sexual violence against women in America.[9]

As Table 8.1 indicates, there is a wide discrepancy between the various studies as to the type and prevalence of sexual violence committed in the United States.

One study was conducted by the National Victims Center, entitled *Rape in America: A Report to the Nation*, and it caused an uproar across America when it was

TABLE 8.1   Sexual Violence and Women

Study	Sample	Collection Method	Measured Phenomena and Prevalence Rate
Burt[a]	328	Interview	Completed rape—24 percent lifetime
Essock-Vitlae & McGuire[b]	300	Interview	Rape—8 percent since age eighteen
Kilpatrick and associates[c]	2004	Telephone	Forcible rape including attempts—8.8 percent lifetime
Riger & Gordon[d]	693	Telephone	Rape or sexual assault—2 percent of telephone sample
National Victims Center[e]	4008	Telephone	Rape—14 percent lifetime
Russell[f]	930	Interview	Completed rape—24 percent
Sorenson and associates[g]	1444	Interview	Sexual assault—13.5 percent
Winfield and associates[h]	1157	Interview	Sexual assault—5.9 percent lifetime
Wyatt[i]	248	Interview	Completed rape—25 percent for Blacks and 20 percent for Whites

a. M. R. Burt, Attitudes Supportive of Rape in American Culture (Final Report, Grant #ROIMH29023), National Institute of Mental Health, (National Center for the Prevention and Control of Rape, Washington, D.C.) 1979.
b. S. M. Essock-Vitlae & M. T. McGuire, "Women's Lives Viewed from an Evolutionary Perspective," I. Sexual Histories, Reproductive Success, and Demographic Characteristics of a Random Sample of American Women, 6 *Ethnology and Sociobiology,* 137–154 (1985).
c. D. G. Kilpatrick, C. L. Best, L. J. Veronen, A. E. Amick, L. A. Villeponteaux & G. A. Ruff," Mental Health Correlates of Criminal Victimization: A Random Community Survey," 53 *Journal of Consulting and Clinical Psychology,* 866–873 (1985).
d. S. Riger & M. T. Gordon, "The Fear of Rape; A Study in Social Control," 37 *Journal of Social Issues,* 71–92 (1981).
e. D. G. Kilpatrick, C. N. Edmunds, & A. K. Seymour, *Rape In America: A Report to the Nation,* (National Victims Center, Arlington, Va.) 1992.
f. D. E. H. Russell, *Sexual Exploitation,* (Sage, Beverly Hills, Calif.) 1884.
g. S. B. Sorenson, J. A. Stein, J. M. Siegel, J. M. Golding, & M. A. Burnam, "Prevalence of Adult Sexual Assault: The Los Angeles Epidemiologic Catchment Area Study," 126 *American Journal of Epidemiology,* 1154–1164 (1987).
h. I. Winfield, L. K. George, M. Swartz, & D. G. Blazer, "Sexual Assault and Psychiatric Disorders Among a Community Sample of Women," 147 *American Journal of Psychiatry,* 335–341 (1990).
i. G. E. Wyatt, "The Sociocultural Context of African American and White American Women's Rape," 48 *Journal of Social Issues,* 77–92 (1992).

released in April 1992.[10] The National Victims Center relied on a comprehensive study entitled "The National Women's Study" to gather their information. This report was based on a national sample of 4008 women who were interviewed regarding their experience with rape. The report indicated that rape occurred at a much higher incidence than previously accepted.

Sexual violence is a serious and continuing problem in the United States and around the world. As Kilpatrick's report indicates, rape is one of the most underreported crimes in the United States. In 2002, only 39 percent of sexual assaults were reported to law enforcement.[11]

Two out of every one thousand children were confirmed as having been victims of sexual assault. Approximately 9 percent of all high school students reported that they had been raped. Among college students, approximately 25 percent reported being attacked or actually raped. Finally, more than 300,000 women and 90,000 men reported that they had been raped within the last year. One in six women reported experiencing an attempted or completed rape some time during their lives.[12]

These figures indicate that rape in America is more common than previously thought, and rape is only one form of sexual violence that is perpetrated against women. Sexual violence can happen to any woman, at any time and in any place. No one is completely secure from this type of assault. The following sections examine different aspects of this form of sexual violence.

Stranger Rape

There are still myths regarding the crime of rape. Some of these myths hold that women really want to be raped, that they like rough sex, and when they go braless they are asking for sex. These myths apply to stranger, marital, or acquaintance rape situations.

Definitions

Carnal knowledge of a female was one of the first terms used to connote sexual violence. It was defined as *penile–vaginal penetration*.[13] *Black's Law Dictionary* defines *carnal knowledge* as "coitus; copulation; the act of a man having sexual bodily connections with a woman; sexual intercourse."[14]

Traditional penal codes reflected this bias and misunderstanding of the crime of rape. Criminal codes are enacted by each state and the federal government setting forth various definitions of crime. This has resulted in a patchwork of different definitions applied to basically the same act. In an effort to establish uniformity within the area of criminal law, a distinguished group of scholars and attorneys worked together for several years in drafting a Model Penal Code (MPC). The purpose of this code was to set forth the most reasoned thinking on various crimes and encourage states to adopt these definitions of the various crimes so uniformity would be established throughout the United States. The MPC defines rape as:

> *A male who has sexual intercourse with a female, not his wife, is guilty of rape if:*
>
> (a) *he compels her to submit by force or by threat of imminent death, serious bodily injury, extreme pain or kidnapping to be inflicted upon anyone, or*
> (b) *he has substantially impaired her power to appraise or control her conduct by administrating or employing without her knowledge drugs, intoxicants or other means for the purpose of preventing resistance, or*

(c) the female is unconscious, or

(d) the female is less than 10 years old. Rape is a felony of the second degree unless (i) in the course thereof the actor inflicts serious bodily injury upon anyone, or (ii) the victim was not a voluntary social companion of the actor upon the occasion of the crime and had not previously permitted him sexual liberties, in which case the offense is a felony of the first degree.[15]

The drafters of the MPC were not purposefully discriminating against women. However, it is clear that the MPC perpetuated the bias of the times. A reading of the MPC reveals several flaws: the statute is gender biased, does not punish acquaintance rape as seriously as stranger rape, and does not provide for marital rape. The MPC only prohibits men from raping women. It makes no provision for female rape of a man. Secondly, although it "allows" that an acquaintance might rape his companion, this form of rape is not as serious as stranger rape, therefore it will not be punished as harshly. Finally, it would not be a crime for a husband to rape his wife under the code. Some states adopted the provisions of the code and others have modernized their criminal statutes relating to the crime of rape. Many statutes now define the crime of ***rape*** as "an unlawful act of sexual intercourse with another person against that person's will by force, fear, or trick."[16]

These statutes are gender neutral: either a man or a woman may commit the crime. Secondly, the very definition allows for the charging and prosecution of marital rape. Finally, a person may be prosecuted for acquaintance rape under this statute. The only area that is not covered by these statutes is insertion of an object into the vagina during the assault.

Some authorities define rape as the penetration by a penis or other object into the mouth, vagina, or anal openings by force or fear.[17] There is a small but growing movement among the states to adopt this more modern definition of rape. Part of the rationale for the expanded definition is that rape is not a sexual crime, rather it is a violent assault on the victim and any type of forced penetration should be punished. This definition attempts to punish all forms of sexual assault. Additionally, it attempts to provide uniformity in an area where each state has adopted differing statutes regarding sexual violence. Other authorities suggest doing away with the term *rape* and using instead *sexual assault* or *sexual battery* and prohibiting oral, vaginal, or anal penetration by force or fear.[18] Someday we may move toward a more comprehensive definition of this type of sexual violence, but at present the great majority of statutes define rape in a manner similar to that discussed here. This definition in turn triggers reporting requirements by professionals in certain instances. Therefore, the definition set forth here is used for purposes of clarity and conformity with existing statutes. It should not give the impression that forcible anal intercourse or oral copulation is not a crime in most states. Under most statutes, these are considered separate offenses distinct from the crime of rape.

Legal Aspects

Rape carries with it certain physical, mental, and legal consequences. Many times during a rape the offender will perform or attempt to perform a variety of acts including vaginal, oral, and anal sex. As mentioned, each of these acts is considered a separate and distinct crime.

The crime of rape requires penetration of the penis into the vagina. The offense is complete on the slightest entry into the victim; therefore, it is possible for a woman to be raped and still retain her hymen. There is no requirement that the offender ejaculate for the crime to be complete.

As indicated, rape may be committed by force, fear, or trick. Forcible rape involves the offender using brute force to overpower the victim. He may use his fists, clubs, or other objects to strike the victim prior to raping her. The second situation occurs when the offender threatens the victim and she submits out of fear for her safety. This type of rape may not leave any physical scars, torn clothing, or other signs of physical violence. The third type of rape occurs when the offender tricks the victim. This is a broad category that includes sex with incompetents as well as the use of drugs and alcohol to render the victim incapable of consenting.

Victims are not the only ones asking rapists to wear condoms. The *New York Times* conducted an informal survey of rape crisis centers and concluded that more rapists are wearing condoms.[19] Rapists are not wearing condoms out of concern for the victim, they are wearing them to avoid receiving AIDS from the victim and to hinder prosecution. Condoms make the job of the prosecutor harder because there is no access to semen from which DNA samples might be obtained. The use of condoms by rapists reinforces the theory that the crime is a planned act of violence rather than an impulsive act.

Once the crime is complete and if the victim reports the offense to the authorities, the criminal justice system begins its slow and methodological prosecution of the offender. The rape victim will have to testify in open court about the incident. As late as the early 1960s, rape victims were treated as the criminals in sexual assault cases and defense attorneys were allowed to ask questions regarding their previous sexual experiences. There were a variety of theories that allowed for admission of this type of "evidence." Two of the more common theories involved the victim's reputation: (1) Because she had intercourse with other

---

FOCUS: Did She Consent When She Asked Him to Wear a Condom?

One common defense in rape cases is that the victim consented. This is especially true in fear or trick rapes, when the victim suffers no outward physical injuries.

In Texas, a recent rape trial caught the attention of the nation. The victim was single and lived alone. One evening after she returned from a friend's party, she looked up and saw the defendant with a knife in his hand; he had entered through a sliding glass door. He approached her and demanded sex. The victim, fearing for her life, consented and asked the offender to wear a condom, which she supplied. The defendant was later arrested and tried for the crime of rape. He claimed the act was consensual in nature and pointed to the victim supplying him with a condom as proof of his assertion. The jury did not buy his story, and he was convicted of rape.

persons, she was therefore likely to have consented during this act. (2) Because of the proof that she was a person of loose morals, she was therefore willing to have sex with anyone, including this defendant. These antiquated and biased rules are no longer accepted in our judicial system. All fifty states and the federal government have adopted *rape shield laws*, which are statutes that prohibit the defendant or his attorney from questioning the rape victim regarding her previous sexual history or introducing any other evidence concerning her past sexual practices.[20]

Victim Selection

As with so many other aspects of sexual assault, we are not certain why certain rapists select certain victims. This is one of the many subjects in this area that needs further research. One study attempted to answer this question by interviewing convicted sexual predators. Stevens used other convicted felons to conduct a survey of sixty-one sexual offenders incarcerated in a maximum security prison.[21] Stevens trained thirteen incarcerated violent offenders enrolled in his class at a maximum security prison as student interviewers. They conducted interviews with convicted sexual predators, which resulted in sixty-one valid interviews.

The average respondent was thirty-two years old and had served seven years in prison at the time of the interview. The average rapist had attended eighth grade and was employed in a menial type of job before his arrest. The subjects averaged 3.4 prior adult arrests. Fifty-six percent of the sample was Black, 42 percent White, and 2 percent Hispanic.

The author cautions against accepting the word of criminals. However, the data show some interesting results: The most common characteristic for selecting victims was that the victims were perceived as "easy prey," meaning that the victims were thought to be vulnerable. In other words, either these predators selected victims who they thought could or would not resist an attack or an opportunity presented itself which allowed them to attack the victim.

Some of the predators viewed young women as easy prey. One predator talked about attacking sixty or seventy victims by scouting financial districts and looking for middle-class working women. Still other predators found that female shoppers were easy prey. They identified them by their demeanor. One predator stated, "If she's not watching what's happening all around her, then [she] doesn't know how to handle herself, how to use the things around her to hurt me, or get me caught." Finally, other predators wait for situations to develop in which the victim puts herself in a vulnerable position. For example, one predator attacked a woman in the parking lot by threatening to harm her young child unless she cooperated.

Stranger rape is a violent physical assault on women; however, it is not the most common form of sexual assault. Recent studies have indicated that more women are raped by persons they know than by strangers. The next section examines this form of sexual violence—acquaintance rape.

Acquaintance Rape

Introduction

Intimate sexual violence includes marital and acquaintance rape. These forms of assault are not isolated incidents that occur to only a few women. *Rape in America* reported that only 22 percent of all women raped were sexually assaulted by someone they had never seen before or did not know![22] Nine percent of all victims were raped by their husbands or ex-husbands, 10 percent by boyfriends or ex-boyfriends, and 21 percent by other nonrelatives such as friends or neighbors. The remaining percentages were composed of fathers or stepfathers, other relatives, and a "not sure" category of 3 percent. This report indicates that approximately 683,000 women were raped in a one-year period. Using the figures provided in this report, that means in one year 61,470 women were raped by their husband or ex-husband, 68,300 women were raped by their boyfriend or ex-boyfriend, and 143,430 women were raped by other known acquaintances.

The Focus box illustrates forms of sexual violence faced by women on a daily basis. Some men and defense attorneys would argue that situations 1 and 3 were clearly not rape and that a man should not be responsible for getting inside the mind of his date. Depending on what further facts are added, situation 1 may have involved the use of force and therefore qualify as a sexual assault and rape. Situation 2 is clearly a rape by trick situation in which the victim was unable to give consent. Situation 3 may be classified as rape, because many authorities argue that when a woman says no, the advances by the man must stop. Others will argue that it may be rape depending on the victim's state of mind.

FOCUS: When Is It Rape?

1. A couple attending college decides to break up. They have been intimate for three years, engaging in oral, anal, and vaginal sexual activities. One week after they separate, the man arrives at the woman's apartment intoxicated and states they are going to have sex. The woman insists the relationship is over; however, the male gets angry, punches the wall, and demands sex. The woman knows he will not hit her and is therefore not frightened for her own safety, but she gives in and they engage in sexual relations.

2. On a third date, the man double-shots his date's drinks. She is not an experienced drinker and passes out while they are engaged in heavy petting. The man proceeds to have intercourse with her.

3. A couple has been dating for three weeks. They both have had several drinks and are intoxicated. They engage in heavy petting and the woman responds physically, but says "Please darling, no." The man continues his sexual advances and the woman continues to respond physically, but also continues to say no. They finally engage in intercourse.

Are any of these examples acquaintance rape? Why? Who is responsible in these situations? Are both parties at fault?

Sexual violence in dating relationships is not a new topic to social scientists and other professionals. As early as 1957, Kanin studied college students' sexual aggression. He found that over half of all college women (50 to 60 percent) reported being offended by sexual aggression whereas only 20 to 30 percent of college men admitted to such aggressive behavior.[23] This indicates a serious lack of empathy on the part of male college students as to what is appropriate behavior. Whereas a majority of the women found the acts aggressive, only 20 to 30 percent of the men found them to meet their definition of sexual aggression. Other researchers have confirmed these percentages and come to the conclusion that the double standard still exists in America.[24] This attitude in turn leads to situations in which date rape can and does occur.

One of the most controversial rape studies was conducted by Mary Koss, who was then a professor at Kent State University. Koss was contacted by *Ms.* magazine and commissioned to conduct a national rape survey. Koss and her associates interviewed more than three thousand women nationwide. They concluded that 15.4 percent of the respondents had been raped, and 12.1 percent were victims of attempted rape—a total of 27.5 percent of respondents had been victims of sexual assault. This percentage led to the "one-in-four" victims of rape slogan. Koss's study became one of the most widely cited articles on rape. It also became, and still is, one of the most controversial articles on rape.[25]

A more recent study of acquaintance rape was conducted by the Bureau of Justice Statistics.[26] The authors utilized the National College Women Sexual Victimization Study, which had a sample of 4,446 women who were attending a two- or four-year college or university. The study found 2.8 percent of the sample had experienced a completed rape or attempted rape. This equaled 27.7 rapes per 1,000 female students during the academic year. This statistic would place the numbers at "only" 1 in 36 college women. However, the authors point out that these statistics are misleading because the data is for only 6.91 months instead of for a full year. This limited time frame may lead to the conclusion that nearly 5 percent of college women are victimized in any given calendar year (2.8 + 2.8 = 5.6), and since a college career now typically lasts 5 years, the percentage of rapes or attempted rapes in colleges and universities could be as high as 20 to 25 percent. The "one-in-four" figure again appears as a statistic.

Although sexual aggression in dating relationships has been studied for over thirty years, Americans still have problems in accepting the concept of rape by a person known to the victim. There are still individuals who want to believe that rape is committed in some dark alley by a sadistic monster and only "nice girls" who resist and whose resistance was overcome by physical force can be raped.

In assessing sexual violence during dating or courtship, Lloyd explained that sexual violence in a dating relationship does not necessarily lead to the breakup of the relationship.[27] Many victims reported that the relationship continued for some time after the violence. Lloyd also explained that violence in a dating situation occurs in a context of control by the aggressor.

Stranger rape at one time was thought to be the most common form of sexual violence. However, we now understand that intimate violence is more frequent than suspected. One survey reported that on a Midwestern campus 100 percent of all rapists knew their victims.[28]

Definition

Similar to marital rape, date or acquaintance rape situations are covered by the general definition of rape as set forth in the previous section. However, for purposes of explaining this special type of sexual violence, *acquaintance rape* is defined as the unlawful sexual intercourse accomplished by force or fear with a person known to the victim who is not related by blood or marriage.

The following actual cases[29] illustrate the continuing problems faced by victims of acquaintance rape:

- A young woman reports to the police that she was kidnapped and raped by a former boyfriend. He had beaten her in the past, leading to his arrest on at least one occasion. The prosecutor resists bringing rape charges because of the victim's prior relationship with her assailant and offers the man a plea to reduced charges—a misdemeanor assault for which the attacker receives a six-month sentence and eighteen months probation. Less than a year later, the attacker brutally rapes and almost kills another woman.

- A group of young men meet a woman in a bar at night; they surreptitiously slip a tablet of LSD in her drink before leaving the bar with her. At the home of one of the young men, they slip her four more doses of LSD. The woman is then repeatedly raped with objects as a group cheers and takes pictures, which are later destroyed. One assailant stops the attack when someone suggests raping the woman with a statue of Christ. Three of the attackers are given immunity for providing statements helpful to the prosecution; one defendant pleads to evidence tampering and delivery of illegal drugs; he serves three months of an eight-month sentence in jail, with eight years probation. Not one of the defendants is convicted of sexual assault.

- A woman ends her engagement with a man. Several weeks later, he goes to her house and they get into an argument in his car. She tells the police that he dragged her into the back seat of the car and raped her. After the attack, she goes to the hospital and files a police report. The prosecutor in the case accepts the defendant's plea to "unlawful restraint"—a fourth-degree felony with a two-year sentence—saying, "It's not like she didn't have sex with him before." The attacker serves six months and one day in jail.

Acquaintance rape will continue to be a serious problem in America as long as we socialize men to view women as inferior members of society who really want to be chased, conquered, and dominated. We must learn to view women as equals in interpersonal, social, and professional relationships.

Marital Rape

A recent article in the *Journal of the American Medical Association* discusses the various forms of family violence with a subsequent recommendation that the American Medical Association undertake a campaign to sensitize its members to marital rape.[30] The recommendation includes training and dissemination of protocols on identifying and treating victims of marital rape. As discussed, the medical community is slowly becoming aware of the need to respond to intimate sexual violence. Although there is more awareness now of marital and acquaintance rape primarily because of the media, many people, including professionals, have difficulty with the concept that a man can be accused and convicted of raping his wife or that a date who "consented" the evening before can raise the specter of rape the next day. Although the perception is slowly changing, there still remain those who believe sex is a matter of right in marriage or other intimate relationships.

Yllo cited several disturbing trends in marital rape.[31] She reported data from recent studies indicated that approximately 10 to 14 percent of wives were forced by their husbands to have sex against their will. She further illustrated that because of the sexual nature of marriage, marital rape has not been regarded as a serious form of assault. Finally, Yllo stated that many rape crisis shelters and battered women's shelters often feel that marital rape is the responsibility of some other organization.

Other studies indicate that marital rape accounts for appropriately 25 percent of all rapes. Studies dealing with battered women indicate that between one third and one half of battered women are raped by their partners at least once. One study reported that while women of all ages were raped by their partners, almost two thirds of the spouses were first raped by their husbands when they were under the age of 25. Finally, women who were raped by their husbands are likely to be raped repeatedly—often twenty times or more during the marriage or relationship.[32]

Historical Perspective

For centuries our society has believed that a man is entitled to sex with his wife. A man could not be charged or convicted of raping his wife in eighteenth century England. Wives were considered chattel and clearly subordinate to the husband.[33] Fathers had a property right or interest in their daughter's virginity and husbands in their wives' fidelity. The rape of an unmarried woman destroyed her value as a suitable bride and sexual mate. The rape of a married woman was an infringement on the property rights of her spouse and a disgrace to her husband.

The marital exemption for rape can be traced to Sir Matthew Hale, a seventeenth-century English jurist. Hale was the chief justice of King's Bench from 1671 to 1675. A book based on his writing was published after his death in 1736.[34] Geis in his review of early English common law indicated that Sir Matthew Hale's statement helped establish a precedent for spousal immunity from rape when he held: "But the husband cannot be guilty of rape committed by himself upon his lawful wife, for by their mutual matrimonial consent and contract the wife hath given up herself in this kind unto the husband which she cannot retract."[35]

Blackstone, the great English legal scholar, helped to perpetuate this reasoning. He stated that the legal existence of a woman is suspended during marriage, or at the very least incorporated into that of her husband. Blackstone's argument served to continue the legal fiction of unity of the person on marriage. Therefore, a wife was deemed to have irrevocably consented to sex when and where her husband wished.[36] This philosophy continued in England and elsewhere almost to modern times. R. E. Martin pointed out that Winston Churchill's mother could not refuse her husband's sexual advances even though he was suffering from incurable syphilis.[37]

The feminist movement in the 1970s sought to change the laws to allow for charges to be brought against a husband who raped his wife. It was not an easy victory. State- and congressional-elected officials made such comments as: "But if you can't rape your wife, who can you rape?" and "[T]he Bible doesn't give the state permission anywhere in the Book for the state to be in your bedroom. . . ." [38] Unbelievable as it may seem now, there was a great deal of resistance to passage of any laws that would delete spousal immunity from the books and thus allow a wife to charge her husband with rape. Through the efforts of several dedicated groups and individuals, laws began to be amended to define marital rape as a specific crime.

As mentioned, many rape statutes now allow for the prosecution of a husband who rapes his wife. Therefore there is no separate legal definition of marital rape. However, for purposes of explaining and distinguishing this form of sexual violence from stranger rape, *marital rape* is defined as the unlawful sexual intercourse with a spouse or ex-spouse against her will by means of force or fear.

Finkelhor and Yllo conducted extensive research in the area of marital rape and classified marital rapes into three categories: force-only rapes, battering rapes, and obsessive rapes. A force-only rape occurs when the husband attempts to gain control over the type and frequency of sexual activity within the marriage. Finkelhor and Yllo compare this type of rape with Groth and Birnbaum's power rape. A battering rape involves the husband attempting to humiliate and degrade his spouse. These types of marital rapes are very similar to Groth and Birnbaum's anger rapes. The last type of marital rape is the obsessive rape. These rapes involve sexual sadism, fetishes, and forcible anal intercourse. This type of rape is similar to Groth and Birnbaum's sadistic rape.[39]

Factors Contributing to Marital Rape

Just as there are a number of theories as to why spousal abuse and stranger rape occur, so are there a variety of theories dealing with factors that encourage or promote marital rape. Previous chapters have discussed factors that increase the risk of family violence, including child physical and sexual abuse, spousal abuse, and marital rape. The following discussion focuses on factors and forces within our society that specifically encourage or contribute to marital rape. These factors include our historical perspective toward the family, spousal immunity, economics, and our culture's preoccupation with violence.

Historical Perspective toward the Family.   For generations the family has been viewed as the last stronghold of absolute privacy. What happened in the wedding bed was believed to be no one else's business. This concept of family privacy has caused delays and problems in researching issues such as marital rape. Additionally, women were raised with the belief that they had to "submit" to their husbands' sexual advances. Only recently have we begun to study the dynamics within the family bedroom, and many women now understand that they do not owe sex on demand to their spouse.

Spousal Immunity.   As mentioned, early common law established the proposition that a husband could not be accused of raping his wife. Rape of a stranger was considered a violent and unspeakable act; however, rape of a wife was unknown. The wife was considered to be part of the husband, and therefore he was immune from charges of rape brought by his spouse. Only recently have spouses been able to bring charges of rape against their husbands.

Economics.   Similar to other causes of family violence, economics and dependency play a role in promoting marital rape. In some marriages, both spouses are aware of the wife's economic dependency. Some men argue that they provide the paycheck so the wife must take care of the home. This "taking care of the home" includes, in the man's mind, sex on demand—any kind of sex.

Preoccupation with Violence.   Violence and its effect on families have already been discussed in detail earlier in this text. Because some films, books, and television programs devalue women, it is easier for men to utilize violence as an acceptable form of sexual expression.

Although none of these factors may be the single or sole cause for marital rape, they contribute along with other factors to a general climate of violence in America that promotes sexual violence against women.

Stalking

Stalking may be defined as a knowing, purposeful course of conduct directed at a particular person that can cause a reasonable person to believe that she or he or a member of his or her family is in danger of physical injury or death.[40] Stalking may involve a celebrity, a complete stranger, or an individual who is related to the stalker by marriage or other intimate or casual relationship. Stalking may happen to a person who forms a relationship with the stalker or is found by the stalker on the Internet or other electronic or print media.

Cyberstalking involves sending e-mails or hacking into e-mails or other personal accounts while pursuing the victim on the Internet. Cyberstalking has become more prevalent as our society increasingly relies on the use of computers and the Internet. In many ways, cyberstalking and identity theft are the new crimes of the twenty-first century. Some cyberstalkers may obtain the victim's personal data using the Internet and then attempt to destroy their credit or cause

---

FOCUS: Statistics on Stalking

- One in twelve women and one in forty-five men will be stalked during their lifetime.
- Seventy-seven percent of female victims know their stalker, and 64 percent of male victims know their stalker.
- Eighty-seven percent of stalkers are men.
- Thirteen percent of college women have been stalked.

- Three in ten college women reported being injured emotionally or psychologically from being stalked.
- Seventy-six percent of femicide victims had been stalked by the person who killed them (femicide is the murder of a woman).

Sources: Bonnie Fisher, Francis Cullen, & Michael Turner, *Sexual Victimization of College Women*, National Institute of Justice, U.S. Department of Justice, Washington, D.C. (2000); Patricia Tjaden & Nancy Thoennes, "Stalking in American: Findings from the National Violence Against Women Survey," National Institute of Justice, U.S. Department of Justice, Washington, D.C. (1998); and Judith McFarlane et al., "Stalking and Intimate partner Femicide," 4 *Homicide Studies* 3(4), Sage Publications (1999).

other harm. For instance, in a West Coast university, an ex-boyfriend accessed the university's registration Web site and disenrolled his former girlfriend from all of her classes without her knowledge or consent. This was a clear attempt on his part to injure or hurt his former girlfriend.

Stalking is composed of six elements that must be met before an act or a series of acts can be classified as stalking:

1. The stalker must have knowledge that the acts undertaken by him or her will place the victim in fear of injury.
2. The acts must be conducted in a purposeful or conscious manner that a reasonable person would believe will cause the victim fear.
3. The perpetrator must engage in more than a single act in order to be classified as a stalker.
4. A stalking crime is judged by a reasonable person standard, not by what the victim may feel. In other words, it is judged by what a reasonable person would think or feel if the reasonable person was in the particular situation that the victim has experienced.
5. The conduct by the perpetrator must consist of acts that would cause the victim to fear injury or death as a result of the perpetrator's actions.
6. The actions of the perpetrator must be directed at the victim or his or her immediate family, including spouses, children, or parents. Many stalkers may also attack the victim's pet as a way of intimidating or threatening the victim.

The four most common types of stalking behaviors are (1) *erotomania*; (2) *love obsessional*; (3) *simple obsessional*; and (4) *false victimization syndrome*.[41] The erotomaniac stalker has a delusional disorder. Often, the victim is a person such as a public figure or celebrity who does not know the stalker. The stalker believes that the victim would love him or her back if not for external influences. These individuals do not accept any opposing evidence or suggestions and remain delusional for a long time of period.

The characteristics of love obsessional stalkers are similar to the ones of erotomanic stalkers. The main difference between the erotomanic stalker and the love obsessional stalker is that the latter has a primary psychiatric diagnosis. The love obsessional stalker often engages in activities such as writing, telephone calling, or other activities to contact the victim so the victim will acknowledge the existence of the stalker.

Simple obsessional stalkers have been involved in a prior relationship with the victim. This relationship could be a former spouse, cohabitant, boyfriend or girlfriend, employer, or neighbor. This type of stalking occurs after the relationship has ended or when the stalker perceives that the victim has mistreated him or her. The simple obsessional stalker attempts to solve the problem or seek revenge by stalking the victim.

False victimization syndrome is the fourth classification of stalking. It occurs when a victim believes that he or she is being stalked but in fact there is no stalking. This is the rarest classification of stalking. Although it is not truly stalking, it is included for the purpose of comparison and understanding the stalking process.

Responses to stalking vary, but one of the most common responses is the use of protective or restraining orders, which are court orders directing the perpetrator to stay away from and have no contact with the victim. The National Stalker and Domestic Violence Reduction Act established a database of all civil restraining orders in the National Crime Information Center database in an effort to facilitate the use of one state's restraining order in another state.

There is a continuing controversy over the effectiveness of restraining orders. In *Castle Rock vs. Gonzales,* the United States Supreme Court refused to allow a domestic violence victim to sue Castle Rock Police Department for failure to enforce a restraining order against her former husband.[42] The husband kidnapped the children, murdered them, and was eventually killed by the police. The mother filed a civil action against the city, but the Supreme Court held that the victim's due process rights had not been violated because there was no personal entitlement to police protection despite the existence of a restraining order.

Sexual Harassment

The title of this section was purposely chosen. Sexual harassment is the overall umbrella under which specific forms of sexual violence take place. Although it is true that men have been targets of sexual harassment, most victims are women. Because sexual harassment is a form of violence against women, it is included in this chapter to allow for comparison between sexual violence within the family and sexual violence in the workplace. Only by understanding the full spectrum of sexual violence can we begin to respond appropriately to it.

We have faced discrimination in America since its founding. Lincoln began the process of doing away with discrimination when he freed the slaves, and for decades our courts have held that one citizen should not discriminate against another simply because of skin color. However, that battle still goes on in coffee shops that refuse to serve people of color, banks that decline to make home loans to persons living in certain locations, and many service-related businesses such as automobile dealers who simply ignore persons of different races. Discrimination against women simply because of their sex is one bias that is also reaching our collective consciousness. One offensive form of this discrimination is sexual harassment. Employment-based sexual harassment is dehumanizing and it changes the focus of employment from the woman's work performance to her sex. Additionally, it degrades women by reinforcing their traditionally inferior role in the workplace. The following sections will provide a brief overview of sexual harassment.

Introduction

Sexual harassment is a widespread phenomenon. One of the first work-related surveys of 9,000 women found that nine of ten women reported instances of sexual harassment.[43] Probably the most comprehensive survey of sexual harassment ever done was conducted by the United States Merit System Protection Board in 1980. The board surveyed 23,000 federal employees and stated that 42 percent of all women reported being the subject of some form of sexual harassment.[44]

Demands for sexual favors in exchange for continuing employment have long been a common abuse of personal power in the workplace. The clandestine squeeze on the factory floor, the stolen kiss in the copy room, or the lewd suggestion regarding sex have been commonplace in American businesses for years. Until recently, the victim of such sexual violence has two choices: agree or lose her job. Additionally, she was led to believe that the activities that she found offensive were in reality common practice in the workplace. There was no legal recourse for victims of sexual harassment until the 1980s.

In 1964, we began the long process of outlawing all forms of discrimination. Congress passed Title VII of the Civil Rights Act of 1964 which prohibited employment discrimination based on race, color, religion, sex, pregnancy, or national origin.[45] Title VII provides that:

> *It shall be an unlawful employment practice for an employer—*
>
> 1. *to fail or refuse to hire or to discharge any individual, to otherwise to discriminate against any individual with respect to his compensation, terms, conditions, or privileges of employment, because of such individual's race, color, religion, sex, or national origin; or*
> 2. *to limit, segregate, or classify his employees or applicants for employment in any way which would deprive or tend to deprive any individual of employment opportunities or otherwise adversely affect his status an employee, because of such individual's race, color, religion, sex, or national origin.*[46]

Even though the language of the statute was clear, women continued to be exposed to discrimination because they were pregnant at the time or might become pregnant in the future. This continuing discrimination caused Congress to pass the Pregnancy Discrimination Act of 1978 which prohibited discrimination based on pregnancy, childbirth, or other related medical conditions.[47]

Many scholars believe the Civil Rights Act of 1964 was the basis for the current prohibition against sexual harassment. However, Congress never directly addressed that issue when it passed the act. In fact, sex was added as a prohibited classification in a last-minute attempt by opponents to block passage of the legislation.[48] Rather, courts and administrative agencies have used the Civil Rights Act as the foundation on which to base their rulings regarding sexual harassment.[49]

Definitions

There are a number of definitions of sexual harassment. From a traditional perspective, sexual harassment is a demand that a subordinate, usually a woman, grant sexual favors to retain a job benefit.[50] A more encompassing definition defines *sexual harassment* as the imposition of any unwanted condition on any person's employment because of that person's sex. Under this definition, harassment includes jokes, direct taunting, disruption of work, vandalism or destruction of property, and physical attacks.[51] Sexual harassment occurs in a wide variety of forms, including rape, pressure for sexual favors, sexual touching, suggestive looks or gestures, sexual joking or teasing, and the display of unwanted sexual material.

Sexual harassment may occur in either of two forms: quid pro quo harassment or hostile environment harassment. These are not mutually exclusive situations. Many times they will overlap and both forms may be present in the workplace.

Quid pro quo harassment occurs when an agent or supervisor of the employer uses his position to induce a female employee to grant him sexual favors. The exchange of continued employment or job benefits for sex suggests the name quid pro quo. The essence of a quid pro quo harassment is that the victim must choose between suffering economic disadvantage or enduring sexual advances.[52]

Hostile environment harassment occurs when unwelcome conduct of a sexual nature creates a hostile working environment. The conduct usually involves a series of incidents rather than a single episode of harassment. The essence of a hostile working environment form of harassment is that an individual is forced to work in an environment that, although it does not cause direct economic detriment, results in psychological or emotional harm or humiliation.

Barnes v. Costle established the principle that sex-based assignments or sexual advances in which the employer enforces the demand by threat of discharge or other adverse economic consequences violate Title VII of the Civil Rights Act.[53] In *Barnes,* the plaintiff alleged that she was hired as an administrative assistant to the director of the agency's equal employment opportunity division at the Environmental Protection Agency. Shortly after commencing employment, the director solicited her to join him after hours at social functions and stated that if she cooperated with him in a sexual affair her employment status would be enhanced. She refused these advances and her position was abolished. The appellate court held that such actions were a clear violation of Title VII of the Civil Rights Act.

In 1980, the Equal Employment Opportunity Commission (EEOC) adopted regulations in the form of guidelines that prohibited discrimination based on sex. These guidelines specifically state that an individual's response to unwelcome conduct of a sexual nature may not be made on the basis of any adverse employment decision.[54] Although the EEOC guidelines are not binding, they have been held to constitute a body of experience and informed judgments to which courts and litigants may properly resort for guidance.[55]

It wasn't until 1986 that a case concerning sexual harassment based on a hostile working environment was decided. In *Meritor Savings Bank v. Vinson,* the United States Supreme Court held that a working environment that is hostile to women may violate Title VII of the Civil Rights Act even without any question of economic detriment. In *Meritor,* the victim was hired by the bank as a teller and eventually advanced to the position of assistant branch manager. She alleged that a supervisor subjected her to sexual harassment for over four years. This harassment included sexual intercourse, fondling her in front of other employees, exposing himself to her, and even following her into the ladies' restroom. The Supreme Court upheld the victim's claim of sexual harassment based on the theory that the actions of the aggressor established a hostile working environment.

In 1993, the Supreme Court again addressed the issue of sexual harassment when it decided *Harris v. Forklift Systems, Inc.*[56] The Court extended its ruling in *Meritor* to include conduct that does not actually cause psychological injury. In *Harris,* the Court held that Title VII is violated when a workplace is permeated with unwelcome discriminatory intimidation, ridicule, and insult that are so severe or pervasive as to alter the conditions of the victim's employment. In essence, the court held that sexual harassment can occur if the environment can reasonably be perceived as hostile or abusive. The Supreme Court acknowledged that there is no clear line that determines whether a working environment is hostile, but noted that some factors can be examined as part of the circumstances of any case. These factors include frequency of the discriminatory conduct, severity of that conduct, whether it is physically threatening or humiliating or a mere offensive utterance, and whether it unreasonably interferes with an employee's work performance.

Tangri, Burt, and Johnson established three models or types of sexual harassment: the natural/biological model, the organizational model, and the sociocultural model.[57] Using data from the initial Merit Systems Protection Board 1980 survey, they partially tested these models.

The *natural/biological model* assumes that sexual behavior in the workplace is an extension of human sexuality. It is assumed that men and women possess strong sex drive, but the man whose sex drive is stronger takes the role of the aggressor. From this perspective, sexual harassment is not discriminatory in nature; it is simply the result of natural biological mating urges. This model presupposes that all sexual advances are mutual in nature and part of a courtship or mating behavior. We now understand that all advances are not in fact part of a courtship, and therefore this model fails to explain sexual harassment.

The *organizational model* is a result of the workplace environment which provides opportunities for sexual aggression. From this perspective, sexual harassment becomes an issue of power, not sex. This power is derived from the formal roles in an organizational context. For this model to be valid, only those women in positions of low hierarchical power would be targets of sexual harassment. Women have been harassed in a variety of positions, some of which were considered high on the organizational scheme. Therefore this model does not adequately explain sexual harassment.

The *sociocultural model* views sexual harassment as reflecting the more dominant position of men in our culture in which they are the source of economic and political power. This model suggests that sexual harassment is the result of a patriarchal power system in which men rule society. From this perspective, sexual harassment is based on the personal power of gender, in which men are dominant. Power is an important factor in sexual harassment. The male aggressor may control advancement, benefits, and even continued employment.

Sexual harassment doesn't exist only in the workplace. It has been called one of the best-kept secrets on college campuses, and some feminists are concerned that certain professors have used their position of power to obtain sexual favors from students. Dziech and Weiner list the following actions they consider inappropriate behavior by professors:

- *Staring, leering, ogling.* These behaviors may be surreptitious or obvious. Professors, who by the very nature of their occupation must look at and/or observe students, should not cross over the boundaries of reason.

- *Frequently commenting on personal appearance of the student.* In an academic setting, professors should refrain from discussing apparel and physical characteristics of students.

- *Touching out of context.* Touching of students should be minimal and only to the extent necessary to carry out certain types of instruction.

- *Excessively flattering and praising the student.* This behavior, with others listed here, is especially seductive to students with low self-esteem or high expectations. By convincing the student that she is exceptional, the professor gains psychological access to her.

- *Injecting a "male versus female" tone into discussions with the student.* This type of disparaging remark about women and their abilities is a clear signal of a bias or negative perception on the part of the professor.

- *Persistently emphasizing sexuality in all contexts.* Pervasive emphasis on sex inside or outside the classroom is inappropriate.[58]

This discussion should not be construed to label every professor as a potential sexual harasser. However, even in academia, the controversy about professor–student relationships continues to be debated. In April 1993, the University of Virginia Faculty Senate was considering a policy that would prohibit faculty members from dating students. Representatives of the American Civil Liberties Union (ACLU) questioned the appropriateness of the actions, stating that the university might be infringing on privacy and associational rights of teachers. The ACLU instead recommended that the university beef up its sexual harassment codes. The University Faculty Senate proceeded to approve the no-dating policy. Many universities have sexual harassment codes and some are beginning to adopt a no-dating policy between students and faculty members. The relationship between students and faculty members is one of power. When a professor uses his position to extract sexual favors from a student, this becomes a serious quid pro quo form of sexual harassment.

Simply having agencies and courts establish procedures and processes to handle sexual harassment cases does not eliminate this behavior. The perception of women must be changed and they should be viewed as equals instead of sex objects. Only when women are approached as partners and equals will sexual harassment stop.

Summary

Sexual violence is a complex and far-ranging topic. The study of sexual violence has been and will continue to be hindered by a lack of agreement among the different professions on terminology and research methodology. All professionals agree that sexual violence continues to be a serious problem in the United States. Recent studies have indicated that women are more at risk from someone they know than from the stranger lurking in the darkness. Also, the consequences of any type of sexual violence are severe and in many instances long-lasting. We really should begin to think about a "war on rape" in addition to the "war on drugs."

We are slowly advancing in our perception of rape victims. No longer can only "nice" girls be raped. We have accepted that rape is a violent physical assault that has very little if anything to do with sexual gratification. Our legislatures have passed rape shield laws that now provide some protection to the victims of rape. These laws bar questions to the victim which require her to explain her previous sexual experiences to the judge and jury. As long as men rape women, lawyers will raise consent as a defense. However, as we become more educated as a nation, that rationalization will stop bearing creditability.

Sexual harassment continues to be a form of sexual violence in the United States and will continue as long as men view women as sexual trophies or playthings instead of equals. Only by continuing our education of society can we hope to put an end to this form of sexual violence.

Key Terms

Sexual violence is any intentional act or omission that results in physical, emotional, or financial injury to a woman.

Rape is an unlawful act of sexual intercourse with another person against that person's will by force, fear, or trick.

Rape shield laws are statutes that prohibit the defendant or his attorney from questioning the rape victim regarding her previous sexual history or introducing any other evidence concerning her past sexual practices.

Acquaintance rape is the unlawful sexual intercourse accomplished by force or fear with a person known to the victim who is not related by blood or marriage.

Marital rape is the unlawful sexual intercourse with a spouse or ex-spouse against her will by means of force or fear.

Sexual harassment is the imposition of any unwanted condition on any person's employment because of that person's sex.

Discussion Questions

1. Why is it so hard to define sexual violence?

2. In your opinion, what is the most acceptable theory on the cause of sexual violence? Justify your answer.

3. Should the definition of rape include more than sexual intercourse? Why? Why not?

4. Is victim selection an important issue in studying sexual violence? Isn't this a form of blaming the victim?

5. Should we call rape between nonstrangers "acquaintance rape"? Does that terminology degrade the crime into something less than what it is?

6. Should there be a requirement for independent evidence to support a charge of marital rape? Why? Why not?

Suggested Readings

D. J. Graney & B. A. Arrigo, *The Power Serial Rapist: A Criminology—Victimology Typology of Female Victim Selection*, (Charles C. Thomas Publisher Ltd., Springfield, Ill.) 2004.

A. P. Giardina, E. Datner, J. Asher, B. W. Giradin, D. K. Faugno & M. J. Spencer, *Sexual Assault Victimization Across the Life Span: A Comprehensive Clinical Guide and Color Atlas for Professions who Deal with Sexual Assault* (G. W. Medical Publishing, St. Louis, Mo.) 2003.

L. F. Alarid & P. Cromwell (eds.), *In Her Own Words: Women Offenders' Views or Crime and Victimization* (Roxbury Publishing, Los Angeles) 2005.

T. K. Logan, R. Walker, C. E. Jordan & C. G. Leukefeld, *Women and Victimization: Contributing Factors, Interventions and Implications* (American Psychological Association, Washington, D.C.) 2005.

Enforcement of Protective Orders (U.S. Department of Justice, Office for Victims of Crime, Washington, D.C.) 2002.

P. Phillips, *Marx and Engels on Law and Laws*, (Barnes and Noble, Totowa, N.J.) 1980.

K. Millett, *Sexual Politics*,(Abacus, London) 1972.

S. Brownmiller, *Against Our Will: Men, Women and Rape*, (Penguin Books, New York) 1975.

L. Kelly, *Surviving Sexual Violence*, (University of Minnesota Press, Minneapolis) 1988.

D. E. H. Russell, *Sexual Exploitation*, (Sage, Beverly Hills, Calif.) 1884.

D. Russell, *The Politics of Rape*, (Stein and Day, New York) 1975.

D. Symons, *The Evolution of Human Sexuality*, (Oxford University Press, Oxford) 1979.

C. McCaghy, *Deviant Behavior: Crime, Conflict, and Interest Groups*, (Macmillian, New York) 1976.

A. N. Groth & J. Birnbaum, *Men Who Rape*, (Plenum Press, New York) 1979.

H. Wallace & C. Roberson, *Principles of Criminal Law*, (Longman, White Plains, New York) 1995.

R. E. Martin, *The Life of Lady Randolph Churchill*, (New York American Library, New York) 1969.

D. Finkelhor & K. Yllo, *License to Rape*, (Holt, Rinehart & Winston, New York) 1985.

B. Lindemann & D. D. Kadue, *Sexual Harassment in Employment Law*, (Bureau of National Affairs, Washington, D.C.) 1992.

A. M. Jaggar & P. S. Rothenberg, (eds.), *Feminist Frameworks*, 3rd ed. (McGraw-Hill, New York) 1993.

Endnotes

1. D. Russell, *The Politics of Rape,* (Stein and Day, New York) 1975.
2. D. Mosher & R. Anderson,"Macho Personality, Sexual Aggression and Reactions to Guided Imagery of Realistic Rape," 20 *Journal of Research in Personality,* 77–94 (1987).
3. D. Symons, *The Evolution of Human Sexuality,* (Oxford University Press, Oxford) 1979.
4. C. McCaghy, *Deviant Behavior, Crime, Conflict and Interest Groups,* (MacMillian, New York) 1976.
5. J. Rabkin, "Epidemiology of Forcible Rape," 49/4 *American Journal of Orthopsychiatry,* 634–647 (1979).
6. A. N. Groth, A. W. Burgess & L. L. Holmstrom, "Rape: Power, Anger, and Sexuality," 134:11 *American Journal of Psychiatry,* 1239 (November 1977).
7. A. N. Groth & J. Birnbaum, *Men Who Rape,* (Plenum Press, New York) 1979.
8. For an excellent in-depth discussion of these issues see, M. P. Koss, "Detecting the Scope of Rape," 8/2 *Journal of Interpersonal Violence,* 198–222 (June 1993).
9. M. P. Koss, "Detecting the Scope of Rape," 8/2 *Journal of Interpersonal Violence,* 200–203 (June 1993).
10. Personal communication with Christine N. Edmunds, co-author and project director, National Victims Center, Washington, D.C.
11. Criminal Victimizations 2002, Bureau of Justice statistics, U.S. Department of Justice, Washington, D.C. (2003).
12. *Sexual Violence: Fact Sheet,* National Center for Injury Prevention and Control, Centers for Disease Control, Atlanta, Ga. (December 30, 2005).
13. L. B. Bienen, "Rape III—National Developments in Rape Reform Legislation," 6 *Women's Rights Law Reporter,* 171–213 (1981).
14. H. C. Black, *Black's Law Dictionary,* (West Publishing Co., St. Paul, Minn.) p. 213 (1990).
15. Model Penal Code Section 213.1 (American Law Institute, Chicago) 1985.
16. H. Wallace & C. Roberson, *Principles of Criminal Law,* (Longman, White Plains, New York) 1994.
17. D. G. Kilpatrick, C. L. Best, B. E. Saunders & L. J. Veronen, "Rape in Marriage and in Dating Relationships: How Bad Is It for Mental Health?" 528 *Annals of the New York Academy of Sciences,* 335–344 (1988).
18. M. P. Koss, "Detecting the Scope of Rape," 8/2 *Journal of Interpersonal Violence,* 198 (June 1993).
19. Craig Wolff, "Rapists Increasingly Using Condoms," *The Fresno Bee,* A-7 (August 22, 1994).
20. See *Michigan v. Lucas,* 111 S. Ct. 1743 (1991) where the United States Supreme Court upheld the constitutionality of these statutes. See also, *Vermont Statute,* Title 13, Chapter 72, Section 3255 (3)(A)(B) for an example of a rape shield law.
21. Dennis J. Stevens, "Predatory Rapist and Victim Selection Techniques," 3¼ *The Social Science Journal,* 421 (1994).
22. D. G. Kilpatrick, C. N. Edmunds & A. K. Seymour, *Rape in America: A Report to the Nation,* (National Victim Center, Arlington, Va.) 1992.
23. E. Kanin, "Male Aggression in Dating–Courtship Relationships" 63 *American Journal of Sociology,* 197–204 (1957).
24. Mary P. Koss & Sarah L. Cook, "Date and Acquaintance Rape Are Significant Problems for Women," Richard J. Gelles and Donileen R. Loseke, (eds.), *Current Controversies on Family Violence,* (Sage, Newbury Park, Calif.) 1993.
25. Christina Sommers, "Researching the 'Rape Culture' of America," LeadershipU; available online: www.leaderu.com/real/ri9502/sommers.html. A recent review of Internet blogs finds continuing dialogue and debate on Koss's methodology and findings (Archive for the "Mary Koss controversy," www.amptoons.com).
26. Bonnie Fisher, Francis Cullen, and Michael Turner, *The Sexual Victimization of College Women,* Bureau of Justice Statistics, U.S. Department of Justice, Washington, D.C. (December 2000).

27. Sally A. Lloyd, "Physical and Sexual Violence during Dating/Courtship," in Richard J. Gelles, (ed.), *Vision 2010: Families & Violence, Abuse, & Neglect,* (National Council on Family Relations, Minneapolis) 1995.

28. T. Meyer, "Date Rape: A Serious Campus Problem That Few Talk About," *Chronicle of Higher Education,* A 15 (5 December 1990).

29. *The Response to Rape: Detours on the Road to Equal Justice,* (Majority Staff of the Senate Judiciary Committee), May 1993, pp. 18–19.

30. Council of Scientific Affairs, "Violence Against Women," *Journal of the American Medical Association,* 3/84 (267/23) (June 17, 1992).

31. Kersti Yllo,"Marital Rape," in Richard J. Gelles, (ed.), *Vision 2010: Families & Violence, Abuse, & Neglect,* (National Council on Family Relations, Minneapolis) 1995.

32. Raquel K. Bergen, *Marital Rape,* VAWnet, National Resource Center on Domestic Violence (March 1999).

33. See Comment, "Abolishing the Marital Exemption to Rape: A Statutory Proposal, *U. Ill. L. Rev.* 201 (1983).

34. M. Hale, *The History of the Pleas of the Crown* (1736). The first American edition of the book, *Pleas of the Crown,* was published in 1874. See Comment, "Sexual Assault: The Case for Removing the Spousal Exemption from Texas Law," 38 *Baylor Law Review,* 1941 (1986).

35. G. Geis, "Rape and Marriage: Historical and Cross-Cultural Considerations," Paper presented at the annual meeting of the American Sociological Association, New York (1980). See also M. Hale, *The History of the Pleas of the Crown,* (1736) p. 629.

36. L. D. Waggoner, "New Mexico Joins the Twentieth Century: The Repeal of the Marital Rape Exemption," 22 *N. M. L. Rev.,* 551 (1992).

37. R. E. Martin, *The Life of Lady Randolph Churchill,* (New York American Library, New York) 1969.

38. J. Schulman, "The Marital Rape Exemption in the Criminal Law," 13/6 *Clearinghouse Review* (1980).

39. D. Finkelhor & K. Yllo, *License to Rape,* (Holt, Rinehart & Winston, New York) 1985.

40. See H. Wallace, *Family Violence: Legal, Medical, and Social Perspectives,* 4th ed., Allyn & Bacon, Boston, Mass. (2005).

41. M. A. Zona, K. K. Sharma & J. Lane, "A Comparative Study of Erotomanic and Obsessional Subjects in a Forensic Sample," 38 *Journal of Forensic Science,* p. 894 (July 1993).

42. 125 .Ct.417(2005).

43. Safran, "What Men Do to Women on the Job: A Shocking Look at Sexual Harassment," *Redbook,* 149 (Nov. 1976). Redbook received over 9000 responses to their questionnaire regarding sexual harassment.

44. "Sexual Harassment in the Federal Workplace—Is It a Problem?" (Merit System Protection Board 1981); see also W. Pollack, "Sexual Harassment: Women's Experience vs. Legal Definitions," 13 *Harv. Women's L.J. 35* (Spring 1990) for a discussion of this and other surveys.

45. *42 U.S.C. 2000e to 2000e-17 (1964).*

46. *42 U.S.C. 2000e-2(a) (1982).*

47. *42 U.S.C. 2000e(k) (1982).*

48. *Wilson v. Southwest Airlines Co.,* 517 F. Supp. 292 at 297 fn. 12 (N.D. Tex. 1981).

49. *Meritor Saving's Bank v. Vinson,* 106 S.Ct. 2399, 2404 (1986).

50. B. Lindemann & D. D. Kadue, *Sexual Harassment in Employment Law,* (Bureau of National Affairs, Washington, D.C.) 1992.

51. See note, "The Dehumanizing Puzzle of Sexual Harassment: A Survey of the Law Concerning Harassment of Women in the Workplace," 24 *Washburn L.J.,* 574 (1985).

52. See *Barnes v. Costle,* 561 F.2d 983 (D.C. Cir. 1977).

53. 561 F.2d 983 (D.C. Cir. 1977).

54. 29 C.F.R. ss 1604.11(a).

55. *Meritor Saving's Bank v. Vinson,* 106 S.Ct. 2399, (1986).

56. 114 S.Ct. 367 (1993).

57. S. Tangri, M. Burt & L. Johnson, "Sexual Harassment at Work: Three Explanatory Models," 38 *Journal of Social Issues,* 33–54 (1982).

58. B. W. Dziech & L. Weiner, "The Lecherous Professor," in A. M. Jaggar and P.S. Rothenberg, (eds.), *Feminist Frameworks,* 3rd ed. (McGraw-Hill, New York) 1993, pp. 323–327.

9

SPOUSES AS VICTIMS

Chapter Outline

Introduction to Spousal Abuse
> *Definition*
> *Extent of the Problem*
> *Dynamics of Battering*

Theories on Spousal Abuse
> *Social Stress*
> *Power*
> *Dependency*
> *Alcohol*
> *Pregnancy*
> *Marriage*

The Criminal Justice Response to Spousal Abuse
> *Introduction*
> *Factors Affecting Police Response*
> *Arrest of Abusers*
> *The Minneapolis Experiment*
> *Other Replications*

Summary

Key Terms

Discussion Questions

Suggested Readings

Learning Objectives

After reading this chapter, you should be able to:

- Explain why victims stay in abusive relationships
- Distinguish between the cycle theory of violence and the battered woman syndrome
- Define and give examples of the Stockholm syndrome
- Understand the various theories of spousal abuse
- Explain the advantages and disadvantages of mandatory arrest policies for those who assault their spouses

Introduction to Spousal Abuse

There is probably no more misunderstood form of violence than spousal abuse. Gelles has published a series of *Domestic Violence Factoids,* which are statements or sound bites used by various individuals or agencies when discussing family violence.[1] Gelles explained that many of these statements have taken on a life of their own and are presumed to be true or accurate. In many instances, this "truth" is based on misinterpretation or faulty analysis of research. The following are some of these factoids and Gelles's response:

Domestic violence is the leading cause of injury to women between the ages of fifteen and forty-four in the United States—more than car accidents, muggings, and rapes combined.

> *Gelles explained that as good a sound bite as this statement is, it is simply not true. The actual research that this statement is based on was a small survey of only one emergency room, and the authors of the study stated that domestic violence* may *be a more common cause of emergency room visits than car accidents, muggings, and rapes.*

The March of Dimes reports that battering during pregnancy is the leading cause of birth defects and infant mortality.

> *Gelles responded that the March of Dimes knows of no such study.*

Nationally, 50 percent of all homeless women and children are on the streets because of violence in the home.

> *Gelles stated that this factoid can be attributed to Senator Biden, but there is no actual published scientific research supporting this figure.*

There are nearly three times as many animal shelters in the United States as there are shelters for battered women and their children.

Gelles indicated that although this is another great sound bite, there is no verified count of either type of shelter.

As this discussion indicates, there is still a great deal of misinformation and controversy surrounding spousal abuse. These factoids should not be interpreted to mean that spousal abuse is not a serious and deadly problem. It is. However, to understand this form of violence, we must base our knowledge on facts or theories that are accepted within the various professions that deal with spousal abuse, not on sound bites.

Definition

There is no clear, single definition of spousal abuse. Different authorities include different acts within their definition and some authorities have established levels of spousal abuse. They categorize spousal abuse into two forms of violence. The lessor forms include yelling and throwing things and the more severe include striking and hitting.

As the practicum below indicates, there are shades of grey in any situation, and reasonable people may disagree as to what constitutes spousal abuse. For purposes

---

FOCUS: An Epidemic of Family Violence

Violence is not only as American as apple pie—it is often as homemade. Statistics as recent as 2003 continue to point out the crisis facing our society in regards to family violence.

- Approximately 1.5 million women and 800,000 men were raped and or physically assaulted, or both, by an intimate partner in recent years.
- Nearly two-thirds of all women reporting the crime of rape, assault, or stalking since the age of 18 were victimized by someone they were married to, knew, or had dated.
- The number of violent crimes committed by intimates against females actually declined from 1993 to 2001. This form of family violence dropped from 1.1 million nonfatal violent crimes committed by an intimate in 1993 to 588,490 crimes in 2001.

- Intimate partner violence made up 20 percent of all nonfatal violent crimes experienced by females in 2001.
- Simple assault was the most common type of crime committed among intimate partners.
- In recent years, intimate partners killed about 33 percent of all female murder victims and about 4 percent of all male murder victims.

Source: Callie Marine Rennison, "Intimate Partner Violence 1993–2001," *Crime Data Brief*, Bureau of Justice Statistics, Washington, D.C. (February 2003); and P. Tjaden and N. Thoennes, *Full Report of the Prevalence, Incidence, and Consequences of Intimate Partner Violence Against Women: Findings from the National Violence Against Women Survey*, report from a grant funded by the National Institute of Justice and the Centers for Disease Control and Prevention, Washington, D.C. 2000.

of this chapter, *spousal abuse* is defined as any intentional act or series of acts that cause injury to the spouse. These acts may be physical, emotional, or sexual. Spouse is gender neutral and therefore the abuse may occur to a man or woman. The term includes those who are married, cohabitating, or involved in a serious relationship. It also encompasses individuals who are separated and living apart from their former spouses. Although there is some disagreement regarding the exact definition of spousal abuse, all scholars and authorities agree it exists. The next section will examine the extent of this form of family violence.

Extent of the Problem

Depending on whose study is reviewed, the extent of spousal abuse varies. In their landmark study of 8,145 families, Straus and Gelles estimated that just over 16 percent, or one in six American couples, experienced an incident of physical assault during 1985. Projecting that number to the 54 million couples in America in that year leads to a startling figure of approximately 8.7 million couples who were involved in spousal abuse.[2] Other scholars point out that 20 percent of all women who go to emergency rooms for treatment have been battered.[3] These authorities cite figures that pertain to physical violence. As the definition here indicates, spousal abuse also includes psychological and sexual abuse. When a woman is emotionally abused, she may not go to an emergency room or even report the acts because she may believe she deserved the treatment and therefore it is not abuse. "After all, he didn't hit me" is a common refrain in some spousal abuse cases.

Although it is true that the definition of spousal abuse is gender neutral and in fact men can be battered by women, most of the victims of spousal abuse are women. In 1977, Steinmetz presented a paper entitled "The Battered Husband

---

PRACTICUM: Spousal Abuse

Which of the following, in your opinion, would be considered spousal abuse?

- A man is upset at his girlfriend, who is late for a date. He calls her lazy and irresponsible.
- During a date, the man takes his date's arm and steers her to an exit, commenting that she is stupid for not seeing that this is the fastest way to leave the theater.
- A couple living together while attending college get into a yelling match, with each of them calling the other names.
- The same couple's argument escalates and the woman throws a textbook at her male friend. It misses and strikes the television.

- During a heated argument, the man grabs the woman's arms and shakes her.
- A husband yells at his wife and calls her an obscenity after she overdraws the bank account, causing him to bounce a check.
- The husband does not allow his wife access to any funds after she bounced three checks and almost caused him to lose his job at the bank.
- The wife is tired and wants to sleep, but the husband forces her to engage in sex.
- The wife does not enjoy anal sex, stating that it hurts her, but the husband forces her to engage in it once a month.

Syndrome." This presentation was the basis for an article dealing with husbands who are battered.[4] Steinmetz's research, which was widely publicized in the media, claimed that men were abused at a far greater rate than previously believed. Steinmetz went even further and claimed that wives abused their husbands more often and more severely than vice versa. This claim was attacked by feminists, professionals, and scholars. In 1988, Steinmetz and Lucca published a follow-up article discussing husband battering in more detail.[5] In this article, they continued to assert that husbands are battered and concluded that all forms of violence must be prevented by placing greater emphasis on changing the attitudes and values of a society that glorify violence.

One result of Steinmetz's position is the acknowledgment that both parties in an abusive relationship need to be evaluated. Some studies indicate that there are higher levels of female aggression by women toward their spouses than previously thought.[6] However, the type and severity of aggression is different than that experienced by women. As Campbell explained, most authorities agree that the detrimental effects of abuse affect women disproportionately.[7] Furthermore, Campbell stated that gender inequity is a significant risk factor in battering.

Although it may be true that some men are abused by women in an intimate relationship, the majority of all abuse is inflicted by men. Therefore the remainder of this chapter examines the abused from the perspective of women as the victims.

The National Institute of Justice and the Centers for Disease Control undertook a comprehensive survey to determine the nature and extent of spousal abuse. Between November 1995 and May 1996, they contacted 8,000 women and 8,000 men via telephone. The results of this survey support previous samples that indicate spousal abuse is a serious and on-going phenomenon. This survey, entitled the National Violence Against Women Survey, indicated that approximately 7.7 percent of all the female respondents had been raped by their intimate partner at some time in their lives. Using the U.S. Census population, this translates into nearly 7.8 million women who have been raped by an intimate partner during their lives. The survey also found that 22.1 percent of all female respondents had been physically assaulted by their intimate partner at some time during their lives.[8]

One surprising result of some of these studies is the indication that spousal abuse may have declined in recent years. There are several explanations for this apparent decline. One is the existence of shelters for women who are abused. This escape valve allows them an option to escape an abusive relationship. Another is the widespread publicity that has occurred in recent years about spousal abuse. A third possible explanation is more effective punishment and better treatment for the assaultive partner.[9] Although the incidence of spousal abuse may be declining, many scholars believe its severity is increasing. Even with a decline in the number of reported cases in recent years, this form of family violence is still prevalent and requires any professional to be familiar with the nature and dynamics of spousal abuse.

Dynamics of Battering

One often-asked question is, "Why does the victim stay in an abusive relationship?" The reasons that women stay with abusive partners are complex and multifaceted.

A number of theories attempt to explain the dynamics involved in battering. This section will briefly discuss some of the more well-known concepts in this area.

Lenore E. Walker is one of the leading authorities in the area of spousal abuse. She coined the term "cycle theory of violence" as a result of her research in the area of battered women.[10] This concept does not attempt to explain the cause of spousal abuse, rather it examines the dynamics of this form of family violence.

The *cycle theory of violence* sets forth the dynamics of battering in spousal abuse. Walker's theory has three distinct phases: the tension-building phase; the explosion or acute battering phase; and the calm, loving respite phase. These phases can vary in length and intensity depending on the relationship.

Tension-Building Phase.   As the tension-building phase implies, tension increases within the relationship, at which time the husband may engage in minor battering of his spouse. The wife attempts to calm him by agreeing to his demands, becoming more nurturing, or simply attempting to stay out of his way during this phase. The victim may rationalize that perhaps she is really at fault and deserves the abuse, accepting the batterer's faulty logic as her own. Women who have been in a battering relationship for an extended time know only too well that the minor battering will increase in time. A woman may try to withdraw more from the abuser in an attempt to avoid more conflict, but the tension in the relationship will continue to increase until the batterer explodes in a fit of rage.

Explosion or Acute Battering Phase.   During the explosion or acute battering phase, the abuser loses control and engages in major incidents of assaultive behavior. The intense, violent aggression is what distinguishes this phase from the minor or occasional battering that takes place in the first phase. When the first serious attack is over, both parties may feel shock, disbelief, and denial. For example, the woman may attempt to minimize her injuries.

Calm, Loving Respite Phase.   The calm, loving respite phase is characterized by contrite loving acts on the part of the abuser. The batterer may understand that he has gone too far during the previous phase and will beg forgiveness and promise never to let it happen again. The woman will want to accept the abuser's promises that he can change and that his loving behavior is an inducement for her to stay in the relationship.

Walker's theory is generally accepted both in academia and in the legal system. Her explanation for the dynamics of battering has been cited in numerous court decisions that deal with battered spouses.

Walker also presented the concept of the "Battered Woman Syndrome."[11] Some authorities prefer the term battered "woman's experiences" because they believe that the former (1) implies that there is one syndrome that all battered women develop; (2) has pathological connotations that suggest that battered women suffer from some sort of sickness; (3) does not make clear that, according to expert testimony, domestic violence refers to more than women's psychological reactions to violence; (4) focuses attention on the battered woman rather than on the batterer's coercive behavior; and (5) creates an image of battered women as suffering victims rather than active survivors.[12] However, because most court cases and the majority of experts still refer to this experience as the battered woman syndrome, that term is used in this text. According to Walker, the *battered woman syndrome* theorizes that victims of spousal abuse gradually become immobilized by fear and believe they have no other options. As a result, these women stay in the abusive relationships, coping the best they can. The battered woman syndrome involves one who has been, on at least two occasions, the victim of physical, sexual, or serious psychological abuse by a man with whom she has an intimate relationship. It is a pattern of psychological symptoms that develop after someone has lived in a battering relationship. This is a gradual process of conditioning in which the victim feels both helpless and hopeless and, according to Walker, is one of the main reasons why spouses stay in these situations longer than people would expect. The abuse tends to follow the three-stage cyclical pattern of tension building, acute explosion, and loving contrition. The following responses are typical of women suffering from the battered woman syndrome: (1) traumatic effects of victimization induced by violence; (2) learned helplessness deficits; and (3) self-destructive coping responses to the violence.[13]

Very similar in dynamics to the battered woman syndrome is a condition referred to as the *Stockholm syndrome*, which is a phenomenon that occurs when persons who are held as hostages, captives, or prisoners of war begin to identify with the captors. These victims are isolated, mistreated, and in fear for their lives. They become helpless, confined to the area in which they are ordered to stay, and dependent on their captors to supply everything they need to survive. They begin to develop positive feelings for their captors.[14] The syndrome was named after an incident in Stockholm, Sweden, where four bank employees were held hostage in the bank's vault for 131 hours by two perpetrators. When the victims were finally freed, they expressed gratitude toward the offenders for sparing their lives.

NiCarthy indicated that the dynamics of spousal abuse are very similar to techniques used to control or brainwash prisoners of war. NiCarthy wrote, "As stated in a report published by Amnesty International, these techniques induce 'dependency, dread and debility.' To the extent that a person is victimized by these techniques, she or he tends to become immobilized by the belief that she or he is trapped, cannot escape."[15] This heightening of fear, helplessness, dependency, and dread are all intertwined in the definition and dynamics of spousal abuse.

Dutton and Painter developed the *traumatic bonding theory* to explain why battered women stay in abusive relationships.[16] This theory holds that when a woman finally leaves an abusive partner, her immediate fears begin to diminish and her hidden attachment to her abuser begins to manifest itself. Emotionally drained and vulnerable, she becomes susceptible to her partner's loving contrite pressure to return. As her fears lessen and the needs previously provided by her partner increase, she may decide to give him another chance.[17]

Dutton's theory is based on the concepts of power distribution and emotional bonding that focus on the dynamics of the abusive relationship rather than on any personality defect or socioeconomic status of the victim. Dutton states that these two features—the existence of a power imbalance and the intermittent nature of the abuse—can explain why abused women stay with their abusers or even return to the relationship. Dutton theorized that when power imbalances exist in a relationship, the person of low power feels more negative in her self-appraisal, more incapable of fending for herself, and thus in need of the person with more power. This cycle of dependency and lowered self-esteem repeats itself over and over and eventually creates a strong affective bond to the high-power person.[18]

The second factor in traumatic bonding is the intermittent nature of the abuse. This occurs when the abusive partner periodically abuses the submissive partner by threats or physical acts. The time between these incidents is normally characterized by normal, socially acceptable behavior. Thus, the victim is subjected to negative arousal and the relief or release associated with its removal. This situation of alternating negative and pleasant conditions is known within learning theory as "partial or intermittent reinforcement." Dutton states that this situation is highly effective in producing persistent patterns of behavior associated with strong emotional attachment to the abuser that is hard to change or modify.[19]

These four theories or concepts are only a few of the many reasons advanced for why battered women stay in abusive relationships. At this time, controversy continues regarding why victims stay in these relationships. Victim services providers must understand these concepts so that they can educate not only the public but also members of the criminal justice profession.

Theories on Spousal Abuse

If we knew the causes of spousal abuse, we could correct them. To date, no one has yet come forward with a definitive answer to this problem. However, numerous scholars in different professions have studied this form of family violence and have

---

FOCUS: Animal Abuse and Spousal Abuse: Is There a Relationship?

Several researchers have examined this issue and found various relationships between abuse of animals and abuse of intimate partners. Ascione, in 1998, reported that female victims of spousal abuse consistently reported that their adult partner had threatened or actually hurt or killed one or more of their pets. In 2000, he conducted a replication of the first study. This replication involved 100 female victims and a companion group of 117 nonbattered females.

Both groups had pets. Ascione's figures are chilling. He found that 54 percent of the battered females, compared to only 5 percent of the nonbattered females, reported that their partner had hurt or killed their pets. Flynn found a similar pattern when he studied female pet owners who were victims of abuse. These studies point out the need for authorities to consider the overlap between abuse of animals and abuse of an intimate partner.

Source: Adapted from Frank R. Ascione, *Animal Abuse and Youth Violence*, Office of Juvenile Justice Programs, Washington, D.C. (September 2001).

developed a variety of reasons or causes for this type of abuse. Although several theories and studies exist in the area of spousal abuse, space dictates that only a few of the more well-known theories can be discussed.

Social Stress

The family system in America is a system of contradictions. Americans retreat from the city streets to their homes and install bars on their windows to keep out the violence. Yet the family structure is one of the most violent settings a person is likely to encounter.

For purposes of this discussion, a family is a group of persons who cohabitate. Marriage is not a requirement. Within this living arrangement, forces converge to cause stress. This increased level of stress in turn leads to a high rate of violence within the family. Many times this violence is directed at the spouse in the form of physical assaults. It should be pointed out that stress does not cause violence; it is one of the many responses available to persons who suffer from stress.

Family life has a different set of behaviors than other social settings. How the members within a family setting dress, talk, and act in their home is different from when they attend social functions. Additionally, violence in the form of physical punishment is accepted by many as a characteristic of the family. Parents can and do slap infants' hands to teach them to not touch the hot coffee pot. Thus, this form of physical violence may be used on loved ones for their own benefit. When stress occurs, there is already a preconditioned response or behavior that has been used, and therefore it is easier to use when one is under pressure.

Power

Power is the ability to impose one's will on another and make life decisions. Couples who share power or are equals in the decision-making process have the lowest level of both conflict and violence.[20] When a conflict arises, these families display the greatest resistance to the use of violence.

One characteristic of family violence is the use and abuse of power. Additionally, battered women report a feeling of powerlessness as a result of the spousal abuse they have suffered. If the husband desires power and control in the relationship, this represents one factor that may indicate a potential for violence.

Dependency

Some authorities argue that our society has fostered women's dependency. Women's financial and social success in many instances has been dependent on the man they marry. Although this is beginning to change, the "glass ceiling" still remains for the most part an impregnable barrier. A few examples illustrate this point: there are only two female United States Supreme Court justices, only six women are United States senators, and only a small percentage of women are chief executive officers of major corporations.[21] Statistically, after a divorce a man's standard of living increases, while a woman's declines.[22]

The meaning of marital dependency is subject to debate, but the most common meaning includes economic dependency. The wife has little or no earning power and is therefore dependent on her husband for the necessities of life. A variation on this theme of economic dependency results from the presence of children. Although a woman may be able to leave an abusive relationship and make ends meet, the addition of children multiplies the difficulties inherent in any separation. A third factor in dependence is society's expectation of women as caregivers and the further hidden message that a woman is not whole until she is married.[23]

Thus, *marital dependency* is a multifaceted concept that involves economic, emotional, and societal forces that result in a woman being dependent on her spouse for support. This dependency on a man and marriage for economic, emotional, and other support increases a woman's tolerance for physical abuse.

Straus and Gelles and their associates conducted an in-depth study of dependency and violence and reported that women whose dependency on marriage is high tend to suffer more physical violence than women whose dependency is low. Dependent wives have fewer alternatives to marriage and fewer resources within the marriage with which to cope or modify their husbands' behavior.[24] This dependency is a pair of "golden handcuffs" that bind the spouse to the abusive partner.

Alcohol

There is a common perception that men who drink alcohol beat their spouses. Therefore, so the reasoning goes, alcohol causes violence. Movies, books, and to some extent our own personal experiences support the concept that alcohol causes problems in relationships. The relationship between alcohol and abuse has been studied extensively, and several theories regarding alcohol and its relationship to violence exist. A few of the more common theories are listed here.

Disinhibition Theory.   The disinhibition theory is based on the principle that alcohol releases inhibitions and alters judgment. Medical evidence regarding the effects of alcohol on the central nervous system supports this theory. However, recent research into the disinhibition theory reveals that alcohol interacts with individuals based on varying individual expectancies, which is only one aspect of the alcohol–violence equation.[25]

Social Learning and Deviance Disavowal Theory.   Coleman and Straus argued that individuals learn violence by observing others who drink and become violent. This violent behavior is excused, pardoned, or justified because the individual was drunk and therefore not accountable for his or her actions.[26] Other scholars have suggested that individuals use alcohol to increase their sense of power and as an excuse for the exercise of unlawful force against others.[27]

Integrated Theoretical Models. Pernanem's research into alcohol and violence indicates numerous factors that interact in alcohol and violence. These factors may include the inherent conflict present in marriages.[28] A second factor is our society's expectation that drinking is an acceptable and expected form of male behavior.

These theories and studies have attempted to determine if alcohol causes spousal abuse. At this stage, there is no definitive answer, but a link between the two is apparent. However, there are persons who drink and do not abuse their spouses, so it would appear that alcohol by itself cannot be defined as the cause of spousal abuse.

Pregnancy

Pregnancy and spousal abuse is a controversial subject, and studies indicate that there is a relationship between the two.[29] Despite this linkage, the question still remains of whether pregnancy contributes to domestic violence or whether it is simply another factor to be considered. Most studies are based on small samples and have internal validity problems; however, the Straus and Gelles survey of violence, using the National Family Violence Survey, determined that the rates of violence were higher for households in which the female partner was pregnant.[30] Subsequently, the authors concluded that previously reported associations between pregnancy and violence were not valid and that age is a more critical factor in determining violence than pregnancy. Young women have higher pregnancy rates and they experience violence more often than older women. Women under the age of twenty-five appeared to be at the highest level of risk.

Marriage

"The marriage license as a hitting license" was adopted in the early 1970s by Straus and Gelles when they discovered that married couples suffered assault at a much greater rate than strangers.[31] They reasoned that the common law tradition that allowed a husband to discipline his wife was alive and well in this modern age. However, more recent studies indicate that the highest rate of assault is among cohabitating couples. Additionally, violence is most severe in homes of cohabitating couples.[32]

Age may also be a factor, because dating and cohabitating couples tend to be younger than married couples. However, other research indicated that age and marital status have no relationship to violence. Therefore, significant relationships, whether they involve dating, cohabitation, or marriage, place women at risk. As indicated, cohabitating couples may be at a higher risk than married couples. In a more recent evaluation of the National Family Violence Survey, Straus and Gelles set forth the following factors as having more impact on the degree of risk a woman faces in a cohabitating relationship.

Isolation.   Couples who are living together may be more isolated than married couples. Part of this isolation may be because of the stigma society attaches to cohabitation over marriage. This isolation allows for spousal abuse because of the lack of a supporting network of friends or family available for the abused spouse.

Autonomy and Control.   Some persons prefer cohabitation over marriage with the thought that they can retain their own independence. However, any living arrangement brings with it duties, obligations, tensions, and the resulting disagreements. Some authorities point out that when the issue of control arises, violence occurs.[33] As the relationship becomes more serious, the issue of control becomes more important and violence is more likely to occur.

Investment in the Relationship.   Cohabitating couples may share some characteristics that trigger violence while lacking others shared by married couples who stop the conflict from escalating into physical violence.[34]

As with other theories of spousal abuse, more study and research needs to occur before we can understand whether women who enter into any significant relationship are at risk of spousal abuse. This section discussed various theories of spousal abuse, and it is clear that as of now we have not discovered a cure for this type of abuse. The cause of this type of violence may never be determined; therefore, it is necessary for professionals in the field to understand the criminal justice response to spousal abuse.

The Criminal Justice Response to Spousal Abuse

Introduction

There are excellent texts and research material that discuss police and domestic violence.[35] This material provides an in-depth scholarly examination of the causes, effects, and police responses in this area. The purpose of this section is to acquaint readers with an overview of policing of spousal assault cases. This will allow them to have an understanding of some of the existing controversies in this highly debated area of domestic violence.

The term *spousal assault* is used to distinguish this form of family violence from spousal abuse. From a legal perspective, the term *spousal assault* is inaccurate. As will be discussed later in this chapter, in a majority of states an assault does not involve any physical injury to the victim. However, to be consistent with other professionals and writers in the field of family violence, *spousal assault* is used and defined as the act of intentionally inflicting physical injury on the spouse or other person who is cohabitating with the abuser. It is distinct and yet a part of spousal abuse in that all the dynamics that cause spousal abuse may be present in spousal assault. However, this form of assault may occur without the existence of the other forms of abuse, such as emotional or psychological injury, that typically accompany spousal abuse.

FOCUS: Two Cases of Indifference

Thurman v. City of Torrington,
595 F. Supp. 1521 (Conn. 1984)[36]

Starting in October 1982 and continuing until June 1983, Tracey Thurman repeatedly contacted the Torrington, Connecticut, police department begging for protection from her estranged husband, Buck. Tracey signed several sworn complaints against Buck; however, the police department considered the incidents a family matter and did not respond to them in the same manner as they did to "stranger assaults."

On the day of the final beating, Buck stabbed Tracey repeatedly. A police officer arrived and asked Buck for the knife but did not arrest or restrain him in any manner. Buck gave the officer the knife and then proceeded to stomp on Tracey's head in front of the officer. He then went inside the house and returned with their son and cursed and kicked Tracey in the head. This series of blows left her partially paralyzed. Other officers arrived, and they did not arrest Buck until he tried to assault Tracey as she lay on the ambulance stretcher.

Tracey filed suit in federal court against the City of Torrington, its police department, and all twenty-four officers that she had contacted over the years about Buck's assaultive acts. She alleged that the police department and its officers had been negligent in responding to her and, further, that they had violated her constitutional rights to equal protection under the law by treating her differently than they would persons who were assaulted by strangers.

The jury awarded Tracey $2.3 million in damages. Although the city's insurance company paid the judgment, it indicated that it might not pay any future awards of any police department that refused or failed to educate their officers about domestic violence.[37]

Castle Rock v. Gonzales, 125 U.S. 417 (2005)

In 1999, the Castle Rock Police Department refused to enforce a protective order Jessica Gonzales had obtained against her husband, Simon, as part of a divorce decree. The order allowed for visitation on alternate weekends. One late afternoon, Mr. Gonzales kidnapped all three of the children while they were playing outside. Mrs. Gonzales contacted the Castle Rock Police Department to enforce her protective order; however, the agency took no action.

At 3:30 the next morning, Mr. Gonzales appeared at the police station and opened fire and was killed by the officers. Upon examining the truck he had arrived in, the officers discovered the dead bodies of all three of the children.

Mrs. Gonzales sued the town of Castle Rock, alleging the police had failed to enforce her protective order as mandated by state law and had therefore violated her due process rights. The U.S. Supreme Court, in a surprise decision, held that Mrs. Gonzales's due process rights had not been violated, since she had not had personal entitlement requiring the police to enforce the protective order.

Similar to many other areas of domestic violence, police response to spousal assault is still being researched and studied. As with so much of domestic violence and other criminal acts, we simply do not have the answers to the problem. Scholars such as Cynthia Bowman would even argue that we do not yet even understand what questions to ask.[38]

If spousal assault were like any other crime, the police response would be fairly simple: investigate, arrest, charge, and cooperate with the district attorney in the prosecution of the perpetrator. Unfortunately, spousal assault involves certain factors that make it unique. These factors are explored in detail in this chapter. These forces all interact to cause law enforcement agencies to respond differently to spousal assault than they do to robberies, rapes, and other crimes of violence.

As the Thurman case described in the Focus box illustrates, spousal assault can have serious consequences for both the victim and any professionals who are involved with either the abuser or the victim. However, we are slowly beginning to acknowledge that spousal assault is one of the crimes society has ignored. Part of the reason for society's reaction to this form of domestic violence is the perceived difficulty in responding to physical assaults between adult family members. Another factor is our inability to classify those who assault their spouses into any identifiable category. Finally, as with other forms of family violence, we cannot with any certainty predict who will be the aggressor or victim in the area of spousal assault.

Factors Affecting Police Response

Law enforcement's acknowledgment and response to spousal assault have been slow in coming. Even today there are police officers who would rather not get involved in a "family matter." This should not be surprising in that the battering of women has existed for thousands of years. As indicated in Chapter 8, women were considered chattel, and it was perfectly proper to "discipline" spouses as long as there was no permanent injury inflicted upon the wife.[39] There is clear evidence that numerous early laws accorded men rights and power over women.[40] The privacy that families enjoyed behind the closed doors of the home continued into modern times.

The *Journal of Marriage and the Family* did not even discuss spousal assault until 1971.[41] Slowly, however, scientific data emerged that indicated criminal violence occurred behind those closed doors. By the mid-1970s, numerous other studies began to elevate spousal abuse to the status of a national social problem.

Feminist groups, scholars, and others raised a hue and cry regarding this form of criminal conduct. Between 1975 and 1980, forty-four states passed some sort of legislation on domestic violence. Despite the existence of laws regarding spousal abuse, studies have indicated that police have been reluctant to enforce violations of this type of criminal conduct.[42]

No one single factor has resulted in this hesitation or reluctance to enforce the laws in the area of spousal assault. Scholars have examined this phenomenon in detail and have noted a series of influences that have affected police agencies' enforcement of spousal assault. These factors include call screening, beliefs regarding financial hardship on the family in the event of an arrest, the family argument theory, the classification of spousal assault as a misdemeanor, the victim's preference not to arrest, and perceived danger to the police in domestic violence situations.

Numerous police departments engage in *call screening*, which is downgrading by the law enforcement agency of the priority assigned to domestic violence calls for service. Call screening results in a slower response time by the police officer than for other calls of the same or similar seriousness. This dynamic allows the abuser to beat the victim and leave the scene of the crime before the arrival of the officers. In addition, the failure of police to respond in a timely manner may increase the power of the abuser over the victim and lead the victim to believe that she is truly alone and helpless.

Police officers were and are reluctant to arrest the abuser in the mistaken belief that an arrest would pose a financial hardship on the family. An *arrest* is the taking of a person into custody in the manner prescribed by law. In addition, many law enforcement officers believe arrest is a futile act in view of the lack of prosecution and lenient sentences imposed (if at all) by the courts.

Many officers would arrest only if, in their opinion, the injury to the victim was severe. This is clearly not the law; however, it illustrates the thinking and reluctance of police to intervene in a "family argument."[43]

Until recently, another factor affecting the decision to arrest was the statutory limits on arrests for certain types of crimes. Traditionally, criminal violations are divided into two major classifications: felonies and misdemeanors. In the United States, this distinction is spelled out by statute or state constitution.[44] A *felony* is considered the most serious type of crime and is usually punished by imprisonment in state prison. Many statutes provide that all other crimes are misdemeanors. A *misdemeanor* is considered less serious and is punished by incarceration in local jails not to exceed one year. Normally, police may arrest persons who have committed felonies based on reasonable grounds or probable cause. *Probable cause* is that set of facts that would lead a reasonable person to believe a crime has been committed by the suspect. This felony arrest may occur even if the officers did not personally witness the offense. Misdemeanor arrests, on the other hand, require the officers to witness the crime. If they did not see the offense committed, they could request the victim to make a citizen's arrest, and then on behalf of the citizen they would take the perpetrator into custody.

This distinction in the nature and classification of crimes had a direct impact on the ability of police officers to make arrests for domestic violence assaults. Many domestic violence disputes involve a battery. Most statutes define a *battery* as the unlawful application of force to the person of another.[45] Battery is the unlawful touching of another, whereas assault does not require any physical touching of the other person.[46] Absent serious injury, many state laws define battery as a misdemeanor. Thus until recently, officers could not make an arrest for spousal assault unless they witnessed the act or the victim was willing to make a citizen's arrest.

The victim's preference not to file charges also affected the police officer's decision not to arrest the offender. Several studies have indicated that many times victims of spousal assault did not want the police to make an arrest.[47] This resulted in the officers admonishing the offender and leaving the scene of the crime.

Many police officers perceive family disputes as potentially dangerous situations in which both parties, the abuser and the victim, may turn on the officer. Although there are conflicting studies as to whether family disputes are in fact more dangerous to police officers, the fact that many officers believe this to be the case can result in a delay in responding to these types of calls for service.[48] This perception may cause officers to delay in responding to spousal assault calls until they have a backup unit.

In the last several years, many states have passed mandatory arrest statutes that require the officer to arrest the suspect. These laws allow police to make arrests for misdemeanors not committed in their presence. The passage of these laws and their effectiveness is a subject of debate within the field of criminal justice. The following section discusses the factors that resulted in the passage of these statutes.

Arrest of Abusers

In recent years, victims of family violence have turned to the courts in an attempt to require law enforcement departments to provide effective intervention and protection against spousal assault. Increasingly, courts have begun to listen and rule in their favor both on constitutional and tort grounds. However, lawsuits and personal liability did not result in the amendment of various state statutes mandating arrest of abusers. This development started in 1984 with a federally funded experiment in Minneapolis.

The Minneapolis Experiment

In the area of policing and domestic violence, there is probably no more controversial study than the Minneapolis Experiment dealing with the effect of arrest on those who batter their spouses. The dean of policing and domestic violence, Lawrence Sherman, was the architect of the 1984 Minneapolis Domestic Violence Experiment. This study was the first controlled evaluation of the effect of arrest on individuals who commit assaultive types of crimes against their spouses.[49]

The Police Foundation and the Minneapolis Police Department joined forces to conduct a controlled experiment to test the effectiveness of arrest on prevention or deterrence of domestic violence. Funded in part by the National Institute of Justice, the experiment utilized a lottery system of three possible actions by police when dealing with domestic violence.

Police officers responding to a domestic disturbance were required to utilize one of the following options:

1. arrest with at least one night incarceration
2. send the offender away from the scene of the disturbance or arrest him if he refused to leave
3. give the couple some form of advice, including mediation

The officers were not allowed to select which of these options would be used, rather they carried a pad of forms that listed the available options. When they encountered a situation that met the experiment's criteria, they were required to utilize the option listed on the top form.

The experiment involved only misdemeanor batteries in which both the victim and the suspect were present when the officers arrived at the scene of the disturbance. Cases involving serious threats or danger to the victim were excluded, as were situations in which the victim demanded the officers arrest the suspect.

After the officers finished their assignment, they turned in a brief report to the researchers for follow-up. The research staff utilized two measures to determine the amount of repeated violence by the offenders: official police reports and victim interviews. Official police reports were monitored to determine if the suspect committed another similar offense within a specified time period. In addition, the research staff contacted the listed victims and conducted a detailed interview with subsequent interviews for a period of twenty-four weeks after the initial offense.

The experiment produced a sample of 314 cases that met all the criteria. The results indicated that the arrest option produced the lowest percentage of repeated violence of all the alternatives. Official police reports revealed that 10 percent of the arrested suspects committed a subsequent offense, 24 percent of those suspects who were sent from the home repeated acts of violence against their spouse, and 19 percent of the suspects who were advised by the officers committed another offense. Interviews with victims produced even more dramatic percentages: 19 percent of the arrest suspects, 33 percent of those suspects sent from the home, and 37 percent of those advised by the officers committed another offense.

Based on the results of the study, Sherman and his colleagues made three recommendations. The first and probably the least controversial was to change existing laws to allow the police to make warrantless arrests for misdemeanor spousal assaults not committed in their presence. The second recommendation was read to suggest that mandatory arrest was the preferred option in most cases of domestic violence. The final recommendation suggested that additional experiments be conducted in other cities to validate the results of the Minneapolis study.

The Minneapolis Experiment acted as a change agent within the criminal justice system. Armed with its results, advocates of mandatory arrest and other sanctions were able to find support in various state legislatures for long overdue reform of criminal statutes dealing with domestic violence. Eleven states adopted legislation that authorized warrantless arrest in misdemeanor domestic violence cases, and another sixteen states enacted mandatory arrest laws in family violence situations.[50]

Prior to the experiment, only 10 percent of police departments serving cities over 100,000 in population encouraged their officers to make arrests in domestic violence situations. Within five years of the announcement of the results of the experiment, 84 percent of all major police departments in the United States had adopted a policy that stated arrest was the preferred option in domestic violence situations.[51]

The Minneapolis Experiment was hailed as a breakthrough study of domestic violence and criticized by a number of prominent scholars as inadequate and flawed.[52] In retrospect, it may not matter whether the results of the study were accurate; its greatest contribution may be that it generated an incredible amount of debate within academia and the law enforcement profession regarding how we should respond to domestic violence.

Other Replications

One direct result of the Minneapolis Experiment was the funding of additional replications by the National Institute of Justice. Five additional studies were undertaken in the following locations: Metro-Dade (Miami), Colorado Springs, Milwaukee, Omaha, and Charlotte. What was consistent about these additional studies was the finding of inconsistency in the deterrent effect of arrest.

The Metro-Dade Experiment established two major categories with two subgroups under each of these categories. The two major subdivisions were those suspects who were arrested and those who were not arrested. Each of these groups were further divided into subgroups that did or did not receive follow-up counseling by specially trained police officers.[53] The Metro-Dade Experiment clearly supports the theory that arrest is a deterrent to future domestic violence.

The Colorado Springs Experiment employed four options in its replication: (1) arrest and issuance of a restraining order; (2) counseling for the offender and issuance of a restraining order; (3) issuance of a restraining order; and (4) restoring order at the scene of the crime without arrest or use of a restraining order. The Colorado Springs Experiment supports the hypothesis that arrest in some situations does in fact act as a deterrent to future violence.[54]

The Milwaukee Experiment was carried out in a city that in May 1986 had adopted a citywide policy of mandatory arrest for domestic violence cases.[55] However, the study did not involve arrests of all offenders, rather it utilized three options: full arrest, short arrest, or warning. The full arrest involved taking the suspect into custody pursuant to existing policy and allowing him bail in the amount of $250. The short arrest required officers to arrest the suspect but allowed him to be released on his own recognizance preferably within two hours after arrest. The warning option utilized a standard warning of arrest if the officers had to return to the location at any time during the same day.

The results were obtained by a review of police records and follow-up interviews with the victims. The researchers found that there was a clear initial deterrent effect in both the full arrest and short arrest situations as compared with the warning only option. However, this deterrence did not last and there appeared to be no long-term difference between the arrest options and warning option.

The original Minneapolis Experiment and these three replications may lead one to conclude that arrest does in fact deter either short-term or long-term spousal assault. Unfortunately, the Omaha and Charlotte replications came to the opposite conclusion. These studies were conducted in the same manner as the other replications and indicated that arrest does not deter future violence.

The Omaha Experiment randomly assigned eligible police calls regarding domestic violence into three categories when both the suspect and the victim were present.[56] These classifications were arrest, separation, or mediation. In those cases in which the suspect had already left the scene of the crime when the police arrived, the police randomly assigned him to a warrant or no warrant group.

The police relied on five conditions when making their determination of whether to include the suspect within the experiment: (1) the existence of probable cause to arrest for misdemeanor assault; (2) a clearly identifiable victim and suspect; (3) both the victim and suspect were adults; (4) the victim and the suspect must have cohabitated some time during the year preceding the assault; and (5) neither party had an outstanding arrest warrant. Although the Omaha Experiment excluded felony domestic violence cases, a majority of the calls for service involved physical injuries to the victim.

The results of the experiment were measured in two ways: review of police reports and victim interviews. Contrary to the Minneapolis Experiment, the Omaha study concluded that arrest of a suspect at the scene of the domestic assault did not have any greater deterrent effect than the other two options.[57] However, the issuance of a warrant for an offender who was absent from the scene of the crime at the time the officers arrived did appear to extend significantly the time frame in which the victim was free from further violence in comparison with those situations in which the police simply informed the victim that she had the right to obtain a warrant for the suspect.

The Charlotte Experiment tested three distinct alternatives to domestic violence.[58] Police responses included advising the couple, issuing a citation to the offender, or arresting the offender. Excluded from the study were situations in which the victim insisted on the arrest of the suspect, the suspect threatened or assaulted the officer, or the officer believed the victim was in imminent danger. Similar to the other replications, the Charlotte Experiment evaluated the effect of these alternatives using only two methods: police reports and victim interviews. The results indicated no significant difference in the deterrent effect of advising, citing, or arresting the offender.

In 2001, the National Institute of Justice and the Centers for Disease Control conducted a scientific evaluation of the results of the 1984 Minneapolis Experiment and its five replications.[59] Because of the inconsistent and conditional findings of the previous studies, scholars and policymakers reevaluated the deterrent effect of arrest using an approach that was more statistically sound. The study pooled incidents from the five replications, computed comparable independent and outcome measures from common dates intentionally embedded in each experiment, and standardized the experimental design and statistical models.

This method of reevaluating the data produced the following significant results:

- Arresting batterers was consistently related to reducing subsequent aggression against female partners.
- The research found no relationship between arresting the perpetrator and an increased risk of subsequent aggression against the female partner.

This study reexamined the Minneapolis replications and found evidence of a consistent and direct, though modest, deterrent effect of arrest on aggression by males against their female partners. This effect existed for the first several days after the incident regardless of the length of incarceration and lasted up to one year after the incident. The research also pointed out that a minority of perpetrators continued their violence regardless of the intervention that occurred.

As a result of these studies and other factors, many police departments have adopted policies that encourage or mandate the arrest of a spouse abuser. To ensure the effectiveness of these policies, some police departments have created special domestic violence units, trained personnel on the dynamics of spousal abuse, and created sophisticated tracking and monitoring communication systems.[60]

For arrest to be an effective domestic violence intervention policy, there must be a coordinated and integrated response to the problem on the part of the criminal justice system. If police, prosecutors, judges, and probation and parole agencies all respond appropriately and the victims feel that the system is committed to protecting them and their children, we will have taken a major step forward in responding to this type of violence.[61]

Summary

Although spousal abuse has been intensely researched in the past years, it is still one of the most commonly misunderstood issues within family violence. Our society has placed women in inferior and subordinate positions throughout history, and even today some segments of our society continue to treat them as property rather than partners. These beliefs contribute to the interpersonal dynamics that result in violence against women. The nature and extent of spousal abuse is staggering. Current figures indicate women today are being brutalized at alarming numbers.

One common question asked by both professionals and laypersons is, "Why does the victim stay in such a relationship?" It is clear today that there are a number of dynamics that occur in a battering relationship. These dynamics many times bind victims to their abusers more tightly than if they were handcuffed to them.

There are numerous theories to explain why men batter women. In fact, there are so many theories that entire textbooks are devoted to explaining them. Yet no one theory is accepted by all scholars, practitioners, or professionals in the field as the theory that explains spousal abuse. Even though no one theory prevails, professionals should be aware of the more common and well-known studies of spousal abuse. They include studies of social stress, power, dependency, alcohol, pregnancy, and marriage.

The criminal justice system is still searching for ways to respond to spousal abuse. As a result of a number of factors, there are mandatory arrest policies in effect in a number of jurisdictions. This may stop the immediate battering but will not solve the problem. We must continue to search for ways to prevent this type of abuse. Only by stopping it before it occurs can we grow as a nation and society.

Key Terms

Spousal abuse is any intentional act or series of acts that cause injury to the spouse. These acts may be physical, emotional, or sexual. Spouse is gender neutral and therefore the abuse may occur to a man or a woman. The term includes those who are married, cohabitating, or involved in a serious relationship. It also encompasses individuals who are separated and living apart from their former spouse.

Cycle theory of violence sets forth the dynamics of battering in spousal abuse.

Battered woman syndrome theorizes that victims of spousal abuse gradually become immobilized by fear and believe they have no other options. As a result, these women stay in the abusive relationships coping the best they can. The battered woman syndrome involves one who has been, on at least two occasions, the victim of physical, sexual, or serious psychological abuse by a man with whom she has an intimate relationship. It is a pattern of psychological symptoms that develop after somebody has lived in a battering relationship.

Stockholm syndrome is a phenomenon that occurs when persons who are held as hostages, captives, or prisoners of war begin to identify with the captors.

Traumatic bonding theory explains why battered woman stay in abusive relationships. This theory holds that when a women finally leaves an abusive partner, her immediate fears begin to diminish and her hidden attachment to her abuser begins to manifest itself. Emotionally drained and vulnerable, she becomes susceptible to her partner's loving contrite pressure to return. As her fears lessen and the needs previously provided by her partner increase, she may decide to give him another chance.

Power is the ability to impose one's will on another and make life decisions.

Marital dependency is a multifaceted concept that involves economic, emotional, and societal forces that result in a woman being dependent on her spouse for support.

Spousal assault is used and defined as the act of intentionally inflicting physical injury on the spouse or other person who is cohabitating with the abuser.

Call screening This is downgrading by the law enforcement agency of the priority assigned to domestic violence calls for service.

Arrest is the taking of a person into custody in the manner presented by law.

Felony is considered the most serious type of crime and is usually punished by imprisonment in state prison.

Misdemeanor is considered less serious and is punished by incarceration in local jails not to exceed one year.

Probable cause is that set of facts that would lead a reasonable person to believe a crime has been committed by the suspect.

Battery is the unlawful application of force to the person of another.

Discussion Questions

1. Can you narrow the definition of spousal abuse? What would you exclude and why?

2. Do we really know the extent of spouse abuse? Why is it important how many spouses are abused?

3. Which of the theories regarding the dynamics of battering do you believe is the major reason spouses stay with their abuser? Justify your answer.

4. Isn't Dutton's theory of traumatic bonding just another form of the battered woman syndrome? Why? Why not?

5. Which of the theories regarding spouse abuse do you believe is the major reason one spouse abuses the other?

6. What can we do to improve the criminal justice system's treatment of abused spouses?

Suggested Readings

D. A. Hines & K. Malley-Morrison, Family *Violence in the United States: Defining Understanding, and Combating Abuse* (Sage, Newsbury Park, Calif.) 2004.

K. Little, *Family Violence: An Intervention Model for Dental Professionals* (U.S. Department of Justice, Office of Victims of Crime, Washington, D.C.) 2004.

M. A. Straus & R. J. Gelles, *Physical Violence in American Families,* (Transaction Publishers, New Brunswick, N.J.) 1990.

V. B. Hasselt, R. L. Morrison, A. S. Bellack & W. Frazier, (eds.), *Handbook of Family Violence,* (Plenum, New York) 1988.

R. J. Gelles, (ed.), *Vision 2010,* (National Council on Family Relations, Minneapolis) 1995.

R. T. Ammerman & M. Hersen, (eds.), *Case Studies in Family Violence,* (Plenum, New York) 1991.

L. E. Walker, *The Battered Woman,* (Harper & Row, New York) 1979.

L. E. Walker, *The Battered Woman Syndrome,* (Springer, New York) 1984.

D. J. Sonkin, (ed.), *Domestic Violence on Trial,* (Springer, New York) 1982.

M. D. Pagelow, *Family Violence,* (Praeger, New York) 1984.

D. G. Dutton, *The Domestic Assault of Women,* (UBC Press, Vancouver, B.C.) 1995.

E. S. Buzawa & C. G. Buzawa, (eds.), *Domestic Violence: The Changing Criminal Justice Response,* (Auburn House, Westport, Conn.) 1992.

A. M. Jaggar & P. S. Rothenberg, (eds.), *Feminist Frameworks,* 3rd ed. (McGraw Hill, New York) 1993.

L. W. Sherman, *Policing Domestic Violence,* (The Free Press, New York) 1992.

F. G. Bolton & S. R. Bolton, *Working with Violent Families,* (Sage, Newbury Park, Calif.) 1987.

W. R. LaFave & A. W. Scott, Jr., *Criminal Law,* 2nd ed. (West Publishing Co., St. Paul, Minn.) 1986.

R. M. Perkins & R. N. Boyce, *Criminal Law,* 3rd ed. (Foundation Press, Inc., New York) 1982.

M. Steinman, (ed.), *Women Battering: Policy Responses,* (Anderson Publishing Co., Cincinnati) 1991.

Endnotes

1. R. J. Gelles, *Domestic Violence Factoids,* http://www.umn.edu/mincava/factoid.htm (file created October 16, 1995).

2. M. A. Straus & R. J. Gelles, *Physical Violence in American Families,* (Transaction Publishers, New Brunswick, N.J.) 1990, pp. 96–98.

3. E. Stark & A. Flitcraft, "Violence Among Intimates: An Epidemiological Review," in V. B. Hasselt, R. L. Morrison, A. S. Bellack, & W. Frazier, (eds.), *Handbook of Family Violence,* (Plenum, New York) 1988, pp. 292–317.

4. Suzanne Steinmetz, "The Battered Husband Syndrome," 2 (3/4) *Victimology,* 499–509 (1978).

5. S. K. Steinmetz & J. S. Lucca, "Husband Battering," *Handbook of Family Violence,* V. B. Van Hasselt, R. L. Morrison, A. S. Bellack, & M. Hersen, (eds.), (Plenum, New York) 1988.

6. K. D. O'Leary, J. Barling, I. Arias, A. Rosenbaum, J. Malone & A. Tyree, "Prevalence and Stability of Physical Aggression between Spouses: A Longitudinal Analysis," 57 *Journal of Consulting and Clinical Psychology,* 263–268 (1989).

7. Jacquelyn Campbell, "Violence Toward Women: Homicide and Battering," in Richard J. Gelles, (ed.), *Vision 2010,* (National Council on Family Relations, Minneapolis) 1995.

8. *Costs of Intimate Partner Violence Against Women in the United States,* Department of Health and Human Services, Centers for Disease Control and Prevention, Atlanta Ga. (March 2003).

9. E. W. Gondolf & E. R. Fisher, "Wife Battering," *Case Studies in Family Violence,* R. T. Ammerman & M. Hersen, (eds.), (Plenum, New York) 1991, pp. 273–274.

10. L. E. Walker, *The Battered Women,* (Harper & Row, New York) 1979.

11. L. E. Walker, *The Battered Woman Syndrome,* (Springer, New York) 1984.

12. See *People v. Humphrey,* 96 *Daily Journal D.A.R.* 10609 at 10612 where the California Supreme Court addressed this issue.

13. M. A. Douglas, "The Battered Women Syndrome," in D. J. Sonkin, (ed.), *Domestic Violence on Trial,* (Springer, New York) 1982.

14. M. D. Pagelow, *Family Violence,* (Praeger, New York) 1984, p. 308.

15. G. NiCarthy, *Getting Free: A Handbook for Women in Abusive Relationships,* (Seal Press, New York) 1986, pp. 117–118.

16. D. G. Dutton & S. L. Painter, "Traumatic Bonding: The Development of Emotional Attachments in Battered Women and Other Relationships of Intermittent Abuse," 6 *Victimology*, 139 (1981).

17. D. G. Dutton, *The Domestic Assault of Women*, (UBC Press, Vancouver, B.C.) 1995.

18. Id. at p. 190.

19. Id. at p. 191.

20. Demie Kurz, "Battering and the Criminal Justice System: A Feminist View," in Eve S. Buzawa & Carl G. Buzawa, (eds.), *Domestic Violence: The Changing Criminal Justice Response*, (Auburn House, Westport, Conn.) 1992.

21. For an excellent discussion of these issues, see K. Spiller, "The Feminist Majority Report: Corporate Women and the Mommy Track," in A. M. Jaggar & P. S. Rothenberg, (eds.), *Feminest Frameworks*, 3rd ed. (McGraw Hill, New York) 1993, pp. 316–318.

22. See K. Newman, "Middle-Class Women in Trouble," in A. M. Jaggar & P. S. Rothenberg, (eds.), *Feminist Frameworks*, 3rd ed. (McGraw Hill, New York) 1993, pp. 319–323.

23. M. Roy, "A Current Study of 150 Cases," in M. Roy, (ed.), *A Psychological Study of Domestic Violence*, (Van Nostrand Reinhold, New York) 1977.

24. D. S. Kalmuss & M. A. in Straus, "Wife's Marital Dependency and Wife Abuse," in M. A. Straus & R. J. Gelles, *Physical Violence in American Families*, (Transaction Publishers, New Brunswick, N.J.) 1990, pp. 379–380.

25. K. J. Sher, "Subjective Effects of Alcohol: The Influence of Setting and Individual Differences in Alcohol Expectancies," 46 *Journal of Studies on Alcohol*, 137–146 (1985).

26. D. H. Coleman & M. A. Straus, "Alcohol Abuse and Family Violence," *Alcohol, Drug Abuse and Aggression*, E. Gottheil, K. A. Druley, T. E. Skoloda & H. M. Waxman, (eds.), (Charles C. Thomas, Springfield, Ill.) 1983, pp. 104–124.

27. D. C. McClelland, W. N. Davis, R. Kalin & E. Wanner, *The Drinking Man*, (Free Press, New York) 1972.

28. K. Pernanem, "Theoretical Aspects of the Relationship between Alcohol Use and Crime," *Drinking and Crime: Perspectives on the Relationships Between Alcohol Consumption and Criminal Behavior*, J. J. Collins, Jr., (ed.), (Guilford Press, New York) 1981.

29. A. Helton, "Battering during Pregnancy," 86 *American Journal of Nursing*, 910–913 (1986).

30. R. J. Gelles, "Violence and Pregnancy: Are Pregnant Women at Greater Risk of Abuse?" in M. A. Straus & R. J. Gelles, *Physical Violence in American Families*, (Transaction Publishers, New Brunswick, N.J.) 1990, p. 282.

31. M. A. Straus & R. J. Gelles, "How Violent Are American Families? Estimates From the National Family Violence Survey and Other Studies," in G. T. Hotaling, D. Finkelhor, John T. Kirkpatrick & M. A. Straus, (eds.), *New Directions in Family Violence Research*, (Sage, Beverly Hills, Calif.) 1988.

32. J. E. Sets & M. A. Straus, "The Marriage License: A Comparison of Assaults in Dating, Cohabitating, and Married Couples," in M. A. Straus & R. J. Gelles, (eds.), *Physical Violence in American Families*, (Transaction Publishers, New Brunswick, N.J.) 1990, pp. 227–244. Published earlier in 4 *Journal of Family Violence*, 161–180 (1989).

33. J. E. Stets & M. A. Pirog-Good, "Violence in Dating Relationships," 50 *Social Psychology Quarterly*, 237–246 (1987).

34. See J. E. Sets & M. A. Straus, "The Marriage License: A Comparison of Assaults in Dating, Cohabitating, and Married Couples," in M. A. Straus & R. J. Gelles, *Physical Violence in American Families*, (Transaction Publishers, New Brunswick, N.J.) 1990, pp. 227–244.

35. See for example, Lawrence W. Sherman, *Policing Domestic Violence*, (The Free Press, New York) 1992; Frank G. Bolton & Susan R. Bolton, *Working with Violent Families*, (Sage, Newbury Park, Calif.) 1987; and Eve S. Buzawa & Carl G. Buzawa, (eds.), *Domestic Violence, The Changing Criminal Justice Response*, (Auburn House, Westport, Conn.) 1992.

36. The judgment was later reduced to $1.9 million.

37. M. Buddy & K. Taylor, "Please, Somebody Help Me," *20/20 News*, January 23, 1986.

38. See Cynthia Grant Bowman, "The Arrest Experiments: A Feminist Critique," 83/1 *Journal of Criminal Law and Criminology*, 201–208 (1992) in which Bowman argues that current research in the area of spousal assault is flawed because it is usually conducted from the

abuser's perspective, ignores feminist thinking, and does not consider various social factors.

39. Lisa A. Frisch, "Research That Succeeds, Policies That Fail," 83/1 *Journal of Criminal Law and Criminology,* 209 (1992).

40. For an excellent discussion of these laws see, Arnold Binder & James Meeker, "The Development of Social Attitudes Toward Spousal Abuse," in Eve S. Buzawa & Carl G. Buzawa, (eds.), *Domestic Violence, The Changing Criminal Justice Response,* (Auburn House, Westport, Conn.) 1992.

41. John E. O'Brien, "Women Abuse: Facts Replacing Myths," 33 *Journal of Marriage and the Family,* 362–398 (1971).

42. Edna Erez, "Intimacy, Violence and the Police," 39 *Human Relations,* 265–281 (1986).

43. Eve S. Buzawa & Carl G. Buzawa, *Domestic Violence, The Criminal Justice Response,* (Sage, Newbury Park, Calif.) 1990, p. 44.

44. Wayne R. LaFave & Austin W. Scott, Jr., *Criminal Law,* 2nd ed. (West Publishing Co., St. Paul, Minn.) 1986, p. 30.

45. Rollin M. Perkins & Ronald N. Boyce, *Criminal Law,* 3rd ed. (Foundation Press, Inc., New York) 1982, p. 152.

46. Wayne R. LaFave & Austin W. Scott, Jr., *Criminal Law,* 2nd ed. (West Publishing Co., St. Paul, Minn.) 1986, p. 684.

47. See Donald Black, *The Manners and Customs of Police,* (Academic Press, New York) 1980, p. 189.

48. For an excellent discussion of this area see, Sherman, *Policing Domestic Violence,* pp. 30–31.

49. Lawrence W. Sherman & Richard A. Berk, "The Specific Deterrent Effects of Arrest for Domestic Assault," 49 *American Sociological Review,* 261 (1984).

50. Jacob R. Clark, "The Minneapolis Study: Policy Gets Made Despite Cautions," *Law Enforcement News,* 9 (March 31, 1993).

51. J. David Hirschel & Ira Hutchinson, "Police-Preferred Arrest Policies," in Michael Steinman, (ed.), *Women Battering: Policy Responses,* (Anderson Publishing Co., Cincinnati) 1991, p. 59.

52. See Delbert S. Elliot, "Criminal Justice Procedures in Family Violence Crimes," in Lloyd Ohlin & Michael Tonry (eds.), *Family Violence,* (University of Chicago Press, Chicago) 1989,

p. 458 which cites the study as a landmark study on the effectiveness of alternative police responses to family violence and compares that position with Richard Lempert, "Humility is a Virtue," 23 *Law & Society Review,* 146 (1989) which argues that the experiment lacked a scientific basis.

53. Antony Pate, Edwin E. Hamilton & Annan Sampson, *"Metro-Dade Spouse Abuse Replication Project, Draft Final Report,* (National Institute of Justice, Washington, D.C.) 1991.

54. Richard A. Berk, Alec Campbell, Ruth Klap & Bruce Western, "A Bayesian Analysis of the Colorado Springs Spouse Abuse Experiment," 83/1 *Journal of Criminal Law and Criminology,* 170 (1992).

55. Lawrence W. Sherman, Janell D. Schmidt, Dennis P. Rogan, Douglas A. Smith, Patrick R. Gartin, Ellen G. Cohn, Dean J. Collins & Anthony R. Bacich, "The Variable Effects of Arrest on Criminal Careers: The Milwaukee Domestic Violence Experiment," 83/1 *Journal of Criminal Law and Criminology,* 137 (1992).

56. Franklyn W. Dunford, David Huizinga & Delbert S. Elliot, "The Omaha Domestic Violence Police Experiment," Final Report to the National Institute of Justice, (National Institute of Justice, Washington, D.C.) 1989.

57. Id. at p. 34.

58. J. David Hirchel, Ira W. Hutchinson III, Charles W. Dean, Joseph J. Kelly & Carolyn E. Pesackis, "Charlotte Spouse Assault Replication Project." Final Report to the National Institute of Justice, (National Institute of Justice, Washington, D.C.) 1991.

59. This section is adapted from C. D. Maxwell, J. H. Garner, and J. A. Fagan, *The Effects of Arrest on Intimate Partner Violence: New Evidence From the Spouse Assault Replication Program,* National Institute of Justice, Washington, D.C. (June 2001).

60. *Grants to Encourage Arrest Policies,* (Office of Justice Programs, Washington, D.C.) 1996.

61. B. J. Hart, "Coordinated Community Approaches to Domestic Violence," presented at the Strategic Planning Workshop on Violence Against Women, sponsored by the National Institute of Justice in Washington, D.C., March 31, 1995.

10

CHILD VICTIMS

Chapter Outline

Discussion Questions

Suggested Readings

Learning Objectives

After reading this chapter, you should be able to:

- Distinguish between the different types of physical child abuse
- Recognize when poor parenting becomes child neglect
- Understand the dynamics involved in child sexual abuse
- Distinguish between the different theories regarding child abuse
- Explain some excuses used by parents to justify the acts of aggression between siblings
- Understand the controversies surrounding the topic of ritualistic child abuse

Types of Child Abuse

Physical Child Abuse

Is a parent unfit or considered abusive if, while bathing his one-year-old daughter, she slips from his grasp and hits her head against the faucet causing a cut over her eye that requires two stitches? Is this child abuse? Although some might blame the father for not being alert to that possibility, others would not classify him as a child abuser. Accidents happen. They are a part of growing up and, painful as they may be to the parent and the child, they are part of a normal, healthy relationship. Thus, not all injuries sustained by children can be classified as child abuse. If not all injuries are child abuse and parents have a right to inflict corporal punishment on children as a form of discipline, how do we draw the line and define physical injuries to children?

Numerous authorities have defined child abuse. Part of the problem in this area has been the continued struggle to agree on what the term *child abuse* means. Van Hasselt, Pagelow, Gelles, and other scholars in the field have excellent discussions and definitions of this condition.[1] For purposes of this text and ease of understanding, we have accepted the following definition: *physical child abuse* may be defined as any act which results in a nonaccidental physical injury by a person who has care, custody, or control of a child.

There are two key aspects to this definition—the act is intentional or willful and the act resulted in a physical injury. An accidental injury does not qualify as child abuse. In the previous example, an accidental slip in a bathtub would not qualify as child abuse even if the child received an injury that required several stitches. Child abuse as discussed in this chapter is manifested by physical injury that can be proved or documented. Simply yelling at the child is not child abuse within the meaning of this definition. Nor is spanking the child on the hand, the

---

PRACTICUM: When Is It Child Abuse?

Situation 1: A three-year-old boy is running around the supermarket, knocking down cans of food and does not stop when his grandmother asks him to. The grandmother takes the child by the arm and the child starts yelling, "You're hurting me!" Assume there is no physical injury to the child. Is it child abuse? What if the child is just acting out?

Situation 2: The father leaves the four-year-old child in the fenced-in backyard with the family pet, a collie. The child hits the dog, who bites her arm. Assume there is no history of aggression on the part of the dog. Is it child abuse?

Situation 3: A mother is babysitting the next door neighbor's five-year-old girl. She has a six-year-old boy. She decides to give them a bath together. The boy keeps touching the girl's genital area. Is it child abuse?

Situation 4: An older brother decides to tease his younger sister. When their parents are gone, he holds her down and tickles her until she cries. Is it child abuse?

---

face, or the buttocks if those acts do not result in a physical injury that can be documented. Although it is true that any form of spanking causes injury in the form of pain and some trauma to the child, unless the force is sufficient to leave marks, most medical and legal authorities will not classify these acts as child abuse. This lack of a clear definition is part of the problem of physical child abuse. The next section addresses the issue of child neglect, an area that is even more emotional and hard to define.

Child Neglect

In the past twenty years, numerous texts, articles, and studies have dealt with the subject of neglect. The literature runs the gamut from examining assessment techniques of neglect[2] to listing the different forms of this abuse.[3] Except for rare instances, child neglect does not receive the public attention that child sexual and physical abuse generates. Part of the reason for this lack of emphasis may lie in the definition and nature of child neglect.

Child neglect is the negligent treatment or maltreatment of a child by a parent or caretaker under circumstances indicating harm or threatened harm to the child's health or welfare. Although this appears at first glance to be a simple and straightforward statement, it covers a wide range of activities or omissions that impact on the physical and emotional well-being of a child. At what point does mere inattention or lack of knowledge translate itself into child neglect? This definition would require an act or omission that results in harm or threatens to cause harm to the child's health or welfare. This act or omission may be physical or psychological. A strict interpretation of this definition would require that parents or caretakers guard their children like prisoners. However, this is unrealistic because children are mobile. They get into drawers, cabinets, and every corner in the house

Momentary inattention ———————————————— Gross action or inaction

FIGURE 10.1   Child Neglect Continuum

and yard. Therefore, as Figure 10.1 illustrates, we are dealing with a continuum that stretches from momentary inattention to gross inaction.

Somewhere on the line in Figure 10.1, acceptable parenting ends and child neglect begins. Although no specific place on this line establishes child neglect, it is a common form of child abuse. The next section addresses another aspect of child abuse—sexual abuse of children.

Sexual Child Abuse

Child sexual abuse is sexual exploitation or sexual activities with children under circumstances which indicate that the child's health or welfare is harmed or threatened.[4] This definition includes inappropriate sexual activities between children and adults. The inappropriate behavior may be between family members or between a stranger and the victim. *Intrafamilial sexual abuse* includes incest and refers to any type of exploitative sexual contact occurring between relatives. *Extrafamilial sexual abuse* refers to exploitative sexual contact with perpetrators who may be known to the child (neighbors, babysitters, live-in partners) or unknown to the child.[5]

One major problem with this definition is the requirement that the child be harmed. From a legal perspective, harm to the victim is not an element of the crime of child sexual abuse. If certain physical acts occur, the crime is complete. In criminal proceedings, it is not necessary to prove that the perpetrator intended to harm or actually harmed the child. However, this definition is useful in exploring the consequences of child sexual abuse, and retaining the requirement of an injury to the child will allow for such a discussion.

The following acts are examples of child sexual abuse: exposing one's sexual organs to the child, voyeurism, touching the sex organs of the child, mutual or self-masturbation with the child, oral sex, intercourse, and anal sex. In addition, allowing the child to view or participate in pornographic or obscene movies is considered child abuse.

Child sexual abuse may be distinguished from rape in that the perpetrator may use a variety of different "techniques" to achieve the objective of sexual gratification. Rape normally involves sexual acts as the result of force or fear. Child abuse offenders may also use force or fear; however, they also employ other pressures or influences to accomplish their goal. These actions include manipulation of the child (psychologically isolating the child from other loved ones), coercion (using adult authority or power on the child), force (restraining the child), threats or fear (informing the child if he tells, no one will love him).[6]

Extent of the Problem

Physical Child Abuse

The physical battering of children is not a new phenomenon. Children have suffered trauma at the hands of their parents and caretakers since the beginning of recorded history. In Egypt, upon the birth of Moses, the pharaoh ordered the death of all male children. King Herod also ordered infanticide on a large scale when Jesus was born.

Early history records the practice of burying infants alive in foundations of buildings and bridges.[7] Excavations of Canaanite dwellings have uncovered jars of infant bones in the foundation of buildings.[8] Although officially outlawed, this practice continued in seventeenth-century Europe, and children were found buried in the foundations of London Bridge.

Plato (428–348 B.C.) and Aristotle (348–322 B.C.) both urged the killing of infants born with birth defects. Children with birth defects, female infants, and the children of poor families were killed as a matter of course several hundred years before the birth of Christ. In Rome, the law of the Twelve Tables prohibited raising a child with a defect or deformity. In Sparta, infants were examined by a local council of elders, who had the power to throw those children considered unfit into a canyon.[9]

Infanticide was not the only form of abuse practiced by early civilizations. During the Middle Ages, families would often mutilate or sever limbs from children so as to make them more effective beggars. The histories of the European school system are filled with records detailing beatings and abuse by teachers inflicted on their young charges.

The industrial revolution was characterized by repeated maltreatment of children. Young children were forced to work long hours under inhumane conditions in factories or other heavy industries. Many were beaten, shackled, or starved to force them to work harder at their tasks.

In 1874, an eight-year-old child named Mary Ellen Wilson was discovered by a social worker to have been beaten and starved by her adoptive parents. The worker referred the case to the New York Police Department, which refused to take any action because there were no laws on the books that addressed the abuse of children by their parents or caretakers. In an effort to save the child, the city filed charges against the caretakers utilizing a statute that prevented cruelty to animals. The adoptive mother was sentenced to one year in jail, and the resulting publicity surrounding Mary Ellen's plight led to the formation of the Society for the Prevention of Cruelty to Children in 1875.

From this beginning, we have expanded our concern and care for abused children. Every state has laws preventing the physical abuse of children. The phenomenon of child abuse has generated many studies. One commonly cited study was conducted by the American Association for Protecting Children. In 1996, the Third National Incidence Study of Child Abuse and Neglect was released by the Department of Health and Human Services.[10] One of the most reliable sources of information regarding child abuse and neglect, the report indicated that an estimated 1,553,800 children were abused or neglected in 1993. This figure represented a 67 percent increase since 1986. That child abuse is a continuing problem is supported by other recent statistics. For example, the National Child Abuse and Neglect Data System (NCANDS) reported an estimated 1,400 child fatalities in 2002. A child fatality is the death of a child caused by an injury resulting from abuse or neglect or in which abuse or neglect was a contributing factor. Some researchers even take the position that there is no method of obtaining reliable data in this field.[11] Even the federal government has failed to establish standards for reporting child abuse. The FBI's Uniform Crime Reports (UCR) is the accepted method of reporting crimes on a nationwide basis. The UCR publishes crime statistics reported by 16,000 law enforcement agencies. However, it provides no specific information on crimes against children. With the exception of murder, the UCR does not list the victim's age. The National Center on Child Abuse and Neglect (NCCAN), a division within the U.S. Department of Health and Human Services, has commissioned studies to provide a national estimate of the incidence of child maltreatment.

Many authorities believe that the number of reported cases of child abuse is only the tip of the iceberg. This is particularly true for those children between the ages of twelve and nineteen. This age group is far less likely than younger victims to report crimes, especially when the offender is not a stranger.[12] Part of the problem with determining the magnitude of physical child abuse may have something to do with the definition itself.

By defining the characteristics or hallmarks of physical child abuse differently, the research data can also differ significantly. Researchers select their sample populations based on criteria that differ from scholar to scholar and study to study. Some social scientists view physical child abuse in the context of determining whether the child is "at risk," whereas those working in the criminal justice field emphasize physical evidence. This multifaceted approach to understanding physical child abuse presents both problems and opportunities for growth. As mentioned earlier, the problem is reaching consensus on the definition of physical child abuse and how we respond to it. The opportunities for growth are based on the premise that professionals can and should learn from each other. The social worker may learn of the difficulties in proving certain types of abuse while at the same time teaching the prosecuting attorney to accept the seriousness of a situation that might not otherwise be apparent from a legal perspective.

Child Neglect

Some scholars have stated that child neglect is the most common form of maltreatment. According to Green, the reported cases of neglect in New York outnumbered those of physical abuse by 11 to 1 in 1987.[13] A more recent study confirms prior research that neglect is more prevalent that other forms of child abuse. In 2002, Prevent Child Abuse America issued a joint report with the Centers for Disease Control that indicates in 2000, there were 879,000 cases of child maltreatment with

515,800 (63 percent) categorized as neglect.[14] Child neglect is an important topic all professionals should understand. Neglect is less obvious than physical or sexual abuse and it may continue for years without any outsider even being aware that the child they see daily is a victim. Neglect has many faces, forms, and appearances. There are serious cases in which a child's life is threatened and more mundane acts when the child is simply neglected on a daily basis.

Child Sexual Abuse

The American people have a widespread interest in child sexual abuse; however, the true magnitude of this problem is difficult to establish. There is a general agreement among both scholars and professionals in the field that the incidence of child sexual abuse reporting is understated.[15] Estimates on the number of child sexual abuses vary from source to source. Finkelhor's 1979 study of 796 college students indicated that 19 percent of the women and 9 percent of the men had been subjected to sexual abuse as children.[16] A later study by Finkelhor of 521 Boston parents indicated that 15 percent of the women and 6 percent of the men had been sexually abused by the age of sixteen.[17] Russell's survey of 930 San Francisco women found that 28 percent had been victims of child sexual abuse before the age of fourteen.[18] In 1985, the *Los Angeles Times* conducted a random survey of 2627 adults across the United States. The survey revealed that 27 percent of the women and 16 percent of the survey participants had been molested as children. The total percentage (combining men and women) for those who suffered child sexual abuse was 22 percent.[19] In 1991, researchers came to the conclusion that as many as 10 to 15 percent of all boys and 20 to 25 percent of all girls had experienced at least one instance of sexual abuse prior to the age of eighteen.[20]

Rape in America, which was published by the National Victims Center, indicates sexual violence occurs at a much higher rate than previously expected.[21] This study was discussed in more detail in Chapter 8 dealing with women and sexual violence, but it illustrates that sexual violence is still a major problem in America. Based on this study, the National Victims Center estimates at least 12.1 million women in the United States have been subjected to sexual violence as children or adults.

Many authorities are reporting a dramatic drop in the number of reported child abuse cases. The Office of Juvenile Justice and Delinquency Programs reported that the number of child sexual abuse cases substantiated by child protective services (CPS) dropped from approximately 150,000 cases in 1992 to 89,500 cases in 2000.[22] This is a 40 percent drop in cases in an eight-year period.

Although the figures may vary from study to study regarding the types and incidents of child sexual abuse, there is some agreement among researchers that the classification of offenders shown in Table 10.1 is a valid estimate.[23]

The true extent of child victimization is unknown; however, simply discussing this subject raises our awareness and makes it more likely that we will acknowledge its existence. Professionals must not only be aware that it occurs, they should also have a basic understanding of some of the more common theories dealing

TABLE 10.1   **Classification of Offenders**

Stranger as the offender	approximately 8–10 percent
Family member as the offender	approximately 47 percent
Acquaintance as the offender	approximately 40 percent

with causation of child abuse. The next section examines one popular theory in this area, the cycle of violence.

Child Fatality Review Teams

Despite a growing awareness of child abuse, we continue to experience child fatalities. Deaths of children due to illness or accidents can be, for the most part, easily identified; however, it is much harder to track deaths that result from physical assault or neglect. The NCANDS estimates that 1,400 child fatalities occurred in 2002.[24] Many researchers believe that deaths due to abuse and neglect are underreported since some of these deaths are labeled as accidents. Additionally. many states differ on the definition of key terms such as *child homicide, child abuse,* and *child neglect*.

In response to various concerns regarding child fatalities, a number of organizations and jurisdictions have formed child fatality review teams composed of a variety of professionals from different backgrounds who review child fatalities. The team members vary among jurisdictions, but usually include the medical examiner, a pediatrician, a representative from the district attorney's office, law enforcement and child protective services members, and other professionals as appropriate.

The teams integrate the separate disciplines with specific roles and mandates to insure services do not overlap or conflict. Teams also gather statistics to determine whether or not patterns exist that increase the likelihood of child fatalities and serious injuries within the community. There are generally two types of reviews: prospective and periodic. Prospective reviews usually occur within 72 hours of the death and are designed to assist the death investigation and delivery of services. Period reviews are designed to evaluate and discuss all deaths within a designated time frame.[25]

Cycle of Violence

Some scholars would argue that the most effective method of stopping child abuse is to break the cycle of violence. The cycle of violence theory is discussed as a distinct and separate aspect of child abuse. Simply separating it from the other theories should not imply that this is the definitive answer to why people commit aggressive acts, rather it is singled out for examination because professionals and laypersons constantly refer to it as a scientifically accepted fact. As with other causes or theories of family violence, there is no way to prove or disprove the cycle of violence theory. However, because of the widespread acceptance of this theory, it is necessary to explore fully both the premises on which it is founded and the criticisms directed to it.

The cycle of violence concept has generated continuing controversy among researchers for several decades. Scholars have attempted to determine whether violent tendencies can be inherited from the family of origin as a result of observing it or being a victim. Other scholars have attempted to explain criminal behavior by reference to this cycle.[26]

Definitions

The most commonly used term to describe the process involved in this concept is *cycle of violence;* however, this theory is also known as the "intergenerational transmission of violence theory." Because many authors, researchers, and commentators use the former, that is the term that will be used in this text. The ***cycle of violence theory*** asserts that violent behavior is learned within the family and bequeathed from one generation to the next. This theory holds that children who are victims of child abuse or who witness violent aggression by one spouse against the other will grow up and react to their children or spouses in the same manner. The childhood survivor of a violent family develops a predisposition toward violence in his or her own family. Thus, so this theory holds, we have a never-ending chain of violence that is passed from one generation to the next. There have been numerous studies on the cycle of violence, and the results of these studies will be discussed later in this section.

Cycle of Violence and Family Violence

The sources for most studies of the cycle of violence theory are case studies, clinical interviews, self-reporting, and agency records. One widely cited study in support of the cycle of violence theory is Steele and Pollock's research which appeared in Helfer and Kempe's *The Battered Child Syndrome* in 1968.[27] Their study involved sixty parents who were referred to them as a result of their children being treated for child abuse. Steele and Pollock gathered data by testing and interviewing the parents. The parents stated that as children they had experienced intense, pervasive, continuous demands from their own parents. Lost within the conclusions of the study was the fact that some parents were physically abused and others were not. The researchers had cautioned against drawing too many inferences from their research; however, their study is constantly cited as evidence supporting the cycle of violence theory.

Straus conducted an extensive study by interviewing 1,146 families with children.[28] The results of the study indicated an 18 percent rate of generational transmission of violence. The results of this study may have been low because the researchers limited the definition of abuse to physical acts that occurred during adolescence. As discussed in Chapter 2, child abuse is more likely to occur at a younger age with a gradual tapering off in incidents as the child reaches the teenage years.

During this same time period, Hunter and Kilstrom interviewed 282 parents of newborn infants.[29] These researchers followed the parents and determined that the intergenerational transmission of violence was 18 percent. However, 82 percent of the parents who were abused as children did not abuse their offspring. Those parents appeared to be able to break the cycle of violence because of social support, healthy children, and a more supportive relationship with one of their own parents. Hunter and Kilstrom's study is suspect because it examined only infants who had been admitted to an intensive care nursery. In addition, there was no extended follow-up of the families or their children.

In 1984, England and Jacobvitz concluded a major study of 160 single-parent mothers.[30] Each mother had at least one child under the age of five. The sample was divided into three groups: severe physical child abuse, including being struck by objects or burned; borderline child abuse, including weekly spankings; and, finally, those children who were being raised by another caretaker. The researchers found a 70 percent intergenerational transmission of violence for those mothers who had suffered severe abuse as a child.

In 1990, Cappell and Heiner analyzed 888 childrearing families and measured the incidence of aggression in the respondent's families.[31] The presence or absence of aggression was classified into family member relationships: husband to wife aggression, wife to husband aggression, and respondent to child aggression. These researchers found that women who witnessed or experienced violence as children were more likely to discipline their own children aggressively. Perhaps more important, these scholars suggested that children who are raised in a violent family learn or inherit vulnerability. Cappell and Heiner theorize that this intergenerational transmission of vulnerability causes men and women to provoke violence, accept violence as normal, and select aggressive partners. These scholars rightfully explain that this research is limited because the same group was composed only of intact couples.

Cycle of Violence and Aggression

Dodge and his associates examined the effect of the cycle of violence on development of aggressive tendencies in children.[32] They studied a representative sample of 309 four-year-olds in kindergarten. This research was multisite in nature, with children being selected from Nashville and Knoxville, Tennessee, as well as Bloomington, Indiana. The researchers interviewed the mothers, evaluated the children, and received responses regarding the children's behavior from school personnel, peer ratings, and direct observation.

They found that children who had been physically abused were more aggressive toward other children than those who had not been harmed.[33] The teacher-rated aggression index for abused children was 93 percent higher than for nonabused children. The researchers also found that abused children were less able to process information and solve interpersonal problems. Although the authors accurately point out several caveats to their study, it does demonstrate the harm inflicted on children by abuse.

This harm may translate into future acts of aggression that take the form of crime against society. One comprehensive study in this area of child abuse and delinquency was undertaken by Widom in 1989.[34] She followed 1,575 cases from childhood through young adulthood. The study compared arrest records of two groups:

- One group was composed of 908 children with documented histories of abuse or neglect.
- The control group was composed of 667 children with no reported incidents of child abuse.

These groups were tracked through official records over the next fifteen to twenty years. The children were eleven years old or younger at the time of the abuse; therefore, an inherent weakness in the Straus research was avoided. The study classified abuse into three distinct areas: physical, sexual, and neglect cases. Court and probation records were the source of data for the initial acts of abuse, and subsequent arrest data were obtained from federal, state, and local law enforcement agencies.

The study found that children who had been abused were more likely to commit crimes as juveniles and adults than the control group. Further, these children were arrested more often for violent crime (11 percent) than the nonabused children (8 percent). Those children who were physically abused were more likely to be arrested for a violent crime. Interestingly, this study pointed out that the next biggest arrest rate for violent crimes was for those children who had been neglected.

As this discussion illustrates, the cycle of violence theory continues to dominate the literature. This and other theories of family violence will continue to be researched in an attempt to find the cause of family violence, predict its occurrence, and search for a cure.

Other Theories Regarding Child Abuse

Theories of Physical Child Abuse

Rather than attempt to describe all acceptable theories of the causes of child abuse, this section will set forth one model that encompasses several different theories. Cynthia Crosson Tower established a series of categories that grouped several theories into three distinct models: (1) the psychopathological model; (2) the interactional model; and (3) the environmental–sociological–cultural model.[35]

The *psychopathological model* stresses the characteristics of the abuser as the primary cause of abuse. The abuser's personality predisposes the abuser to injure the child. This model includes three separate approaches to child abuse: (1) the psychodynamic model; (2) the mental illness model; and (3) the character-trait model.

The psychodymanic model is based on the work of C. Henry Kempe and Ray Helfer. This model theorized that a lack of bonding between the parent and child is an important factor in child abuse. This theory assumes that the abuser was part of a cycle of parental inadequacy. These individuals are unable to bond with children and when a crisis occurs, they respond with abusive acts. This model also assumes the abuser will engage in role reversal. In other words, the parents expect the child to nurture them instead of vice versa.

The mental illness model sets forth the proposition that the parent's mental illness is the primary cause of child abuse. This is an easy theory for laypersons to accept because its easy to believe that anyone who would repeatedly beat or torture a child must be crazy. Justice and Justice suggested this model as a viable category.[36] Although some scholars have found abusive parents to be mentally disturbed, many others argue that abusive parents do not fit any existing psychiatric classification. For example, Kempe found that fewer than 5 percent were psychotic.

The character-trait model focuses on specific traits of abusers without regard to how they acquired these traits. Scholars such as Merrill and Delsordo have categorized abusive parents by specific traits that cause child abuse.[37] Merrill's study included such traits as hostility, rigidity, passivity, dependence, and competitiveness. Delsordo's categorization of abusive parent's traits included mental illness, frustration and irresponsibility, and severe disciplinarian and misplaced abuse.

The *interactional model* views child abuse as a result of a dysfunctional system. This category of abuse focuses on the following factors in child abuse: (1) the role of the child, (2) chance events, and (3) the family structure.

The role of the child and the perceptions of the parent toward that child are viewed as a cause of child abuse by some scholars. Martin suggests that abuse not only requires a certain type of adult, but also that certain acts of the child trigger the abuse. If the parent has certain expectations that the child does not meet, abuse may occur.[38]

"Chance events" is the somewhat inaccurate name given to events which prevent the parent from bonding with the child. This lack of attachment is viewed as a predisposition toward child abuse. Lynch suggests that difficulties in pregnancy, labor, or delivery can have a bearing on the attachment of the mother to the child.[39]

The family structure model theorizes that child abuse is a result of a dysfunctional family. The adult members of the family blame the child for their own shortcomings, and this leads to abuse.

The *environmental–sociological–cultural model* views child abuse as a result of stresses in society that are the primary causes of abuse. This category of abuse includes the following causes of child abuse: (1) the environmental stress model; (2) the social learning model; (3) the social psychological model; and (4) the psychosocial systems model.

The environmental stress model accepts the proposition that factors such as lack of education, poverty, unemployment, or occupational stress result in child abuse. As these outside forces build, the parent or caretaker is unable to cope and reacts by hitting or injuring the child.

The social learning model emphasizes the inadequacy of the parenting skills of abusive parents. These parents never learned appropriate responses to childrearing and therefore their lack of skill leads to frustration. This frustration in turn causes abusive behavior.

The social psychological model assumes stress results from a number of social and psychological factors including marital disputes, unemployment, or too many or unwanted children. These factors induce stress that causes the individual to react to the child in an abusive manner.

The psychosocial systems model stresses that abuse results from interactions within the family. The family as a system is out of balance and incapable of caring for the child. The child becomes the target for family members' frustration, and abuse is the result.

As this discussion indicates, several theories attempt to explain who the abusers are and why they abuse children. Although no authority can point to one single cause of child abuse, it is clear that it continues to occur. The causes of child physical abuse are multifaceted; therefore, it is necessary to review who are the victims or recipients of this violence to attempt to understand this phenomenon more fully.

Theories of Child Neglect

Are poor children neglected and rich kids well cared for? Unfortunately, a substantial number of people in society equate poverty with neglect, but simply being poor does not make a neglectful parent. There are children who live at the edge of poverty or below the poverty level and are loved and nurtured. On the other hand, there are children who live in $1 million homes but are neglected or psychologically abused on a daily basis. The causes of neglect are varied and wide ranging.

Polansky and his colleagues in their classic text, *Damaged Parents: An Anatomy of Child Neglect*, established three major causes of neglect: (1) economic causes, (2) ecological causes, and (3) personalistic causes.[40] The *economic theory* suggests that neglect is caused by stress as a result of living in poverty. The *ecological theory* views the family behavior and neglect as a result of social causes. The *personalistic theory* attributes child neglect to individual personality characteristics of the caretakers.

Numerous studies have indicated that poverty is an important factor in the parents' ability to care for their children, and the question must be asked, "Does poverty cause neglect, or is poverty the result of the parents' inability to function?"[41]

Some scholars have indicated that families who neglect their children live in an environment that is unfriendly and characterized by low morale and hopelessness.[42] As indicated, the issue is whether environment causes neglect or whether the environment is a characteristic of the parents' inability to function.

The more reasoned approach seems to be that of the personalistic theory. In this approach, neglect is viewed as being caused by complex maladaptive interactions and/or lack of essential caretaking behaviors that are influenced by the level of parental skill, knowledge deficits, and other stress factors.[43] The following is a list of some important characteristics of parents or caretakers who neglect their children:[44]

> Inability to plan: These parents lack the ability to establish goals, objectives, and direction. These parents may have low frustration levels and little ability to delay gratification.
>
> Lack of knowledge: Parents have little or no knowledge about children's needs, housekeeping skills, cooking, and so on.
>
> Lack of judgment: Parents may leave a young child alone and unsupervised.
>
> Lack of motivation: Parents lack energy, have little desire to learn, and have no other standard of comparison. These parents are apathetic or ineffective in that they are withdrawn and feel that nothing is worth doing.

There are other models that profile personalities of neglectful parents or caretakers, and no one study or theory has gained universal acceptance. The next section examines an even more controversial subject—the reason why perpetrators molest young children.

Theories of Child Sexual Abuse

Numerous studies indicate that child abusers do not fit any stereotype. The common lay perception that all abusers are ugly old men who prey on children is simply not true, but researchers have attempted to find a common thread or factor that connects all child abusers. They have examined the degree of violence, the age of the victim, the age and education of the offender, preoffense social and occupational adjustment, alcohol abuse, physiological responses of offenders, and aggression. Conti reviewed the literature in this area and described the following factors that were considered important when evaluating characteristics of abusers:[45]

1. Measurement of sexual arousal is essential to discriminate between various categories of sexual offenders.
2. The role of sexual fantasies with children is important due to its connection to deviant sexuality. Fantasies about children coupled with masturbation during these fantasies serve as a form of rehearsal for contact with the victims.
3. The types of rationalizations used by adult offenders who have sexual relations with children commonly take the form of statements or thoughts to the effect: "A child who doesn't resist really wants to have sex," or "Having sex with a child is the best way to teach her about sex," or "You become closer to the child when you share sex with him," and so on.

In addition to the various forms of psychopathology present in child abuse, Finkelhor established four factors involved in sexual abuse.[46] He called this theory the *four preconditions model of sexual abuse,* which establishes preconditions that create a personal and social context for expressing sexually abusive behaviors:

(1) motivation to abuse sexually; (2) overcoming internal inhibitors; (3) factors predisposing to overcome external inhibitors; and (4) factors predisposing to overcome the child's resistance.

Precondition I: Motivation to Abuse Sexually.   The motivation to abuse a child sexually includes emotional congruence, sexual arousal, and blockage. Emotional congruence involves satisfying an emotional need by relating to the child in a sexual manner. Sexual arousal occurs when the child becomes the source of sexual gratification. Blockage occurs when other alternative forms of sexual satisfaction are not present, not available, or less satisfying. The motivation to abuse a child is based on individual as well as sociological grounds. Individual explanations include the need for power and control, unconscious reenactment of a previous childhood trauma, and biological abnormality. Sociological reasons include the male-oriented society that demands male dominance, child pornography, and erotic portrayal of children in the media.

Precondition II: Overcoming Internal Inhibitors.   The perpetrator must overcome internal controls that would prevent him from sexually abusing the victim. Some of these controls are overcome by use of alcohol or drugs, existing psychosis, inability of the offender to identify with the needs of the victim, weak criminal sanctions against offenders, and child pornography.

Precondition III: Factors Predisposing to Overcome External Inhibitors.   These conditions are outside the control of the perpetrator. These factors include social situations such as the type and amount of supervision a child receives, lack of a parental figure who is close to or protective of the victim, and unusual sleeping or living arrangements. Additionally, the lack of social support for mothers, barriers to equality, and erosion of the family's social networks contribute to the ability of the offender to overcome external inhibitors.

Precondition IV: Factors Predisposing to Overcome the Child's Resistance. These factors concern the victim's ability to resist the sexual advances. The child may be emotionally insecure, deprived, or lacking in sexual experience or knowledge. The victim may feel powerless, or a situation of trust exists between the offender and the victim.

There is no distinct or clear answer as to why adults sexually abuse children. The offender may commit these acts for a variety of reasons. Both psychological forces and social structure enter into this complex mesh of forces to allow individuals to engage in sexual activities with young victims.

We traditionally think of the abuser as a man and the victim as a girl. However, studies indicate that boys may be the victim of sexual abuse at a higher rate than previously thought. One study in San Jose, California, indicates a rise in the reported incidents of sexual abuse of boys.[47] Between 1970 and 1975, only 5 percent of the reported victims of sex abuse were boys. However, this figure rose to over 22 percent by 1986.[48]

Boys who are victims of abuse may not report the acts or incidents for several reasons. First, boys may not want to be viewed as victims or sissies or be perceived as weak. Second, boys normally do not have to account for their movements and are given greater degrees of freedom and less protection through supervision and therefore parents may not notice unusual behavior that may indicate sexual abuse. And third, our stereotypes lead us to look for abuse with girls, not with boys.[49]

The high-risk years for child sexual abuse range from between four and nine years old.[50] At the former age, children are naive and sexually curious, and by the time they reach the age of nine, their loyalty, desire to please, and trust of adults are traits manipulated by offenders to accomplish their goal of molestation. Generally, sexual abuse is terminated by the time the child reaches fourteen. This termination occurs because the victim may threaten the offender with disclosure or engage in activities, such as running away, that would lead authorities to suspect abuse.[51]

Contrary to popular belief, the actual physical attractiveness of the female child has little if anything to do with whether the child is a victim of molestation. Additionally, the seductiveness of the female child is now discounted as a contributing factor in sexual abuse situations. Although we may be able to dispel certain stereotypes about female victims, there needs to be more research on the issue of male victims. Two scholars have isolated at least one factor that may identify why certain male children are molested. Finkelhor and Porter suggested that the less assertive boys are more likely to be victims of sexual abuse.[52]

Children are at a higher risk of sexual abuse if they are socially isolated, left alone, and unsupervised. If the mother is absent from the home for long periods, either because of work or other commitments, the child is more likely to be abused. Some authorities theorize that the presence of a stepfather in the home adds to the risk of sexual abuse.[53] These factors establish situations in which the child becomes vulnerable to the perpetrator.

We are still researching and learning about the characteristics of those who abuse and why certain children are chosen for abuse over others. Misconceptions and stereotypes have contributed to the confusion in this very important area. We do not have all the answers on why and who is involved in child sexual abuse, but we are making progress.

There are normally two situations or factual patterns that occur in child sexual abuse: one is a sudden, violent assault by a stranger and involves the use of force or fear, and the other involves sexual activities by a perpetrator known by the child. The former is the classic rape of the victim, which is discussed in detail in Chapter 8. This section discusses those situations in which the offender knows or is related to the victim. As with most relationships, child sexual abuse requires interaction between the perpetrator and the victim. There is often a progression of acts that lead to the sexual encounter. Tower established five stages or phases of child sexual abuse: the engagement phase, sexual interaction, the secrecy phase, the disclosure phase, and the suppression phase.[54]

The engagement phase involves the perpetrator gaining access to the victim. This access may occur as a result of a living arrangement, a trip, babysitting, or any other situation in which the offender has an opportunity to discuss sex with the child without supervision of any other adult. The adult may offer rationalizations or attempt to convince the victim that sex is proper. Comments such as "This is how daddies teach their daughters about sex" and "You will make me and your mommy happy by doing this" are examples of verbal communications that occur during this stage. The perpetrator may engage in what appears to be "accidents" to see how the child responds. Acts such as walking in while the child is bathing or allowing the child to see the adult nude or view the offender's genitals are examples of these types of actions. If the child reacts negatively to these tentative approaches, some offenders will back off and try another approach.

The sexual interaction phase involves actual sexual contact. This may range from viewing the child nude or having the child observe the adult without clothes, fondling the child and vice versa, oral sex, or sexual penetration. Groth established two categories of sexual contacts: pressured sex and forced sex.[55]

Pressured sex involves the perpetrator attempting to convince the child to engage in sexual activity. This is accomplished by bribing or rewarding the child with attention, praise, or material goods. If the child refuses the advances, the perpetrator will not resort to force to achieve sexual contact. Forced sex involves the threat of harm or use of force to complete the act. The perpetrator may use his position of authority as an adult to obtain compliance from the child. Other offenders will carry out the act in the traditional sexual assault form of rape.

The secrecy phase involves the perpetrator convincing the child to remain silent about the acts. This allows the offender to continue with sexual relations over an extended period of time. The adult may threaten, blackmail, or bribe the child to remain silent. The most common tactic is intimidation.[56] Statements such as "If they found out, your daddy would have to leave you and your mommy" are common forms of threats that may occur during this stage of sexual exploitation.

The disclosure phase may occur relatively soon after the act or at a later time when the victim is an adult. The disclosure may occur accidentally when the participants are observed in the act of sex or when the child visits a physician and is diagnosed as the victim of sexual abuse. Intentional disclosure involves the child informing someone of the actions of the perpetrator. Many victims of sexual abuse do not disclose its existence until they are adults and out of the reach, authority, or power of the offender. Occasionally, adult women will disclose the activity because they are afraid the perpetrator may be molesting a younger brother or sister.

The suppression phase occurs after disclosure or discovery of the abuse and involves caretakers attempting to force the child to recant the accusations of abuse. If the molester is a father figure or sole support for family, pressure may be brought on the child to keep quiet. Some families will promise the child that it will not happen again. Other techniques involve telling the child that a loved one will go to prison if the child continues to tell others of the molestation. The purpose of these activities is to get the child to recant so that no action will be taken by the authorities.

This discussion has focused on the progression of sexual abuse. In these situations, the offender is usually known to the victim. These activities may occur with a relative or a caretaker who is associated with the family. Child sexual abuse is a serious form of victimization that has longlasting consequences for the victim. However, there are other forms of child abuse that also have long-term consequences for their victims. The next section addresses some of these special types of child abuse.

Special Types of Child Abuse

Sibling Abuse

Sibling abuse is probably the most common form of family violence in the United States. Gelles and Cornell stated this fact in another manner when they wrote that the most commonly victimized family members are siblings.[57] If sibling abuse is in fact the most common form of family violence, why is there such a reluctance on the part of society and professionals to discuss it? There are very few texts devoted exclusively to this topic. Most academic articles dealing with child abuse may include as an afterthought a discussion of sibling abuse. Two areas of sibling abuse that are being examined in some detail are incest and the abuse of a sibling by parents.

There are a variety of reasons for this lack of discussion regarding sibling abuse. We consider sibling aggression to be a normal part of growing up. As the Focus box indicates, we have all heard excuses for sibling aggression. They are common refrains in families with more than one child. As a society we tend to minimize sibling aggression. Yet early studies in New York and Philadelphia indicated that 3 percent of all homicides committed in those cities were committed by siblings against siblings![58] In another classic study of sibling abuse, Steinmetz found that parents did not consider their children's physical aggression toward siblings as abuse. They would even talk with friends, neighbors, and relatives about the aggression—viewing it as an inevitable part of siblings growing up.[59]

No one has accurate figures on the nature, type, or extent of sibling abuse. However, most authorities agree that it is the most common form of family violence. The popular media first addressed this issue in 1979 with a report in *U.S. News & World Report* that stated 138,000 children aged three to seventeen had used a weapon on a sibling within the last year.[60] In a 1980 study, Straus, Gelles, and

---

FOCUS: Sibling Abuse and Excuses

How many of the following excuses have you heard used to justify one sibling's acts toward another?

Don't worry about it, its just normal sibling rivalry.

They were just playing doctor.

Kids will be kids.

He really didn't mean to hurt his sister; he loves her.

It's only normal childhood curiosity.

Kids are always calling each other names.

I told him not to hit her again.

They will grow out of it.

Steinmetz reported that 82 percent of parents of children surveyed considered sibling violence to be the most common form of intrafamily violence.[61] In another early study, Steinmetz (1981) found that a clear majority of children used physical violence to resolve conflict with their siblings.[62]

In 1988, Pagelow presented the findings of her study of 1025 college students at three university campuses in southern California at the annual meeting of the Pacific Sociological Association. Pagelow's survey revealed that almost half of the siblings living at home at the age of twelve were either aggressors or victims of violent acts of kicking and punching. Ten percent said their siblings beat them, and 4 percent stated that their siblings had threatened them with a gun or knife or used a gun or knife against them.

In 1992, Carson and Daane presented the results of their study of 3357 students in an Indiana school district at the annual meeting of the American Sociological Association. Seventy-four percent of the students approved of hitting their sibling if they were reacting to being hit first. Forty-three percent approved of striking their sibling if that sibling broke the stereo. Thirty-eight percent believed it was appropriate to hit their sibling if that sibling made fun of the aggressor in front of friends. Almost one-quarter of all students surveyed approved of hitting their sibling if there was an argument and the other sibling did not listen to reason.

These and other studies indicate that sibling abuse is a common form of family violence. Its existence can no longer be denied; however, we are still studying its nature, causation, and extent. As with many other forms of family violence, there is no one single definition of sibling abuse.

The question then must be, do we really need a separate definition of sibling abuse, or would other definitions within this text cover most if not all of the situations that arise in which children commit acts of violence toward their siblings? Earlier in this chapter, *physical* child abuse was defined as any act that results in a nonaccidental physical injury by a person who has care, custody, or control of a child. Many acts of sibling abuse occur when the older or more powerful sibling has care or control over the victim. However, there are acts of sibling abuse that occur within the home when parents are present but unaware of the acts of the abusing sibling. Therefore, the definition of physical child abuse does not cover all situations that might arise in sibling abuse. Although it is possible to draft a broad definition of child abuse that would cover acts of sibling abuse, by defining it as a separate and distinct form of child abuse, its importance in any study of family violence is highlighted.

Sibling abuse is any form of physical, mental, or sexual abuse inflicted by one child in a family unit upon another. This definition covers the various types of abuse that will be discussed later. Additionally, it does not require that the children be related by birth. There are situations in which children from different marriages end up in the same household. Finally, the definition uses the term *child*. This term requires further explanation. There are reported incidents of one sibling abusing the other after they have reached the age of eighteen. However, it appears that the vast majority of abuse occurs when the victim and/or the abuser are under the age of adulthood. Therefore, *child* is defined as a person under the age of legal majority.

This age is typically stated to be eighteen. It should be clear that this definition does not include abuse of different children within the same family by an adult member of the household.

Munchausen Syndrome by Proxy

One type of child abuse has recently become a topic of discussion.[63] *Munchausen syndrome by proxy* is defined as a psychiatric disorder whereby individuals intentionally produce physical symptoms of illness in their children. It is still being researched but has surfaced as a diagnosis in a number of cases.[64]

The term "Munchausen syndrome" was coined by Richard Asher in 1951 to describe patients who fabricated histories of illness. These individuals described complex medical histories and often displayed symptoms of the alleged disease. These fabrications invariably led to complex medical interventions and hospitalizations. Asher named this disorder after Baron von Munchausen. Hieronymous Karl Fredrich von Munchausen was an eighteenth-century German baron and mercenary officer in the Russian cavalry. The baron was famous for dramatizing his "amazing" adventures. Some might describe him as a world-class teller of tall tales.

There is some debate as to who first used the term Munchausen syndrome by proxy. Money used it in 1976 to describe four children who were so severely abused that they were dwarfed.[65] However, in 1977 Meadow also used the term to describe the more commonly accepted definition of this form of abuse. Meadow examined two children who were being poisoned by a parent. The parent knew what was happening but encouraged the medical professionals to search for a diagnosis. This diagnostic process was painful and dangerous to the children.[66]

The warning signs of the disorder include repeated hospitalizations and medical evaluations without definitive diagnosis; inappropriate symptoms and/or medical signs that are inconsistent; signs and symptoms that disappear when away from the parent; a parent who welcomes medical tests of the child, even if they are painful; increased parental uneasiness as the child recovers; and a parent who is less concerned with the child's health and more concerned about spending time with hospital staff.[67]

Today, professionals in the field have come to the conclusion that Munchausen syndrome by proxy is of continuing concern. Some authorities predict that 10 percent of these child victims will die at the hands of their parents.[68] Professionals in the field must recognize this form of child victimization and respond accordingly.

Ritual Abuse

On a daily basis, we are beginning to hear tales of horror and disgust involving children being victimized in so-called satanic cults. Adults who were victims are coming forward and shedding light on this new form of family violence. Just as we were slow in accepting the fact that fathers were molesting their young daughters, so are we as a society hesitant to believe that many of the described practices of ritualistic abuse occur. Child abuse, neglect, and sexual molestation are difficult to accept, but satanic ritualistic abuse not only causes harm to our children, it also strikes a cord in our collective consciousness as to the evil that is perpetrated by our species. It is for these reasons that we must examine this controversial and highly emotional issue.

Professionals are only now beginning to treat survivors of ritualistic abuse. However, controversy rages as to the validity of many of the claims made by these survivors and the extent of their abuse. Other scholarly works in the field are silent or only briefly touch on this new issue.[69] Even though this is a relatively new form of family violence and we are still researching its causes and consequences, it is included in this text for purposes of familiarizing students with the general nature and types of ritualistic abuse.

During the early twentieth century one of the most important figures in the development of magic and mysticism appeared. His name was Aleister Crowley and he published the book *Magick in Theory and Practice.*[70] Crowley's book was a "how to" for neophytes who wanted to experiment with magic. It told them what to do, what to say, and how to feel. For those who were unable to achieve the desired psychological state, Crowley recommended the use of various drugs including hashish, mescaline, or cocaine.

The 1960s and 1970s were decades of rebellion in the United States. The Age of Aquarius was upon us. The concept of mind-expanding drugs gained widespread acceptance. During this period of change, it was popular to question authority and beliefs. The advent of birth control, the first stirrings of the women's movement, and the breakdown of traditional roles all combined to force change in America. Magic, free love, and drugs were accepted tenets in our life.

During this period, Anton LaVey established the Church of Satan and drafted *The Satanic Bible.* Although he was denounced as a fraud by some, LaVey had a far greater impact than most people were willing to admit. He took the position that individuals could make a conscious choice to live in a world without God, and then he thrust this idea upon the general public.[71] A passage from *The Satanic Bible* illustrates the logic and allure of LaVey's teaching:

> *Satanists are encouraged to indulge in the seven deadly sins as they need hurt no one; they were only invented by the Christian Church to [e]nsure guilt on the part of its followers. Their Christian Church knows that it is impossible for anyone to avoid committing these sins, as they are things which we, human beings, most naturally do.*[72]

It should be stressed that the Church of Satan does not condone ritualistic child abuse. It is listed in the telephone pages and has its headquarters or grotto in San Francisco.

In 1980, the reading public was shocked by a book that brought the specter of satanism and ritualistic abuse directly into their homes. *Michelle Remembers,* a book written by psychiatrist Lawrence Pazder and Michelle Smith, recounts a tale of satanism and ritual abuse that happened to Michelle as a child at the hands of a satanic cult in Victoria, Canada.[73] The book describes how Michelle recovered her memories during therapy. One memory included a claim that she was a designated bride of Satan and was to be presented to him at a ceremony that occurs only every twenty-eight years during the Year of the Beast. One of the most controversial portions of *Michelle Remembers* details how she resisted Satan's attempts to claim her with the help of the Virgin Mary.

In the late 1980s, tales began to surface of massive sexual abuse at daycare centers. Americans were angered and repulsed by allegations of ritualistic child abuse allegedly perpetrated on scores of preschool children by Peggy McMartin Buckey and her son, Raymond Buckey, at the Virginia McMartin Preschool in Manhattan Beach, California. Several children testified that they had been subjected to satanic rituals, including animal sacrifices and sexual abuse inside churches. After one of the longest and most expensive trials in the United States, all the defendants were acquitted. Although the defendants were found not guilty, the trial raised our consciousness regarding this new form of child abuse.

The nature and extent of allegations of sexual abuse of children in daycare settings in recent years is a controversial subject among clinicians. Cases of sexual abuse in daycare often involve numerous factors that differ from what clinicians are typically confronted with in cases of intrafamilial sexual abuse. These factors include the young age of the child victims, the involvement of multiple victims and multiple perpetrators, women as perpetrators, use of extreme threats, and in some cases ritualistic activities.[74]

Ritualistic child abuse in daycare centers is a particularly disturbing type of reported daycare center abuse. Children who have been ritualistically abused describe participation in group ceremonies, use of chants and songs, adults dressed in costumes and masks, threats with supernatural powers often involving Satan or demons, the sacrifice of animals, the ingestion of blood, feces, and urine, and murders.[75]

The definition of ritualistic child abuse is still evolving. One of the most cited definitions was established by the Los Angeles County Commission for Women in 1989. This commission set forth the following definition of ***ritual abuse***:

> *A brutal form of abuse of children consisting of physical, sexual, and psychological abuse, and involving the use of rituals. Ritual does not necessarily mean satanic. However, most survivors state that they were ritually abused as part of satanic worship for the purpose of indoctrinating them into satanic beliefs and practices. Ritual abuse rarely consists of a single episode. It usually involves repeated abuse over an extended period of time.*[76]

As the definition states, ritualistic child abuse does not have to involve religion. However, most of the survivors claim the ritualistic abuse was definitely tied to satanic worship. All rituals are not evil. The word *ritual* is defined simply as the established form for a ceremony, a system of rites, any formal and customarily repeated act or series of acts.[77] It is only when ritual is combined with abuse that we as a society can intervene. We have established that ritualistic child abuse involves long-term repeated abuse of the most severe form. These abuses may be inflicted and believed justified because of certain religious tenets held by the cult or organization.

It would be easy to explain satanism as the creation of a deranged mind. Doing so would permit us to dismiss it as something so out of the ordinary that it doesn't bear thinking about, except in a curious nonanalytical way. But this approach does not allow for a complete understanding of this form of family violence. Although historians still dispute the historic nature and extent of satanism and many present-day scholars continue to discount stories of ritualistic child abuse, the fact remains that more people are coming forward and claiming to be victims of this type of abuse. It is therefore imperative that professionals in the field have a general understanding of ritualistic abuse.

Summary

At this stage in the development of our society, we cannot prevent all forms of child abuse, so we must be alert to its existence and understand some of the more common theories on how and why it occurs. We have won half the battle if we are aware that child abuse occurs in all segments of our society. On the other hand, we must be willing to accept reasonable explanations of injuries. Children are active human beings—as such they will trip, fall, and run into objects. Our goal is to be able to distinguish between a normal injury and a nonaccidental one. This ability may save a child's life.

In many instances, there is no clear line between simply poor parenting and neglect. Each situation must be evaluated on its own merits, and professionals must look at the totality of the circumstances in determining whether the child is a victim of neglect. The causes of neglect are varied and do not simply rest on the assumption that poverty is the cause. The rich and famous can, and do, subject their children to acts that are clearly child neglect.

Child sexual abuse is one of the most emotional areas of family violence. It is a crime that occurs in secret and may last only moments or for years. Even the definition of child sexual abuse is shrouded in controversy. Although we cannot explain why it occurs, some scholars have established certain theories or characteristics regarding child sexual abuse.

Unlike other forms of child abuse, sexual molestation may not leave scars that are visible to other persons. Sexual abuse in children takes many forms. Scholars have established certain steps or a progression in the nonviolent sexual abuse of children. These include a gradual increase in sexual activity culminating in intercourse.

The consequences of child sexual abuse are traumatic and long lasting, and various scholars have attempted to study the ramification of this type of child maltreatment. Although disagreement exists among these authorities, all agree that it is a serious problem that must be studied and hopefully a solution found to ease the pain of the survivors of sexual abuse.

The victimization of children is an emotional and complex topic. Not only are children kidnapped, raped, and killed by strangers, sometimes they face a worse fate in their own homes. Understanding the types, extent, and theories surrounding child abuse will benefit any professional who works in the criminal justice field.

Key Terms

Physical child abuse may be defined as any act which results in a nonaccidental physical injury by a person who has care, custody, or control of a child.

Child neglect is the negligent treatment or maltreatment of a child by a parent or caretaker under circumstances indicating harm or threatened harm to the child's health or welfare.

Child sexual abuse is sexual exploitation or sexual activities with children under circumstances which indicate that the child's health or welfare is harmed or threatened.

Intrafamilial sexual abuse includes incest and refers to any type of exploitative sexual contact occurring between relatives.

Extrafamilial sexual abuse refers to exploitative sexual contact with perpetrators who may be known to the child (neighbors, babysitters, live-in partners) or unknown to the child.

Cycle of violence theory asserts that violent behavior is learned within the family and bequeathed from one generation to the next.

Psychopathological model stresses the characteristics of the abuser as the primary cause of abuse. The abuser's personality predisposes the abuser to injure the child.

Interactional model views child abuse as a result of a dysfunctional system.

Environmental–sociological–cultural model views child abuse as a result of stresses in society that are the primary causes of abuse.

Economic theory suggests that neglect is caused by stress as a result of living in poverty.

Ecological theory views the family behavior and neglect as a result of social causes.

Personalistic theory attributes child neglect to individual personality characteristics of the caretakers.

Four preconditions model of sexual abuse establishes preconditions that create a personal and social context for expressing sexually abusive behaviors.

Sibling abuse is any form of physical, mental, or sexual abuse inflicted by one child in a family unit upon another.

Child is defined as a person under the age of legal majority. This age is typically stated to be eighteen.

Munchausen syndrome by proxy is a psychiatric disorder whereby individuals intentionally produce physical symptoms of illness in their children.

Ritual abuse is a brutal form of abuse of children consisting of physical, sexual, and psychological abuse, and involving the use of rituals. Ritual does not necessarily mean satanic. However, most survivors state that they were ritually abused as part of satanic worship for the purpose of indoctrinating them into satanic beliefs and practices. Ritual abuse rarely consists of a single episode. It usually involves repeated abuse over an extended period of time.

Discussion Questions

1. If a child is injured and the physician is uncertain of whether the injury is physical child abuse, should the physician alert the police? Why? Why not? Would it make any difference if the physician knew the parents and had been to their home for a social event?

2. What is the most serious form of physical child abuse? Why?

3. If a child has been seriously injured by his mother, should that child ever be returned to the mother's care? Why?

4. Should convicted child abusers be required to inform all social partners of their crimes? What if the criminal is dating someone who has small children and she asks him to watch her children while she goes to work for the day?

5. Based on your reading, what is the single most important cause of neglect? Why?

6. Based on your reading of this chapter, can you provide a more comprehensive definition of child sexual abuse? What about a more specific definition?

7. If you were a professional working in an environment that includes young children and you observed a child exhibiting symptoms that led you to suspect child sexual abuse, what would you do?

8. Should we punish or treat child molesters? Because some would argue that you can never cure a pedophile, does this mean we should lock the offender up forever?

Suggested Readings

Vincent B. Van Hasselt, et al., (eds.), *Handbook of Family Violence,* (Plenum Press, New York) 1988.

R. T. Ammerman & M. Hersen, *Assessment of Family Violence,* (John Wiley & Sons, New York) 1992.

R. Helfer & C. H. Kempe, (eds.), *The Battered Child,* 2nd ed. (University of Chicago Press, Chicago) 1974.

G. Gerber, C. Ross & E. Zigler, (eds.), *Child Abuse: An Agenda for Action,* (Oxford University Press, New York) 1980.

R. Ammerman & M. Hersen, (eds.), *Case Studies in Family Violence,* (Plenum Press, New York) 1991.

D. Cicchetti & V. Carlson, (eds.), *Child Maltreatment,* (Cambridge University Press, Cambridge, Mass.) 1989.

J. L. Mullings, J. W. Marquart & D. J. Hartley (eds.), *The Victimization of Children,* (Hawthorn Press, New York) 2003.

L. A. Fontes, *Child Abuse and Culture: Working with Diverse Families,* (The Guilford Press, New York) 2005.

Child Physical and Sexual Abuse: Guidelines for Treatment, (National Crime Victims Research center and Center for Sexual Assault and Traumatic Stress, Charleston, S. C.) 2004.

T. P. Doyle, A. W. R. Sipe & P. J. Wall, *Sex, Priests, and Secret Codes: The Catholic Church's 2000-Year Paper Trail of Sexual Abuse,* (Bonus Books, Los Angeles, Calif.) 2006.

J. E. B. Myers, *Meyers on Evidence in Child, Domestic and Elder Abuse,* (Aspen Publishers, New York) 2005.

D. Finkelhor, *Child Sexual Abuse: New Theories and Research,* (Free Press, New York) 1984.

D. G. Kilpatrick, C. N. Edmonds & A.K. Seymour, *Rape in America: A Report to the Nation,* (National Victims Center, Arlington, Va.) 1992.

Cynthia Crosson Tower, *Understanding Child Abuse and Neglect,* 2nd ed. (Allyn & Bacon, Boston) 1993.

N. Polansky, M. Chambers, E. Buttenwieser & D. Williams, *Damaged Parents: An Anatomy of Child Neglect,* (University of Chicago Press, Chicago) 1981.

M. A. Straus, R. J. Gelles & S. K. Steinmetz, *Behind Closed Doors: Violence in the American Family,* (Doubleday, New York) 1980.

D. K. Sakheim & S. E. Devine, *Out of Darkness,* (Lexington Books, New York) 1992.

Endnotes

1. See, for example, Vincent B. Van Hasselt, et al., (eds.), *Handbook of Family Violence,* (Plenum Press, New York) 1988.
2. R. T. Ammerman & M. Hersen, *Assessment of Family Violence,* (John Wiley & Sons, New York) 1992.
3. J. Meyers, *Evidence in Child Abuse and Neglect,* 2nd ed. (John Wiley & Sons, New York) 1992.
4. This is a shortened version of the definition contained in the Child Abuse Prevention and Treatment Act of 1974, which is one of the most widely adopted statutes defining child sexual abuse.
5. D. A. Wolfe, V. V. Wolfe & C. L. Best, "Child Victims of Sexual Assault," in V .B. Van Hasselt, R. L. Morrison, A. S. Bellack & M. Hersen, (eds.), *Handbook of Family Violence,* (Plenum Press, New York) 1988.
6. J. R. Conte, "Victims of Child Sexual Abuse," in R. T. Ammerman & M. Hersen, (eds.), *Treatment of Family Violence,* (John Wiley & Sons, New York) 1990, pp. 64–65.
7. S. Radbill, "A History of Child Abuse and Infanticide," in R. Helfer & C. H. Kempe, (eds.), *The Battered Child,* 2nd ed. (University of Chicago Press, Chicago) 1974.
8. C. F. Potter, "Infanticides," in M. Leach, (ed.), *Dictionary of Folklore, Mythology and Legend,* vol. 1, (Funk & Wagnalls, New York) 1949.
9. N. C. Sorel, *Ever Since Eve: Personal Reflections on Childbirth,* (Oxford University Press, New York) 1984.
10. Andrea J. Sedlak & Diane D. Broadhurst, "Executive Summary of the Third National Incidence Study of Child Abuse and Neglect," Department of Health and Human Services, Washington, D.C. (1996).
11. R. Uviler, "Save Them from Their Saviors: The Constitutional Rights in the Family," in G. Gerber, C. Ross & E. Zigler, (eds.), *Child Abuse: An Agenda for Action,* (Oxford University Press, New York) 1980, pp. 147–155.
12. U.S. Department of Justice, Bureau of Justice Statistics, *Criminal Victimization in the United States, 1987,* (Government Printing Office, Washington, D.C.) 1989, Table 4.
13. Arthur H. Green, "Child Neglect," in R. Ammerman & M. Hersen, (eds.), *Case Studies in Family Violence,* (Plenum Press, New York) 1991, p. 135.
14. *Monitoring Child Neglect: Summary of Discussions of a Meeting Co-sponsored by the Centers for Disease Control and Prevent Child Abuse America,* Prevent Child Abuse America and Centers for Disease Control, Chicago, Ill. (March 29, 2002).
15. C. R. Hartman & A. W. Burgess, "Sexual Abuse in Children: Causes and Consequences," in D. Cicchetti & V. Carlson, (eds.), *Child Maltreatment,* (Cambridge University Press, Cambridge, Mass.) 1989, p. 98.
16. D. Finkelhor, *Sexually Victimized Children,* (Free Press, New York) 1979.
17. D. Finkelhor, *Child Sexual Abuse: Theories and Research,* (Free Press, New York) 1984.
18. D. Russell, *Rape in Marriage,* (Macmillan, New York) 1982.
19. L. Timnick, "22% in Survey Were Child Abuse Victims," *Los Angeles Times,* 1 (25 August 1985).
20. Friedrich, Grambsch, Broughton, Kuiper, & Beilke, "Normative Sexual Behavior in Children," 88 *Pediatrics,* 456 (1991).
21. D. G. Kilpatrick, C. N. Edmonds & A. K. Seymour, *Rape in America: A Report to the Nation,* (National Victims Center, Arlington, Va.) 1992.
22. David Finkelhor & Lisa Jones, "Explanations for the Decline in Child Sexual Abuse Cases," *Juvenile Justice Bulletin,* Office of Justice Programs, Washington, D.C. (January 2004).
23. C. R. Hartman & A. W. Burgess, "Sexual Abuse of Children," pp. 98–99.
24. Child Abuse and Neglect Fatalities: Statistics and Interventions, U.S. Department of Health and Human Services, (2004); available online: www.childwelfare.gov/pubs/factsheets/fata-lity.cfm
25. Lauren Perrotto, "Prospective vs. Retrospective in Child Fatality Review," *Unified Response,* Inter-Agency Council on Child Abuse and Neglect Associates, (Winter 2004), El Monte, Calif.

26. L. J. Siegal, *Criminology,* 3rd ed. (West Publishing Co., St Paul, Minn.) 1989, p. 188.

27. B. Steele & V. Pollock, "A Psychiatric Study of Parents Who Abuse Infants and Small Children," in R. Helfer & C. H. Kempe, (eds.), *The Battered Child Syndrome,* (University of Chicago Press, Chicago) 1968. It is interesting to note that later editions of this classic book on child abuse do not contain the article. For example, see the 4th edition published in 1987.

28. M. A. Straus, "Family Patterns in a Nationally Representative Sample," 3 *International Journal of Child Abuse and Neglect,* 23 (1979).

29. R. Hunter & N. Kilstrom, "Breaking the Cycle in Abusive Families," 136 *American Journal of Psychiatry,* 1320 (1979).

30. B. England & D. Jacobvitz, "Intergenerational Continuity of Parental Abuse: Causes and Consequences." Paper presented at the Conference on Biosocial Perspectives in Abuse and Neglect, York, Maine (1984).

31. C. Cappell & R. B. Heiner, "The Intergenerational Transmission of Family Aggression," 5(2) *Journal of Family Violence,* 135 (1990).

32. K. A. Dodge, J. E. Bates & G. S. Pettit, "Mechanisms in the Cycle of Violence," 250 *Science,* 1678 (December 1990).

33. Id. at p. 1681.

34. C. S. Widom, "The Cycle of Violence," *Research in Brief, National Institute of Justice* (U.S. Department of Justice, Washington, D.C.) October 1992.

35. Cynthia Crosson Tower, *Understanding Child Abuse and Neglect,* 2nd ed. (Allyn and Bacon, Boston) 1993.

36. B. Justice & R. Justice, *The Abusing Family,* (Human Services Press, New York) 1976, p. 37.

37. See J. D. Delsordo, "Protective Casework for Abused Children," 10 *Children,* (1963) 213–218.

38. H. P. Martin, (ed.), *The Abused Child,* (Ballinger, Cambridge, Mass.) 1976.

39. M. Lynch, "Risk Factors in the Child: A Study of Abused Children and Their Siblings," in H. P. Martin, (ed.), *The Abused Child,* (Ballinger, Cambridge, Mass.) 1976, pp. 43–56.

40. N. Polansky, M. Chambers, E. Buttenwieser & D. Williams, *Damaged Parents: An Anatomy of Child Neglect,* (University of Chicago Press, Chicago) 1981, p. 21.

41. See L. Young, *Wednesday's Children,* (McGraw-Hill New York) 1964; and S. N. Katz, *When Parents Fail,* (Beacon Press, Boston) 1971.

42. I. Wolock & B. Horowitz, "Child Maltreatment and Maternal Deprivation Among AFDC Families," 53 *Social Service Review,* 175–184 (1979).

43. D. J. Hansen & V. M. MacMilian, "Behavioral Assessment of Child Abuse and Neglectful Families: Recent Development and Current Issues," 14 *Behavior Modification,* 225–278 (1990).

44. H. B. Cantwell, "Child Neglect," in C. H. Kempe and R. E. Helfer, (eds.), *The Battered Child,* (University of Chicago Press, Chicago) 1980, pp. 183–197.

45. See J. Conti, "The Effects of Sexual Abuse on Children: A Critique and Suggestions for Future Research," 10 *Victimology: An International Journal,* 110–130 (1985); and J. Conti, I. Berliner, & J. Schurman, "The Impact of Sexual Abuse on Children: Final Report," Available from the authors at the University of Chicago, 969 E. 60th Street, Chicago, Ill., 60637.

46. D. Finkelhor, *Child Sexual Abuse: New Theories and Research,* (Free Press, New York) 1984.

47. E. Porter, *Treating the Young Male Victims of Sexual Assault,* (Safer Society Press, Syracuse, N.Y.) 1986.

48. Id.

49. A. N. Groth, *Men Who Rape,* (Plenum Press, New York) 1979.

50. D. J. Gelinas, "The Persisting Negative Effects of Incest," 46 *Psychiatry,* 312–322 (1983).

51. C. A. Courtios, "Studying and Counseling Women with Past Incest Experience," 5, *Victimology: An International Journal,* 322–334 (1980).

52. D. Finkelhor, *Child Sexual Abuse* See note #51 (1984) and E. Porter, *Treating the Young Male Victim of Sexual Assault.* See note #45 (1986).

53. D. Finkelhor, *Child Sexual Abuse,* (Free Press, New York) 1984.

54. C. C. Tower, *Understanding Child Abuse and Neglect,* 2nd ed. (Allyn and Bacon, Boston) 1993.

55. A. N. Groth, *Men Who Rape*, (Plenum Press, New York) 1979.

56. E. D. Farber, J. Showers, C. F. Johnson, J. A. Joseph & L. Oshins, "The Sexual Abuse of Children: A Comparison of Male and Female Victims," 13 *Journal of Clinical Child Psychology*, 294–297 (1984).

57. Richard J. Gelles & Claire Pedrick Cornell, *Intimate Violence in Families*, 2nd ed. (Sage, Newbury, Calif.) 1990, p. 85.

58. See M. Bard, "The Study and Modification of Intrafamily Violence," in J. L. Singer, (ed.), *The Control of Aggression and Violence*, (Academic Press, New York) 1971 for study of homicides in Philadelphia; and M. Wolfgang, *Patterns in Criminal Homicide*, (John Wiley, New York) 1958 for the study of homicides in New York.

59. S. K. Steinmetz, *The Cycle of Violence: Assertive, Aggressive, and Abusive Family Interaction*, (Prager, New York) 1971.

60. "Battered families: A growing nightmare," *U.S. News & World Report*, 60–61 (15 January, 1979).

61. M. A. Straus, R. J. Gelles & S. K. Steinmetz, *Behind Closed Doors: Violence in the American Family*, (Doubleday, New York) 1980.

62. S. K. Steinmetz, "A Cross-Cultural Comparison of Sibling Violence," 2 (3/4) *International Journal of Family Psychiatry*, 337–351 (1981).

63. See for example, David D. P. Jones, "The Syndrome of Munchausen by Proxy," 18 *Child Abuse and Neglect*, 769 (1994).

64. E. J. Kudsk & J. A. Nolan, "Munchausen Syndrome by Proxy: The Case for Adult Victims," paper presented at the annual meeting of Academy of Criminal Justice Sciences, Boston, (March 1995).

65. J. Money, "Munchausen's Syndrome by Proxy: Update," *Journal of Pediatric Psychology*, 583 (November 1986) discussing an earlier article that appeared in the *Bulletin of the American Academy of Psychiatry and the Law* in 1976.

66. R. Meadow, "Munchausen Syndrome by Proxy: The Hinterland of Child Abuse," *The Lancet*, 351 (1977).

67. S. J. Boros & L. C. Brubaker, "Munchausen Syndrome by Proxy," *FBI Law Enforcement Bulletin*, 16 (June 1992).

68. Id. at p. 20.

69. See D. Cicchetti & Vicki Carlson, (eds.), *Child Maltreatment*, (Cambridge University Press, Cambridge, Mass.) 1989; C. C. Tower, *Understanding Child Abuse and Neglect*, 2nd ed. (Allyn and Bacon, Boston 1993); R. T. Ammerman & M. Hersen, *Assessment of Family Violence*, (Wiley & Sons, New York) 1992 which do not discuss ritual abuse; and compare C. C. Kent, "Ritual Abuse," *Case Studies in Family Violence*, R. T. Ammerman & M. Hersen, (eds.), (Plenum Press, New York) 1991; and D. K. Sakheim & S. E. Devine, *Out of Darkness*, (Lexington Books, New York) 1992 which covers the entire realm of ritualistic abuse.

70. A. Crowley, *Magick in Theory and Practice*, (Dover, New York) 1924. Reprinted in 1976.

71. C. Raschke, *Painted Black: Satanic Crime in America*, p. 123.

72. A LaVey, *The Satanic Bible*, (Avon Books, New York) 1969, p. 77.

73. M. Smith & L. Pazder, *Michelle Remembers*, (Congdon & Lattes, New York) 1980.

74. For an excellent discussion of this area, see S. J. Kelly, R. Brant & J. Waterman, "Sexual Abuse of Children in Day Care Centers," 17 *Child Abuse & Neglect*, 71–89 (1993).

75. Id.

76. *Ritual Abuse: Definitions, Glossary, the Use of Mind Control*. (Ritual Abuse Task Force. Los Angeles County Commission For Women) September 15, 1989).

77. *Webster's Ninth New Collegiate Dictionary* (Merriam-Webster Inc., Springfield, Mass.) 1987, p. 1018.

11

ELDER VICTIMS

Chapter Outline

Learning Objectives

After reading this chapter, you should be able to:

- Discuss the nature and extent of elder abuse in the United States
- Define issues that affect the validity of examining the problem of elder abuse
- Explain the different causation theories of elder abuse
- Describe the various types of criminal victimizations and their impact on elders

Elder Abuse

Although we became aware of certain forms of family violence in the 1960s and 1970s, it wasn't until the 1980s that the plight of elder victims entered our national consciousness as a problem that must be dealt with. One of the first studies dealing with elder abuse was published in 1979. Block and Sinnott entitled their work "The Battered Elder Syndrome: An Exploratory Study." They contacted twenty-four agencies in Maryland and surveyed 427 professionals and 443 elders. They found twenty-six cases of elder abuse. Unfortunately, the study went no further, but it was the first step in the long process of recognizing that elders can be victims of family violence.[1] By 1988, the research examining elder abuse consisted of over two hunderd research papers.[2] Today, that number continues to expand rapidly. Although several problems exist in the study of elder abuse, defining the term itself and determining its extent are two of the most controversial and difficult to resolve.

Extent of the Problem

How pervasive is elder abuse? Domestic elder abuse, like other forms of family violence, occurs behind closed doors in the privacy of the home. One significant study of elder abuse published in 1988 by Pillemer and Finkelhor involved 2,020 Boston elders who were sixty-five and older and living on their own or with their families. This research found a rate of thirty-two abused elders per thousand. The results of this survey would translate into over 1 million abused elders in the United States in 1988.[3]

Estimates on the nature, type, and prevalence of elder abuse continue to vary widely. In 1989, one congressional committee estimated that 1.5 million cases of elder abuse occur each year.[4] More shocking is the fact that this figure has steadily increased by 0.5 million each year since 1980.[5] Callahan claims that between 4 and 10 percent of all elders suffer abuse.[6] Other researchers believe the figure is higher, contending that only one in six incidents of elder abuse is ever reported to the authorities.[7]

In February 2006, the National Committee for the Prevention of Elder Abuse and the National Adult Protective Services Association released its survey of *Abuse of Adults Age 60+.*[8] The findings show an alarming 19.7 percent increase in the total number of reported cases of elder and vulnerable adult abuse and neglect cases. Additionally, the report indicates that there has been a 15.6 percent increase in sustained or provable cases since 2000. Over 52 percent of the perpetrators of abuse were female. The most common relationship of the victims to the perpetrators was parent–adult child.

Controversy continues regarding who is the abused and who is the abuser—is it the children who abuse the parents? or the elder's wife? or the husband? This confusion is further illustrated by the fact that some authorities believe that victims are primarily women over the age of seventy-five,[9] whereas others believe that the wife is the one who perpetrates the abuse.[10] Other scholars argue that adult children inflict abuse on their parents. The Boston survey indicated elders were abused more by their spouses than by their children. This result is somewhat skewed once it is understood that elders live with spouses more than adult children and therefore the chance is greater of being abused by a spouse than by an adult child. Although both men and women may be victims of elder abuse, the abuse inflicted by husbands is more severe than that inflicted by wives. More research is necessary to determine the extent and nature of elder abuse, but the central issue is that abuse is likely to be inflicted by the people with whom the elder is living.

There is a continuing failure to report and act on this form of abuse and Decalmer lists two major factors that may contribute to this failure:

1. There is a failure to understand the size, severity, and nature of the problem because of the conflicting definitions of elder abuse.
2. The number of controlled studies and the case reporting methods that are used in most of the research in this area have produced difficulties in estimating the true extent of the various acts of abuse and neglect.[11]

In addition, methodology and sampling procedures differ from study to study. Some research focuses on the elderly population, other studies examine agency records, and still other investigations poll professionals. As a result, there are no definitive figures that are accepted by all scholars and researchers.

Definition

The term *elder abuse* was first used during congressional hearings in the late 1970s. The House Select Committee on Aging, chaired by Representative Claude Pepper (the Pepper Commission) examined the mistreatment of the elderly and introduced the term *elder abuse* to the nation.[12] However, coining a term does not always clearly define the parameters for the scholars and professionals trying to do the research.

Some scholars, when examining elder abuse, have included persons under the age of sixty in their research, whereas others simply include everyone who is over the age of sixty regardless of the circumstances.[13] Well-respected authorities defined elder abuse as occurring only between those who share a residence with the victim, and in other studies out-of-home caretakers were included.[14] The debate, confusion, and inability to agree on any acceptable conceptual framework from which to study elder abuse continue to cause problems in this area.

In an effort to clarify this confusion, some authorities attempted to develop a list of definitions involving abuse of the elderly by establishing typologies. Unfortunately, these typologies lacked uniformity and resulted in more confusion. Hudson and Johnson pointed out that some typologies differed considerably in defining neglect, whereas others classified withholding of personal care as physical abuse and/or psychological abuse.[15] As a result of this continuing confusion, other researchers began to attempt to frame the definition of elder abuse from a conceptional perspective. For example, some scholars placed the issue of elder abuse within the broad category of inadequate care.[16] However, the same problems that were faced in trying to establish an acceptable typology were present in the effort to conceptualize the whole issue.[17]

Several prominent scholars including Wolf, Pillemer, and Godkin subsequently distilled these various definitions down to a multifaceted definition that classified elder abuse into five areas:

1. *Physical abuse* includes the infliction of physical pain or injury, physical coercion, sexual molestation, or physical restraint.
2. *Psychological abuse* includes the infliction of mental anguish.
3. *Material abuse* includes the illegal or improper exploitation and/or use of funds or resources.
4. *Active neglect* includes the refusal or failure to undertake a caretaking obligation.
5. *Passive neglect* includes the refusal or failure to fulfill a caretaking obligation.[18]

This discussion clearly illustrates the difficulty in attempting to define the term *elder abuse* and helps to explain the continuing scholarly debate and controversy. Based on this confusion and conflict, a simple, clear definition of elder abuse may not be possible. However, for purposes of consistency with other definitions contained in this text, *elder abuse* is defined as conduct that results in the physical, psychological, or material harm, or neglect or injury to an elder. This definition applies both to domestic and institutional abuse. *Material* in the context of elder abuse refers to the exploitation or use of resources. An *elder* is a person sixty-five years or older. The initial age determination of sixty-five years is based on common acceptance of that age by most authorities, scholars, and professionals.[19] This age group may be further subdivided into those between sixty-five and seventy-five who are called the young-old and those above seventy-five who are referred to as the old-old.[20]

Elder abuse can occur in a domestic or institutional setting. Pillemer and Moore explained that despite two decades of state and federal regulation of nursing homes, abuse of the elderly still occurs on a regular basis.[21] The focus of this section will be on the domestic abuse aspect of this form of violence, as more research has been done in this area. However, abuse of the elderly in nursing homes and long-term care institutions is a fact of modern life and should not be forgotten or overlooked when considering the overall plight of the elderly in our society.

Theories of Elder Abuse

Authorities may disagree as to the exact cause of elder abuse, but they generally agree that it is similar to other forms of family violence and that it crosses all social and economic lines. Most researchers agree that elder abuse is not an isolated event, rather it is a repetitive pattern of acts by the abuser toward the victim.

Cycle of Violence

The cycle of violence or intergenerational transmission of violence theory was discussed in detail in Chapter 10. Galbraith argues that it has proven ineffective in predicting elder abuse.[22] Wolf and Pillemer also point out that those who abuse elders do not necessarily grow up in families characterized by violence.[23]

Psychopathology

The *psychopathology theory* is based on the premise that abusers suffer from mental disorders that cause them to be violent. Wolf found a high prevalence of mental illness among elder abusers.[24] This approach seems to have greater validity in explaining elder abuse than in explaining either child or spousal abuse. Researchers have found psychopathology present in cases of physical and verbal abuse of elders.[25] Other scholars indicate that a number of abusers have had previous hospitalizations for serious psychiatric disorders, such as schizophrenia and other psychoses.[26]

Social Exchange Theory

One *social exchange theory* assumes that dependency in relationships contributes to elder abuse; that is, increased dependency of the victim on the abuser results in acts of violence. Other research studies support this theory.[27] The abuser's financial dependency on the victim also has been found to be a factor in a number of studies of elder abuse.[28]

The loss of mutual resources between the elder and the caretaker also contributes to the deterioration of the relationship. This results in the caretaker perceiving the relationship as unfair, with a subsequent increase in hostility toward the elder.[29]

A second social exchange theory assumes that the dependency of the abuser on the elder victim causes abuse. This concept focuses on adult children becoming dependent on the elder for material rewards, such as housing and finances. Because these children perceive themselves as weaker and less powerful than the elder, abusing the elder is a way to equalize the balance of power and gain control over the relationship.[30]

Family Stress Theory

The family stress theory is one of the most widely accepted theories of elder abuse.[31] The *family stress theory* is based on the premise that providing care for an elder induces stress within the family. This stress may take many forms, including economic hardship, loss of sleep, intrusions into normal family privacy routines, and other activities which may cause the caregiver to feel resentment toward the elder. Adult children may have to give up economic security to provide care for an aged parent or other close relative. In addition, the physical toll of caring for an ill elderly person can sometimes overwhelm the adult child, which results in a loss of control and subsequent abuse.[32] However, even this theory is subject to controversy. Phillips suggests that stress levels may not be as important a factor in causing elder abuse as previously believed.[33]

Neutralization Theory

The *neutralization theory* was originally developed by Sykes and Matza to explain juvenile delinquency in our society.[34] This theory views the delinquent as being affected by the norms and values of a larger social system rather than a counterculture. This concept holds that delinquents show guilt and shame for their antisocial behavior.[35] To commit criminal or antisocial acts, persons develop techniques of neutralization. These techniques are rationalizations or justifications for their behavior. Matza established five techniques that allow individuals to justify their acts:

1. *Denial of responsibility.* The person may claim that something else, such as alcohol, made him commit the criminal act.
2. *Denial of injury.* Juveniles may believe that even though they violated the law, no one was really hurt. For example, theft of an automobile is okay because the owner's insurance company will replace it with a new model anyway.
3. *Denial of victim.* Delinquents may claim that the victim had it coming and therefore their acts were justified under the circumstances.
4. *Condemnation of the condemners.* Juveniles may shift the blame to others, calling them corrupt or incompetent.
5. *Appeal to higher loyalty.* Some offenders claim they violated the law to satisfy a higher authority or goal.

Tomita has applied the neutralization theory to elder abuse and suggests that, although it cannot be used to establish a direct cause, it may viewed as reasons employed by abusers to justify their acts.[36] She examines each technique of neutralization and explains how it is utilized by the perpetrators to justify their abuse of elders.

1. *Denial of responsibility.* In these situations, the abuser claims the mistreatment was caused by forces beyond his control, such as poverty, bad parents, and so on.
2. *Denial of injury.* The abuser rationalizes that the injury was not really that serious because the victim did not have to go to the emergency room. In material abuse situations, the abuser justifies her actions by stating that the parent can afford to give away property or assets.
3. *Denial of the victim.* Abusers may state that the victim doesn't need help, that she is only attempting to gain attention. For example, the abuser may refuse to dress

the victim, claiming the victim feigns disability because she wants attention, when in reality, the victim cannot dress herself.

4. *Condemnation of the condemners.* In these situations, the abuser condemns protective services or other agencies for interfering with the family.

5. *Appeal to higher loyalty.* The abuser may believe he must act a certain way to satisfy his spouse.

As this discussion illustrates, several theories attempt to explain why people abuse the elderly. Just as with other causes of family violence, no single theory is universally accepted by all scholars. Continued research is needed in this area to determine if a cause can be established.

FOCUS: Triads

Community Involvement in Fighting Elder Victimization

A new concept that emphasizes community cooperation in combating elder victimization is succeeding in a number of areas throughout the nation. This innovative concept is the triad program.

Triads are formed when the local police and sheriff's department agree to work cooperatively with senior citizens to prevent the victimization of the elderly in the community. The three groups share ideas and resources to provide programs and training for vulnerable and often fearful elderly citizens.

A triad program usually begins when a police chief, a sheriff, or a leader in the senior citizen community contacts the other two essential participants to discuss a combined effort. Although each entity may already have programs in place to reduce the victimization rate among the elderly, the three-way involvement of traids adds strength, resources, and greater credibility.

Most traids include representatives from agencies that serve older persons, such as the Agency on Aging, senior centers, and Adult Protective Services. Law enforcement leaders then invite seniors and those working with them to serve on an advisory council, often called Seniors and Lawmen Together (SALT).

Some triads establish programs to prevent elder abuse through education and to address the plight of seniors in personal care homes. For example, in Columbus, Georgia, the plight of some seniors in such facilities came to the attention of a very active SALT council. Learning that older residents were suffering from abuse and neglect, the SALT council devised a strategy to investigate specific situations.

To begin, the council enlisted the assistance of the sheriff's office and the police and health departments. Through these agencies, a search warrant of the homes was obtained, proper lodging and care was arranged for those seniors living in unhealthy and unsafe conditions, and a plan for more careful monitoring of such homes was initiated.

The essence of the triad program is cooperation. This program allows the service providers—law enforcement—to work together with the consumers—senior citizens. Through positive programs that affect safety and quality of life, mutual respect and appreciation evolves between the law enforcement community and citizens.

Source: Adapted from Betsy Cantrell, "Triad, Reducing Criminal Victimization of the Elderly," *FBI Law Enforcement Bulletin,* 19–23 (February 1994).

Elder Victimization[37]

Even with programs such as triads, the incidence of elder victimization continues to escalate in our society. This section will examine a few of the more common crimes committed against elders. Not only are elders preyed upon by family members because of their frail condition, they are also prime targets for certain kinds of criminals who seek easy targets.

Sexual Assault

For many elderly women who were raised during a time when sexual matters were never discussed publicly, becoming a victim of a sexual assault can be a traumatic experience that the elder is not able to process. Some elders are still surrounded with embarrassment about sexual activity and have never discussed it even with their children. To these elders, the thought of having to discuss sexual acts in public is unthinkable. Many older victims believe it is the worst form of lost dignity. They may experience shame in discussing the case or participating in a medical examination with law enforcement officers present. They may have been required to perform sexual acts that they have never participated in before, which only adds to the humiliation.

Elderly rape victims often sustain injuries different from those experienced by younger victims. Vaginal linings are not as elastic as those of younger women because of hormonal changes. This may cause increased sexual trauma including infections, bruising, and tears that never fully heal. More alarmingly, many elders have brittle bones, such as the pelvis and hips, that can be more easily broken or crushed by the weight of the rapist.

Intervention with the elderly is critical and may afford the victims some choices they may not have otherwise had. For example, victim assistance professionals can offer to work with the victim on a relocation plan if that is her desire and she has the financial ability to move from the place of the attack. If the elder agrees, the victim services provider can work with family members to help educate them about the special needs of the victim as a result of the crime. If there is no family, close contact should be maintained with the victim to help increase her feelings of self-worth.

Other Violent Crimes

Elder victims are the least likely to be physically injured during the commission of a violent crime. However, if they are injured, these injuries tend to be more serious because of their frailty and aging bodies. Bones become more brittle with advanced age and break more easily than those of a twenty year old. One study points out that when elders are physically injured during a violent crime, they are twice as likely as any other age group to be seriously injured and require hospitalization.[38] However, the elderly as a whole are significantly less likely than younger age groups to become victims of most types of crime, including violent crime.[39] This may be because they are not as mobile and therefore do not go out in public as much as their younger counterparts and therefore are not as easily approached or victimized.

Most homicide victims over the age of sixty-five were killed during the commission of another felony and were more likely to be killed by a stranger. The elderly are also less likely to protect themselves during the incident and may suffer injuries that younger victims would avoid. A purse snatcher may cause a younger victim to stumble and regain her stability, whereas the same incident may cause an elderly victim to fall and break her hip.

Fraud

The elderly are targeted for crimes involving finances more than any other victim population. Although elderly victims may not sustain any physical injury as a result of this type of crime, the psychological impact can be devastating. The loss of one's entire life savings can create severe and debilitating depression. Many victims blame themselves for the loss and because of this can suffer additional health problems relating to depression such as loss of appetite, decreased interest level, increased withdrawal, and diminished sleep. Some victims feel ashamed that they didn't recognize the "con" and become reluctant to report the crime because they think family members will blame them for mismanagement of their funds and seek to terminate their financial independence.

A majority of the elderly live on fixed incomes and the impact of a financial crime can be devastating to them. They may lose their life savings and even their homes. This may result in the loss of their independence, which many elderly people value more than money itself.

Victim services providers can provide the elderly and their families with information on the victim's right to file civil actions against the perpetrator. The elderly may need help in rearranging their finances as a result of the loss. The courts should be asked to allow for an expiated payment schedule on any restitution plan. The elderly victim may need the funds now, not three or five years from now.

Burglary

For many of the elderly, the home becomes the center of their world as they gradually lose friends and their own mobility. They retire from jobs, family members begin to die, and outside activities decrease due to increasing physical or mental limitations. This imposed isolation explains, in part, why a majority of the elderly are victimized near or in their homes.

The loss of certain possessions, especially those that have sentimental value, can have a great impact on an older person. The loss of other material items such as televisions can further restrict an elder's outside contact with the world. Many victims may want to relocate after a burglary but may not have the financial ability to do so. Once their home has been invaded, they may never feel safe again.

Victim services providers should work with other organizations in the community to assist elderly victims. The local law enforcement agency may provide advice and assistance in evaluating the elder's home to determine if other points of entry should be made more secure. Neighborhood Watch participants should be alerted to the fact that their neighbor was victimized and to increase their vigilance of any suspicious activity which might involve the perpetrator returning to an "easy target." Additionally, every Agency on Aging operates an information and referral line that can refer the elderly to a variety of services.

Summary

Elder abuse has become still another form of violence in our society. Authorities cannot agree on a definition, and as a result the outcome of different studies vary widely regarding the nature, cause, and extent of this type of violence. Elder abuse, like other forms of family violence, is not an isolated event, rather it is a pattern of behavior that increases both in intensity and frequency over time. The rich, poor, college educated, and uneducated suffer from elder abuse. The dynamics and etiology of this type of abuse are still being theorized, with some theories holding more promise than others. Continued research is of paramount importance if we are to understand and intervene in this type of behavior.

It is a grim fate that awaits our maturing population: that after years of productivity and work, we could face the prospect of being beaten and shamed by other members of our society. As a society, we owe it to ourselves and those who will come after us to actively pursue detection and prevention of this form of violence.

Key Terms

Elder abuse is defined as conduct that results in the physical, psychological, or material harm, or neglect or injury to an elder.

Material in the context of elder abuse refers to the exploitation or use of resources.

Elder is a person sixty-five years or older.

Psychopathology theory of elder abuse is based on the premise that abusers suffer from mental disorders that cause them to be violent.

Social exchange theory of elder abuse assumes that dependency in relationships contributes to elder abuse.

Family stress theory regarding elder abuse is based on the premise that providing care for an elder induces stress within the family.

Neutralization theory was originally developed by Sykes and Matza to explain juvenile delinquency in our society. This theory views the delinquent as being affected by the norms and values of a larger social system rather than a counterculture.

Discussion Questions

1. Is elder abuse more or less serious than child abuse? Why?

2. Do you agree with the definition of elder abuse contained in the text? Draft another definition that you believe is more appropriate, and justify your answer.

3. Which of the theories discussing elder abuse do you favor? Why?

4. What is the most serious type of crime that an elder can experience? Why?

5. What is more important in your mind for an elderly victim—independence or security from further victimization? Why?

Suggested Readings

R. B. Wallace, (ed.), *Elder Mistreatment: Abuse, Neglect, and Exploitation in an Aging America,* (National Academies Press, Washington, D.C.) 2003.

B. Brandl, C. B. Dyer & C. J. Heiser, *Elder Abuse Detection and Intervention: A Collaborative Approach,* (Springer Publishing Co., New York) 2006.

M. J. Mellor & P. J. Brownell, (eds.), *Elder Abuse and Mistreatment: Policy, Practice, and Research,* (Haworth Social Work, Binghamton, N.Y.) 2005.

E. Podnieks, (ed.), *Elder Abuse: Selected Papers from the Prague World Congress on Family Violence,* (Haworth Press, Binghamton, N.Y.) 2005.

L. Curtis, *Partnering with Faith Communities to Provide Elder Fraud Prevention, Intervention, and Victim Services,* (U.S. Department of Justice, Office for Victims of Crime, Washington, D.C.) 2005.

L. A. Stiegel, *Elder Abuse Fatality Review Teams,* (U.S. Department of Justice, Office of Victims of Crime, Washington, D.C.) 2005.

B. Schlesinger & R. Schlesinger, (eds.), *Abuse of the Elderly: Issues and Annotated Bibliography,* (University of Toronto Press, Toronto) 1988.

Peter Decalmer & Frank Glendenning, (eds.), *The Mistreatment of Elder People,* (Sage, London, England) 1993.

V. B. Van Hasselt, et al. (eds.), *Handbook of Family Violence,* (Plenum Press, New York) 1988.

R. S. Wolf & K. A. Pillemer, *Helping Elderly Victims: The Reality of Elder Abuse,* (Columbia University Press, New York) 1989.

R. Filenson & S. R. Ingman, (eds.), *Elder Abuse: Practice and Policy,* (Human Sciences Press, New York) 1989.

R. T. Ammerman & M. Hersen, (eds.), *Assessment of Family Violence, A Clinical and Legal Sourcebook,* (John Wiley & Sons Inc, New York) 1992.

M. R. Block & J. D. Sinnott, (eds.), *The Battered Elder Syndrome: An Exploratory Study,* (University of Maryland Center on Aging, College Park, Md.) 1979.

Endnotes

1. M. R. Block & J. D. Sinnott. "The Battered Elder Syndrome: An Exploratory Study," (Center on Aging, University of Maryland) 1979.

2. B. Schlesinger & R. Schlesinger, (eds.), *Abuse of the Elderly: Issues and Annotated Bibliography,* (University of Toronto Press, Toronto) 1988.

3. K. A. Pillemer & D. Finkelhor, "The Prevalence of Elder Abuse: A Random Sample Survey," 28(1) *The Gerontologist,* 51 (1988).

4. U.S. House of Representative, Select Committee on Aging, "Elder Abuse: Curbing a National Epidemic," (Hearings) (Washington, D.C. GPO) December 10, 1990.

5. Id.

6. J. J. Callahan, "Elder Abuse: Some Questions for Policymakers," 28 *The Gerontologist,* 453–458 (1988).

7. J. I. Kosberg, "Preventing Elder Abuse: Identification of High Risk Factors Prior to Placement Decision," 28 *The Gerontologist,* 43–50 (1988).

8. Joanne M. Otto, *Abuse of Adults Age 60+,* National Committee for the Prevention of Elder Abuse and the National Adult Protective Services Association, Boulder, Colo. (February 2006).

9. U.S. House of Representative, Select Committee on Aging, "Elder Abuse: A Decade of Shame and Inaction" (Hearings) (Washington, D.C. GPO) May 1, 1990.

10. K. A. Pillemer & D. Finkelhor, "The Prevalence of Elder Abuse: A Random Sample Survey," 28(1) *The Gerontologist,* 51 (1988).

11. Peter Decalmer & Frank Glendenning, (eds.), *The Mistreatment of Elder People,* (Sage, London, England) 1993, p. 35.

12. "Elder Abuse," 1(17) Infolink, (National Victims Center, Washington, D.C.) 1992.

13. Karl Pillemer & J. J. Suitor, "Elder Abuse," V. B. Van Hasselt, et al. (eds.), *Handbook of Family Violence,* (Plenum Press, New York) 1988.

14. Compare M. R. Block & J. D. Sinnott. "The Battered Elder Syndrome: An Exploratory Study," (Center on Aging, University of Maryland) 1979 with S. Steinmetz & D. J. Amsden, "Dependent Elders, Family Stress and Abuse," T. H. Brubaker, (ed.), *Family Relationships in Later Life* (Sage, Beverly Hills, Calif.) 1983.

15. M. F. Hudson & T. F. Johnson, "Elder Abuse and Neglect: A Review of the Literature," in C. Eisdorfer, et al. (eds.), 6 *Annual Review of Gerontology and Geriatrics* (Springer, New York) 1986.

16. T. A. O'Malley, H. C. O'Malley, D. E. Everitt & D. Sarson, "Categories of Family-Mediated Abuse and Neglect of Elderly Persons," 32(5)

Journal of the American Geriatrics Society, 362–369 (1984).

17. Id.

18. See R. S. Wolf & K. A. Pillemer, *Helping Elderly Victims: The Reality of Elder Abuse* (Columbia University Press, New York) 1989; and M. A. Godkin, R. S. Wolf & K. A. Pillemer, "A Case-Comparison Analysis of Elder Abuse and Neglect," 28(3) *International Journal of Aging and Human Development,* 207–225 (1989).

19. R. Bachman, "Elderly Victim," *Special Report, Bureau of Justice Statistics,* (U.S. Department of Justice, Washington, D.C.) 1992.

20. M. D. Pagelow, *Family Violence,* (Praeger, New York) 1984, p. 359.

21. K. A. Pillemer & D. W. Moore, "Abuse of Patients in Nursing Homes: Findings from a Survey of Staff," 29(3) *The Gerontologist,* 314 (1989).

22. M. W. Galbraith, "A Critical Examination of the Definitional, Methodological and Theoretical Problems of Elder Abuse," in R. Filenson & S. R. Ingman, (eds.), *Elder Abuse: Practice and Policy,* (Human Sciences Press, New York) 1989, pp. 35–42.

23. R. S. Wolf & K. A. Pillemer, *Helping Elderly Victims: The Reality of Elder Abuse,* (Columbia University Press, New York) 1989.

24. R. S. Wolf, C. Strugnell & M. Godkin, *Preliminary Findings from Three Model Projects on Elder Abuse,* (University of Massachusetts Medical Center, (Worcester, Mass.) 1982.

25. T. Hickey & R. L. Douglas, "Mistreatment of the Elderly in the Domestic Setting: An Exploratory Study," 71 *American Journal of Public Health,* 500–517 (1981).

26. R. S. Beckman & R. D. Adelman, "Elder Abuse and Neglect," in R. T. Ammerman & M. Hersen, (eds.), *Assessment of Family Violence, A Clinical and Legal Soucebook,* (John Wiley & Sons Inc, New York) 1992, p. 238.

27. J. L. Davison, "Elder Abuse," in M. R. Block & J. D. Sinnott, (eds.), *The Battered Elder Syndrome: An Exploratory Study,* (University of Maryland Center on Aging, College Park, Md.) 1979, pp. 49–55.

28. R. S. Wolf, M. Godkin & K. A. Pillemer, *Elder Abuse and Neglect: Report from the Model Projects,* (University of Massachusetts Medical Center,

University Center on Aging, Worchester, Mass.) 1984.

29. S. K. Steinmetz, *Duty Bound: Elder Abuse and Family Care*, (Sage Publications, Newbury Park, Calif.) 1988.

30. G. J. Anetzberger, *The Etiology of Elder Abuse by Adult Offspring*, (Charles C. Thomas, Springfield Park, Ill.) 1987.

31. S. K. Steinmetz, *Duty Bound: Elder Abuse and Family Care*, (Sage Publications, Newbury Park, Calif.) 1988.

32. R. J. Gelles, "An Exchange/Social Control Theory," in D. Finkelhor, G. Hotaling, R. J. Gelles & M. A. Straus, (eds.), *The Dark Side of Families: Current Family Violence Research*, (Sage, Beverly Hills, Calif.) 1983.

33. L. Phillips, "Theoretical Explanations of Elder Abuse: Competing Hypotheses and Unresolved Issues," in K. Pillemer & R. Wolf, (eds.), *Elder Abuse: Conflict in the Family*, (Auburn House Publishing Co., Dover, Mass.) 1986.

34. G. M. Sykes & D. Matza, "Techniques of Neutralization: A Theory of Delinquency," 22 *American Sociological Review*, 664–670 (1978).

35. J. F. Short, Jr. & Fred Strodtbeck, *Group Process and Gang Delinquency*, (University of Chicago Press, Chicago) 1965.

36. S. K. Tomita, "The Denial of Elder Mistreatment by Victims and Abusers: The Application of Neutralization Theory," 5(3) *Violence and Victims*, 171 (1990).

37. This section has been adapted from Ellen Alexander, "Elderly Victims of Crime," *National Victim Assistance Academy Text*, (Office for Victims of Crime, Washington, D.C.) 1996, which was funded by a federal grant.

38. *Elder Victimization*, (Bureau of Justice Statistics, Washington, D.C.) 1987.

39. *Highlights from 20 Years of Surveying Crime Victims, 1973–1992*, (Bureau of Justice Statistics, Washington, D.C.) October 1993.

12

HATE CRIMES

Chapter Outline

Cultural Awareness
  Introduction
  Cultural Awareness Training

Hate Crimes
  Introduction
  Legal Aspects of Hate Crimes
  Identifying Bias Crimes
  Typology of Offenders

Cultural Awareness Case Study

Summary

Key Terms

Discussion Questions

Suggested Readings

Learning Objectives

After reading this chapter, you should be able to:

- Explain why it is important to understand different cultures
- List the elements of an effective cultural diversity program
- List the indicators of bias crimes
- Explain the different types of bias crime offenders

FOCUS: Hate Crimes in America

- In New York, a white teenage boy was arrested for chasing two Hispanic girls with a baseball bat while yelling racial slurs.
- In Kansas, a developmentally disabled woman is raped by a caretaker.
- In Woodland Hills, California, posters depicting swastikas and KKK symbols are discovered at California State University, Hayward. These posters urge homosexuals to "go back to your closets."
- A number of African-American places of worship are burned.
- There is a reported rise in the militia movement in America.
- White supremacist groups have become more visible and active in the last ten years.
- In 1994, the Southern Poverty Law Center listed more than 270 hate groups as being active in the United States.

To understand hate crimes fully, victim services providers must be sensitive to cultural issues. Each victim of a crime needs to be treated as an individual. However, some victims face more difficult tasks than others, necessitating a more comprehensive approach from the service provider. This difficulty may arise because of the nature of the crime; that is, a murder victim's family will suffer more trauma than the victim of a car theft. Other victims face difficult times because they are from special populations that are different from the established cultures in our country. This difference may be based on skin color, sex, religious beliefs, sexual orientation, or a number of other factors that make people culturally different. This text cannot possibly address all the issues facing the victims who are members of special groups. Its purpose is to examine selected special victim populations and suggest specific methods professionals should use when responding to crimes committed against them.

Cultural Awareness

The United States has traditionally been a melting pot of different peoples who have come to its shores and taken their unique place in our society. We pride ourselves on our diversity and multiculturalism. However, the other side of this coin reflects a darker side to our relationship with these groups. Clashes between ethnic and racial minority groups and other more established cultures in the United States have escalated over the last ten to twenty years. Additionally, new refugees, recent immigrants, and other minority groups are prime targets for certain types of perpetrators. These victims face an almost overwhelming task when attempting to pursue redress in the criminal or civil justice system. Victim services providers need to be aware of these issues when dealing with these victims.

Introduction

Simply saying to those who work in the criminal justice system that a victim comes from a different culture and is different from the rest of us does not automatically guarantee sympathetic treatment and/or an understanding response to that victim's special needs. Stereotyping must be guarded against, and relying on third-hand information when responding to the needs of minority victims should be avoided. Different cultures may not be as homogeneous as they appear on the surface, and care should be taken to not attribute characteristics to special populations based on conversations or interactions with one member of the group. The person being interviewed may be advocating personal beliefs, which may not represent the feelings of other members of that particular culture. It is essential that professionals working in the criminal justice profession be both culturally sensitive and careful to validate their information if possible.

Cultural awareness can be defined as the understanding an individual has regarding different cultures. The term *culture* includes different races, religions, genders, ages, physical disabilities, and gay or lesbian issues. Therefore, cultural awareness encompasses a wide range of issues, any of which may confront those working within this field. The next section will provide some guidelines for professionals to use when evaluating cultural awareness programs or setting up such training programs.

PRACTICUM: Cultures and Misunderstanding[1]

The Officer's Perspective

A Nigerian cab driver runs a red light. An officer pulls him over in the next block, stopping the patrol car at least three car lengths behind the cab. Before the officer can exit his patrol car, the cabbie gets out of his vehicle and approaches the officer. Talking rapidly in a high-pitched voice and making wild gestures, the cab driver appears to be out of control.

The officer steps from his vehicle and yells for the cab driver to stop, but the cabbie continues to advance until he is about two feet from him. The cab driver does not make eye contact and appears to be talking to the ground. Finally, the officer arrests the cabbie for disorderly conduct and resisting arrest.

The Cab Driver's Perspective

Although most Americans know to remain in their cars, the Nigerian exited his cab to show his respect by not troubling the officer to leave his own vehicle. The Nigerian ignores the command to stop advancing on the officer because in his eyes he is not even close to the officer. The social distance for conversation in Nigeria is much closer for conversations than in the United States. For Nigerians, it may be less than fifteen inches, whereas two feet represents a comfortable conversation zone for Americans.

Anglo-Americans expect eye contact during conversation; the lack of it usually signifies deception, rudeness, defiance, or a means to end a conversation.

In Nigeria, however, people often show respect and humility by averting their eyes. The Nigerian believes he is sending a message of respect by averting his eyes and talking to the ground.

1. Is either party at fault in this encounter?

2. Is the officer responsible for understanding other cultures? Is the cabbie responsible for conforming to the standards of the country in which he is working?

3. List ways to avoid such situations.

Cultural Awareness Training

The Practicum indicates how important cultural awareness or sensitivity training is within the criminal justice system. This is an emerging area to which victim services providers can contribute greatly, and in which they should take the lead. They should become knowledgeable regarding different cultures within their community and be prepared to conduct training sessions regarding the customs and traditions of those cultures and their responses to crime and the criminal justice system.

They have an opportunity to provide a valuable service to future victims by ensuring that those in the criminal justice system respond appropriately to members of different cultures. Occasionally, law enforcement agencies will contact victim services providers and ask that they provide cultural awareness or sensitivity training to members of their organization. Unfortunately, this request for training occurs after an incident involving a minority victim has resulted in adverse publicity being directed toward the department. The victim services providers should use this request as an opportunity to "train the trainers" regarding what is an appropriate cultural awareness training program.

No single technique or program will work for all agencies. Professionals may find themselves adapting programs or training techniques to fit specific situations. There are a number of different techniques that may be used to train professionals in the area of cultural awareness.

St. George lists a variety of factors that trainers should consider when conducting cultural awareness training.[2] These factors include multidimensional learning from several perspectives, learning that is relevant and structured to meet specific needs, that is behavior-based, so that students express their feelings by actions, that is empathetic to the feelings and concerns of community minority members, that is practical in nature, and that allows for controversy and provides follow-up support.

Shusta and his associates recommended a multifaceted cultural awareness training program.[3] They suggested that the trainer should use a variety of training aids and techniques to accomplish the objective of teaching cultural awareness. These techniques include the following strategies:

Lectures.   Lectures should be interspersed between other activities and include local demographics. This information may be obtained from city and county departments, housing authorities, state and federal census data, and community-based organizations. Lectures should introduce students to cultural-specific information about the various subcultures within a community.

Role-playing.   Role-playing should include communication skills. Role-playing is intended to create a realistic environment in which the participants may interact and be trained to respond in an appropriate manner.

Simulations.   The purpose of simulations is to allow the participants to identify their own feelings and thereby achieve a better understanding of others. A number of commercial simulation packages specifically designed for cultural awareness programs are on the market.

Work Groups or Presentations.   The work group or presentation aspect of a cultural awareness program allows the participants to discuss various issues. Small groups are a useful technique that allow participants to express their feelings more freely than if they were in a large group.

Critical Incidents or Case Studies.   In critical incidents or case studies, participants are asked to bring in news stories of actual conflict expressing hate or bias based on ethnicity, gender, or sexual orientation. An experienced facilitator interjects comments and asks questions of the students regarding their reactions to the incidents. Students discuss how they would have responded to the situation and how they can avoid similar situations in the future.

Local Culture Video Profiles and Cross-Cultural Films.   Local agencies or universities might cooperate in producing a video that examines local cultural groups. Students might be assigned to write the script, direct, or even act in the video. In this day of inexpensive camcorders, videos are relatively easy to make and show. Students learn by researching local information for the production.

Experiential Assignments.   Students are assigned to spend time in a minority community or work environment. They return to class and explain their reactions and feelings based on their experience.

Interactive Computer Video.   Probably the most innovative tool available to trainers is the interactive computer video. Students use computers and computer disks (CDs) to move through interactive sessions dealing with cultural issues. Students cannot progress from one stage until they have successfully completed all tasks at prior steps.

As indicated, many scholars advocate cultural awareness training as a continual process. An example of one successful cultural awareness project is the federally funded Head Start program. This program teaches parenting skills to families, provides medical and social services to children, and prepares them for school. Congress has established a series of performance standards for Head Start programs.[4] Some of these performance standards are excellent examples of continuing cultural awareness training. Although these standards obviously apply to a preschool classroom setting, they are easy to modify to make them relevant to a variety of situations. Samples of Head Start performance standards are listed here:

> *45 Code of Federal Regulations 1304.2-2 Education Services and Objectives and Performance Standards*
> *(c) The education services component of the plan shall provide for a program which is individualized to meet the special needs of children from various populations by:*
> *(1) Having a curriculum which is relevant and reflective of the needs of the population served.*

This standard can be accomplished by including in each classroom materials and activities that reflect the cultural background of the children. Examples of materials include books, records, posters, maps, dolls, and clothing. Activities may include celebrating cultural events and holidays, serving food related to other cultures, and enjoying stories, music, and games representative of children's background.

> *(2) Having staff and program resources reflective of the racial and ethnic population of the children in the program.*

This standard may be accomplished by having an adult present who speaks the primary language of the children and who is knowledgeable about their heritage. This adult may be a teacher or aide, other member of the center staff, a parent or family member, or a volunteer.

> *(3) Include parents in the curriculum development and having them serve as resource persons.*

Parents can be valuable resources in planning which activities reflect the children's heritage. Teachers may request suggestions from parents on ways to integrate cultural activities into the program. For example, parents may wish to plan holiday celebrations; prepare foods unique to various cultures; recommend books, records, or other materials for the classroom; act as classroom volunteers; or suggest games, songs, and art projects that reflect cultural customs.

As this discussion indicates, there is no easy answer to the problem of dealing with minority populations. Feelings, perceptions, and past experiences all enter into our reactions to those who are different from us. Unfortunately, some members of our society do more than simply feel uncomfortable around members of other cultures or other minority groups. As indicated in the Focus box at the beginning of this chapter, some groups engage in acts of violence directed at special populations. The next section discuss hate crimes and their impact on our society.

Hate Crimes

Introduction

Hate violence has a long history in the United States. However, some sources suggest that it has increased in the recent past.[5] Accurately measuring the number of hate crimes that are committed is extremely difficult because the Hate Crime Statistics Act of 1990, although it requires reporting, is still a relatively new procedure. Additionally, two other factors contribute to the lack of meaningful statistics in this area: the lack of training by law enforcement causes many officers to fail to recognize incidents of racial violence, and there is natural reluctance on the part of many victims of hate crimes to report such incidents to law enforcement agencies[6] (Table 12.1).

TABLE 12.1   Bias Crimes by Motivation and Type as Reported
              to the FBI for 2004

Bias Motivation	Incidents	Offense	Victims
Race	4042	4863	5119
Religion	1374	1480	1586
Sexual Orientation	1197	1406	1482
Total	7649	9035	9528

Source: *Hate Crime Statistics, 2004*, Federal Bureau of Investigation, U.S. Department
of Justice, Washington, D.C. (2004).

Acts of racial violence reflect a racial prejudice or interpersonal hostility that is based on the view that different cultures do not merit treatment as equals or that they deserve blame for various problems within society. Many minority cultures are viewed in a certain manner.[7] These stereotypes are race-based generalizations about a person's behavior or character that are typically not substantiated in scientific data. This stereotyping may act as a trigger to violence in different cultures. Stereotyping does not cause violence; however, physical violence is easier to perform on a dehumanized victim. Attackers may believe that the minority is "invading their turf." This may occur when a minority family moves into a traditional neighborhood and has not had any previous experience with that particular culture. Attackers may also claim that minority cultures are taking jobs that rightfully belong to "real" Americans. These and other rationalizations deny minority cultures status as accepted citizens.

Persons of color and certain religious groups have traditionally been the target of hate crimes. These groups have been victimized both on a national and international scale. They continue to be victimized today. For example, in New York in 1988, 30 percent of all bias incidents were committed against African-Americans and another 30 percent were perpetrated against Jews. In Los Angeles in that same year, the majority of racial incidents were against African-Americans, and more than 90 percent of religiously motivated incidents were against Jews.[8] The arson of African-American churches is but another example of the continuing victimization of persons of color.[9]

Disabled persons are also victims of hate or bias crimes. As the number of disabled persons in our nation has increased, so too has the number of hate crimes and abuse against them. Some perpetrators seek out disabled victims because their disability makes them "easy prey" for this type of offender. An example is a developmentally disabled woman with the intellectual ability of a seven-year-old child who may be sexually assaulted by a caretaker. A ***disabled person*** is one who has a physical or mental impairment that substantially limits one or more of the major life activities of that individual, or that person has a record of such impairment, or that person is regarded as having such an impairment. Major life activities include walking, seeing, hearing, speaking, breathing, learning, and working.

Antigay and antilesbian violence became a national issue with the murders of San Francisco Mayor George Moscone and City Supervisor Harvey Milk. Their deaths became symbols of both the strength of the homosexual community and the hostility that is directed at them. Attacks against gays infected with HIV/AIDS have increased in the last several years.[10]

Women also have been the subject of hate and bias crimes. They continue to be targets of violence because of their gender. Many states include gender as a classification within their hate crime statutes. Crimes against women, including sexual assault and spousal abuse, are discussed in Chapter 8. The next section examines the conflict between the First Amendment of the U.S. Constitution, which protects freedom of expression, and prosecuting hate or bias crimes.

Legal Aspects of Hate Crimes

Prosecuting a perpetrator for violation of a hate crime raises several emotional and constitutional issues. The First Amendment prohibits the federal government and the states from enacting any law that unduly regulates a person's freedom of expression.[11] However, from the founding of our nation, the Supreme Court has held that such freedom of expression is not unlimited. There are situations in which conduct or other activities, although expressing beliefs or thoughts, are outside the scope of First Amendment protection.

Hate crimes deal with both the expression of beliefs and action. The expression of beliefs reflects hatred or loathing toward a certain group, and the action is criminal in nature. Thus, crafting a criminal statute that regulates hate crimes is no easy task. In 1992, the Supreme Court struck down a local hate crime ordinance in St. Paul, Minnesota, which criminalized the use of hate symbols, such as the burning of a cross, on the grounds that it violated an individual's right to freedom of expression.[12]

On June 11, 1993, in *Wisconsin v. Mitchell,* the U.S. Supreme Court unanimously upheld the constitutionality of Wisconsin's hate crime statute, which increased penalties for crimes motivated by hate or bias.[13] Todd Mitchell was a nineteen-year-old Black who was outraged over a scene in the film *Mississippi Burning* that depicted a young black child being attacked by a white racist. Upon seeing a fourteen-year-old white boy, Mitchell asked his companions if they wanted to "get that white boy." They attacked the white boy, leaving the victim comatose for four days with possible brain damage. Mitchell was convicted for aggravated battery, and the sentence was doubled from two to four years after it was proved he had intentionally selected his victim based on race. Mitchell challenged the constitutionality of the hate crime enhancement statute, claiming that it violated the First Amendment guarantee of freedom of expression.

The U.S. Supreme Court upheld the statute, stating bias or hate crimes were valid for three main reasons:

1. While the government cannot punish an individual's abstract beliefs, it can punish a vast array of depraved motives for crime, including selecting a crime

victim based on race, religion, color, disability, sexual orientation, national origin, or ancestry;

2. Hate crimes do not punish thoughts, rather they address the greater individual and societal harms caused by bias-related offenses in that they are more likely to provoke retaliatory crimes, inflict distinct emotional harms on their victims, and incite community unrest; and

3. Hate crime penalty enhancement laws do not punish people because they express their views.

As indicated, laws prohibiting certain conduct will be considered constitutionally valid. Nonthreatening bigoted expression is still protected as long as it does not evolve into bias-motivated action. When such beliefs are the basis for hate or bias crimes, professionals in the field should be able to identify them. The next sections discuss factors that may indicate that the offense was a hate crime.

Identifying Bias Crimes

To identify hate or bias crimes, we must first define these offenses. In this text, hate crime and bias crime are used interchangeably. Finn and McNeil define hate crimes as "words or actions designed to intimidate an individual because of his or her race, religion, national origin or sexual [preference]."[14] In the Hate Crimes Statistics Act of 1990, *bias crimes* are those offenses that are motivated by hatred against a victim based on race, religion, sexual orientation, ethnicity, or national origin.[15] Many states have also adopted hate crime statutes that prohibit the same or a similar type of conduct. As indicated, hate or bias crimes are not new; what is new is that we are beginning to recognize these crimes and respond to them.

Recognizing bias crimes involves an evaluation of a number of factors. There is no generally accepted foolproof list of indicators that indicate the offense is motivated by bias or hate of a particular group. However, the Office for Victims of Crime has identified seven general categories that should be examined when evaluating criminal acts.[16] These factors include cultural differences, written or oral comments, use of symbols, representation of organized hate groups, prior hate crimes, victim–witness perceptions, and lack of other motive. Depending on the situation, one of these factors standing by itself may strongly indicate that the offense may be classified as a bias or hate crime. Conversely, several of these indicators may not present conclusive evidence that the crime was motivated by hate or bias. Each case should be evaluated on its own merits.

Racial, Ethic, Gender, and Cultural Differences

Is the victim of a different culture than the offender? Investigators may not be able to establish this fact from the victim. They may have to look for other indicators that point to any cultural differences between the victim and the offender. These other factors include the cultural diversity of a number of locations, including the place of attack, the victim's home, or the workplace. Inquiry should be made as to whether the victim was engaged in activities that represent or promote a group, such as a gay rights march. Did the incident occur on a date that has a special significance to certain cultures, such as Martin Luther King's birthday? Even if the victim is not a member of any recognized cultural or ethnic minority, that person may have supported such a group and the attack may be in reprisal for that activity. Finally, questions must be asked as to whether there is a history of violence between the victim's culture and any other group.

Written or Oral Comments or Gestures
Inquiry should be made as to whether the attackers made any comments or gestures before, during, or immediately after the attack. These comments may refer to the victim's race, sexual orientation, or gender. Likewise, the attackers may make certain gestures indicating their own affiliation with another group.

Drawings, Markings, Symbols, and Graffiti
Care should be taken to look for any drawings or symbols that may indicate membership in a group. These may be on the victim's house, place of work, house of worship, or where the attack occurred.

Representations of Organized Hate Groups
Sometimes hate groups will call members of the media and take credit for a bombing, burning, or other act of violence. They may also leave their trademark at the scene of the crime. For example, a burning cross may be found outside the victim's home.

Previous Existence of Bias or Hate Crime Incidents
Did the incident occur in a location where previous hate crime have occurred? If there have been a series of crimes involving victims of the same culture, or the incidents occurred in the same location that is frequented by members of a specific culture, those facts may indicate that the crimes are motivated by hate or bias. Interview the victims to determine if they have received previous harassing mail or phone calls based on their affiliation or membership in a group.

Victim–Witness Perception
Victims should be questioned to determine if they perceive the crime as motivated by bias. This may not always be accurate, but the victims' input in this area is always critical.

Lack of Other Motives
If there is no other motive for the incident and the victim is a member of minority culture, the fact that it may be motivated by bias or hatred of that group should always be considered.

As indicated, the presence or absence of these factors does not establish the existence of a hate-related crime. In fact, there are several caveats that must be exercised when evaluating these crimes. These caveats might appropriately be called false-positive factors. These factors include the following:

Requirement for a Case-by-Case Assessment.   Each crime must be evaluated on its own merits. The existence or nonexistence of bias or hate as the motivation for the offense must be evaluated in light of all facts and circumstances surrounding the crime.

Misleading Facts.   Care must be taken not to rush to judgment in what appears to be a hate crime. There may be other facts that negate this first impression. For example, the victim may tell the officers that the perpetrator used a racial epithet during the assault. Further investigation may reveal that the victim and the offender were both of the same race or culture.

Feigned Facts and Hoaxes.   Some offenders may leave hate symbols in an effort to give the false impression that the offense was motivated by bias or hatred when in fact is was simply an ordinary crime. Other perpetrators may leave symbols or signs of certain groups as a hoax or to mislead investigators.

On occasion, determining whether the offense is really a hate crime may be difficult. Even if police officers cannot prove that the offense was a hate crime, the victim may believe that hate or bias was in fact the motivation. The effect of such crime on victims is unique and in many cases more devastating than other crimes because of the psychological impact on the victim.[17]

The victim must live with the realization that the crime was not a random act of violence; rather, the victim was targeted or selected for victimization based on beliefs, race, culture, religion, or sexual preference. Bias crimes are "message crimes" that send a message of terror to the victim because the victim is different from the majority of other Americans. Some victims of bias crimes may not have any community support systems within their communities. They may have recently arrived in the United States and may not have developed a support base within the general community or their specific culture. Other victims may fear discovery of their status and therefore decline to report suspected hate crimes. This aspect of this type of victimization is especially true for closeted gays and lesbians, undocumented aliens, and those who suffer from other disabilities such as HIV/AIDS infection.

Bias crimes also impact the victim's immediate community and culture. Such crimes increase tension with the minority community and raise the specter of retaliation by members of that community. As a result of these factors, bias or hate crimes pose special problems for victim services providers.

Typology of Offenders

Understanding more about those who commit hate crimes allows victim services providers to help the victim understand some of the dynamics involved in this type of crime. Although research is still being developed in this area, Levin and McDevitt have established three categories of offenders: thrill-seeking offenders, reactive offenders, and mission offenders.[18]

The thrill-seeking offenders are generally groups of teenagers who are not otherwise associated with any other formal hate group. They engage in these acts for a variety of reasons, including an attempt to gain a psychological or social thrill or rush, a desire to be accepted by others, or to be able to brag about the act at a later time. Almost any member of a minority group may be a target of these groups. They generally operate outside of their own area or neighborhood and actively look for targets and opportunity. Because these attacks are random and usually fail to follow any pattern, it is often difficult to identify the perpetrators of these types of hate crimes.

The reactive offenders have a sense of entitlement concerning their rights or lifestyle that does not extend to the victim. They usually do not belong to any organized hate group but may associate with one to mitigate a perceived threat to their way of life. When a victim acts in such a manner as to cause these offenders to feel that their lifestyle is threatened, they may react with violence. They will commit hate crimes to send a message to the victim and/or the victim's community that will cause the victim to stop whatever action is threatening the perpetrator's rights or lifestyle. These crimes normally occur within the offender's own community, school, or place of work. Examples of these types of hate crimes include burning crosses at a minority's new home in a predominately white neighborhood, beating a minority who takes a job in a traditionally white occupation, and other acts of violence directed at maintaining the status quo.

The mission-oriented offenders may suffer from a mental illness, including psychosis. They may experience hallucinations, withdrawal, and impaired ability to reason. These offenders may believe they have received instructions from a higher deity to rid the world of this "evil." They typically have a sense of urgency about their objectives and believe that they must act before it is too late. The victim is usually a member of a group that is targeted for elimination. These perpetrators will look for victims in the victim's own neighborhood. An example of this type of offender was Marc Lepine, who killed fourteen women at the University of Montreal, stating that he hated all feminists.

Sapp and his associates developed a typology of hate offenders based on their ideology.[19] They believed that ideology is used by hate groups to serve as a symbolic set of ideas that provides the group with a perceived social legitimacy. Ideology is a way of thinking used by a group to express its beliefs and social values. Sapp classified hate groups into three basic categories: Christian conservatism based on the identity movement, white racial supremacy, and patriotism and survival.

Christian conservatism based on the identity movement uses passages in scripture identifying certain groups as superior to others and the notion that a nation, rather than being a geographic, political, or economic entity, is a culture grouped according to bloodlines and shared history. Racial identity thus becomes the basis for national identity.

These groups may adopt a postmillennial view that holds that the second coming of Christ cannot happen until Christians purge the Earth of sin and establish the Holy Land.[20] As Gale points out, this is potentially a blueprint for genocide in that it allows these groups to cleanse the Holy Land of "sinners." Therefore, mass murder of inferiors and those who oppose the groups and their churches is mandated.[21]

FOCUS: What Is Racism?

In 1937, Ruth Benedict penned a definition of racism that is still valid today. "Racism is the dogma that one ethnic group is condemned by nature to congenital inferiority and another group is destined to congenital superiority. It is the dogma that the hope of civilization depends upon eliminating some races and keeping others pure. It is the dogma that one race has carried progress with it throughout human history and can alone ensure future progress. . . . [R]acism is essentially a pretentious way of saying that 'I belong. . . . For such a conviction, in the most gratifying formula that has ever been discovered, for neither my own unworthiness nor the accusations of others can ever dislodge me from my position. . . .' It avoids all embarrassing claims by 'inferior' groups about their own achievements and ethical standards."

Source: Ruth Benedict, "Race: Science and Politics," in Jacques Baryan (ed.), *Race: A Study in Modern Superstition* (MacMillan, New York), 1937, pp. 153–154.

White racial supremacy groups also include racial purity proponents. Racial purity is concerned with the purity of the Aryan race or God's children. Refugees, illegal aliens, legal immigrants, Jews, Blacks, Hispanics, Asians, and non-Christians are all considered a threat to white racial purity theorists. The Ku Klux Klan is an example of a white supremacy group. Its founding fathers stated that its purpose was the maintenance of the supremacy of the white race in the republic because that race is superior to all other races.[22]

Patriotism and survival groups have recently come to the attention of the general public because of the incidents in Idaho and Montana involving various members of militia groups. These groups offer an attractive ideology to some conservative groups in America. They point out the economic troubles, including unemployment, and blame these problems on refugees and other nonwhite groups. They argue that special interests control the government and decry the moral bankruptcy of our leaders.

These groups blame lax courts for encouraging criminals. They target the media because they believe the media glorify criminals and are responsible for the total breakdown of morals in America. Some of these groups use quotes from the Constitution as a basis for their beliefs and argue that they are no longer subject to the laws of the United States.

Bias and hate crimes do not simply happen, they are motivated by a variety of feelings, beliefs, and emotions. The result is intimidation of the individual as well as the community. Victim services providers must understand these crimes and their impact to assist these victims properly.

Cultural Awareness Case Study

You live in a medium-sized community with a wide range of cultures and subcultures. These groups include people from South America and the Far East. Within the last several months, there have been reports of the use of excessive force on the part of law enforcement officers when they encountered these minorities. The minority groups have responded by picketing city hall and threatening recall campaigns against the local elected officials.

You are the local victim–witness coordinator and have spoken at a variety of meetings regarding cultural awareness and its impact on and importance to victims. The chief of police has asked you to assist his department in the establishment of a cultural awareness program. You understand that for such a program to be successful, it must be continuing and multifaceted. Reread the Head Start performance standards listed in this chapter. Revise them so that they could apply to a local law enforcement agency instead of a school setting. For example, instead of a parent providing suggestions, you may want to substitute a leader of a minority group.

Summary

Cultural awareness is more than a series of "politically correct" sayings and posters that hang in an office. Victim services providers are in unique positions to serve both the victims and the criminal justice agencies within the system. They can act as advocates for the victims and as cultural awareness trainers to law enforcement agencies.

Hate or bias crimes continue to happen in this country. Victim services providers must be aware of the dynamics involved in these crimes from both the offenders perspective and the victim's position. The commission of a hate crime not only affects the individual victim, it impacts the victim's entire community. A message of terror is sent to these victims, their families, and their communities. Service providers must be able to offer advice, guidance, and support to these special victims.

Key Terms

Cultural awareness is the understanding that an individual has regarding different cultures.

Disabled person is one who has a physical or mental impairment that substantially limits one or more of the major life activities of that individual or that person has a record of such

impairment or that person is regarded as having such an impairment.

Bias crimes are those offenses that are motivated by hatred and directed against a victim based on race, religion, sexual orientation, ethnicity, or national origin.

Discussion Questions

1. List the various cultures that exist in your city. Explain how they are different from the mainstream population of your area. What do you know of the history and culture of these populations?

2. What is the most important aspect of a cultural awareness program?

3. Save your local newspaper for one week and list all the incidents involving hate crimes. How do these crimes compare with the material listed in the book? Discuss each crime using the criteria set forth in the book.

4. Are there any other groups that you can identify that might be subject to hate crimes?

5. Should membership in organizations that espouse hate doctrine be a crime? Why? Why not?

Suggested Readings

Robert M. Shusta, Deena R. Levine, Philip R. Harris & Herbert Z. Wong, *Multicultural Law Enforcement*, (Prentice-Hall, Englewood Cliffs, N.J.) 1995.

Marlene A. Young, *Victim Assistance Frontiers and Fundamentals*, (Kendall/Hunt Publishing, Dubuque, Iowa) 1993.

Robert J. Kelly, (ed.), *Bias Crimes: American Law Enforcement and Legal Responses*, (Office of the International Criminal Justice Administration, Reading, Berkshire, United Kingdom) 1993.

National Bias Crimes Training for Law Enforcement and Victim Assistance Professionals, Office for Victims of Crime, (U.S. Department of Justice, Washington, D.C.) January 1995.

M. Welch, *Scapegoats of September 11th: Hate Crimes and State Crimes in the War on Terror*, (Rutgers Press, New York) 2006.

P. Connors (ed.), *Hate Crimes (Current Controversies)* (Greenhaven Press, Chicago) 2006.

H. A. Lim, *Race, Bigotry, and Violence: Understanding the Impact of Hate Crimes on Asian Americans*, (ProQuest, Ann Arbor, Mich.) 2006.

R. D. King, *When Law and Society Disagree: Group Threat, Legacies of the Past, and the Organizational Context of Hate Crime Law Enforcement*, (ProQuest, Ann Arbor, Mich.) 2006.

Endnotes

1. Adapted from Gary Weaver, "Law Enforcement in a Culturally Diverse Society," *FBI Law Enforcement Bulletin*, 1 (September 1992).
2. Joyce St. George, "Sensitivity Training Needs Rethinking," 7/347 *Law Enforcement News*, 8–12 (Nov. 30, 1991).
3. Robert M. Shusta, Deena R. Levine, Philip R. Harris & Herbert Z. Wong, *Multicultural Law Enforcement*, (Prentice-Hall, Englewood Cliffs, N.J.) 1995.
4. 45 Code of Federal Regulations 1304 et. seq. (1992).
5. "1990 Audit of Anti-Semitic Incidents," Anti-Defamation League of B'nai B'rith, New York (1991).
6. For example it was not until January 1995 that the Office for Victims of Crime published a *National Bias Crimes Training Manual for Law Enforcement and Victim Assistance Professionals*, (U.S. Department of Justice, Washington, D.C.) 1995.
7. Harry H. L. Kitano, "Asian-Americans: The Chinese, Japanese, Koreans, Philipinos and Southeast Asians," 454 *Annals American Academy of Political & Social Science*, 125 (1981).
8. R. J. Kelly, (ed.), *Bias Crimes: American Law Enforcement and Legal Responses*, (Office of the International Criminal Justice Administration, Reading, Berkshire, United Kingdom) 1993.
9. But see Fred Bayles, "Church Arsons not all Linked to Racism," Associated Press, *Fresno Bee*, A-1 (July 5, 1996) where the reporter points out that after reviewing six years of federal, state and local data, the Associated Press found arsons increasing, but with only random links to racism. Of the seventy-three

African-American church arsons since 1995, fewer than twenty cases had clear links to racism. On the whole, the Associated Press reported that church arsons increased across the nation.

10. Kevin Berrill, "Gay and Lesbian Crime Victims: What We All Can Do," 10/12 *NOVA Newsletter,* 3 (Washington, D.C.).

11. See Edwin J. Delattre & Daniel L. Schofield, "Combating Bigotry in Law Enforcement," *FBI Law Enforcement Bulletin,* 27 (June 1966).

12. *R.A.V. v. City of St. Paul,* 112 S. Ct. 2538 (1992).

13. 113 S. Ct. 2194 (1993).

14. Peter Finn & Taylor McNeil, *The Response of the Criminal Justice System to Bias Crimes: An Exploratory Review,* (Abt Associates, Inc., Washington, D.C.) 1987.

15. Public Law 101–275 (1990).

16. *National Bias Crimes Training for Law Enforcement and Victim Assistance Professionals,* Office for Victims of Crime, (U.S. Department of Justice, Washington, D.C.) January 1995.

17. Marlene A. Young, *Victim Assistance Frontiers and Fundamentals,* (Kendall/Hunt Publishing, Dubuque, Iowa) 1993.

18. Jack Levin & Jack McDevitt, *The Rising Tide of Bigotry and Bloodshed,* (Plenum, New York) 1993.

19. Allen D. Sapp, Richard N. Holden, & Michael E. Wiggins, "Value and Belief Systems of Right-Wing Extremists," in Robert J. Kelly, (ed.), *Bias Crimes: American Law Enforcement and Legal Responses,* (Office of the International Criminal Justice Administration, Reading, Berkshire, United Kingdom) 1993.

20. Normal Geiser, *Moody Monthly,* 129–131 (October 1985).

21. William Gale, *Racial and National Identity,* (pamphlet) (Ministry of Christ Church, Glendale, Calif.) undated.

22. William P. Randel, *The Ku Klux Klan: A Century of Infamy,* (Chilton Books, New York) 1965, pp. 15–16.

13

SPECIAL VICTIM POPULATIONS

read

Chapter Outline

HIV/AIDS Victims
Medical and Psychological Aspects of HIV/AIDS
Victim Service Issues
Specific Victim Populations

Disabled Victims
Introduction
Legal Issues
Types of Victimization
Emerging Issues

Gay and Lesbian Victims
History
Definitions
Gays and Lesbians as Victims of Crime
Intimate Violence
Extent of the Problem
Legal Aspects of Gay and Lesbian Abuse

Prisoners as Victims

Violence in the Schools: From Bullying to Homicide
Introduction
Causation and Theories
Bullying
Fighting
Gangs

Learning Objectives

After reading this chapter, you should be able to:

- Understand the HIV/AIDS disease
- Explain how the HIV/AIDS disease impacts victims of crime
- Distinguish between the various victim populations that are impacted by the HIV/AIDS disease
- Discuss the victimization of disabled persons
- Understand the dynamics involved in gay and lesbian abuse

HIV/AIDS Victims[1]

HIV/AIDS is the black plague of the nineties. It causes normally rational professionals to become emotional at the thought that they may have been exposed to AIDS. We are still learning the consequences of this disease; however, two facts remain constant—persons with AIDS die because of the infection, and at present there is no known cure. It is therefore critical that professionals in victim services understand how to respond to victims that have been exposed to this disease.

Medical and Psychological Aspects of HIV/AIDS

AIDS is the acronym for the medial term *acquired immune deficiency syndrome.* The "acquired" portion of the term means that the condition is not a birth defect but is acquired from another person after birth. "Immune deficiency" means that the immune system is repeatedly attacked by infections and diseases until it becomes so weak that it cannot perform its job. "Syndrome" means that a series of signs or symptoms occur together and characterize this particular abnormality. The term AIDS is be used only when the person has become seriously ill and has fulfilled the Centers for Disease Control's criteria for a formal diagnosis as AIDS. Otherwise, the more correct description HIV positive to describe persons who have the HIV disease or infection.[2]

HIV stands for *human immunodeficiency virus,* which overcomes and destroys the body's natural immune system. As the immune system deteriorates, the person's body is unable to protect itself from infections and diseases. The person dies from a disease or infection. The person does not die from AIDS or HIV; rather death results from one or more of the infections that overcome the person's weakened immune system.

There are two primary types of HIV: HIV-1 is the most common and deadly, and HIV-2 acts in the same way as HIV-1 but reproduces more slowly. Almost all infected persons in the United States suffer from HIV-1. Once a person is infected with HIV, there is no known cure. The progression of the disease can be slowed with medication, but it cannot be stopped. Most cases result in death; however, some persons, known as "nonprogressive long-term survivors," have the virus, but it does not destroy their immune system and they do not become sick and die from the disease. Researchers continue to study these individuals in an attempt to learn why the virus affects them differently than it does the majority of the infected population.[3]

HIV has various phases, running the spectrum from wellness to illness.[4] Normally, the virus replicates itself in the lymph glands and then begins to dump copious amounts of itself into the bloodstream, thus setting the stage for progression of the disease. There are five phases in the HIV infection:

Phase 1.   Asymptomatic incubation period, which lasts from four to six weeks. Phase 1 is often called the window period because the infected person has HIV present and replicating in the blood but generally has no detectable symptoms. This is a dangerous period because infected persons have no idea that they are contagious. At some point during this phase, the first antibody is produced, and the infected person converts from HIV negative to HIV positive. This conversion is called the *seroconversion.*

Phase 2.   Acute primary infection, which lasts from one to two weeks. During phase 2, the person experiences some symptoms of early infection but may not recognize the cause of the symptoms. For example, the person may attribute aches, pains, and swollen glands to the flu. The infected person has sufficient antibodies in his or her system to detect the HIV virus during this phase.

Phase 3.   Asymptomatic phase, which lasts three to fifteen years. This phase is characterized by seemingly good health while HIV continues to replicate in the blood and certain tissues and begins slowly to erode the body's immune system. The length of this phase varies among people depending on a number of factors, including the person's overall general health, self-care, and medical treatment received.

Phase 4.   Symptomatic phase with persistent, generalized lymphadenopathy, which lasts one to three years. Serious symptoms signal the beginning of phase 4. Infections that a healthy person would fight off will make an HIV-positive person ill. The symptoms for this phase include fever, night sweats, diarrhea, enlargement of the lymph glands, weight loss, oral lesions, fatigue, rashes, and cognitive slowing.

Phase 5.   AIDS case, which lasts from one to three years. This condition meets the Centers for Disease Control's criteria for the definition of AIDS. As the person approaches death (end-stage AIDS), it is common to have multiple symptoms. The person dies as a result of infections and disease.[5]

HIV is not transmitted by animals or insects or by using swimming pools or hot tubs. It cannot be transmitted after contact with an infected person's clothes or use of the same toilet seat, eating utensils, drinking glasses, or telephone. There has never been a case in which HIV was transmitted by kissing or CPR. For HIV to be passed from one person to another, there must be an infected party, an uninfected party, and a route of entry to get particles of the virus from the donor to the recipient. HIV has been found in blood, semen, saliva, serum, urine, tears, breast milk, vaginal secretions, lung fluid, and cerebrospinal fluid. However, its presence in those fluids does not mean it is transmissible via those fluids. The three most common routes of HIV transmission are sexual transmission, blood-to-blood transmission, and mother-to-child transmission.

Most cases of HIV transmission occur as a result of sexual activities. Anal intercourse carries the highest risk of transmission because the fragile tissues of the anus and rectum may tear as a result of the friction of intercourse. Vaginal intercourse is also a high-risk practice with an infected person. Oral sex with a man or woman, although lower in risk than anal or vaginal intercourse, may also transmit the virus. Because of the violent nature of most sex crimes, there is a great concern that victims may be exposed to HIV.

Blood-to-blood transmission can also occur in a variety of ways. Using infected needles can transmit the disease. This method of transmission is common among drug users and is of concern to health workers who receive needle sticks during their work with patients. The virus may be transmitted when contaminated blood or body fluids come into contact with open wounds. This is an area of concern in domestic violence cases when one party may get infected blood into an open wound of another person.

Mother-to-child transmission occurs when the virus is transmitted to the fetus of a pregnant woman. This is the most common form of pediatric transmission. A newborn may also become infected as a result of breast-feeding from an HIV-positive mother.

AIDS and HIV present social, psychological, and medical problems. AIDS has changed our view of public health and has affected how we judge others. People with HIV disease respond like all others in a crisis situation. Learning that one has HIV is a severe stressor because of the inevitable result—death. Service providers must understand that there is no right or wrong way to respond to this life-threatening disease.

When individuals learn they are infected with HIV, they may react with a wide range of emotions similar to those experienced by victims of crime. The trauma of victimization is discussed in detail in Chapter 5. Once they have passed through these emotions, they must face the physical, social, and psychological aspects of living and dying with this disease. As death becomes more imminent, AIDS victims begin to plan for their death. This process becomes difficult and sometimes impossible because they may be coping with HIV-related dementia.

HIV-induced is the presence of a dementia that is judged to be the direct pathophysiological consequence of the HIV disease. The major features of this type of dementia are forgetfulness, slowness, poor concentration, and difficulties with problem solving. The infected person may exhibit apathy and social withdrawal and occasionally experience delirium, delusions, or hallucinations.[6]

Victim services providers must remember that AIDS is a medical disease that has additional social and psychological aspects. Because some victims of crime may become infected by the virus, professionals must be knowledgeable regarding the disease and be prepared to address sensitive issues. The next section will examine some of these issues.

Victim Services Issues

Since society acknowledged the existence and impact of HIV, victim services providers have attempted to deal with its impact on the victims they serve. Most service providers focused solely on victims of rape. However, with the passage of time and expansion of knowledge regarding the disease, victim services providers now must understand how HIV affects victims of child sexual abuse and other violent crimes. Service providers must also be ready to deal with persons who are infected with the disease and who are victimized. Additionally, they must respond to family members, friends, and colleagues of these victims who bring their own concerns, biases, and feelings to their interactions with victim services providers.

HIV/AIDS is a medical condition, and therefore a person's HIV status is considered confidential information. Victim services providers must always remember that they may not disseminate the medical status of a victim suffering from this disease without his or her express permission. Victim providers must be able to explain the consequences to victims of disclosing or not disclosing their condition to others.

Creating a safe and open environment in which a victim, family member, friend, or colleague will feel secure enough in raising the HIV/AIDS issue is a critical first step in responding to these victims' special needs. In a safe environment, victims receive a message that they are with someone who has some knowledge of the disease and is open to discussing it. Victims must be reassured that the professional is not sitting in judgment on them or their lifestyle.

Displaying AIDS awareness posters in the office may assist in establishing this open environment. Posters can be obtained from local AIDS service organizations, county health departments, and the Centers for Disease Control. Information regarding the disease should be made available in brochures. Many victims have found lists of local AIDS service organizations to be very helpful.[7]

Raising the issue of HIV/AIDS with a victim who may be at risk is one of the most difficult tasks undertaken by a victim services provider. This topic may be made easier by the open and safe office environment. Victims may not want to discuss this topic for a variety of reasons: they may not realize they are at risk; they may understand that they are at risk but be fearful of discussing the risk with anyone; or they may already know they are infected and decide not to disclose that fact.

Victim assistance professionals should take the time to review the victim's risk of infection and motivation for being tested. They should explain the testing process, including the various test results. They may need to consider a collaborative response to a victim's inquiry by using a local AIDS service provider. Victim services providers should never deliver the victim's HIV/AIDS test results. This would possibly introduce an uncomfortable aspect to an already existing relationship because the victim professional may become a constant reminder of the moment the positive results were delivered to the victim.[8]

One controversial issue in the criminal justice field today involves involuntary testing of offenders. In recent years, several states have passed laws that give victims of sexual assault access to information about the HIV status of their offender.[9] These laws apply to those arrested, convicted, or who have pled guilty to crimes involving sexual penetration or other exposure to an offender's bodily fluids. At the federal level, sexual assault victims can request an order requiring the HIV testing of the defendant if the court finds there is probable cause to believe that the defendant committed the offense, that the victim has received appropriate counseling, and that the information is necessary for the health of the victim.

If the offender is positive, it does not mean that the victim will have contracted the virus, but simply learning of the offender's status may cause the victim unnecessary emotional upheaval. The victim must also be tested to be absolutely sure that the virus was or was not transmitted. Other professionals fear that imposing mandatory testing on offenders will lead to mandatory testing of other groups or professions. This continues to be a hotly debated topic.[10] The Practicum, that follows lists distinct classes of persons in our society. Discuss the advantages and disadvantages of mandatory testing of these persons.

If we adopt mandatory testing of offenders and other groups for the HIV/AIDS disease, isn't it also reasonable to test those groups for additional diseases, such as all other sexually transmitted diseases?

Professionals in this field normally work with persons who have already experienced the trauma of victimization. Most victim assistance providers do not encounter a person who has a life-threatening illness such as HIV/AIDS. When they work with these victims, it is with the knowledge that the victim will surely die as a result of this disease. It is therefore critical that everyone in the criminal justice system understand the effect on victims of HIV/AIDS.

Specific Victim Populations

Victim services providers must not only understand the HIV/AIDS disease but also be able to relate to specific victim populations who might be exposed to the disease. This section focuses on those victims for whom HIV/AIDS is a concern. The victim

---

PRACTICUM: Who Should Undergo Mandatory Testing for HIV/AIDS?	
Sexual predators	Professional athletes
Physicians, dentists, nurses	Law enforcement personnel
Members of the military	All persons above the age of fifteen

populations include victims of rape, child abuse victims, family violence victims, and HIV-positive persons who are victimized.

Victims of Rape

Even as enlightened as we like to think our society is about crime and victimization, victims of rape are still reluctant to report such assaults. Although many victims have experienced difficulty disclosing their rape to their significant partners, the additional factor of possible exposure to HIV may make disclosure even more difficult. The grieving process that normally occurs after a rape may now be extended and deepened because of the added fear regarding HIV.[11] These issues will continue to confront victim services providers as they work with victims of rape until we find a cure for the HIV/AIDS disease.[12]

Child Victims

The Centers for Disease Control reports that there were 6,209 pediatric cases of AIDS in the United States as of the end of 1994. Children who are sexually assaulted are considered to be at higher risk than adult victims of sexual assault. This increased risk is based on two factors: (1) child victims may be repeatedly assaulted over a long period of time by the same perpetrator; and (2) children are at a greater risk of injury during penetration and as a result there is a higher likelihood of transmission of the virus during the sexual act.

Victim services providers must assist parents in making informed decisions regarding how much information to give to a young child who has been sexually assaulted by an HIV-positive perpetrator. The victim services provider should work closely with the AIDS service provider regarding counseling and other support techniques for both the child and the parents.[13]

Family Violence Victims

Family violence occurs every day from the mansions of Brentwood to the slums of New York. This type of violence crosses all ethnic, social, and sexual boundaries. Some family violence victims are forced to participate in drug usage with the abuser and his friends. Additionally, the abuser may be using drugs or engaging in sexual acts with multiple partners that exposes him to the disease. He can then pass the virus along to his partner during "consensual" sexual relations. The victim's request for use of a condom or other device may be met with violence by the abuser.

Shelters for battered women have traditionally been places of sanctuary for these victims. The spread of HIV/AIDS disease has added another complication to the heavy burden carried by these shelters. Victim services providers must ensure that staff working in the shelters understand the medical and legal aspects of the disease so as not to traumatize further those residents who are HIV-positive.

HIV-Positive Persons Who Are Victimized

Persons who are HIV-positive are no different from the rest of society as it relates to becoming a victim of a violent crime. What is different is that some persons have been victimized merely because of their real or perceived HIV status. Other HIV-positive victims must decide if they are going to disclose their status to authorities when reporting crimes of violence.

HIV-related violence covers a wide spectrum of acts from simple verbal abuse, to harassment, to job discrimination and actual physical attacks. The person's appearance may suggest that he or she is at risk of carrying HIV. Certain groups, such as homosexuals, drug users, and those wearing AIDS support ribbons and other symbols, have suffered HIV-related violence.

A person who is living with HIV must expend a great deal of energy on day-to-day survival, including taking medications, attending medical appointments and treatment sessions, and going to support groups. Suffering criminal victimization with its attendant responsibilities of reporting the crime, interviewing with law enforcement officers, attending court, and facing the perpetrator can add a tremendous amount of stress to the victim's life. This increased stress can dramatically impact the victim's health. For this and other reasons, HIV-positive victims may decide not to pursue reporting victimization. Still others may report, but as the burdens of appearing in court increase, they may opt to drop the charges. Victim services providers must be aware of the dynamics of this form of victimization and respond accordingly by supporting the victim.

Disabled Victims

Introduction

Disabled victims have the same rights as any other victim; however, they remain one of the largest categories of victims to be neglected by our criminal justice system.[14] This is because they are not afforded the same type of access, legitimacy, or respect as other victims. For example, as the Practicum "Disability and Crime" illustrates, some material in the criminal justice system is in several different languages, but very few agencies may have information in Braille. This section will provide victim services providers with an overview of some of the problems faced by disabled persons.

Crimes against persons with developmental and other severe disabilities is a problem similar to other forms of violence.[15] Some research indicates that the level of violence against children and adults with developmental and other severe disabilities is as much as five times higher than against the general public, that such crimes are reported at a much lower rate, and that there are indications of lower rates of prosecution and conviction.[16]

One of the first issues confronting victim services providers is how to respond to victims of crimes who also have a disability.[17] Each type of disability may require a different response on the part of the victim services provider. For example, a victim with a hearing impairment has different needs than a victim with a sight impairment. However, certain rules apply to all crime victims who are disabled.

PRACTICUM: Disability and Crime

It was late in the evening when John was returning home from the local convenience store with a carton of milk and some other groceries. It was cold and rainy, and John was hurrying as fast as he could to reach his apartment, when two persons grabbed him from behind and pulled him into an alley.

They took his wallet, trashed his bag of groceries, and proceeded to kick him in the ribs, legs, and head. Several other people walked by the attack but did nothing to render assistance. The perpetrators fled only when they heard a police siren. John gave a report to the police and was informed by the investigating officer of his right to contact the local victim–witness office. Several days later, John went downtown to that office. He had to ride ten stories in a crowded elevator and was late for the scheduled appointment. Once inside the office, he was asked to have a seat and waited approximately thirty minutes before he finally was interviewed regarding his victimization. After the interview with a victim services provider, John wanted to take some of the information home so he could study his rights as a victim more closely. Unfortunately the office did not have any pamphlets in his language—John was blind.

1. What are the issues faced by a victim services provider in this situation?

2. What problems did John encounter? How would you attempt to solve those problems? Assume you do not have any additional funds in your agency.

- Look directly at the victim when speaking. Deliberately averting your eyes is impolite and can be uncomfortable.
- Feel free to ask a disabled victim how you should act or communicate most effectively if you have any doubts about correctness in the situation.
- Address and speak directly to the disabled person, even if the person is accompanied or assisted by a third-party nondisabled person.
- Feel free to offer physical assistance to a disabled person, such as offering your arm if the need arises, but do not assume the person will need it or accept it.
- Ask a disabled victim about any personal needs that will require special services or arrangements, and then attempt to make arrangements to meet those needs.
- Do not stare or avoid looking at a visible disability or deformity or express sympathy to the disabled victim.
- Do not tell the disabled victim you admire his or her courage or determination for living with the disability. The disabled person doesn't want to be thought of as a hero.
- Do not avoid humorous situations that occur as a result of a disability. Take your cue from the victim.[18]

These suggestions should be used as guidelines when working with disabled persons. Victim service professionals must understand that the disabled person, like all other victims, is an individual and must be approached and interacted with as a separate and distinct individual. For years, people with disabilities tolerated discrimination and hardship as a result of society's reaction to their disability. Congress finally addressed this issue when it enacted the Civil Rights Act of 1964 and the Americans with Disabilities Act of 1990.

Legal Issues

There are approximately 43 million Americans with one or more disabilities. These disabilities may be mental, physical, or both. They may be congenital (occurring at birth) or adventitious (occurring after birth). As indicated earlier in this chapter, a *disabled person* is one who has a physical or mental impairment that substantially limits one or more of the major life activities of that individual, or that person has a record of such impairment, or that person is regarded as having such an impairment. This definition is founded on the language contained in the Americans with Disabilities Act (ADA) of 1990. This is one of the most comprehensive pieces of civil rights legislation passed by Congress since the Civil Rights Act of 1964. The ADA was enacted by Congress to protect the employment and accessibility rights of persons suffering from disabilities. Any agency receiving any type of governmental funding (federal, state, or local) must comply with the provisions contained in the ADA.

Some authorities state that persons with developmental and other severe disabilities represent approximately 10 percent of the population of our country (1.8 percent developmental disabilities, 5 percent adult onset brain impairment, 2.8 percent severe major mental disorders). As many as 30 percent to 40 percent of all families may have loved ones or close friends with developmental or other severe disabilities. These numbers may increase as our population ages. Fifteen percent of Americans over the age of fifty-five have cognitive disabilities, and 25 percent of those over the age of seventy-five suffer from this form of disability.[19]

Disabilities covered by the law include physical and mental impairments. Physical disabilities include physiological disorders or conditions, disfigurement, or loss of use of any body system. Specific examples include cerebral palsy, epilepsy, multiple sclerosis, AIDS/HIV infections, cancer, heart disease, and diabetes. Mental impairments include any mental or psychological disorder, such as mental retardation, organic brain syndrome, emotional or mental illness, and specific learning disorders.

Victim services providers must anticipate serving disabled victims. They must work with local governmental agencies and be prepared to provide a wide variety of services to those disabled persons in need of their help. They should become familiar with the ADA and be spokespeople for disabled victims within the criminal justice system.

Types of Victimization

Disabled persons can be victimized in the same way as other persons; however, their response to crime is different from other victims. Crimes against disabled persons are underreported for a number of reasons: There may be communication and mobility barriers; the disabled person may be unable to report the crime because of a mental or developmental reason, or the person may be dependant on others to do so; and finally, some reporting agencies fail to record the fact that the victim was disabled.[20]

One researcher reported that 60 percent of all persons who have mental disabilities become victims of crime sometime during their life, and 60 percent of all hearing-impaired women will be victims of sexual assault.[21] Another source indicates that many disabled people do not receive any form of sex education, and some of them are socialized to obey others without question. Consequently, they do not complain or report acts of sexual maltreatment.[22] Disabled individuals in institutions are twice as likely as those in the community to be abused.[23]

Although the data are extremely limited, there is reason to believe that substantial numbers of disabled persons are victims of domestic abuse. These studies also indicate that hearing-impaired women have a high probability of becoming victims of domestic violence.[24] For years, professionals have acknowledged that there is a higher risk of child abuse if the child is suffering from a disability.[25]

Emerging Issues

The realization that disabled victims present unique challenges to those in the criminal justice system is just being acknowledged at local, state, and federal jurisdictions. California has assembled a task force to study these issues, and this group has formulated a series of recommendations regarding the treatment of disabled crime victims.[26] These recommendations still need further study and revision, but they represent an important first step in this newly emerging area of victimization of the disabled. The following is a brief summary of these recommendations.

The Legal Process

Each service provider should have a criminal justice coordinator. Knowledgeable service professionals and disability advocates should be available to assist the police, prosecutors, and courts. Each developmental disabilities regional center and other primary care or case management service agencies should have a twenty-four-hour phone number to respond to requests for information on an emergency basis. Criminal justice organizations should have specialized staff for cases involving persons with disabilities. This will allow for the gathering of information and building of expertise by those in the system. It will also provide a single point of contact for service organizations. There should be sentence enhancements when disabled persons are victims. This protects those who cannot protect themselves. Regular and relatively comprehensive training on disabled victims should occur for police, prosecutors, judges, defense attorneys, probation officers, victim–witness officers, and others in the criminal justice system.

Reporting laws should be amended to require mandatory reporting of possible crimes against disabled victims. Persons that deal with the disabled on a regular basis should receive training in recognizing criminal acts against these victims and how to report them. Multidisciplinary teams including disabled victims should be formed in all local jurisdictions. These teams should meet on a regular basis to address various problems encountered by disabled victims. These teams should review sudden, unexpected deaths or major traumatic injuries to the disabled when the death or injury occurs in an institution, residential or other service facility.

Victim Support
Each community should develop multidisciplinary teams to provide victim support cooperatively. Each team should include, as a minimum, victim services providers, sexual assault advocates, and service providers who work with the disabled. All case management agencies should have a designated staff person to serve as an advocate for disabled victims. There should be a coordinated public relations campaign to encourage disabled victims to report all crimes committed against them.

Risk Reduction and Prevention
Curriculums and required training for residential programs, vocational training, day programs, recreational programs, and special education should be modified to include personal safety training skills for disabled persons. This training should include self-defense skills, individual rights, assertiveness training, social skills, and training about the criminal justice system. All education and service plans for disabled clients should include a personal safety plan as a component. Crime prevention should involve the client, service providers, family, and friends. Special training should be conducted for family members on how to overcome isolation, facilitate attachments, support family relationships, and increase and improve communication skills of the client and family members. Safer living environments are necessary to prevent victimization of the disabled. The more connected and integrated these persons are with their community, the lower the risk of victimization. Steps should be taken to break down the traditional barriers that exist between the disabled and the community. Adult protective service agencies should have adequate resources to investigate reported abuse of the disabled.

Institutional Abuse
There is a critical need to improve standards for screening and hiring of staff in institutions that serve the disabled. Staff training in institutions needs to be improved and updated. Use of the "buddy system" for mentoring new and problem employees should be implemented. Advocacy systems that are independent of any institutional provider should be created and supported. Ombudsperson programs need to be expanded to address these concerns. Administrators and professional staff must be actively present in all institutions to monitor and supervise staff and the clients. Management staff must be held accountable for abuse that occurs in their institutions and yet must also be encouraged to report such abuse. They must look beyond individual cases and accept the moral and professional responsibility to care for these individuals.

Gay and Lesbian Victims

This section is included because gay and lesbian victimization is often overlooked. One unique aspect of their victimization deals with intimate violence between gay and lesbian couples. Some people respond negatively to the discussion of this type of aggression. To accept that reaction is to deny reality and fail to anticipate issues that affect many professionals who work in the area of victim services. The fact of the matter is that gays and lesbians are victims of crime and they do live, work, and love with same-sex partners.

History

The history of the gay and lesbian struggle for equal treatment does not necessarily belong in a text on victimology. However, society's reactions to same-sex living arrangements need to be explored for professionals to understand some of the dynamics involved in a gay or lesbian relationship. Understanding these relationships will allow professionals to react properly when faced with a situation that involves gay or lesbian victimization.

Historically, homosexual behavior can be traced back to ancient Greece, where homosexuality was viewed as natural in many segments of Greek society. Plato's *Symposium* extolled the virtues of homosexual behavior and indicated that homosexual lovers would make the best soldiers.[27] One scholar indicates that homosexuality was not considered socially deviant behavior until the time of Thomas Aquinas and St. Augustine, both of whom argued that it was unnatural because it did not lead to conception.[28] In 1980, the DSM-III-R reclassified homosexual behavior as an alternative sexual lifestyle rather than deviant behavior. This view is not accepted by all members of our society. Even in the medical community there remains a core of professionals whose opinion is that homosexuality is unnatural sexual behavior.

Definitions

Homosexual, gay, lesbian—these terms evoke strong emotional responses from certain segments of our society. However, to discuss gay and lesbian victimization accurately, one needs to put that response aside and start with a clear understanding of what these terms mean.

- *Homosexuality* is defined as the manifestation of sexual desire toward a member of one's own sex.
- *Gay* is defined as a male homosexual or a socially integrated group oriented toward and concerned with the welfare of homosexuals.
- *Lesbian* is defined as a female homosexual.[29] Lesbianism is believed to have been named for the Isle of Lesbos, where the practice of lesbianism was reputed to have been general in ancient days.

Even these terms are subject to debate and interpretation, especially among members of the gay and lesbian community itself. If the gay and lesbian community cannot agree on certain definitions, it becomes very difficult to research victimization within those communities.

Gays and Lesbians as Victims of Crime

Antigay and antilesbian violence is a pervasive problem throughout the United States.[30] Research, surveys, studies, and community-based analyses of gay and lesbian victimization have all indicated that gay men and lesbian women are victimized at a higher rate than the general population.[31]

Additionally, the discovery and spread of AIDS with its high mortality rate has affected the homosexual community disproportionately and has generated additional fear, hatred, and discrimination against members of the gay and lesbian community. Although victimization existed before the discovery of AIDS, evidence suggests that the spread of this virus within the homosexual community has increased the prejudice that already existed.

Since 1984, the National Gay and Lesbian Task Force Policy Institute has produced an annual report on gay and lesbian violence.[32] This report uses data collected from programs in nine cities—Boston, Chicago, Columbus, Detroit, Minneapolis/St. Paul, New York, Portland, Los Angeles, and San Francisco.

Over one-third of all hate crimes committed against gay or lesbian victims involved two or more perpetrators. Data indicate that gay and lesbian offenses involve a higher number of perpetrators per incident than other hate crimes. The FBI lists the average perpetrator–victim ratio for all forms of hate crimes as 1 to 1.19.[33] Gay and lesbian victims are often surprised and outnumbered by their assailants, and therefore fighting back may not be a viable option.

Forty-three percent of the incidents involved physical assaults. The level of injury suffered by the victims was high, with only 37 percent escaping without any injury, 28 percent suffering minor injuries, 16 percent requiring outpatient medical treatment, 17 percent requiring admission to the hospital, and 3 percent of the attacks resulting in the death of the victim. These figures dispel the myths that the majority of hate crimes against gay or lesbian victims involve simple intimidation or verbal threats.

In the past thirty years, there has been a considerable body of knowledge and research accumulated on sexual coercion in heterosexual relationships. Marital rape is discussed in depth in this text in Chapter 8. However, there is very little research into the area of gay men as victims of nonconsensual, or forced, sex. Waterman and her associates conducted one of the first studies of sexual coercion in gay male and lesbian relationships.[34] The results of their research indicate that forced sex is a considerable problem for gay men.

Hickson and his associates reviewed incidents of nonconsensual sexual activity among 930 gay men living in England and Wales.[35] Hickson points out that the vast majority of research dealing with sexual assault on men has focused on prison populations. The presumed sexual orientation of men who rape other men has been subject to some debate. Hickson correctly states that men rape other men for the same reasons they rape women, and that male rape is rarely, if ever, a homosexual problem. Of the 930 men interviewed, 257, or 27 percent, stated that they had been subjected to nonconsensual sex at some point in their lives. After deleting 10 of the men who were assaulted by women, and 28 respondents who declined to discuss the event or could not remember the details, the remaining 219 subjects' sexual history was examined.

Hickson's research indicated a broad range of different types of sexual assaults on gay men. These assaults included older men touching younger boys, sexual assault of the victim by a heterosexual man after the victim had identified himself as gay, and a large number of assaults that occurred between gay men.

Just as female victims of male battering are reluctant or incapable of reporting or leaving the abusing spouse, so are same-sex victims. However, gay and lesbian victims face additional problems when it comes to disclosure or detachment from the abuser. Many of these problems are unique to the lesbian or gay community and have contributed to a lack of academic research in this area of victimology.

Intimate Violence

As indicated earlier, gays and lesbians live together as same-sex partners. These living arrangements sometimes result in one of the partners becoming a victim of intimate violence. As more gays and lesbians acknowledge this form of abuse, it will be incumbent upon professionals to understand the dynamics that are involved and to offer support and treatment to the victims.

Gay and lesbian couples face the same kind of violence that occurs in a heterosexual relationship. Some authorities refer to gays and lesbians who live together as a family as a *nontraditional family*. By some estimates, there are several million nontraditional families in the United States.[36] Many of these families include children from previous marriages, adoptions, or artificial insemination of a lesbian partner. These are family units in every aspect except for the issuance by the state of a marriage license. Polikoff states that these nontraditional families are defined by their sharing of emotions and their financial interdependence in the relationship.[37]

Gay and lesbian couples have struggled for years to be accepted in society and accorded the same rights as heterosexual couples. The U.S. Census Bureau annual survey in 1990 revealed 4.47 million households of unmarried adults with 1.6 million of this number composed of members of the same sex.[38] One complex issue facing these couples is gay or lesbian abuse.

In comparison to other forms of family violence, there is very little research in the area of lesbian and gay abuse. However, some scholars in academia have set forth definitions of gender-specific abuse. For example, Hart defines lesbian battering as "that pattern of violent and coercive behaviors whereby a lesbian seeks to control the thoughts, beliefs or conduct of her intimate partner or to punish the intimate for resisting the perpetrator's control over her."[39] Island and Letellier published one of the first studies on gay abuse and defined gay domestic violence as "any unwanted physical force, psychological abuse, material or property damage inflicted on one man by another."[40] Both definitions involve dynamics similar to heterosexual spousal abuse. Some authorities might argue that gay and lesbian abuse should have its own definition because of the nature of the relationship; however, if one accepts that position, then heterosexual couples who live together but are not married should have their own definition of abuse. To approach this topic in such a manner would be to splinter all relationships into separate groups and lose sight of the overall dynamics that are involved in an abusive relationship. The definition of family violence used in this text does not require that the parties be married or even be of different sexes. *Family violence* is defined as any act or omission by persons who are cohabitating that results in serious injury to other members of the family. Because this term covers gay and lesbian abuse, it will be used to promote the fact that this type of aggression is in fact a form of family violence.

To acknowledge that lesbian and gay couples face many of the same problems as heterosexual couples is to accord a legitimacy to their status. There is a segment of the population that refuses to accept same-sex relationships as a legitimate expression of society's values. This viewpoint is only one reason why there is so little research in this area of family violence. However, there are other reasons for the failure to explore this type of aggression. Many of these reasons are unique to the lesbian and gay community and are discussed later in this section.

Extent of the Problem

The true extent of lesbian and gay family violence has never been accurately determined. Some researchers argue that battering within same-sex relationships is the same as it is for heterosexual couples, approximately 25 to 35 percent.[41] Other authorities have stated that domestic violence is the third most severe health problem facing gay men.[42]

The lesbian and gay communities themselves have contributed in some instances to the lack of hard scientific evidence concerning this form of family violence. Lesbian communities may be reluctant, for ideological reasons, to admit that one woman can batter another. To do so is contrary to the idea of a peaceful woman-centered world. However, there is more discussion within the lesbian community regarding battering than in the gay community. Gays may be reluctant to discuss gay abuse because very simply, as one scholar put it, "the gay community would rather not know."[43]

When Yale University conducted a study dealing with battered women and the effectiveness of restraining orders, they discovered that gay and lesbian abuse was so extensive they needed to include this segment of the population in the study.[44] There is a great deal of conflict among authorities as to whether gay men or lesbians are the more violent of the two. Some researchers claim that lesbians seem to be more aggressive than gay men or heterosexual women.[45] Other authors state that there is some evidence to support the theory that violence may occur more frequently between gay men than lesbians.[46] However, all parties to this debate agree that these conclusions are tentative at best, and more empirical research needs to be conducted in this area. Although there has been no definitive study on the different types of abuse suffered by gay couples, there is support for the proposition that they suffer the same type of abuse as lesbian couples.

There is still a great deal of misinformation regarding AIDS, its effect, and how it may be acquired. Gay or lesbian victims who are HIV positive may feel that they do not have any support system available to them other than the abusing partner. Also, if the abuser has AIDS or is HIV positive, the victim may feel a great deal of remorse at the thought of reporting the partner to law enforcement agencies or otherwise abandoning him or her.[47]

The abuser may also prevent the victim from disclosing the abuse or leaving the relationship by threatening to "out" the victim. *Outing* is disclosure of the victim's sexual preference. The abuser may threaten to tell the victim's friends, family, or others unless the victim agrees to conceal the abuse. Even if the victim is open about sexual preference, the batterer may exploit fears of sexist and heterosexual stereotypes to convince the victim that reporting the incident is useless.

Lesbian and gay victims face additional pressure from their peers within the gay community. Some authorities point out that the gay community's failure to acknowledge family violence within its ranks is based on a fear that acknowledgment of such behavior will lead to increased derision from the heterosexual community by adding credence to the homophobic attitude that gay men and lesbians are deviates.[48]

Another problem facing lesbian and gay victims is the critical shortage of support services and/or organizations that offer support for same-sex victims of family violence. Specialized counseling services for gay and lesbian victims of family violence are available in only a few cities: New York, San Francisco, Seattle, and Minneapolis.[49] No city has established an emergency shelter specifically for gay men or lesbian victims of family violence.[50] Although some lesbian victims may be able to use battered women's services and/or shelters, this option is not available to gay men.

Legal Aspects of Gay and Lesbian Abuse

Gay and lesbian victims face additional hurdles when they attempt to prevent further abuse by their partners. These obstacles include outdated, and in many cases homophobic, attitudes by law enforcement officers, attorneys, and even members of the judiciary system. Simply reporting the incident may cause the victims to suffer more humiliation and pain from a system that is ill equipped to deal with this form of family violence.

Law enforcement officers and members of the judicial system have historically been reluctant to acknowledge gay and lesbian abuse. In many instances, this leaves the victims without assistance from the legal system. Therefore, abused gays and lesbians are generally less likely to report incidents of domestic violence to the police.

There are reported cases in which members of the judiciary system have made comments reflecting their negative feelings toward gay and lesbian couples. In *Constant A. v. Paul C.A.* the court awarded custody of the children to the father stating, ". . . once the father established the mother's lesbian relationship and his own legitimate and stable heterosexual relationship, a presumption arose favoring the preferability of the traditional relationship."[51]

Although many professionals in the criminal justice system are aware of the dynamics involved in male battering of women, they may be unwilling to accept the fact that these same kinds of dynamics are operating in same-sex battery. This lack of knowledge on the part of police and the judicial system works to the advantage of the abuser this way: it is not uncommon for the abuser to claim that he or she is in fact the victim. Because many gay and lesbian couples may be the same size physically, the stereotypical view that the larger person is always the aggressor in a relationship may prevent professionals from seeing the facts as legitimate. Even assuming professionals within the criminal justice system are willing to act on allegations of same-sex battering, the laws in sixteen states do not cover same-sex, nonrelated cohabitants.

Some states make certain sex acts criminal even when they occur between consenting adults. In *Bowers v. Hardwick,* the U.S. Supreme Court upheld the right of states to impose criminal sanctions on acts that occur in the privacy of one's bedroom.[52] Although sodomy statutes among consenting adults are criminal in only six states, misinformation and fear may allow the perpetrator to threaten the victim with disclosure of certain sex acts that might be considered criminal. As stated in *Baker v Wade,*

> *the existence of these criminal laws, even if they are not enforced . . . does result in stigma, emotional stress and other adverse effects. The anxieties caused to homosexuals—fear of arrest, loss of jobs, discovery, etc.—can cause severe mental health problems.*[53]

This discussion may lead one to believe that there is no hope for gay and lesbian victims. This is not the case. Therapists are beginning to discuss gay and lesbian relationships more often.[54] Those in academia continue researching issues of gay and lesbian victimization.[55] An example of a local program that provides support for victims of gay and lesbian abuse is the New York City Gay and Lesbian AntiViolence Project. It provides a number of services for gay and lesbian victims including:

- Telephone counseling and crisis intervention
- Short-term in-person counseling
- Assistance in obtaining orders of protection
- Police advocacy and precinct accompaniment
- Crime victims' compensation filing and advocacy
- Court advocacy, monitoring, and accompaniment
- Information and referrals
- Community education and outreach
- Volunteer training

- Hospital accompaniment
- Advocacy with other service agencies

These activities are similar to those offered to heterosexual victims by a number of social service agencies. As more gays and lesbians accept that it is all right to come out of another closet and admit that they have been victims, the sooner we will accept this form of aggression as a part of the totality of the circumstances that must be addressed when studying victimology.

Prisoners as Victims

We have known for a number of years that inmates who are incarcerated may be victimized. It seems that we just have not cared enough to seriously address the issue of prisoners as victims. There are many forms of inmate victimization; however, this section focuses on sexual violence perpetrated by one inmate on another. One estimate places the number of inmates who have been sexually assaulted over the past twenty year in excess of 1 million.[56] Various efforts to address this form of violence and victimization have not solved this immense social problem.

In 1994, the United State Supreme Court, in *Farmer vs. Brennan*, held there was no legitimate penological purpose that is served by allowing rape to occur within prisons.[57] Further, the court held that inmates who are raped as a result of deliberate indifference by prison officials suffered cruel and unusual punishment within the meaning of the eighth Amendment of the U.S. Constitution. Unfortunately, this ruling that established possible liability for prison officials has done little to stop prison rape.

New inmates are more vulnerable to prison rape than are recidivists who have prior imprisonment experiences and knowledge. The latter group of inmates has learned of safety zones, such as gang membership and religious group affiliations, that insulate them from sexual violence. New inmates do not know of these zones and are judged vulnerable by sexual predators. This vulnerability may show up in the way a new inmate walks, his speed in finding acquaintances, and his actions in the dining hall. The characteristics of prison rapist are somewhat unclear, but several patterns are beginning to emerge. The perpetrators are younger and frequently larger or stronger than their victims and generally are more assertive and more at home in the prison environment. Typically, many of them have been convicted of crimes of a more violent nature than the crimes of their victims.[58]

With a national jail and prison population of 2 million at mid-year 2002, the United States likely exposes tens of thousands of male inmates to rape and consequently to HIV/AIDS and other STDs. The release of inmates from jails and prisons—estimated at 11.5 million persons in 1998—transforms the consequences of male rape from a correctional matter into a public health crisis. Inmates experience stigmatization by other inmates and staff as well as physical and mental trauma. Civil rights litigation on behalf of the victims rarely succeeds, and damage awards in successful litigation are usually small.[59]

On September 4, 2003, President Bush signed the Prison Rape Elimination Act (PREA) of 2003. This law establishes a zero tolerance for rape and sexual assault in prisons. The law requires several actions by the Department of Justice, including collection of statistics, establishment of a review panel, and training.

One interim finding regarding sexual activities in prison is that it takes many forms: (1) the traditional sex assault incident with use of force or fear, (2) services for services (sex for protection), and (3) services for property (sex for cigarettes or commissary items). Some of these activities are considered as equal and consensual, however, others involve force and fear or emotional and incentive driven pressure.[60]

In the 2004 survey, there were more than 5,500 allegations of sexual violence. Prison systems reported 42 percent of all allegations, local or private juvenile facilities 23 percent, local jails 21 percent, and state juvenile system 11 percent. Sexual violence in confinement situations includes nonconsensual sexual acts, abusive sexual acts, staff sexual misconduct, and staff sexual harassment. Nonconsensual sexual acts include contact of any person without his or her consent and involve rape, sodomy or oral copulation. Abusive sexual contacts encompasses contact of any person who is unable or unwilling to consent, including intentional touching directly or through clothing of the genitalia, anus, groin, breast, inner thigh, or buttocks. Staff sexual misconduct is any sexual act directed at an inmate by an employee, volunteer, or agency representative. Staff sexual harassment involves repeated verbal comments of a sexual nature to an inmate by a staff person.[61]

Allegations involving inmate sexual violence at local and state agencies are usually investigated by outside authorities. However, investigations of staff sexual misconduct were left to prison authorities in 43 percent of the cases. Less than 20 percent of all the inmate allegations of nonconsensual sexual acts were substantiated or found to have occurred. In juvenile facilities, approximately 33 percent of alleged nonconsensual sexual acts were substantiated. Males comprised 90 percent of the victims and perpetrators in nonconsensual sexual acts in prison.

Caution is needed when viewing the 2004 report. There still exists a difference in definitions regarding the sexual activity of inmates. Some institutions lack effective reporting mechanisms, while others do not have uniform procedures for recording allegations.[62]

The PREA is a substantial step forward in addressing sexual violence within U.S. prisons. Future surveys and information will assist us in understanding this complex and often misunderstood form of sexual violence.

Violence in the Schools: From Bullying to Homicide

Introduction

School violence is an emotional and controversial topic in our society. Violence can include bullying behavior, fighting, sexual misconduct, gang activity, and various forms of homicide. This section will briefly examines causes and theories relating to violence in our schools, discusses bullying behavior, studies fighting on school grounds and elsewhere, looks at sexual misconduct on campus, talks about gangs within schools, and finally highlights homicide within schools.

Causation and Theories

A number of theories have been proposed to explain the cause of violence in our schools. For the most part, they are the same theories that address violence in our society: social learning theory, exchange theory, and violence in the media theory to name a few.

Most criminologists and victimologists have known for years that delinquency occurs most often in the company of peers. This phenomena has been labeled *group offending or co-offending.*

The Social Learning Theory.   The primary theme of the social learning theory is that delinquency is learned through peer-group inactions. One of the most prominent social theorists was Edwin Sutherland, who developed a theory that attempted to explain how group relations impact a person's attitudes and behaviors. When applied to youths, this theory assumes that juvenile delinquency is learned from others during the course of their social interaction. Sutherland's famous theory is called, the theory of differential association. It covers criminal acts from traditional street crimes to white collar crime, and juvenile delinquency.

The Exchange Theory.   This theory is based on the premise that people act according to a system of rewards or punishments. The exchange theory, as applied to bullying behavior, is based on a determination of costs and rewards.[63] To paraphrase one expert in the area of family violence, "To put it simply, people [become bullies] because they can."[64] Individuals resort to violence to obtain psychic or material goals as long as what they achieve is outweighed by the cost of aggression.

Violence in the Media.   Violence is an everyday part of our existence. For the most part, our society glamorizes violence. The boxer, football player, and actor are examples of media heroes who are sought after by men and women alike. Video games and their graphic depiction of violence also may desensitize people to the effects of violence and promote an attitude that rewards aggressive behavior in our society.[65]

Bullying

This section discusses the different aspects of bullying. As with many other aspects of victimology, there are conflicting views on what constitutes bullying.

As the situations in the Practicum indicate, many dynamics occur in a school setting. Some may be explained as simple, adolescent behavior, and others are clearly acts of bullying and even criminal in nature. Now let's examine some definitions of bullying.

PRACTICUM: Who Is the Bully?

Which of the following situations do you consider to be acts bullying.

1. Several male students surround a new seventh grade student and demand that he not cross a certain areas of the lawn, stating that the walkway is only for ninth graders. They inform him that they are ninth graders and will be watching to make sure he doesn't walk on that area of the lawn.

2. One female approaches another, grabs her purse, and throws it in the trash stating that she is the only one on campus who can carry that type of purse.

3. Several friends have a disagreement about a girl whom they all like, and decide not to speak to Sam Student, who is dating her. They further agree to ignore him whenever he approaches the group and not to include him in any after-school activities.

4. Several students wait in the restroom and demand money from each student for the privilege of using that restroom.

5. The class is dividing itself into two soccer teams, and no one wants to pick a new student who is very clumsy.

Definition: There is no single accepted definition of bullying. Some researchers attempt to define bullying by classifying actors as the aggressor or the victim. Other academics define bullying as a set of behaviors. One of the classic definitions of bullying was purposed by Olweus, who defined it from the victim's perspective: bullying behavior occurs when a victim is exposed, repeatedly and over time, to negative actions on the part of one or more persons.[66]

Scope: Bullying may be the most common form of school violence. Worldwide estimates range from 10 percent of secondary students to 27 percent of middle school students. Additionally, some researchers report that an astonishing 75 percent of school-aged children report having been bullied at least one time in their life. It appears that bullying is on the rise. Just as importantly, some authorities are suggesting that there is a positive relationship between bullying and more serious forms of violence.

Types: The definition of bullying given above is a very broad and inclusive definition. It typically involves an imbalance of power. It covers teasing, taunting (including name calling and labeling), shoving, stealing, extortion, and a variety of violent acts imposed on a person by one or more others who have more power. This power may be physical size, aggressive behavior, or simply numbers of actors in relation to the victim. Many authorities consider failure to include the victim in school activities such as sports as a form of bullying. However, it may be that such behavior has less to do with bullying and more to do with perceived athletic ability or popularity. No matter what the reason, the person who is the last to be selected or who is not even considered is going to suffer hurt and sometimes humiliation.

Reactions: As a society, we have become increasingly concerned with bullying. The media has conducted extensive investigations and published a wide variety of newspaper articles and television specials regarding bullying. Some academic researchers have purposed various programs that aim to reduce or eliminate bullying on campuses. Others have listed actions to be taken by the victim if bullying behavior occurs. Numerous publications that deal with bullying behavior are available for teachers and students. For example, *At-Risk Resources* offers over 142 books, DVDs, games, and other items that focus on bullying.[67]

We have not solved the problem of bullying. It has existed for years and will likely continue for the immediate future. What is hopeful is that now, for the first time, we are acknowledging it and conducting research to find it causes and how to respond to its victims.

Fighting

Clearly, as the previous discussion indicates, when there is an imbalance of power that leads to aggression, the resulting acts may be defined as bullying behavior. However, when the aggression leads to a physical fight and takes on the character of mutual combat, it becomes a distinct form of violence. Therefore, for purposes of this discussion, *fighting* may be defined as the physical attack of one person by another or others. Fighting goes beyond the shoving, threatening, and taunting typical of bullying. It is physically violent behavior provoked sometimes by bullying, sometimes by personal differences, sometimes by gang disputes—and sometimes by causes that are not easily identified.

Fighting on school grounds may be spontaneous or may be planned. Sometimes, the actual combat is delayed until after school when the combatants meet at a pre-selected place to settle their differences. Fighting may escalate from the use of fists and feet to knives, other weapons, and even guns.

Gangs

Despite our concern over gangs, there is not a widely accepted definition of a gang. Nor is there any agreement when a group of delinquents becomes a gang. In the 1920s. Frederic Thrasher set forth one of the earliest definitions of a gang. He stated that a gangs is an interstitial group originally formed spontaneously and then integrated through conflict. It is characterized by fact-to-face interaction, milling, movement through space as a unit, conflict, and planning.[68] There are a number of other definitions of gangs, including Decker and Van Winkle's which defines gangs as an age-graded peer group that exhibits some permanence, engages in criminal activity, and has some symbolic representation of member.[69]

In 1987, in response to nationwide concern, the United States Department of Justice established a program to study and respond to the gang problem in the United States. Called the National Youth Gang Suppression and Intervention, the project was headed by Irving A. Spergel, and it identified five strategies that were considered as promising practices:

1. Mobilizing community leaders to respond to gang-involved and at-risk youth.
2. Using outreach workers to engage gang members.

3. Providing social, economic, and educational opportunities for gang members.
4. Conducting gang-suppression activities.
5. Help community agencies better address gang problems.[70]

Gangs continue to exist on our streets, in our prisons, and within our schools. Some schools have gone so far as to prohibit the wearing of certain apparel or colors because might indicate gang membership. Gangs will continue to be a problem within our society for the immediate future.

Sexual Assault

Acquaitance rape was discussed in Chapter 8. It is one of the biggest problems facing our campuses today, from middle schools to college campuses.

How do we turn this tide of sexual violence in our schools? We have college classes that deal with family violence. We have women's studies programs or departments that focus on empowering women. Many college campuses have women's resource centers that provide a wide range of support for female students. However, most of these programs do not go far enough. Just as we educate our youth about the history of our country and the form of our government, so should we educate them about sexual violence. Someday, we will have classes in our middle schools and high schools that teach our students about the dynamics of sexual violence, how to prevent it, and what to do when it occurs.

Homicide in Schools

Homicide was discussed in Chapter 7. This section examine it from the perspective of violence within the school. Fewer than 1 percent of all homicides among school-aged children occur on or near school grounds. However, nearly two-thirds of school associated deaths were those of students, approximately one-tenth were teachers or other staff, and one-quarter were community. Eighty percent of school homicide or suicide victims were male. Finally, 28 percent of the deaths occurred inside school buildings, while 36 percent occurred out-doors, and 35 percent occurred off campus.[71]

The Centers of Disease Control conducted a number of studies regarding school violence and produced an excellent report dealing with the myths and realities of youth violence.[72] These misconceptions need to receive wide dissemination so that we can focus on the real causes and reasons for youth violence.

Myth 1: The epidemic of violent behavior of the early 1990s is over, and young people are much safer today.

Fact: While some reports indicate significant reductions since 1993, self-reports by youths reveal that some violent behavior remains high.

Myth 2: Most future offenders can be identified in early childhood.

Fact: Exhibiting uncontrolled behavior as a young child does not predetermine violence in adolescence. The majority of young people who were violent during their adolescence were not out of control in early childhood.

Myth 3: African American and Hispanic youths are more likely than other ethic groups to become involved in violence.

Fact: Race and ethnicity have little bearing on the overall proportion of racial and ethnic groups that engage in nonfatal violent behavior.

Myth 4: A new breed of young super-predators threatens the United States.

Fact: There is not scientific evidence to document the claim of increased seriousness or callousness.

Myth 5: Getting tough with juvenile offenders by trying them in adult criminal courts reduces the likelihood that they will commit more crimes.

Fact: Youths transferred to adult criminal court have significantly higher rates of reoffending and a greater likelihood of committing other felonies than do youths who remain in the juvenile justice system.

These are just some of the myths that exist about youth violence. They show the need for continued research in this critical phase of school violence. Homicide within schools or on school grounds carries a special sort of sorrow. We have witnessed individual students shoot teachers and other students. Some of these acts appear spontaneous, and others have involved careful planning. Just as we are responding to bullying, so must we prevent rather than react to homicide within our schools. There is hope for the future and for our children.

In a few pages, I have attempted to cover a series of topics that could occupy all of our attention for an entire Congressional session. Simply because I presented an overview does not mean that these are easily solved problems. We must, as Mad Eye Moody, character in the Harry Potter series, stated, "maintain constant vigilance." We must continue our crusade to protect our future both on and off the school grounds.

Summary

This chapter is a general overview of a serious issue within the criminal justice system. Special population victimization continues and in some instances is on the increase. Because the United States is becoming more diverse with the passage of each year, victim services providers need to become very aware and sensitive to the needs of these special victims. More important, they need to act as the spokespeople for these victims to individuals and agencies within the criminal justice system.

HIV/AIDS is a terrible disease with deadly consequences for any infected person. Victims of crimes may suffer a second trauma if there is the possibility that they were exposed to the virus during the commission of the crime. Victim services providers must be sensitive to these victims' special needs.

Disabled victims and gay or lesbian victims are only two of the many special populations that exist in the United States. However, their victimization carries special problems and issues that must be addressed by those within the criminal justice system. Because of their status, these victims may not report crimes. Additionally, they may be victimized a second time during the criminal justice process. Victim professionals must be aware of these potential problems when dealing with these special populations.

Key Terms

Disabled person is one who has a physical or mental impairment that substantially limits one or more of the major life activities of that individual or that person has a record of such impairment or that person is regarded as having such an impairment.

Homosexuality is defined as the manifestation of sexual desire toward a member of one's own sex.

Gay is defined as a male homosexual or a socially integrated group oriented toward and concerned with the welfare of homosexuals.

Lesbian is defined as a female homosexual.

Nontraditional family occurs when gays or lesbians live together as a family.

Family violence is defined as any act or omission by persons who are cohabiting that results in serious injury to other members of the family.

Outing is disclosure of the victim's sexual preference.

Discussion Questions

1. Should victims who are HIV-positive be treated any differently than other victims? Why?

2. Should a person suffering from HIV/AIDS be required to disclose that fact to family members? to sexual partners? to workplace associates? to friends?

3. Should there be stiffer criminal penalties for perpetrators who commit crimes when HIV-positive? What if they were unaware of their infection?

4. Explain how you would work with a sight-impaired victim, a hearing-impaired victim, and a victim confined to a wheelchair. What problems or issues do you see that they will face in the criminal justice system?

5. Assume that a gay man has approached you and told you he had been raped by men who called him a "faggot." However, he doesn't want to report the crime to the police because his parents do not know he is gay. What advice can you offer him? What are the issues raised by this situation?

Suggested Readings

Jack Levin & Jack McDevitt, *The Rising Tide of Bigotry and Bloodshed,* (Plenum, New York) 1993.

William P. Randel, *The Ku Klux Klan: A Century of Infamy,* (Chilton Books, New York) 1965.

J. Boswell, *Christianity, Social Tolerance, and Homosexuality,* (Univ. of Chicago Press, Chicago) 1980.

Kerry Lobel, (ed.), *Naming the Violence: Speaking Out about Lesbian Battering,* (The Seal Press, Seattle, Wa.) 1986.

M. J. Elias & J. E. Zins, (eds.), *Bullying, Peer Harassment, and Victimization in the Schools: The Next Generation of Prevention,* (Haworth Press, Binghamton, N.Y.) 2004.

D. Finkelhor, T. P. Cross & E. N. Cantor, *How the Justice System Responds to Juvenile Victims: A Comprehensive Model,* (U.S. Department of Justice, Office of Justice Programs, Washington, D.C.) 2005.

Reporting School Violence, (U.S. Department of Justice, Office for Victims of Crime, Washington, D.C.) 2002.

Endnotes

1. This section has been adapted from *HIV/AIDS and Victim Services: A Critical Concern of the 90s,* sponsored by a grant from the Office for Victims of Crime (National Victims Center, Arlington, VA) February 1996, Chapters II, III, and IV [hereinafter cited as *HIV/AIDS and Victim Services*]
2. *HIV/AIDS and Victim Services* pp. II-1–II-2.
3. *HIV/AIDS and Victim Services* pp. II-3–II-4.
4. *HIV/AIDS and Victim Services* p. II-5.
5. *HIV/AIDS and Victim Services* pp. II-5–II-8.
6. *HIV/AIDS and Victim Services* pp. II-30–II-32.
7. *HIV/AIDS and Victim Services* p. III-3.
8. *HIV/AIDS and Victim Services* p. III-5.
9. See for example, Florida Code Section 960.003 (1) (1994).
10. *HIV/AIDS and Victim Services* p. III-18.
11. *HIV/AIDS and Victim Services* p. IV-7.
12. *HIV/AIDS and Victim Services* pp. IV-21–IV-30.
13. *HIV/AIDS and Victim Services* pp. IV-31–IV-33.
14. Much of the material in this section has been adapted from *Focus on the Future: A Systems Approach to Prosecution and Victim Assistance,* sponsored by a grant from Office for Victims of Crimes, (U.S. Department of Justice, Washington, D.C.) (National Victims Center, Arlington, Va.) 1992.
15. Kathi Wolfe, "Bashing the Disabled: the New Hate Crime," 9/11 *The Progressive,* 24 (Nov. 1995).
16. This paragraph was adapted from the *Draft Report, Criminal Justice Task Force for Persons with Developmental Disabilities, Victim of Crime Section* (Office of Criminal Justice Planning, Sacramento, Calif.) October 1, 1996, p. 1 (hereinafter referred to as *Task Force for Persons with Developmental Disabilities*).
17. L. Merkin & M. J. Smith, "A Community-Based Model Providing Services for the Deaf and Deaf–Blind Victims of Sexual Assault and Domestic Violence," 13(2) *Sexuality and Disability,* 97–106 (1995).
18. "Eight Do's and Don'ts in Working with Disabled Victims of Crime," *Focus on the Future: A Systems Approach to Prosecution and Victim Assistance,* (National Victims Center, sponsored by a grant from the Office for Victims of Crimes, U.S. Department of Justice, Washington, D.C.) 1992, p. C-13.
19. Adapted from *Task Force for Persons with Developmental Disabilities)* p. 1.
20. Cheryl G. Tyiska, "Responding to Disabled Victims of Crime," 8/12 *NOVA Network Information Bulletin,* (NOVA, Washington, D.C.) 1990. p. 10.
21. George Marshall Worthington, "Sexual Exploitation and Abuse of People with Disabilities," 7/2 *Response to Violence in the Family and Sexual Assault,* 43 (1984).
22. *Sexual Exploitation of Handicapped Students: Teachers Training Manual,* (Seattle Rape Relief Disabilities Project, Seattle, Wash.) 1981.
23. Cathy McPherson, "Bringing Redress to Abused Disabled Persons," 8/12 *NOVA Network Information Bulletin,* 14 (NOVA, Washington, D.C., 1990).
24. Louise Melling, "Wife Abuse in the Deaf Community," 7/1 *Response to Violence in the Family and Sexual Assault,* 12 (1984).
25. Denise Aiello & Lee Capkin, "Services for Disabled Victims: Elements and Standards," 7/5 *Response to Violence in the Family and Sexual Assault,* 14, (1984).

26. Adapted from *Task Force for Persons with Developmental Disabilities*, pp. 11–22.

27. W. Masters, V. Johnson & R. Kolodny, *Masters and Johnson on Sex and Human Loving*, (Little Brown & Co., Boston) 1968.

28. J. Boswell, *Christianity, Social Tolerance, and Homosexuality*, Ill., (Univ. of Chicago Press, Chicago) 1980.

29. *Webster's New Collegiate Dictionary*, (G & C Merriam Co., Springfield, Mass.) 1981.

30. Valerie Jenness, "Social Movement Growth, Domain Expansion, and Framing Process: The Gay/Lesbian Movement and Violence Against Gays and Lesbians as a Social Problem," 42/1 *Social Problems*, (February 1995).

31. Gregory M. Herek, "Hate Crimes Against Lesbian and Gay Men," 44/6 *American Psychologist*, (June 1989).

32. *AntiGay/Lesbian Violence in 1994: National Trends, Analysis and Incident Summaries*, (New York City Gay and Lesbian AntiViolence Project, New York) 1994.

33. *Characteristics of Hate Crime in 1992*, (U.S. Department of Justice, Federal Bureau of Investigation, GPO, Washington, D.C., 1993) p. 9.

34. Carolyn K. Waterman, Lori J. Dawson & Michael J. Bologna, "Sexual Coercion in Gay Male and Lesbian Relationships: Predictors and Implications for Support Services," 26/1 *The Journal of Sex Research*, 118 (February, 1989).

35. Ford C. I. Hickson, Peter M. Davies, Andrew J. Hunt, Peter Weatherburn, Thomas J. McManus & Anthony P. M. Coxon, "Gay Men as Victims of Nonconsensual Sex," *23/3 Archives of Sexual Behavior*, 281 (1994).

36. Nan D. Hunter & Nancy D. Polikoff, "Custody Rights of Lesbian Mothers: Legal Theory and Litigation Strategy," 25 *Buffalo Law Rev.*, 691 (1976).

37. Nancy Polikoff, "This Child Does Have Two Mothers: Redefining Parenthood to Meet the Needs of Children in Lesbian-Mother and Other Nontraditional Families," 78 *Georgia Law Rev.*, 459 (1990).

38. Arlene F. Saluter, "Marital Status and Living Arrangements: March 1990," *U.S. Bureau of the Census, Series P-20*, no. 450 (May 1991), p. 73.

39. Barbara Hart, "Lesbian Battering: An Examination," Kerry Lobel, (ed.), *Naming The Violence:*

Speaking Out About Lesbian Battering, (The Seal Press, Seattle, Wash.) 1986, p. 173.

40. David Island & Patrick Letellier, *Men Who Beat the Men Who Love Them*, (Harrington Park Press, New York) 1991, p. 27.

41. Claire M. Renzetti, *Violent Betrayal, Partner Abuse in Lesbian Relationships*, (Sage Publications, Newbury Park, Calif.) 1992, pp. 17–18.

42. Island & Letellier, *Men Who Beat the Men Who Love Them*, p. 14.

43. David Island & Patrick Letellier, "*Men Who Beat the Men Who Love Them,*" at 10, 36.

44. Gary Brown et al., "Starting a TRO Project: Student Representation of Battered Women," 96 *Yale Law Rev.* 1985 (1987).

45. Mac D. Hunter, "Homosexuals as a New Class of Domestic Violence Subjects Under the New Jersey Prevention of Domestic Violence Act of 1991," 31 *University of Louisville Journal of Family Law*, p. 557 (1992/93).

46. Denise Bricker, "Fatal Defense: An Analysis of Battered Women's Syndrome, Expert Testimony for Gay Men and Lesbians Who Kill Abusive Partners," 58 *Brooklyn Law Rev.*, 1379 (Winter 1993).

47. "Violence Against People with HIV/AIDS," Pamphlet prepared by the New York City Gay & Lesbian AntiViolence Project, (New York 1991).

48. Mindy Benowitz, "How Homophobia Affects Lesbians' Response to Violence in Lesbian Relationships," in *Naming the Violence*, p. 200.

49. Phyllis Winfield, "Rare Program Aids Battered Lesbians, Gays: Violence Mirrors Heterosexual Incidents," *Seattle Times*, September 24, 1990, at E3.

50. Judy Mann, "A Grant in Trouble," C3 *Washington Post*, (July 5, 1995).

51. 496 A.2d 1 at 7 (1985).

52. 478 U.S. 186, (1986).

53. 553 F.Supp. 1121 (N.D. Tex. 1982), appeal dismissed, 743 F.2d 236 (5th Cir. 1984), Cert. denied 478 U.S. 1022 (1986).

54. See for example a special section entitled, "Gay and Lesbians Are Out of the Closet," in *The Family Therapy Networker*, (January/February 1991).

55. Gwat-Yong Lie and Sabrina Gentlewarrier, "Intimate Violence in Lesbian Relationships: Discussion of Survey Findings and Practice

Implications," 15 (1/2) *Journal of Social Service Research,* 41 (1991).

56. Stephen P. Teret, "New Hope for Victims of Prison Sexual Assault," 31/4 *Journal of Law, Medicine & Ethics,* 602 (Winter 2003).

57. 511 U.S. 825 (1994).

58. No Escape: Male Rape in U.S. Prisons: Summary and Recommendations, Human Rights Watch, (2001); available online: http://www.hrw.org/reports/2001/prison/report1.html.

59. James E. Robertson, "Rape among Incarcerated Men: Sex, Coercion and STDs," 17 *Aids Patient Care and STDs,* 423 (2003).

60. Morris L. Thigpen & Larry Solomon, *Annual Report to Congress, Prison Rape Elimination Act (PREA),* National Institute of Corrections, Washington, D.C. (September 2004).

61. Allen J. Beck & Timothy A. Hughes, *Sexual Violence Reported by Correctional Authorities, 2004,* Bureau of Justice Statistics, Department of Justice, Washington, D.C. (July 2005).

62. Id. at pp. 4–5.

63. P. M. Blau, *Exchange and Power in Social Life* (Wiley and Sons, New York) 1964.

64. R. J. Gelles, *Family Violence,* 2nd ed. (Sage, Newbury Park, Calif.) 1987, p. 17.

65. See for example, K. Polk's "Male to Male Homicide: Scenarios of Masculine Violence,"

paper presented at the annual meeting of the American Society of Criminology, San Francisco, November 18–23, 1991.

66. D. Olweus, "Bullies on the Playground: The Role of Victimization," in C. H. Hart, (ed.), *Children on Playgrounds: Research Perspectives and Applications,* (State University of New York Press, Albany, N.Y.) 1993 p. 9.

67. At-Risk Resources, The Bureau of At-Risk Youth, Hawthorne, N.Y., 2006.

68. F. Thrasher, *A Study of 1,313 Gangs in Chicago* (University of Chicago Press, Chicago), 1927.

69. S. Decker and B. Van Winkle, *Life in a Gang: Family, Friends, and Violence,* (Cambridge University, Press, New York), 1988.

70. Spergel, *The Youth Gang Problem; A Community Approach,* (Oxford university Press, New York) 1995.

71. *School Violence Injury Fact Book,* Center for Disease Control, available online: www.cdc.gov (April 21, 2006).

72. Youth Violence: A Report of the Surgeon General: The Public Health Approach, Centers for Disease Control, available online: www.mentalhealth.samhsa.gov (April 21, 2006).

14

NEGLIGENCE AND INTENTIONAL TORTS

Chapter Outline

Necessity
Authority of Law

Summary

Key Terms

Discussion Questions

Suggested Readings

Learning Objectives

After reading this chapter, you should be able to:

- Compare and contrast negligence and intentional torts
- Explain the difference between torts and criminal acts
- Distinguish between the torts of assault and of battery
- Explain why the tort of mental distress is important to victims
- Understand the various defenses to negligence and intentional torts

Introduction

This chapter deals with negligence and the intentional torts of wrongful death, assault, battery, false imprisonment, and intentional infliction of mental distress. The great majority of all victim-related issues occur in the area of tort law and therefore it is important to understand the basic rules that apply to an action based on tort.

A tort may be based on negligence or on intentional acts. *Negligence* is a complex legal concept that under certain circumstances holds persons liable for acting, or failing to act, in a certain manner. Many persons, including victims of crime, have been injured because of the negligence of another party.

Many other issues relating to victims arise because of an intentional act of another. Intentional torts include wrongful death, assault, battery, false imprisonment, and intentional infliction of mental distress. Each of these torts requires the perpetrator to act with a certain state of mind or intent. The intent required for these types of injuries requires that the tortfeasor intend to cause some physical or mental effect on another person. There is no requirement that the tortfeasor intend to harm the victim. The intent to harm is irrelevant as long as the tortfeasor intended the act.[1] The law also calls a tortfeasor's actions intentional even if he didn't desire a certain type of occurrence but knew with substantial certainty that it would occur as a result of his actions.

In the majority of intentional torts, a certain doctrine applies. The doctrine of **transferred intent** holds that so long as the tortfeasor had the necessary intent to act in a certain manner toward one person, he will be held liable for torts committed against any other person who happens to be injured. Many states incorporate this doctrine into their criminal codes that establish criminal liability.[2]

The significance of proving intent relates to the award of damages. If the jury finds that the tortfeasor acted intentionally, the jury may award nominal damages even if no injury occurred to the plaintiff. *Nominal damages* are token damages, for example, $1.00. Although this may seem insignificant, many jurisdictions also allow the prevailing party to recover attorneys' fees. In this case, the award of token damages may allow the victim to recover attorneys' fees and the costs of the suit. An intentional tort victim may also recover punitive damages if the jury finds that the defendant's acts were outrageous or malicious. As discussed later in this chapter, punitive damages are to punish the tortfeasor.

Each of these torts has a "companion" criminal act. Although there are differences between the criminal and civil acts, they are similar in many ways. Table 14.1 compares some of the more common criminal acts with their companion civil tort.

One significant difference between a criminal case and a civil case is the amount of evidence necessary to prove the case. Normally the criminal process will have been completed prior to the civil trial. If the defendant is found guilty in the criminal action, this fact may be presented in the subsequent civil action to prove culpability. Even if the perpetrator is found not guilty in the criminal case, the victim still has the right to pursue a civil cause of action because of the difference in the burden of proof between the two types of proceedings. In criminal cases, the government must prove the case beyond a reasonable doubt, whereas in civil cases the plaintiff need only present a preponderance of the evidence. Table 14.2 illustrates the difference between the two levels of proof.

The difference in the burden of proof is important because unlike criminal proceedings, there is no double jeopardy bar to filing a civil action after an acquittal in the criminal case. In criminal cases, the double jeopardy clause of the Fifth Amendment prevents the state from refiling the criminal charges if the defendant is acquitted.[3] This prohibition, however, does not apply to the filing of civil cases. Therefore, even if the defendant is acquitted in a criminal action, a civil intentional tort action may be filed. This is exactly what happened in the O. J. Simpson saga. After Mr. Simpson was acquitted of the double murder of his ex-wife, Nicole Brown Simpson, and her friend, Ronald Goldman, both families of the victims filed civil actions against O. J. Simpson. Both families prevailed in the civil action

TABLE 14.1   A Comparison of Torts and Crimes

Intentional Torts	Crimes
Wrongful Death	Murder Involuntary manslaughter Voluntary manslaughter Negligent manslaughter
Assault	Assault or Stalking
Battery	Battery or any sexual crime such as rape, sodomy, or oral copulation
False Imprisonment	False Imprisonment
Mental Distress	Stalking

TABLE 14.2

Possible Amount of Proof

0 .... 100%

Beyond a Reasonable Doubt

0 .... 90–95%

Preponderance of the Evidence

0 .... 51%

when the jury found Mr. Simpson liable for the wrongful death of Nicole and Ronald.

Victims file civil actions against their perpetrators for a variety of reasons. They may believe that they did not receive appropriate satisfaction as a result of any criminal proceedings. The defendant may have been acquitted or convicted of a lessor charge than the victim believes is proper. Victims may also feel mistreated by the criminal justice system and have a desire to be in control of the proceedings instead of merely being a witness. Many victims may also want to receive more compensation for injuries than is available in the criminal justice system.

Negligence

Introduction

Often we hear others refer to the fact that someone was negligent. The lay or common meaning of the term *negligent* simply means someone was careless or slipshod in performing some act. The term *negligence* in tort law is a far more complex and confusing concept. The legal definition of *negligence* comprises several components including a duty, a breach of that duty, proximate cause, and actual injury. Under the concept of negligence the injured party must show that the tortfeasor had a legal duty that required him to conduct himself according to certain standards, so as to avoid harming others. The plaintiff must also prove that the defendant breached or failed to conform his conduct to that standard. Once these two elements have been established there must be proof that they were the proximate cause or causal link between the defendant's acts and the injury suffered by the plaintiff. Finally, there must be proof of actual damages as distinguished from intentional torts that allow for recovery of nominal damages even without proof of actual injury.

Elements of Negligence

The definition of negligence contains several distinct elements. Each must be proved before the injured party can recover damages. The problem with negligence is that there are many gray areas in each element. For ease of understanding, only basic concepts are discussed in this text.

The injured party must prove that the defendant owed a legal duty to avoid unreasonable risk to others. Courts utilize a balancing test to determine if the defendant's conduct exposed the victim to unreasonable harm. The test is simply whether a reasonable person would have recognized the risk of harm and sought to avoid it.[4]

In applying this test, courts often examine the situation using an objective test. Juries are asked to view the defendant's conduct from a reasonable person's point of view. If a reasonable person of ordinary prudence in the defendant's position would have avoided harming the victim, the defendant is found negligent if the actions injured the plaintiff.

The defendant must fail to conform his conduct to the legal duty. This duty to others many times is determined by the relationship between the defendant and the victim. Some relationships impose a higher standard of care or duty on the defendant than others.

The victim must also show a close causal relationship between the defendant's acts and the injury. This is known as the *proximate* or *legal cause* of the injury. This is the one area of negligence that gives lawyers, judges, and juries the most problems. For example, suppose two drivers are intoxicated and run into each other. Who is at fault? Suppose one driver had two drinks and the other driver had ten drinks? The short answer is that the law will presume that each driver will be held to be a proximate or legal cause of the accident. Therefore, if the defendant has "caused" the injury to the victim, the law may hold him liable. However, the issue is further complicated by another concept that deals with foreseeability of harm.

Foreseeability is viewing harm as a set of dominoes. When the defendant acts in certain ways, his actions cause other effects similar to pushing over one domino in a line. The public policy question is how far down that line of toppling dominoes will the courts look in holding the defendant accountable. The generally accepted rule is that if the injuries were a direct result of the defendant's action, the defendant will be held liable even if the injuries were not the kind one would normally expect as a result of the act.[5] This position is based on several rationales, including that many serious cases arise from single acts of negligence that are caused by large corporations, government, or utilities. These entities are able to bear the burden of compensating the victim who had no reason to guard against that particular loss.

Finally, the victim must suffer actual damage or injury. The extent of the victim's injury may not be easy to determine. This aspect of negligence may require the services of expert witnesses to explain how the victim was injured, the extent of those injuries, and how long they will last.

Victims may not be aware of the true extent of their injuries. Care should be taken when advising victims to settle with insurance companies immediately after an incident. There are some injuries that do not show up right away and most settlement agreements prevent the victim from asking for additional money for other injuries that are discovered after the settlement. Many states allow victims of negligence up to one year before they lose their right to sue. Victims should be advised to consult their own insurance company as well as an attorney and have a thorough medical examination before signing any settlement.

Wrongful Death

Wrongful death actions may be brought based on negligence, strict liability, or intentional acts by the defendant. They are discussed in this chapter because many wrongful death causes of action arise from criminal acts that are based on homicide statutes. When a perpetrator kills the victim, her family must cope with the loss. Additionally, the family may have been deprived of the economic support that the victim would have contributed over her lifetime.

The Parties

In common law, when a person died, his right to recover for any injuries was extinguished upon death. This rule also applied to his heirs so that they were precluded from recovering damages they suffered as a result of the loss of a loved one. Every state has modified this common law rule by adopting survival statutes and wrongful death statutes.

Survival statutes modify the common law rule by allowing the decedent's claim for personal injuries to be brought by his heirs. Many of these states also allow the filing and maintenance of a personal injury action against the defendant's estate if he dies before the filing of the civil case. Most states have special *wrongful death statutes* which allow a defined group of individuals to recover the loss it sustained as a result of the victim's death. The parties that may sue under these wrongful death statutes are the decedent's spouse, children, and parents. Because wrongful death actions are based on statutorily created rights, courts are reluctant to expand the scope of these remedies. Thus, live-in lovers who are not legally married may be denied recovery.[6]

Elements of Damage

Certain types of damages are unique to wrongful death cases and include loss of companionship, sexual intercourse, and moral guidance of the decedent. Some states also allow for grief or other mental suffering of the survivors as an element of damages.

When a child is murdered and a civil action is brought by her parents, it is sometimes hard to establish pecuniary loss on the part of the parents, because it is generally agreed that the cost of raising and educating a child is more than any earning she could be expected to contribute to her parents. However, many courts are now allowing damages for loss of companionship of the child.

A very emotional issue that sometimes arises in wrongful death cases involves the doctrine of unjust enrichment. This common law rule prohibits persons, in wrongful death cases it would be the perpetrator, from profiting from their own wrongdoing. The doctrine of unjust enrichment is implemented by court decisions that are founded upon *Salyer's Rules or Statutes*. These are statutes that prohibit a murderer from profiting from his illegal acts. There are numerous court decisions that prevent intrafamilial killers from gaining an economic advantage because of their actions. For example, in one famous case, a husband murdered his wife and then filed to become the administrator of her estate. As the administrator, he would have been entitled to fees for his services to the estate. The court rejected his claim because he had been convicted of her murder.[7]

Assault and Battery

Assault and battery are common intentional torts. Many laypersons confuse assault with battery and vice versa. It is not uncommon for an assault and battery to occur during the commission of a crime. However, it must be understood that although they are discussed together for purposes of comparison, they are distinct and separate intentional torts. You may have an assault without a battery and you may also have a battery without an assault.

Defined

The tort of *assault* has been defined as the intentional causing of an apprehension or offensive contact.[8] The defendant has committed the tort of assault when he has caused the victim to believe that she will be subjected to harmful or offensive contact. The interest that is being protected is the victim's freedom from apprehension of wrongful contact. Assault can therefore occur even if no actual contact occurs between the defendant and the victim.

The tort of *battery* has been defined as the intentional infliction of harmful or offensive bodily contact.[9] The tort of battery includes touching or contact that causes injury to the victim as well as any bodily contact that is considered offensive. The standard used to determine if the contact is offensive is whether an ordinary person would have been offended by the contact.

Fear versus Contact

As the previous definitions indicate, the key distinction between an assault and battery is whether the victim experienced fear or was touched in a harmful or offensive manner by the defendant. Some states argue whether words alone may constitute an assault. The states requiring more than words mandate that the words be accompanied by some overt act that adds to the threatening character of the words. Other states and the *Restatement of Torts* indicate that there may be situations in which words by themselves without any overt act are sufficient to constitute the tort of assault.[10] This distinction between threats and overt acts was also a dilemma faced by law enforcement agencies who responded to threats made by perpetrators prior to the adopting of the stalking laws. Most criminal assault statutes required that the defendant have the present ability to inflict injury upon the victim. Stalking statutes allow law enforcement to take action based on a threat to harm the victim in the future.[11]

Because the tort of assault protects the peace of mind of the victim, she must be aware of the threat. The victim need only experience apprehension. Apprehension is not necessarily the same emotion as fear. In other words, the victim only need be concerned rather than scared. The threat must be directed at the victim and not a third person. If a family member is threatened, the victim may experience apprehension or even fear, but cannot recover based on the traditional tort of assault. As will be discussed later, the modern tort of infliction of mental distress would apply in these types of situations.

Unlike assault, the tort of battery may be committed even if the victim is unaware of the contact at the time it occurs. For example, the perpetrator may slip something in the victim's drink causing her to pass out. He then engages in sexual intercourse with her. The crime of rape and the tort of battery have both occurred even though at the time of the contact the victim was unconscious.

False Imprisonment

Defined

The tort of *false imprisonment* is defined as the intentional infliction of a confinement. The victim must show that the perpetrator intended to confine her. She must be confined within definite physical boundaries. Simply blocking the victim's path or preventing him from entering a particular place does not meet the requirement of this tort. However, if the victim initially consents to the confinement there is no tort. If the perpetrator is under a duty to release the victim and fails to do so, the tort has been committed. For example, a victim may meet the perpetrator at a bar and agree to a ride home with him. There is no false imprisonment during the ride to the victim's home. Once they arrive at the victim's home and the perpetrator refuses to allow the victim to leave the car unless the victim has sex with him, the tort of false imprisonment occurs. This is true even though the victim agreed to ride in the perpetrator's car.

The Confinement Requirement

The essence of the confinement requirement is that the victim is held within certain limits, not simply prevented from entering certain places. Thus preventing the victim from entering a store is not false imprisonment, whereas holding him in an office within that store would be such a tort. Confining the victim to a locked room clearly meets the definition of this tort. However, there are other instances of more subtle acts that will give rise to the tort of false imprisonment. If the perpetrator threatens the victim with force if he tries to escape from an unlocked building and the perpetrator has the apparent ability to carry out the threat, the tort of false imprisonment is complete. Unlike assault, the tort of false imprisonment may occur if the perpetrator threatens harm to family members if the victim does not remain in a particular room or tries to escape.[12] The threat or duress that confines the victim must be of imminent harm. Threats of future harm are not sufficient. The tort of false imprisonment usually does not occur in a vacuum. Perpetrators usually commit other torts such as assault and battery in connection with the false imprisonment. Victim services providers should always be aware that several intentional torts may arise from one crime. For example, the offense of kidnapping may give rise to the intentional torts of assault, battery, false imprisonment, and mental distress.

Mental Distress

The intentional tort of infliction of mental distress is a relatively new tort. An increasing number of jurisdictions are recognizing that victims suffer mental problems as a result of criminal or other intentional acts and these jurisdictions are allowing these victims to sue for damages alleging infliction of mental or emotional distress. The tort of *mental distress* has been defined as the intentional or reckless infliction, by extreme or outrageous conduct, of severe emotional or mental distress. This tort does not require any physical harm or injury to the victim.

Intent Requirement

Unlike the majority of other intentional torts, the doctrine of transferred intent does not generally apply to the infliction of emotional distress. The most common reason given for precluding the application of this doctrine is that it would open the floodgates of litigation by unrelated parties. Professor Prosser points out that if the doctrine of transferred intent were allowed in emotional distress cases, millions of Americans who witnessed President Reagan being shot on television would be able to sue John Hinckley for infliction of emotional distress.[13]

The courts have fashioned one important exception in this area that deals with family members who witness the defendant injure or harm another family member. However, this exception is quite narrow and requires that the defendant know of the plaintiff's presence so that the infliction of mental distress is a reasonable consequence of the defendant's actions toward the other family member. For example, in a California case, the plaintiff watched the defendant beat up her father, and as a result of observing the beating she suffered severe emotional distress. The court held that because there was no allegation or proof that the defendant knew of her presence, nor that he intended to cause her emotional distress, her claim was invalid and the case dismissed.[14] However, the *Restatement of Torts* would liberalize this position and allow for recovery by victims who witness injury to others even if they are not related so long as the victim suffers physical illness as a result of the incident.[15]

Conduct Requirement

For the victim to recover damages, she must show that the defendant's conduct was extreme and outrageous. The defendant is not liable for insults or hurt feelings. The Restatement of Torts points out that certain conduct does not meet the standard of outrageous. Nonqualifying conduct includes ". . . mere insults, indignities, threats, annoyances, petty oppressions, or other trivialities."[16] The test that is normally applied requires that the conduct be so outrageous in character and so extreme as to go beyond all possible bounds of decency and be regarded as atrocious and utterly intolerable in a civilized society.[17] Once the victim has shown that the defendant's conduct was extreme and outrageous, she must also prove that she suffered severe emotional distress. Most jurisdictions require as a minimum that the victim show that as a result of the defendant's conduct she sought and received medical treatment.

Defenses to Intentional Torts

Simply establishing that the perpetrator injured the victim does not end the inquiry. Just as there are defenses that persons accused of crimes may raise in criminal actions, so are there the same or similar defenses that may be asserted in civil actions. This is especially true if there was no criminal case filed or it was dismissed on a technicality and no conviction or plea entered. If that is the case, then many of the defenses that would have been raised in the criminal case will most likely be used by the perpetrator in the civil case in an attempt to escape liability.

Self-Defense

Just as criminal law recognizes the privilege of self-defense, so does civil law. The rules regarding the use of self-defense are substantially the same in both situations. In understanding self-defense it is important to distinguish between deadly and nondeadly force. A person is justified in using deadly force only to protect oneself or others from what the person reasonably believes is imminent, unlawful deadly force.

The concept of self-defense includes the components of proportionality and necessity. *Proportionality* mandates that the force used in self-defense not be out of proportion to the force necessary to protect the person from the threatened harm. Necessity requires that a person only use force to prevent imminent, unlawful deadly force. Therefore, a person is normally not authorized in using deadly force to combat threats of future harm.

This is the dilemma faced by many battered spouses. There have been numerous cases and articles dealing with situations in which the battered spouse kills her abusing partner.[18] The victim may have attacked and killed the abuser defending herself from his physical assault or in some cases he may threaten her with harm in the future such as when he awakes or returns home. In some cases, she has responded with force as the abuser enters the home or while he is sleeping or passed out. The abused spouse believes in her own mind that she will be killed or seriously injured. She has no doubt regarding the offender's ability to carry out any threats because she has experienced his violent behavior in the past.

When the spouse kills another under a subjective opinion that they face death or danger, several jurisdictions have called this an "imperfect" form of self-defense. The courts are divided in this area with some courts authorizing the use of deadly force and others claiming the use of force was improper with the result that the abused spouse faces criminal charges for homicide.[19] This imperfect self-defense is what the Menendez brothers used in their high-profile murder trial in which they were accused of murdering their mother and father. The brothers alleged that their father was going to kill them when they threatened to expose the fact that he had sexually molested them for years. The jury rejected this defense and found the brothers guilty of homicide.

The general rule is that the nonaggressor or original victim does not have a duty to retreat before using deadly force to defend oneself. However, the aggressor may not normally use deadly force in self-defense of his actions. Most states deny the defense to those who initiate the fight. However, if the aggressor starts the fight, then clearly tries to retreat, deadly force may be used if the retreat is unsuccessful.

Defense of Others

A person is authorized in using force to defend another from imminent attack. The defender is justified in using the same amount or type of force in defending others as in self-dense. Some early cases required the defender to be related to the one being attacked, but modern cases have done away with this requirement and a person can now use force to defend a stranger.

Defense of Property

There is a right to use force to defend both real and personal property. The property owner can only use as much force as is reasonable to protect the property. There is authority for the position that the owner must first make a verbal demand that the perpetrator stop before using force, unless it appears that the harm is imminent or that the request to stop is useless. Although a property owner may use reasonable force to defend property, a person may not use deadly force to protect the property. Nor can a person use any force to reclaim property not in possession. The law does not favor self-help. A person also may not use mechanical devices such as spring guns in defending the home from theft or trespass. Spring guns are triggered to go off when a perpetrator enters the premises. In a widely discussed case, the defendant owned an unoccupied boarded-up farmhouse that had been broken into and vandalized a number of times. The defendant placed a shotgun in a bedroom and rigged it so that when a person entered the bedroom, the gun would discharge. The plaintiff entered the house to steal some jars he thought were antiques. When he entered the bedroom, the gun discharged striking him in the leg. In the civil trial that followed, the plaintiff (intruder) was awarded damages for his injuries and the property owner's claim of defense of property was denied. On appeal, the court stated that a property owner may not use deadly force to defend his property against a trespasser, unless the latter is committing a felony of violence or endangering human life by his act. Further what a property owner may not do directly, he may not do indirectly by a spring gun or other mechanical device.[20]

Consent

If the victim gives consent, the defendant will not be liable for any injuries. The defense of consent is frequently used in sexual assault cases. The perpetrator will claim the victim consented to the sexual acts and if there are physical injuries, the offender will attempt to dismiss them stating that the victim enjoyed or asked for rough sex. A number of sexual assault cases involve situations in which consent is an issue. These areas include lack of capacity to consent, exceeding the scope of consent, and duress causing consent.

Lack of Capacity to Consent.   This situation occurs when for a variety of reasons the victim, as a matter of law, is unable to give consent. Young children are incapable of consenting to sexual acts. For example, a defendant would never raise the issue of consent when the victim of his sexual advances was five years old. Adults who are developmental disabled may also be incapable of consenting to sexual acts. Persons who are unconscious because of excessive drinking or the use of drugs cannot give consent. Thus the male college student who engages in sexual acts with his date who has passed out cannot raise the defense of consent.

Exceeding the Scope of Consent.   If the victim gives actual consent to certain acts, the offender will not be able to raise the defense of consent if he goes substantially beyond the scope of that consent. In these situations the perpetrator argues that the victim consented to having sex and the victim states that she may have consented to certain acts, such as kissing and petting, but not sexual intercourse. Because there may be no physical evidence to support the victim's position, it becomes an issue of credibility in which the victim gives one statement and the perpetrator claims the events occurred in a different manner.

Duress Causing Consent.   Recently in Texas, a woman was in her home alone at night and a stranger entered through a window. The intruder stated he was going to have sex with her. The women fearing that she might get AIDS asked that he wear a condom during the act. She placed the condom on his penis and they engaged in sexual intercourse. Immediately after the perpetrator fled the scene the women called the police and they arrested the offender. He claimed consent arguing that she had invited the acts by urging him to wear a condom. One Texas grand jury refused to indict the defendant for rape; however, a second grand jury did indict him.

Another situation involves the defendant threatening the victim with a weapon and causing her to comply with his demands for sex. In this situation, there may not be any physical evidence that supports the victim's claim of rape, but clearly such a fact pattern meets all the elements of the crime of rape and the torts of assault and battery.

Necessity

The defense of necessity is based on a balancing of the evil that faces a person. For example, a person trapped on a hill during a snowstorm may have a choice of breaking into a cabin or freezing to death. The person understands that he is committing a crime (of burglary or trespass) by breaking into the cabin, but he also realizes that to stay out in the unprotected environment will result in his death. Although the person may have committed a criminal offense in breaking into the cabin, the defense of necessity will allow him to escape punishment. A person cannot raise this defense if the threatened harm will occur sometime in the future. In other words, a person cannot simply enter a store and take food claiming that a snowstorm is coming and he needs food to exist.

Two types of emergencies justify a person in harming another's property: cases of public necessity and cases of private necessity. When the person injures another's property in order to prevent harm to a substantial number of persons or to himself, the defense is based on public necessity. When the person is protecting only his own interest or the interest of a few citizens, the defense is based on private necessity. Public necessity defenses normally arise when the interference or damage to the lands of another is necessary or appears to be necessary to prevent a disaster to the community or a substantial number of persons within the community.[21] Private necessity defenses arise when a person injures private property to protect his property or the person or property of a third party if there is no other way to prevent the harm.[22]

Authority of Law

Acts committed by persons under authority of law are generally considered a valid defense. For example, a law enforcement officer who executes a valid warrant and uses proper procedures in doing so has a defense against a lawsuit based on the tort of false imprisonment by the person arrested. When an officer makes an arrest based on an arrest warrant that is valid on its face and uses proper procedures in making the arrest, the officer will have a valid defense even if it is later shown that the arrest warrant was invalid. Arrests without a warrant are complex and confusing. An officer or private citizen may make an arrest for a felony or misdemeanor which is committed in her presence. An officer may also make a warrantless arrest for a felony not committed in her presence if she has reasonable cause to believe the defendant committed it. The officer is privileged even if it later turns out that no crime was committed or that she arrested the wrong person so long as her beliefs were reasonable at the time of the arrest. Private citizens will lose their immunity if no felony was committed; however, like the officer they will still retain the immunity even if they arrested the wrong person if their beliefs were reasonable.

Summary

A significant number of victims will decide to file a civil lawsuit against the perpetrator who injured them during the commission of a crime. Victims file these actions for a variety of reasons. As a result, victim services providers must be familiar with civil causes of actions that allow victims to recover for their injuries. Negligence is a complex legal doctrine that holds parties liable for injuries suffered as a result of a breach of duty owed to the victim.

Additionally, a number of other torts correspond to the more common criminal offenses. These civil actions include the intentional torts of wrongful death, assault, battery, false imprisonment, and mental distress. Additionally, victim advocates must be familiar with the basic rules regarding liability of joint tortfeasors, issues surrounding the common defenses to these torts, the various types of intent necessary to commit these torts, and the different levels of proof in a criminal and civil case.

The intentional tort of wrongful death is one of the most emotional torts victim services providers must handle. The primary victim of this crime is dead and the remaining victim must deal with grief regarding the loss of a loved one as well as the complexities of pursuing a civil lawsuit. Victim services providers must understand who can recover and be prepared to discuss issues regarding damages which may be available to the remaining family victims.

There are a number of defenses to intentional torts. Many of these civil defenses are the same ones that will be raised in any criminal action. In many homicides, for example, the defendant will claim to have been provoked by the deceased and was simply acting in self-defense. Understanding the various defenses to intentional torts is an important aspect of this area of victims' rights.

Key Terms

Transferred intent holds that so long as the tortfeasor had the necessary intent to act in a certain manner toward one person, that person will be held liable for torts committed against any other person who happens to be injured.

Nominal damages are token damages, for example, $1.00.

Negligence comprises several components including a duty, a breach of that duty, proximate cause, and actual injury.

Survival statutes modify the common law rule by allowing the decedent's claim for personal injuries to be brought by his heirs.

Wrongful death statutes allow a defined group of individuals to recover the loss it sustained as a result of the victim's death. The parties that may sue under these wrongful death statutes are the decedent's spouse, children, and parents.

Assault is the intentional causing of an apprehension or offensive contact.

Battery is the intentional infliction of harmful or offensive bodily contact.

False imprisonment is the intentional infliction of a confinement.

Mental distress is the intentional or reckless infliction, by extreme or outrageous conduct, of severe emotional or mental distress.

Discussion Questions

1. Should we be able to obtain insurance that covers us in the event of a negligent act on our part? If we didn't have insurance, would we be more careful in our actions?

2. What is the most important element in the tort of negligence? Why is it more critical than the other elements?

3. Other than wrongful death, what is the most serious intentional tort? Justify your answer.

4. Should people be held liable for acts of others? Why? Why not?

5. Should we have a "no-fault" tort system and pay those who are injured instead of arguing over who is at fault and which defense may apply? Would such a system save us money?

6. Which is the most important defense to the intentional torts? Why?

Suggested Readings

Wade Prosser, & Schwartz, *Cases and Materials on Torts*, 5th ed. (West Publishing Co., St. Paul, Minn.) 1984 w/1988 Supp.

Endnotes

1. *Vosburg v. Putney*, 50 N.W. 403 (Wis. 1891).
2. See H. Wallace & C. Roberson, *Principles of Criminal Law*, (Longman, White Plains, N.Y.) 1996.
3. The double jeopardy clause applies to state and federal actions. *Benton v. Maryland*, 395 U.S. 784 (1969).
4. *U.S. v. Carroll Towing Co.*, 159 F2d 169 (2nd Cir. 1947).
5. See the classic case of *In Re Polemis*, 3 K.B. 560 (Eng. 1921) for a full discussion of this concept.
6. See *Steed v. Imperial Airlines*, 524 P.2d 801 (Cal. 1974) where the court held that a stepchild was not a heir under the wrongful death statute and therefore could not recover damages even though the child suffered loses of economic support and moral guidance.
7. *Brown v. Blue*, 724 S.W. 2d 400 (Tex. App. 1986).
8. See *Restatement Second of Torts*, Section 21, American Law Institute (1995).
9. See *Restatement Second of Torts*, Section 13, American Law Institute (1995).
10. See *Restatement Second of Torts*, Section 31, American Law Institute (1995).
11. H. Wallace, "A Prosecutors Guide to Stalking," *The Prosecutor*, 26 (January/February 1995).

12. See *Restatement Second of Torts*, Section 40A, American Law Institute (1995).

13. Wade Prosser & Schwartz, *Cases and Materials on Torts*, 5th ed. (West Publishing Co., St. Paul, Minn.) 1984 w/ 1988 Supp, p. 64.

14. *Taylor v. Vallelunga*, 339 P.2d 910 (Cal. App. 1959).

15. See *Restatement Second of Torts*, Section 40A, American Law Institute (1995).

16. See *Restatement Second of Torts*, Section 46, American Law Institute (1995).

17. See *Restatement Second of Torts*, Section 46 Comment d, American Law Institute (1995).

18. See H. Wallace, "The Battered Women Syndrome: Self-defence and Duress as Mandatory Defences?" *The Police Journal*, 133 (April–June 1994). (Note title uses English spelling.)

19. H. Wallace, *Family Violence: Legal, Medical and Social Perspectives*, (Allyn & Bacon, Boston) 1996.

20. *Katko v. Briney*, 183 N.W. 2d 657 (Iowa 1971).

21. For a case dealing with public necessity by public officials, see *Surocco v. Geary*, 3 Cal. 69 (1853); and for a case dealing with public necessity by a private person see *Harrison v. Wisdom*, 54 Tenn. 99 (1872).

22. See *Ploof v. Putnam*, 71 A. 188 (Vt. 1908) for a discussion of the defense of private necessity.

15

INTERNATIONAL ASPECTS OF VICTIMOLOGY

Chapter Outline

Summary

Key Terms

Discussion Questions

Suggested Readings

Learning Objectives

After reading this chapter, you should be able to:

- Be familiar with the evolution of victimology at the international level
- Discuss the various types of international crime victim surveys
- Explain the globalization of crime and its impact on victims
- Understand the role of the United Nations and its response to victims of crime
- Distinguish between the various types of international crime victims
- Describe the various types of nontraditional international victims

Introduction

In the United States, we like to think that we are leaders in the many different aspects of victimology. However, as Chapter 1 explained, many of the original concepts regarding victimology came from different countries. It is therefore important that we understand victimology from an international perspective.

There are entire textbooks devoted to international victimology. *Victimology* is an excellent, if somewhat dated, text that deals with various aspects of international victimology.[1] Additionally, published proceedings of various international conferences offer a global perspective on victimology, a complete analysis of which is beyond the scope of this chapter. However, several key legal, psychological, and social perspectives are briefly analyzed here to provide an overview of international victimology.

History and Leaders in the Field

Any attempt to research and explain the history of international victimology and to discuss its leaders is a complex and controversial task. To mention some early pioneers and developments is to highlight only a few of the many people who have made international victimology what it is today. Victimology at the international level is viewed by some as a type of criminology and accepted by others as a distinct discipline. To complicate matters further, victimology has not matured at the same rate throughout the world. Some countries have victim assistance legislation; others do not. Crime victimization surveys are conducted in some countries and not in others. Therefore, generalizations and broad statements concerning the discipline should be viewed with caution.[2]

Chapter 1 discussed early leaders in the field, such as Von Hentig, Mendelsohn and Schafer, who argued their case for the discipline of victimology. However, it was not until the 1970s that victimology gained an international perspective. A group of criminologists began meeting in early 1973. The first meeting was in Jerusalem and was followed by a second meeting in Boston, Massachusetts, in 1976. The World Society of Victimology (WSV) was formally established in Munster, Germany, in 1979. The WSV agreed to meet every three years. Also in the 1970s, an American criminologist, Emilio Viano, was instrumental in coordinating a series of meeting and symposium. In 1976, he began publishing a journal entitled *Victimology*.

Many of the early leaders in the field participated in the WSV and continued to debate the direction and goals of the discipline of victimology. For example, Dutch criminologist Nagel believed that victimology should remain part of the field of criminology, while Mendelsohn argued for a general multidisciplinary approach that would establish a separate discipline of victimology aimed at reducing human suffering.[3]

The WSV continues to meet every three years at different locations around the world. It holds symposia, offers annual postgraduate courses, and publishes the symposia proceedings. It is actively involved in the implementation of the United Nation's Declaration of Basic Principles of Justice for Victims of Crime and Abuse of Power.[4] It also has a Web site, www.world-society-victimology.de, that contains some of the most extensive information about international victimology. The only other organization that has similar information and research is International Victimology, at www.victimology.nl, a site maintained by the Dutch Ministry of Justice, which works with the United Nations Crime Prevention Project in Vienna. This organization works closely with the WSV but serves a wider audience.

As with any new discipline, there have been advances and periods of inactivity, as well as several attempts—some successful—to establish academic journals in international victimology.[5] As mentioned earlier, Emilio Viano was active during the early years of victimology and is credited with publishing its first journal, *Victimology*, in 1976. This journal was very active in the early years but is now defunct. In 1988, in Argentina, *Victimologia* began publication in Spanish and serves many Latin American countries. In 1989, in conjunction with the WSV, the *International Review of Victimology* was published in Great Britain. This journal is considered by many authorities in the field to be the premiere journal in international victimology.[6] In 1990, the Australasian Society of Victimology published a journal for its members. Other societies and countries have published journals as well, including Croatia, Japan, and Serbia. The most recent addition to victimology publications is *International Perspectives in Victimology*, published in 2004 by the Tokiwa International Victimology Institute.

Early leaders in victimology, at both the national and international levels, established a foundation for exploring the process of crime victimization. Current leaders are building on that foundation to develop ways to prevent victimization, to improve the resources available to crime victims, and to shape our thinking in the future. Many students in class as this text goes to print will, in the next ten to twenty years, take their place among the early and present-day leaders such as

Mendelsohn, von Hentig, Schafer, Jan van Dijk, Emilio Viano, Gerd Kirchhoff, John Dussich, and Marlene Young.

Crime Victim Surveys

Crime victim surveys have both advocates and detractors. They have flaws in recording and at the same time serve as an invaluable source of information. We are all familiar with crime victim survey in the United States. The major surveys are discussed in Chapter 1. This section discusses surveys conducted by and in other countries.

The International Crime Victimization Survey (ICVS) is the most far-reaching survey of crime in the world.[7] The ICVS was established because of the inadequacy of recorded offenses by law enforcement agencies for purposes of comparing crime in different countries and because there was a notable absence of any other standardized method to record international crimes.

The inadequacy of accurate and comparable reporting can be attributed to a number of cultural differences. Definitions of many crimes vary among nations; for example, some countries do not consider domestic violence a crime, while others recognize it as a serious offense. Recording practices also differ among law enforcement agencies: some countries may record multiple crimes by the same perpetrator as a single offense, for instance, while another country records each crime individually. Cultural differences also influence a victim's willingness to report a crime. In countries such as Sudan, for example, rape victims are ostracized and associated with deep shame.[8] In other countries, public trust in the police and justice system is lacking, so victims are fearful of any involvement with these institutions.

A number of countries conduct their own national crime victimization surveys. These surveys attempt to rectify the shortcomings of law enforcement crime surveys by asking questions of citizens about their crime experience or victimization. The ICVS uses this same approach. The survey collects social and demographic information from the respondents that allows for analysis of how risks of crime vary for different groups within a wide range of populations. The ICVS answers a growing need for a fully standardized survey in different countries that uses the same methods of sampling selection, survey procedures, and data analysis.

The survey is managed by a working group and, for each surveyed country, assigns a coordinator who is responsible for the actual survey in that country. Data gathered from the survey is integrated and processed by the criminology department at Leiden University in the Netherlands. The survey contacts between 1,000 and 2,000 households in each country. Samples of 1,000 are drawn from the country's largest city, although some countries use several cities, and some nations include rural samples.

To date, four ICVSs have been completed. The first was conducted in 1989. Fifteen countries and several cities participated in the first survey. The second survey occurred in 1992 and involved eleven countries. The survey was also expanded to include more developing nations. The third survey took place in 1996 and 1997 and was remarkable in its coverage: it included twelve industrial nations, all but one of the counties in central and east Europe, and fifteen developing countries. In 2000, the results of the fourth round of the ICVS were completed. Surveys have been conducted in over fifty countries since 1989. The fifth round of the ICVS is being conducted in fifteen European countries as well as twenty other countries, including the United States, Mexico, New Zealand, and Japan. (Results had not yet been released as this book went to print.)

The International Violence Against Women Survey (IVAWS) is another international survey that provides researchers and countries with information regarding a specific form of victimization: violence against women.[9] The objective of this survey is to assess the level of victimization of women across a number of countries and to promote and implement research on violence against women in countries around the world. It will assist individual countries in implementing their own victimization surveys on violence against women, the results of which would become an important research and policy tool. The project hopes to provide reliable information as the basis of raising countries' awareness of and response to sexual violence. Developing countries might also benefit from surveys like the IVAWS and perhaps will be encouraged to conduct their own surveys.

The IVAWS is coordinated by a collaboration of two United Nations criminal justice agencies: the United Nations Interregional Crime and Justice Research Institute (UNICRI) and the European Institute for Crime Prevention and Control (HEUNI). The third partner is Statistic Canada. The IVAWS uses the data collected from the ICVS, which was developed by the UNICRI. It also draws upon the expertise of HEUNI in projects aimed at preventing domestic violence and on the expertise of Statistics Canada in developing sensitive surveys for measuring violence against women.

The earliest known discussion of the collection of crime statistics at the international level is considered to have been at the General Statistical Congress held in Brussels in 1853. There was one limited, cross-national crime survey that took place during 1937 through 1946. However, it was not until 1970 that a true international crime survey was conducted: the first United Nations Survey on Crime Trends and Operations of the Criminal Justice Systems.[10]

The United Nations Survey on Crime Trends and Operations of the Criminal Justice Systems is another key international survey. However, it deals with crime and the administration of justice rather than with victimization. Nevertheless, it is important to measure and understand all aspects of international crime victimization, including how data is collected regarding the administration of justice in various countries.

The mission of the United Nations Survey on Crime Trends and the Operations of the Criminal Justice Systems is to collect data on the incidence of reported crime and the operations of the criminal justice systems with a view to improving the analysis and dissemination of that information globally.[11]

Several issues are specific to international crime and victimization surveys: (1) using the same methodology in different cultural and social settings, (2) individual country's differing definition of the term *violence*, (3) interpretation and translation of results, and (4) reaching agreements among the participates. Additionally, several ethical concerns specific to victimization surveys include the safety of the respondents and interviewers, emotional trauma resulting from the interview, and interviewer selection and training.

International crime victimization surveys serve a valuable purpose for understanding violence and victimization. We have just started on this process, and much work remains to be done. However, in our rapidly shrinking world, we must continue our efforts to understand the worldwide nature of violence and victimization.

Globalization of Crime and Victims

Our world is constantly shrinking, or to phrase it more positively, we are becoming a globalized community. Progress in transportation technologies—from horse and buggy to jet aircraft—has steadily contributed to our faster, easier access to all parts of the world. And the Internet has all but negated the need to even travel by making communication and information transferral nearly instantaneous.

There are a number of different definitions of *globalization*. Social institutions might define it as the process by which social institutions become adopted on a global scale.[12] From a monetary point of view, it has been defined as the integration of economics and society.[13] Perhaps one of the better definitions was set forth by the Rockefeller Brothers Fund, which stated that globalization is the quantitative and qualitative expansions in transborder flows of activities and ideas. This definition includes both financial and cultural flows.[14]

Crime has also become globalized. Nations have become concerned about threats to their security from crime that originates outside their borders. The solutions to this concern involve international cooperation. This condition of international security is intertwined with the fundamental rights of individuals within countries. One of the important forms of international crime is organized crime. Organized crime has been defined as groups of individuals with stable, generally hierarchical organizations that perpetrate illegal actions in order to enrich themselves without regard to international borders. Some of the more well-known organized crime organizations include the Mafia, the Japanese Yakuza, the Colombian drug cartels, and the Chinese triads.[15]

International crime is always changing and adapting, becoming more diversified each day. It started in traditional fields such as gambling, loan sharking, and prostitution and has evolved into international automobile smuggling, art and archaeological theft, credit card fraud, and other transnational enterprises. Transnational criminal organizations are more concerned about profit than politics, and if they can control the government in various ways, they are content to leave it in power. Corruption of governmental officials is one method by which these organizations accomplish their goals. Corruption undermines the faith citizens have in their government.

A discussion of terrorism and its impact on the victims of terrorism is beyond the scope of this text. However, no discussion of international victimology would be complete without a brief mention of terrorism.

Terrorism has existed for many years, but September 11, 2001, brought home the phenomena of international terrorism to millions of Americans and others around the world. Since that date, other countries and their citizens have been victims of terrorist attacks. During 2005, terrorist attacks killed or maimed persons in Italy, England, and Egypt.

The numerous definitions of terrorism vary among countries and among agencies. Terrorism has been defined as the use of force or violence against persons or property to intimidate or coerce a government, the civilian populations, or any segment thereof in furtherance of political or social objective.[16] The Federal Bureau of Investigation further breaks down terrorism into domestic terrorism and international terrorism. Domestic terrorism is the unlawful use, or threatened use, of force or violence by a group or an individual based and operating entirely within the Untied States or Puerto Rico without foreign direction and whose acts are directed at the U.S. government or its population for the purpose of furthering political or social goals. International terrorism has essentially the same definition, except the acts are committed by a group or by individuals who has some connection to a foreign power or whose activities transcend national boundaries.

As a result of globalization, the threat of terrorism against both Americans and other populations has dramatically increased in the last several years. The use of weapons of mass destruction, such as high-grade explosives and chemical and biological agents, pose significant threats to populations around the world. As a result of these threats, the United States Department of Justice, Office for Victims of Crime (OVC), formed the Terrorism and International Victims Unit (TIVU). This unit is responsible for developing programs and initiatives that will respond to the needs of victims of terrorism, mass violence, and crimes that have transnational effects, such as trafficking of women and children.[17]

The TIVU provides a variety of services to victims of crime. It provides information and benefits to U.S. nationals who are victims of terrorism in other countries. Victims are given assistance in accessing services that may include briefing on the foreign country's criminal justice system. The TIVU makes all the resources of OVC available to victims of terrorism. It serves as the liaison with the U.S. Department of State and other federal agencies responsible of providing assistance to U.S. citizens in other countries.

The TIVU also provides compensation assistance services to U.S. victims in foreign countries. TIVU administers the International Terrorism Victims Compensation Program, which allows U.S. nationals who are victims of terrorism to apply for compensation by filing a claim with a single federal office. This compensation programs seeks to address the unique needs of U.S. national international terrorism victims. Many countries are developing or expanding their compensation programs, and TIVU works with the U.S. Department of State to maintain an *International Crime Victim Compensation Program Directory* that lists the services provided by foreign countries to U.S. nationals who are victims of terrorism while in their country.

The OVC also works with the U.S. Department of State to assist U.S. embassies and consulates around the world. This work is coordinated with the State Department's Office of Overseas Citizens Services, which has established a full-time victim assistance specialist to coordinate these activities and conduct training for departmental personnel who may come into contact with U.S. citizens overseas.

The Office of Overseas Citizens Services in the State Department's Bureau of Consular Affairs is responsible for the welfare and whereabouts of U.S. citizens traveling and residing abroad.

The embassy or consulate overseas offers assistance to U.S. citizens who are victims of crime. They can help American victims replace a stolen passport, contact family and friends in the U.S., and obtain appropriate medical care. The officer assigned to assist victims can also give the victim general information about the local criminal justice system and process and can provide information about local resources, including foreign crime victim compensation programs. Some U.S. victim compensation programs may also be available to the victim. Approximately half the states offer benefits to their residents who are victims of violent crime overseas.

The United Nations

Introduction

In 1945, representatives from fifty countries met in San Francisco to draft the United Nations Charter. The concept and charter was ratified by a majority of the other signatories, and the United Nations came into existence on October 24, 1945.

Don Emmert/AFP/Getty Images

The Charter is the controlling document for the United Nations and sets forth the rights and obligations of its member nations and its organization and procedures. As established in the Charter, the mission of the United Nations is to develop friendly relations among nations; to cooperate in solving international economic, social, cultural, and humanitarian problems; to promote respect for human rights and fundamental freedoms; and to be a center for harmonizing the actions of nations in attaining these ends.[18]

There are six principle organizations within the United Nations: the Security Council, the General Assembly, the Economic and Social Council, the Trusteeship Council, the International Court of Justice, and the Secretariat. The United Nations also has fifteen other agencies and several other programs and bodies. These programs, bodies, and funds—such as the U.N. Children's Fund (UNICEF)—have their own governing bodies and budgets.[19]

One of the most important aspects of the United Nations is its creation of a comprehensive body of laws dealing with human rights. For the first time in the history of our planet, we have an international organization that has provided the world with a universal and internationally protected code of human rights. The foundation for these laws is the U.N. Charter and the Universal Declaration of Human Rights, adopted by the General Assembly in 1948.[20] Every organization and agency of the United Nations is involved in some aspect of protecting human rights. Twenty-eight articles establish basic human rights for all people in the Declaration. These include the right to be born free; freedom from discrimination based on race, color, or sex; life liberty and security of person; freedom from slavery and torture; equality before the law; fair and public trails; freedom of movement within the borders of one's state; the right to marriage and a family; and other important rights that allow peoples of this earth to live in happiness and dignity.[21]

Victims and the United Nations

In 1985, the United Nations adopted its Declaration of Basic Principles of Justice for Victims of Crime and Abuse of Power. This is the United Nations' foundational document pertaining to victims. Victims of crime are defined as "persons who, individually or collectively, have suffered harm, including physical or mental injury, emotional suffering, economic loss or substantial impairment of their fundamental rights, through acts or omissions that are in violation of criminal laws operative within Member States, including those laws proscribing criminal abuse of power."[22] Under this Declaration, victims are entitled to access to justice and fair treatment, and the Declaration includes the requirement that victims be treated with compassion and respect for their dignity. They are entitled to be informed of their role in the criminal justice proceeding as well as the scope, timing and progress of the proceeding. The Declaration urges states to provide victims with financial aid as well as with various victim assistance programs and activities.

The Declaration recommends that offenders or responsible third parties make fair restitution to victims, their families, or when appropriate, their dependents. It urges governments to make restitution part of the criminal codes and argues that when government agents or officials are responsible for the harm or injury, the victim should receive restitution from the nation under whose authority the agents or employees acted.

Compensation is also addressed in the Declaration. It states that when financial support is not available from the offender or other sources, the nations should attempt to provide compensation. It urges nations to establish compensation programs funded by their national treasury.

Victim assistance programs under the Declaration should provide the necessary medical, psychological, and social assistance from either government-based, community-based, or volunteer organizations. Victims should be informed of the availability of these services, and the services should be easily accessible to them.

The Declaration also addresses another form of victimization: victims of abuse of power. This topic is rarely discussed in the United States; it is examined in more detail later in this chapter. Briefly stated, victims of abuse of power are those who suffer harm from acts or omissions that are not criminal in their country but that are considered a violation of international norms relating to human rights.[23]

U.N. Guide for Policymakers on the Implementation of the Declaration of Basic Principles of Justice for Victims of Crime and Abuse of Power

In 1999, the United Nations adopted a Guide for Policy makers on the Implementation of the Declaration of Basic Principles of Justice for Victims of Crime and Abuse of Power. The Guide sets forth "promising practices" that have been used in various jurisdictions to implement the Declaration. The Guide was developed by the United Nations, the Centre for International Crime Prevention, the Office for Drug Control and Crime Prevention, and the OVC.

This Guide sets forth standards that policy makers from various governmental agencies can use to evaluate their own processes and practices. It proposes several ways to improve services to victims of crime. One proposal recommends that a national-level committee, including academic, justice, health, and government officials, be established with the goal of eliminating the barriers faced by victims in the criminal justice system.

U.N. Handbook on Justice for Victims

The Handbook was developed with input from forty countries as a tool for implementing victim service programs and developing victim-sensitive policies for those who come into contact with victims. These persons may include law enforcement officers, prosecutors, judges, health care professionals, correctional personnel, and spiritual leaders, among others. The Handbook addresses the issue of organizations that come into contact with victims of crime. These organizations include civil organizations, human rights commissions, and elected officials and bodies.

The Handbook outlines the steps necessary to develop a comprehensive victim assistance program. It also acknowledges that differences in cultures and in legal systems preclude its recommendations being followed by every nation. It points out that financial resources to assist victims will vary dramatically among countries.

The International Court of Justice

The International Court of Justice is the principle judicial body within the United Nations. It is located at the Peace Palace in The Hague (Netherlands). The Court has two missions: to settle in accordance with international law the legal disputes submitted by member nations and to give advisory opinions on legal questions referred to it by duly authorized bodies and agencies.[24] The Court is composed of fifteen judges elected to nine-year terms of office by the General Assembly and the Security Council. It may not include more than one judge from any country. One third of the seats are elected every three years, and sitting judges may be re-elected. The members of the Court do not represent their countries but rather act as independent magistrates. Only member nations may appear before the Court. In 2005, there were 191 nations entitled to appear before the Court. Nations must agree to abide by the Court's decision before the case will be heard. The case starts with written pleadings exchanged between the parties. An oral phase is next in which agents address the Court in a public hearing. The Court then goes into private session and returns with a verdict. There is no appeal from the Court's ruling. The Court hears a wide variety of cases, including maritime disputes and other jurisdictional issues.

The International Criminal Court

In 1998, the Rome Statute of the International Criminal Court established the International Criminal Court (ICC). The ICC is *not* a part of the United Nations. It is not under its jurisdiction or control. It is an independent international court with its own legal capacity created by an international treaty.[25] The International Court of Justice at The Hague handles only cases between nations. Nations of the world established the court to prosecute and punish *persons* responsible for crimes against humanity, such as genocide and other serious war crimes. The United States signed the Treaty on December 31, 2000.[26]

The Treaty of Rome defines genocide as acts committed with the intent to destroy, in whole or in part, a national, ethnic, or racial or religious group. Genocide includes killing members of a group or preventing births within the group. Crimes against humanity are defined as a widespread or systematic attack directed against any civilian populations. These crimes may include murder, torture, or trafficking in women and children. They also include rape, sexual slavery, and enforced sterilization. War crime is defined as any act that is committed as part of a plan or policy during war. These crimes include conscripting children under the age of fifteen into the armed forces, taking hostages, use of poison gas, and attacking peacekeeping forces.

The Court is composed of eighteen judges who serve for nine years and may not be re-elected for a second term. The ICC deals with individual responsibility for acts of genocide and other violations of human rights. It does not have automatic jurisdiction over all human rights crimes committed by individuals. The crime must have been committed by a person from a nation that ratified the Rome Treaty, the nation must consent to jurisdiction, or the U.N. Security Council must refer the case to the ICC.[27]

In 2002, the United States withdrew its support from the treaty establishing the ICC. The administration was concerned that the ICC would use the treaty to claim jurisdiction to try U.S. military and government personnel for war crimes. As a result, the United States enters into bilateral treaties with states to insure that military and government personnel are not subject to the Court's jurisdiction.

International Victimization

All victims of crime must be treated as individuals with their own special needs. Each classification of crime produces unique categories of victims. All victims are or should be special. We have studied victims of crime from a variety of perspectives: sexual assault victims, child abuse victims, victims of elder abuse, and others. In fact, many of the existing texts in the area of victimology devote entire chapters to these victims. However, from an international perspective, there are certain types of individuals whose victimization either crosses national borders or is caused by those in power within the victim's nation. This class of victims may be known as forgotten victims, special victims, or international victims. *Forgotten victims* is not an accurate term, since we as a society are aware of such victims, but many countries or organizations simply do not act to assist them. As mentioned previously, all victims are special. To accept them in any other manner is to dehumanize them and do away with their status. The term *international victims* has gained acceptance since several international bodies have proposed various actions that address many of these victims. This section briefly analyzes some of these victims.

Trafficking

Trafficking of human beings has existed since early times. In ancient civilizations, people were taken from their own countries and relocated to other countries to be used as slaves for sex or other purposes. In the United States, the practice of invading African nations and abducting blacks from their country to be used as slaves was an accepted part of our culture in many states until the Civil War. Trafficking also occurs within a nation when its citizens are enslaved for cheap labor or other purposes.

There is no simple definition of trafficking that addresses all of its various aspects. Perhaps the most comprehensive definition is contained in the United Nations Protocol to Prevent, Suppress and Punish Trafficking in Persons, especially Women and Children, which states:

> *The recruitment, transportation, transfer, harboring, or receipt of persons by means of threat or use of force or other forms of coercion, of abduction, of fraud, of*

deception, of the abuse of power or of a position of vulnerability or of the giving or receiving of payments of benefits to achieve the consent of a person having control over another person, for the purpose of exploitation. Exploitation shall include . . . prostitution of others or other forms of sexual exploitation, forced labor or services, slavery or practices similar to slavery, servitude or the removal of organs.[28]

Some countries mistakenly believe that this definition and its protocol does not apply to internal acts of trafficking in which persons are not transported across national boundaries. It is clear from a reading of the definition as well as its accompanying explanation that it does apply to internal trafficking.

The Protocol sets forth three purposes: (1) to prevent and combat trafficking in persons, (2) to protect and assist victims of trafficking, and (3) to promote cooperation among nations to achieve these goals.[29] Member nations of the protocol agreed that they have an obligation to criminalize trafficking, create penalties that take into account the seriousness of this crime, and investigate traffickers.

Signatories agree that law enforcement and border control activities will be enhanced by the exchange of information between nations. They also agree to protect victims by initiating measures to avoid immediate deportation of the victims.

The United Nations' approach to trafficking by use of the Protocol is a new move toward fighting trafficking. It contains one of the first comprehensive definitions of trafficking. It combines traditional crime control measures used in the past to investigate drug trafficking and other crime and to prevent trafficking of human beings. Previous efforts to prevent trafficking have focused on the violations of human rights but did not include law enforcement activities to arrest and prosecute offenders.

Generally, trafficking involves a flow of victims from less developed countries to industrialized nations. The largest number of victims are believed to come from South and Southeast Asia. The former Soviet Union may be the newest source for trafficking of persons for prostitution and the sex trade.[30] Traffickers acquire their victims using a number of different ploys. In some countries, traffickers will purchase a child by paying money to the family and promising a better life for the child.[31] Sometimes, women are simply kidnapped and forcibly taken to another country. In other cases, victims are lured by false promises of a well-paying position, such as an au pair, maid, dancer, or domestic worker, in a foreign country. Traffickers may advertise these "opportunities" in local papers.[32]

The most common techniques used in trafficking to obtain and retain victims is the use of force or coercion, which can be direct and violent or indirect and more psychological in nature. Psychological force can include threatening to turn a foreign national over to the immigration authorities. Another form of coercion involves the use of bonds or debts to keep a person under control, often referred to as *bonded labor* or *debt bondage*. Many trafficked victims fall prey to bonded labor as they assume an initial debt as part of their terms of employment. They are kept in debt as the amount owed grows, the original terms of service change, and the employer becomes more coercive. Cultures that discourage confrontation, illiteracy, and power differentials make this form of slavery for low-skilled workers almost impossible to eliminate.[33]

In 2005, it was estimated that between 600,000 and 800,000 persons were victims of international trafficking across borders. Approximately 80 percent of these victims are female, and up to 50 percent are children. These figures do not include trafficking within the borders of a country. It is estimated that including this type of trafficking would raise the total number of cases to between 2 and 4 million.[34] Estimates for international trafficking brought into the United States vary from a low of 45,000[35] to a high of 87,000 annually.[36]

Asian, South American, and Russian gangs are among the major traffickers of people. Chinese and Vietnamese triads, the Japanese Yukuza, and South American drug cartels interact with local networks to provide transportation, housing, and documentation. Profits from trafficking can be used to fund other criminal activity. Trafficking is a lucrative business for organized crime. These organizations incorporate the knowledge, facilities, and networks used for drug smuggling and other goods into moving human victims from one location to another.[37]

Trafficking exacts a terrible cost on its victims, inflicting both psychological and physical harm. Many victims of the sex trade suffer from sexually transmitted diseases, including HIV/AIDS. In many cases, the victim of trafficking may be sold and resold. A child may first be sold as forced labor and then resold to a prostitution ring. Trafficking also costs many nations valuable resource that must be used to treat victims of trafficking. Many of these victims, when rescued, suffer from a variety of illnesses that require public health intervention.

The United Nations regards trafficking as different from smuggling of migrants (which is subject to a different protocol, the Protocol against the Smuggling of Migrants by Land, Sea and Air). The smuggling of migrants, while often dangerous and performed under degrading conditions, involves persons who have consented to the smuggling. Trafficking victims, on the other hand, do not

---

FOCUS: The Facts about Child Camel Jockeys

The trafficking and exploitation of South Asian and African children as camel jockeys has increased dramatically in the Gulf states, which, after the discovery of oil and the associated surge in wealth, transformed camel racing from a traditional Bedouin sport pastime to a multi-million-dollar activity. Today, thousands of children, some as young as three or four, are trafficked from Asia and Africa and sold into slavery to serve as camel jockeys.

These children live in oppressive environments and endure harsh living conditions. They work long hours, live in unsanitary conditions, and receive little food so they do not gain weight and increase the load on the camel they are racing. Their handlers and trainers abuse them, including using beatings and threats. Many of these children are injured or killed by the camels. Once they reach teenage years, they are disposed of because they serve no further use for their masters. Having no skills or education and suffering severe psychological injuries, many of them lead desolate lives and face dim prospects. These victims, like many children who are trafficked, are robbed of their childhood and their future.

Source: Adapted from *Trafficking in Persons Report*, U.S. Department of State, Washington, D.C. (June 2005).

consent or their consent is obtained by fraud and deception. Smuggling usually ends when the migrant worker arrives at his or her location, while trafficking victims endure months, years, and even lifetimes of slavery. Finally, smuggling of migrants by definition crosses international borders, while trafficking may involve transporting the victim across country borders but can also involve moving the victim from one part of the country to another.[38]

We are making slow progress against human trafficking. Progress was seen in the United States with the passage of the Prosecutorial Remedies and other Tools to end the Exploitation of Children Today (PROTECT) Act and the Trafficking Victims Protection Reauthorization Act.[39] These acts increase the punishment for U.S. citizens or permanent legal residents who engage in child sex tourism (CST). CST involves people who travel from their own country to another to engage in commercial sex acts with children. These crimes most often occur in developing countries, where perpetrators seek anonymity and the availability of young child prostitutes.[40] This crime exists because of weak law enforcement, poverty, ease of travel, and the Internet. Using PROTECT, if a U.S. citizen is arrested in a foreign country for sexually abusing children, he or she may be extradited to the United States and face trial and possible punishment of up to 30 years in prison. While the United States and other countries are beginning to address this crime, we still have a long way to go toward eradicating it. Education, tougher laws, and remedies for universal poverty are a few of the steps we must take to reduce or eliminate this form of slavery.

Parental Child Abductions

A wide variety of excellent texts deal with almost all aspects of child abuse. However, most of them, and almost all of the victimology texts, fail to discuss one of the most difficult and frustrating aspects of raising a child—child abduction. Child abduction has been defined as the "taking, retention, or concealment of a child or children by a parent, other family member, or their agent, in derogation of the custody rights, including visitation rights of another family member or their agents."[41]

Many parents whose child is abducted to another country face a daunting task of attempting to regain custody of the child. The parent who abducts the child often has support from family or friends. Some abductors may believe they are rescuing the child from an abusive partner who has placed the child in danger. Others simply feel disenfranchised from American society and want to return to their homeland and take the child with them. Some abductors are victims of spousal abuse and take the child to protect it, while others take the child as a final act of domination and control over his or her partner.

In 1988, the most recent national survey examining child abductions was conducted. This study was called the National Incidence Study on Missing, Abducted, Runaway, and Throwaway Children in America (NISMART).[42] It placed these victims into two broad categories:

> *Broad Scope Cases:* These cases involved a family member who either took the child in violation of a court order or failed to return or release the child at the

end of a visit and kept the child at least overnight. In 1988, there were an estimated 354,100 children abducted under this definition.

Policy Focal Cases: These cases fit the broad scope definition but included at least one of the following characteristics: (1) the abductor attempted to conceal the taking or whereabouts of the child and to prevent contact between the child and the other parent, (2) the child was transported out of the state, or (3) there was evidence that the abductor intended to keep the child permanently.

Approximately 46 percent of all abductions (163,200) fell within this definition, and all international abductions are considered policy focal cases.[43]

According to NISMART, abductors and the parent who was left behind usually differed sharply in terms of background, citizenship, and education. Eighty-three percent were of different nationalities, 69 percent were of different ethnicity, and 62 percent were citizens of another country.[44] Both mothers and fathers were equally likely to be the abductors.

The number of children abducted per incident ranged from one to three, but in approximately 70 percent of the cases, only one child was abducted. Abducted children tended to be young, ranging from five months to about twelve and a half years old, with the mean age of five. It may be that the abductor feels he or she has more control over younger children.

Approximately 41 percent of all abducted children were returned to the left-behind parent. In half of all the cases in which the child was recovered, the separation time was less than one year. In general, separations were shorter in abductions to signatories to the Hague Convention. This treaty is discussed in more detail later in this section. In cases in which the child was recovered, nearly all the left-behind parents had to travel to the country where the child had been taken to bring the child back to the United States.[45]

The recovery of abducted children has taken many forms. Some recoveries were the result of court decisions, others involved law enforcement agencies, others occurred when the abductor voluntarily returned the child, and still others involved the use of mercenaries.

A number of resources are available to parents of abducted children. The most well known is the National Center for Missing and Exploited Children, which has an extensive Web site with detailed information for parent as well as important links to other Web-based resources dealing with abducted children.[46]

One of the most frustrating and unknown aspects of child abduction is that court orders issued in the United States are not automatically honored in other countries. In order to solve this problem, the United States, in 1976, began the process of establishing the Hague Convention on the Civil Aspects of International Child Abduction.[47] The Convention became law in the United States on July 1, 1988, and is in force in over fifty countries around the world. The terms of the Convention apply to wrongful removals or retentions of children in signatory countries.

The Convention is civil in nature and is available to left-behind parents seeking return or visitation of the abducted child. Since it is civil in nature, the parents are the parties to any legal action, not the United States or the government where the abducted child is located.[48] The Convention requires that children who were abducted from one country to another in violation of a valid custody order shall be returned to the country of the left-behind parent who has the custody order. The time within which to petition the country where the child is located is normally one year from the date of the wrongful removal or retention. The left-behind parent may file a petition after the one year, but it is up to the discretion of the court where the child is located whether or not it will act on the petition.

There are a number of exceptions to the mandatory return of the child to the left-behind parent. If the court finds that the child would suffer physical or psychological harm, it may deny return. If the child objects to the return and has reached an age of reason, the court may take his or her desires into consideration. The Convention is silent on the age at which children reach this level of maturity.

Each country establishes a central authority to carry out the duties under the Convention. The central authority in the United States is the Department of State's Office of Children's Issues. The U.S. central authority's role is one of an active facilitator. It seeks to promote cooperation among the parties and various foreign government agencies involved in the case.

Abuse of Power

The Declaration of Basic Principles for Victims of Crime and Abuse of Power establishes the principle that all persons should be free from *abuse of power*. The concept of abuse of power is multifaceted and is not discussed or analyzed in much if any detail in victimology texts in the United States. The United Nations defines abuse of power from the perspective of victims of abuse of power as any person(s), either as an individual or as a group, who suffers harm, including physical, emotional suffering, economic loss or substantial impairment of their fundamental rights, through acts or omissions that do not yet constitute violations of national criminal laws but are considered violations of internationally recognized norms relating to human rights.[49]

The Declaration states further that countries should consider incorporating into their criminal law codes a prohibition of abuse of power and provide victims of this type of abuse with the same remedies available to victims of crime. It further recommends that countries enter into international treaties regarding abuse of power. Finally, it recommends that countries periodically update their criminal codes to prohibit serious abuses of political or economic power.

One manner of examining the Declaration's definition may be to break it down into subsections for purposes of clarity. A victim may be an individual from any walk of life, including a homeowner, a worker, an outspoken writer or poet who criticizes the government, or a deposed leader of a government; or victims may be groups such as minority or religious groups, or abuse of power may even be based on gender. The harm these victims suffer is very broad and includes physical injuries of all types, such as bullet wounds, sexual assault, and even starvation since it has numerous physical consequences.[50] Mental injuries or emotional suffering may include posttraumatic stress disorder, depression, and other mental illnesses or disorders that result from the abuse of power. Victims may also suffer from economic loss that might occur as a result of forced relocation, loss of businesses or homes, or even death of a loved one who provided economic support.

The final and perhaps the most important aspect of the classification of victims of abuse of power in the Declaration of Basic Principles of Justice for Victims of Crime and Abuse of Power deals with their fundamental rights. The Declaration states that they should not suffer substantial impairment of their (human) rights.

The Declaration defines the prohibited acts as those that are not yet violations of national criminal codes but are substantial violations of internationally recognized norms relating to human rights. For example, a country may not have a law prohibiting trafficking of women or children, but as discussed earlier in this chapter, such a practice is not only a violation of human rights norms but in many cases violates treaties between a number of countries.

There is some support for the position that human rights violations can occur under civil law, such as family law dealing with rights of parents or children within the family.[51] Another problem with the Declaration's definition is the use of the term *substantial*. How does one measure a substantial violation versus a minor violation?

The list of possible violations of human rights is long and reflects the suffering of peoples around the world.

Violation of human rights is not a new phenomenon. It has been part of our culture since the beginning of time. It became better known and nations began to raise international concerns about human rights after World War II. In 1948, the United Nations adopted a Universal Declaration of Human Rights.[52] Some of the more important human rights include political and civil rights; rights for children; economic, social, and cultural rights; freedom of opinion and expression; and freedom of religion and belief.

FOCUS: What Happens If the Protectors Commit Abuse of Power Acts?

One of the most terrifying situations for human rights victims is to be victimized by the persons sent to protect them. In 2001, staff members of the United Nations were asked to investigate reports of sexual abuse of women and children refugees by aid workers in West Africa. As the final report to the United Nations indicates, men, women, and children displaced by conflict or other disasters are among the most vulnerable people in the world. After an extensive investigation, several incidents of sexual abuse were confirmed. It must be noted that interviewing victims in these types of situations is extremely hard and there is a high percentage of unreported cases because of fear of retaliation or stigmatization, distrust of authority, and other cultural reasons. As a result of the allegations, the United Nations has improved systems of reporting, investigating, and disciplining offenders.

Source: "Investigation into Sexual Exploitation of Refugees by Aid Workers in West Africa," *Report of the Secretary-General on the Activities of the Office of Internal Oversight Services*, United Nations General Assembly, New York, October 11, 2002.

Another aspect of abuse of power occurs when there is a human rights violation by persons or organizations, and the government fails to protect to protect those victims.[53] The case of *Kaya vs. Turkey* concerned the disappearance, torture, and death of the victim. The European Court of Human Rights addressed this issue when it held:

> *This involves a primary duty of the State to secure [emphasis added] the right to life by putting in place effective criminal-law provisions to deter the commission of offenses against the person backed up by law-enforcement machinery for the prevention, suppression and punishment of breaches of such provisions. It also extends in appropriate circumstances to operational measures to protect an individual or individuals whose life is at risk from the criminal acts of another.[54]*

Since the adoption of the Human Rights Declaration in 1948, the United Nations General Assembly has gradually expanded the human rights laws to cover a wide variety of situations. These rights have slowly gained acceptance in the international community. Education campaigns have informed the peoples of the world of their inalienable rights, and various groups and organizations continue to fight to promote these rights and protect the rights of individuals and groups throughout the world.

Victims of Torture

. . . nor [shall] cruel or unusual punishment be inflicted.
United States Constitution, Eighth Amendment (Bill of Rights)

The OVC refers to *torture* victims as the "invisible population of crime victims."[55] Not only is the United States concerned with the issue of victims who are tortured, but the United Nations has repeatedly addressed this issue. In 1975, it adopted the Declaration on the Protection of All Persons from Being Subjected to Torture and Other Cruel, Inhuman, or Degrading Treatment or Punishment.[56] The United Nations made progress in this area, and in 1984, the General Assembly adopted the Convention Against Torture and Other Cruel, Inhuman, or Degrading Treatment or Punishment, which became effective in 1987.[57]
Torture has been defined as

> *any act by which severe pain or suffering, whether physical or mental, is intentionally inflicted on a person for such purposes as obtaining from him or a third person information or a confession, punishing him for an act he or a third person has committed or is suspected of having committed, or intimidating or coercing him or a third person, for any reason based on discrimination of any kind when such pain or suffering is inflicted by or at the instigation of or with the consent or acquiescence of a public official or other person acting in an official capacity. It does not include pain or suffering arising only from, inherent in, or incidental to lawful sanctions.[58]*

There are a number of international treaties that prohibit the use of torture. These include the Sixth Amendment to the United States Constitution, the U.N. Universal Declaration of Human Rights, and the Geneva Conventions. However, the use of torture continues in many countries. Amnesty International USA conducted an extensive survey regarding the existing use of torture.[59] The survey covered acts of torture from 1997 to 2005. It included 195 countries and territories. It found more than 150 countries still use torture. In more than seventy countries, the use of torture was wide spread and accepted by the government. This number is probably a low estimate because torture is conducted in secret, and there is good reason to suspect a large percentage of torture goes unreported.

The OVC estimates that there are 400,000 torture survivors in the United States. It reports that approximately 30 percent of all refugees are torture survivors. These victims are "invisible" since many torturers tell their victims that no one will believe them, and they are concerned that if they openly discuss their experiences, family members remaining in their native country will be tortured.[60]

A number of treatment centers across the United States offer a variety of services to victims of torture,[61] including basic needs such as food, clothing, and shelter. Additionally, many centers provide psychotherapy, medical services, interpreters, healing groups, case management and other social services, and legal services including assistance with asylum.

There is a critical need for these types of centers. Survivors of torture exhibit a variety of symptoms, including chronic pain in muscles and joints, severe depression and other mental disorders, nightmares, guilt and self-hatred, impaired memory, the inability to form lasting relationships, and thoughts of suicide. Many of these treatment centers report some of the following behaviors are common among survivors of torture:

- Sleeping in chairs so they won't dream
- Inability to eat without vomiting
- Panic attacks whenever they hear an automobile backfire
- Inability to turn off lights at night because in the dark they have flashbacks of the torture[62]

The victims of torture come from all walks of life. They include activists for human rights, labor rights, or other causes. They are targeted victims because they are easily recognizable and available for arrest or confinement. Incarcerated persons other than activists may also be tortured. On occasion, ordinary citizens may be tortured if the government is attempting to control the population by creating a climate of fear and repression.

Torture by its very nature seeks to destroy a person's personality by use of pain or other degrading acts. Torture can take many forms, such as beating, sexual assault of both males and females, suspension upside down, submersion in water, denial of medical treatment, electrical torture on various parts of the body (most often on the genitals of both male and female victims). Torture can also include psychological

---

FOCUS: Leading the Fight Against Torture

One of the leading private organizations at the forefront of the fight against torture is Amnesty International. It is a world wide organization based on voluntary memberships, and it consists of sections, structures, international networks, and affiliated groups that campaign for international human rights. Its vision is a world in which every person enjoys all of the human rights enshrined in the Universal Declaration of Human Rights and other international human rights standards. To accomplish its vision, it undertakes research and action focusing on preventing and grave abuses of human rights. It is independent of any government, political perspective, economic interest, or religious ideology. It does not support or oppose any government or any victims. It is concerned only with the protection of human rights.

Source: Amnesty International: *http://web.amnesty.org/pages/aboutai-statute-eng.*

terror, threats, humiliation, sleep deprivation, mock executions, witnessing torture of others including family members, and being forced to torture others.[63]

The United Nations implements the Convention Against Torture and Other Cruel, Inhuman, or Degrading Treatment or Punishment by a variety of means, including use of the Committee Against Torture. This committee consists of ten international experts who act as a conduit for countries to report to the United Nations on measures they have undertaken to enforce the Convention. The committee also responds to reports or allegations of torture within a country by inviting the country to co-operate in the examination of the information and may, in certain cases, designate one of its members to make a confidential investigation and to report back to the committee.

The Committee Against Torture appoints a Special Rapporteur (expert or scribe appointed to investigate a subject and report on it) to seek information on questions about torture and to quickly respond to those questions. The Special Rapporteur has the authority to ask for information and to request responses from any country that is a member of the United Nations regardless of whether or not it is a signatory to the Convention Against Torture and Other Cruel and Inhuman or Degrading Treatment or Punishment. The Special Rapporteur submits reports to both the Commission on Human Rights and the General Assembly.[64]

Children as Soldiers

The use of children as soldiers is a black mark against humanity.[65] The effects and consequences of children being used as weapons of war last for generations.[66] Almost all civilized nations publicly agree that they should not use *child soldiers*. The great majority of these nations are signatories to various treaties, conventions, and protocols that prohibit or condemn the use of children as soldiers. However, many of them, as well as many non-signatories, continue to use children as soldiers both in external and internal conflicts. Additionally, rebel groups routinely recruit or abduct children for use as soldiers.

The major international standards that prohibit use of children as soldiers are the Convention on the Rights of the Child, the Optional Protocol to the Convention, the Rome Statute of the International Criminal Court, and additional protocols to the four Geneva Conventions.[67]

The Convention to the Rights of the Child contains specific prohibitions that attempt to protect children from serving as soldiers by prohibiting recruitment of children under the age of fifteen. A number of nations decided to build on the principles of the Convention and worked to raise the minimum age for recruitment and participation in the armed forces to eighteen years. The Optional Protocol to the Convention was adopted by the U.N. General Assembly on May 25, 2000, and became effective on February 12, 2002. By 2005, this Protocol had been signed by 115 countries and ratified by sixty-three countries. It outlaws compulsory recruitment of children under the age of eighteen by government or nongovernment forces. It raises the age that children may volunteer for the armed forces to sixteen and requires nations to establish methods to prove that the child's acts were in fact voluntary. It further requires that any nation that does accept volunteers under age eighteen insures that those children do not take part in direct combat operations. Finally, it outlaws the recruitment or participation of any person under the age of eighteen in any insurgency groups or rebel forces under any circumstances.[68] The Rome Statute of the International Criminal Court classifies conscription, enlistment, or use in hostilities of children under age fifteen in internal or external conflicts as a war crime.

Although the United Nations has information that indicates child soldiers are being used in more than thirty countries, the Security Council actions were limited to six armed conflicts, five of which were in Africa. It appears that members of the Security Council are reluctant to interfere with the actions of other sovereign states or have declined to incur the cost of enforcing sanctions against those nations that violate the various international agreements.[69]

Who are child soldiers? The Treaties, Conventions, and Protocols define them by age. The Coalition to Stop the Use of Child Soldiers defines them as any person under the age of eighteen who is a member of or attached to government forces or any other regular or irregular force or armed group.[70] However, some nations allow young people to join their armed forces with the consent of their parents. In many cases, these are truly voluntarily acts by both the parents and the young person. Therefore, it would seem a better definition might be that "a child soldier is any person under the age of sixteen who does not have the voluntary consent of his or her parents and who then becomes a member or is attached to government forces or any regular or irregular force or armed group." In no event shall any person under the age of eighteen be allowed to participate directly or indirectly in armed combat. This definition would undoubtedly raise concern and controversy, but it addresses the realities and practices of modern, industrialized nations many of which allow sixteen- or seventeen-year-old children to join their armed forces with the consent of their parents. Great Britain and the United States are two

---

FOCUS: What Is the Appropriate Age for a Soldier?

The discussion and definition of who is a child soldier raises complex social and cultural issues. In the United States, a person at the age of seventeen may enlist with his or her parent's approval. In the United Kingdom, a person at the age of sixteen may enlist in his or her armed forces.

- What is the appropriate age for a person to become a soldier in their armed forces?

- Does it make any difference that a person sixteen years old cannot drive in many states?

- How about the fact that a person seventeen years old has only been driving for one year?

- Does your opinion change if the person joining the armed forces is doing so to get out of a ghetto and make a better life for himself or herself?

- Would your opinion change if persons under eighteen were allowed to join the military but were prohibited from directly or indirectly being involved in an armed conflict?

- What about the fact that in many states you may join the armed forces at the age of eighteen but cannot drink in a bar or vote?

- Would your answer be different if instead of joining a formal, recognized military, the person was joining a rebel group?

---

examples of nations that allow persons under the age of 18 to enlist in their armed forces with the consent of their parents.

The true extent of the problem is unknown, since like many other issues addressed in this chapter, in many nations, the actions of recruitment and use of children as soldiers is shrouded in secrecy, and outsiders are barred from examining this issue. However, the Coalition to Stop the Use of Child Soldiers estimates that there are more the 120,000 children under the age of eighteen currently participating in armed conflicts in Africa alone. Children are used as solders in other countries, including countries in the Middle East. Some of these children are not more than seven or eight years old.[71] Other estimates state that more than 500,000 children under the age of eighteen have been recruited by state or non-state armed forces or groups in over eighty-five countries.[72] A third source, Amnesty International, USA, states that approximately 300,000 children under the age of eighteen are participating in armed conflicts in thirty different countries.[73] As can be seen from these figures, well-meaning and dedicated organizations report different facts and figures regarding the extent of the problem of child soldiers. What is clear is that the problem is persistent and that it affects our most valuable resource—children.

Children become soldiers in a variety of ways. Some children are drafted or conscripted, others are kidnapped, and others are forced to join armed groups to protect their families from retaliation. The kidnapping may occur in a variety of ways: children may be seized off the street or taken while attending school or living in orphanages. Hunger, poverty, or fear may drive parents to offer their children for service, especially when the armed group offers to pay the child's wages to the family instead of to the child. Sometimes children may "voluntarily" join the armed groups because they may perceive it as the only way to survive.[74]

Children as young as seven years may participate in armed conflict. They may act as porters who carry food or ammunition for the actual fighters. They also act as runners or scouts, sex slaves, cooks, or spies. Girls are especially vulnerable as child soldiers. Many are sexually assaulted, forced to engage in prostitution, or forced to be "wives" of adult combatants. When they reach age ten, their roles may change: they may be given weapons and forced to become soldiers.[75]

Many commanders like using children as soldiers because they are so young they view combat as a game or are not afraid of death. They are also viewed as a consumable commodity that should be used in place of the more dependable adult combatants. Since they are considered so expendable, many child soldiers never receive any training and are often massacred during combat. Additionally, they are easier to mold into effective fighters. Finally, in some countries, there is a shortage of eligible men, so the combatants widen the recruitment base by accepting or abducting children.

Child soldiers have been witnessed committing atrocities during or after combat. Sometimes these acts are committed under the influence of drugs or alcohol or at the urging of the adult soldiers. However, drugs or alcohol alone is not responsible for these acts. A more likely cause of the majority of the atrocities is that the children have suffered systematic abuse by adult combatants and have lived in a pervasive culture of killing and violence. This environment, coupled with threats of deadly retaliation if they do not conform to the beliefs of their adult leaders, is probably the major reason that children are involved in acts of mutilations, killings, and rapes. Some of these acts include beheading a captive and playing catch with her head, gouging out victims' eyes, and cutting off their hands and feet.[76]

The consequences of children serving as soldiers have been explored by a number of different authorities. Daya Somasundaram examined the long-term civil war in Sri Lanka and explains that child soldiers suffer brutalization, deprivation, institutionalized violence, and various brutal sociocultural factors. Psychological injuries include somatization, depression, post-traumatic stress disorder, and severe psychosis.[77]

War, Natural Disasters, and Other Acts of God

Victims of war, natural disasters, and other acts of God are not considered traditional victims. Indeed, they are certainly not classified as crime victims by many organizations. However, they have suffered many of the same consequences as traditional victims. Any chapter dealing with international victimization should briefly discuss these victims for several reasons. Many professionals working with victims of crime may be called upon to assist victims of war, natural disasters, and other acts of God. Additionally, understanding different forms of victimization allows professionals to put service to victims of crime in a more centered perspective. Finally, these people are in fact victims, and we should understand the dynamics as well as how to respond to their needs.

The nature of war has changed over the last several decades. In many countries, formalized, uniformed soldiers do not face each other across a delineated battlefield. External conflicts and internal strife have changed the face of war and its casualties. Civilians may become deliberate targets. Combatants and insurgents may live in civilian villages and use civilians, even children, as human shields. Villages that voluntarily or by force provide logistical support for one side in a conflict may face retaliation by the other.[78]

Victims of war include both civilian and military casualties. These casualties include those who are injured and those who are killed during the conflict. The injury may result from hostile fire or actions or from friendly fire or actions. In the long term, it does not matter who caused the injury or death: the consequences of war linger for generations. War casualties include men, women, and children.

One of the most tragic casualties of war concerns those who are killed or maimed by landmines. Mines continue to cause injury and death long after the original conflict has ended. Children in over sixty-five countries live with the threat of more than ten million landmines still buried in the ground awaiting victims.[79] Additionally, unexploded ordnance continues to litter the ground of many of these countries. Like landmines, unexploded ordnance does not discriminate against friend or foe, adult or child. Children are at higher risk of injury because some of the ordnance looks like balls or other toys. Clearing landmines is a dangerous, time-consuming, and expensive proposition, and many of these mines and unexploded ordnance are located in the world's poorest countries.[80] In an effort to stop the use of landmines, the Convention on the Prohibition of the Use, Stockpiling, Production, and Transfer of Antipersonnel Mines and Their Destruction was drafted and became effective in 1999. As of March 2001, the Treaty has 133 signatories.

One of the modern world's largest natural disasters occurred in December 26, 2004, when a massive undersea earthquake occurred near Indonesia. Measuring 9.0 on the Richter scale, it was one of the strongest earthquakes in the world in forty years. The earthquake caused massive waves, or tsunamis, that devastated several countries. It generated a tsunami that was among the deadliest disasters in modern history.[81] Indonesia, Malaysia, Bangladesh, Somalia, Sri Lanka, India, Thailand, and other countries suffered massive loss of life and destruction of property. Some estimates put the total loss of life at over 250,000.[82]

Countries around the world responded immediately with various forms of assistance. Many nations and organizations sent foreign professionals to work with those who survived the disaster. Others sent funds and other resources to search for survivors. The effects of this massive disaster have yet to be determined, but it is a certainty that the victims will suffer physical, financial, and mental hardship for years to come.

There are a variety of different types of natural disasters or acts of God that cause death and destruction to millions of people in our society. Earthquakes, droughts, epidemics, famine, floods, and volcanic eruptions are just a few such disasters. The effect on victims of natural disaster is much the same as on victims of crime: physical, financial, and mental trauma to those who survive. As a society, we must be trained and ready to respond to these victims just as we are trying to respond to victims of international or domestic crime.

Summary

The academic and professional discipline of victimology is still a young science. This is especially true at the international level. Some countries continue to make strides forward in serving victims of crime, and others continue their victimization of crime victims as well as entire populations.

Just as there were disagreements about the nature and scope of victimology in the United States, so there were different perspectives on victimology at the international level. One of the most significant achievements was the initiation of the International Crime Victims Survey. While there are criticisms regarding the ICVS, it is the most far-reaching survey of crime in the world. Even though there are different definitions of crime in each country and each country has its own unique culture, the ICVS attempts to account for those differences. The survey is managed by a working group, and each country has its own coordinator. While it is a survey of crime, it also provides us with critical information regarding victims.

Other surveys contribute to the understanding of international victimology. The International Violence Against Women Survey assesses the level of victimization of women across a number of countries, and the United Nations Survey on Crime Trends and Operations of the Criminal Justice Systems, while this focused more on crime statistics than on victims, nonetheless provides us with information on how criminal justice agencies in other countries function.

Globalization of our society continues to occur at a rapid pace, opening doors to new ways of communicating, new ways of doing business, and unfortunately, new ways of committing crimes. Commercial use of the Internet allows businesses to access a new population of customers—and criminals to access a new population of victims.

Terrorism has long affected citizens throughout the world, and since September 11, 2001, Americans who once felt insulated from terrorism have realized they too are potential victims of attack. The United Nations and individual nations are responding to this crisis in a variety of ways. The United States, for example, has increased border security, enforced more stringent identification procedures, established the Department of Homeland Security, and on October 26, 2001, passed the controversial Patriot Act.

The United Nations serves a variety of roles in the world. Its mission is to develop friendly relations among nations; to cooperate in solving international economic, social, cultural, and humanitarian problems and to promote respect for human rights and fundamental freedoms; and to be the center for harmonizing the actions of nations in attaining these goals. One of the most important accomplishments of the United Nations was the creation of a body of laws dealing with human rights. In 1985, it adopted its Declaration of Basic Principles of Justice for Victims of Crime and Abuse of Power. The International Court of Justice is the principle judicial body within the United Nations. It settles international disputes among member nations and gives advisory opinions on certain legal questions.

The International Criminal Court was established by the Rome Treaty of 1998. It is not part of the Untied Nations but an independent judicial body that can prosecute individuals for crimes against humanity.

There are a number of crimes that cross national borders. Trafficking in human beings has existed since the establishment of nations. Trafficking today is a multi-million-dollar business that destroys it victims. Generally, trafficking involves moving victims from less developed countries to industrialized nations. Approximately 600,000 to 800,000 are trafficked across borders each year. If trafficking within countries is included, the number rises to between 2 and 4 million victims.

Child abductions by parents is a problem compounded when the abducting parent leaves the country. Attempting to regain custody of the child in these situations is extremely difficult. One response to this problem was the adoption of the Hague Convention on the Civil Aspects of International Child Abduction. This Convention is civil in nature and is available to the left-behind parent. That parent may use the Convention to try to obtain the return of the abducted child.

Abuse of power is a topic that needs more research and discussion. It concerns victims who suffer loss of their fundamental rights by acts or omissions that do not constitute a violation of the country's criminal codes but are considered violations of internationally recognized norms relating to human rights. It may be perpetrated by the government in power, by other groups, or even individuals.

Victims of torture are sometimes referred to as invisible populations or victims. Torture is prohibited by a number of international treaties; however, it continues to exist. One survey found over 150 nations still use torture.

Children as soldiers are another form of international victimization. The effects on our society and the individual victims will last for generations. A number of treaties prohibit using children as soldiers, but like trafficking, abductions, abuse of power, and torture, it continues unabated in our society.

War, natural disasters, and other acts of God sometimes result in mass victimization. While these victims do not meet the traditional definition of crime victims, it is important to understand this form of victimization so that we may better serve all victims worldwide.

International victimology is growing and expanding as an academic discipline. We are continuing to address violations of human rights at the international level. As we gain more knowledge at the international level and as peoples across the world become more aware of the tragedy of victimization, we can begin to solve some of these problems.

Key Terms

Globalization is the quantitative and qualitative expansion in transborder flows of activities and ideas.

Terrorism is the use of force or violence against persons or property to intimidate or coerce a government, the civil populations, or any segment thereof in furtherance of political or social objectives.

Trafficking is the recruitment, transportation, transfer, harboring, or receipt of persons by means of threat or use of force or other forms of coercion, abduction, fraud, or deception; by means of the abuse of power or of a position of vulnerability; or by means of the giving or receiving of benefits to achieve the consent of a person having control over another person for the purpose of exploitation.

Abuse of power is defined in the context of victimization: any person(s), either an individual or as a group, who suffers harm, including physical, emotional suffering, economic loss or substantial impairment of their fundamental rights, through acts or omissions that do not yet constitute violation of national laws but are considered violations of international norms relating to human rights.

Torture is any act that inflicts pain or suffering on a person for the purposes of obtaining from him or a third person information or a confession or punishing him for any reason based on discrimination of any kind.

Child soldiers are any persons under age sixteen who do not have the voluntary consent of their parents and who become members of or are attached to government forces or any regular or irregular force or armed group.

Discussion Questions

1. Discuss the impact of international victimization on victim services in the United States. Is there an impact? In what areas?

2. Compare and contrast the National Crime Victimization Survey with the International Crime Victim Survey.

3. Is the United Nations the proper body to address international victimization? In light of the controversies regarding its existence, should the United States continue as a member? What are the alternatives?

4. What is the difference between the International Court of Justice and the International Criminal Court? Do we need two international courts?

5. Compare trafficking with parental child abduction. What are the differences and the similarities?

6. Do we have abuse of power incidents in the United States? Give some examples.

7. What can we do to eliminate torture as a tool of governments or groups?

8. How can we stop nations from using children as soldiers? At what age should a child be able to join the armed forces?

Suggested Readings

Paul Rock, (ed.,) *Victimology*, (Dartmouth Publishing, Brookfield, Mass.) 1994.

Stanley Meisier, *United Nations: The First Fifty Years*, (Atlantic Monthly Press, London) 1997.

Linda Fasulo, *An Insider's Guide to the UN*, (Yale University Press, New Haven, Conn.) 2003.

Basic Facts about the United Nations, (Bernan Press, Lanham, Md.) 2004.

Kathryn Farr, *Sex Trafficking: The Global Market in Women and Children*, (Worth Publishers, Cranbury, N.J.) 2004.

Craig McGill, *Human Traffic—Sex, Slaves, and Immigration*, (Vision Paperbacks, London) 2003.

David Kyle & Rey Koslowski, *Global Human Smuggling*, (Johns Hopkins University Press, Baltimore, Md.) 2001.

Kamala Kempadoo (ed.), *Trafficking and Prostitution Reconsidered: New Perspectives on Migration, Sex Work, and Human Rights*, (Paradigm Publishers, Boulder, Colo.) 2005.

David Rosen, *Armies of the Young: Child Soldiers in War and Terrorism*, (Rutgers University Press, Piscataway, N.J.) 2005.

John P. Wilson & Boris Drozdek (eds.), *Broken Spirits: The Treatment of Traumatized Asylum Seekers, Refugees, War and Torture Victims*, (Brunner-Routledge, London) 2004.

Karen J. Greenberg & Joshua L. Dratel (eds.), *The Torture Papers*, (Cambridge University Press, New York) 2005.

Andrew Silke, *Terrorists, Victims and Society: Psychological Perspectives on Terrorism and Its Consequences*, (John Wiley & Sons, Hoboken, N.J.) 2003.

Donald Hyndman & David Hyndman, *Natural Hazards and Disasters*, (Brooks Cole, Florence, Ky.) 2005.

R. J. Terrill, *World Criminal Justice, A Survey*, 2nd ed. (Anderson Publishing, Cincinnati) 1992.

H. R. Dammer & E. Fairchild, *Comparative Criminal Justice Systems*, 3rd ed. (Wadsworth publishing, Belmont, Calif.) 2005.

J. Donnelly, *International Human Rights*, (Westview Press, Boulder, Colorado) 2006.

D. P. Forsythe, *Human Rights in International Relations*, (Cambridge University Press, New York) 2006.

Endnotes

1. Paul Rock (ed.), *Victimology*, (Dartmouth Publishing, Brookfield, Mass.) 1994. A new but promising international journal is *International Perspectives in Victimology*, published by the Tokiwa International Victimology Institute in Mito-shi, Japan.

2. See Ezzat A. Fattah, "Victimology, Past, Present and Future," 33 *Criminologie* 1 (2000).

3. Jan J. M. van Dijk, "Introducing Victimology," Available online: www.victimology.nl/rechts.htm. This Web site contains the full text of the article, which is based on the foreword by the same author in Van Dijk, et al., (eds.), *Caring for Crime Victims: Selected Proceedings of the 9th International Symposium on Victimology*, Criminal Justice Press, New York, (1999).

4. See WSV in a Nutshell, available online: www.world-society-victimology.de/wsv/index

5. Much of the history of the development of journals comes from an excellent article by John Dussich, Ph.D. This editorial is contained in the inaugural publication of *International Perspectives of Victimology*. J. Dussich, "Editorial" 1/1 *International Perspectives of Victimology* 1–13 (December 2004).

6. Id.

7. For an in-depth discussion of the International Crime Victim Survey, please refer to the Leiden University Web site at http://ruljis.lei-denuniv.nl (2005).

8. Emily Wax, "Sudanese Rape Victims Find Justice Blind to Plight," Washington Post Foreign Service (November 8, 2004), p. A01; available online: www.washingtonpost.com/wp-dyn/articles/A32621-2004Nov7.html

9. See, for example, Holly Johnson, "The International Violence Against Women Survey: Challenges and Issues in Developing an International Comparative Research Paper," conference paper presented at Evaluation in Crime and Justice: Trends and Methods, ASB House, Canberra, 24–25 March 2003; Accessed from IWS Web site: www.aic.conferences/evalution/johnson.html

10. M. Shaw, J. van Dijk & W. Rhomberg, "Determining Trends in Global Crime and Justice. An Overview of Results from the United Nations Survey of Crime Trends and operations of Criminal Justice Systems, 3 *Forum on Crime and Society*, 35 (2003).

11. Id.

12. *Encarta Dictionary: English,* (North America), www.encarta.msn.com.

13. Available online: www.worldbank.org/economicpolicy/globalization/(8/17/2006).

14. Ernest J. Wilson III, *Globalization. Information, Technology, and Conflict in the Second and Third Worlds*, (Rockefeller Brothers Funds, Inc., New York) 1998.

15. Fulvia Attina, "Globalization and Crime: The Emerging Role of International Institutions,"

Jean Monnet, *Working Papers in Comparative and International Politics*, (February 1997); available online: www.fscpo.unict.it

16. "Terrorism in the United States, 1997," *FBI Bulletin*, Washington, D.C. (1997).

17. *Terrorism and International Victims Unit*, (Office for Victims of Crime, U.S. Department of Justice, Washington, D.C.) 2002.

18. Basic Facts about the United Nations, www.un.org/aboutun/basicfacts/unorg.htm (8/17/2006).

19. Id.

20. Id.

21. Universal Declaration of Human Rights www.un.org/overview/rights.html (8/17/ 2006).

22. *Declaration of Basic Principles of Justice for Victims of Crime and Abuse of Power*, adopted by General Assembly resolution 40/34 of 29 November, 1985. United Nations, New York; available online: www.ohchr.org/english/law/victims. htm

23. Id.

24. International Court of Justice: General Information—The Court at a Glance, available online: www.icj-cij.org/icjwww/igeneral information/icjgnnot.html (8/17/2006).

25. AMICC: What Is the ICC—Structure and Basics, available online: www.amicc.org/icc_structure.html (8/17/2006).

26. U.S. Department of State, Fact Sheet: The International Criminal Court (August 2002), available online: www.state.gov/t/pm/rls/fs/2002/ 23426.htm (6/8/05).

27. What Is the International Criminal Court, www.globalsolutions.org/programs/law_justice/faq_long.pdf (8/17/2006).

28. Article 3, *United Nations Protocol to Prevent, Suppress and Punish Trafficking in Persons*, (November 2000); available online: www.undoc.org/unodc/en/trafficking_protocol.html

29. Id.

30. Francis T. Miko, *Trafficking in Persons: The U.S. and International Response*, Congressional Research Service Report to Congress, Washington, D.C. (June 24, 2005).

31. Michael J. Dennis, "Newly Adopted Protocols to the Conventions on the Rights of the Child," 94 *American Journal of International Law*, 789–796 (October 2000).

32. Id.

33. *Trafficking in Persons Report*, U.S. Department of State, Washington, D.C. (June 3, 2005).

34. Id.

35. "Trafficking in Women and Children a Worldwide Problem," 181/12 *America* 4 (October 23, 1999).

36. "Free the Slaves." 121/19 *The Christian Century,* 6 (September 21, 2001).

37. *Global Progamme Against Trafficking in Human Beings*, Centre for International Crime Prevention, Office for Drug control and Crime Prevention, United Nations at Vienna, (February 1999).

38. Available online: www.undoc.org/undoc/en/trafficking_victims.consents.html; see also "Developments in the Law: The Trafficking Victims Protection Act," 119 *Harv. L. Rev,* 2180 (May 2005).

39. See Pul L. No. 108-193, 117 Stat. 2875 (2003) codified in scattered sections of 8, 18, and 22 USCA.

40. Brenda Platt, "Commercial Sexual Exploitation of Children: A Global Problem Requiring Global Action," 2002/3 *Sexual Health Exchange,* 10 (Summer 2002).

41. Linda Girdner, Chapter 1: Introduction. In *Obstacles to the Recovery and Return of Parentally Abducted Children: Final Report*, L. Girdner & P. Hoff (eds.), Washington, D.C., U.S. Department of Justice, Office of Justice Programs, Office of Juvenile Justice and Delinquency Prevention, pp. 1–3.

42. See D. Finkelhor, G. Hotaling & A. Sedlak, *Missing, Abducted, Runaway, and Throwaway Children in America—First Report: Numbers and Characteristics, National Incidence Studies*, Washington, D.C.: U.S. Department of Justice, Office of Justice Programs, Office of Juvenile and Delinquency Prevention (1990).

43. Janet Chiancone, Linda Girdner & Patricia Hoff, *Issues in Resolving Cases of International Child Abduction by Parents*, Washington, D.C.: U.S. Department of Justice, Office of Justice Programs, Office of Juvenile and Delinquency Prevention, (December 2001).

44. Id. p. 4.

45. Id. p. 4.

46. National Center for Missing and Exploited Children. Available online: See www.missing-kids.com (8/17/2006).

47. Report on compliance with the Hague Convention on the Civil aspects of International child abduction. Available online: http://travel.state.gov/family/abduction/hague_issues/hague_issues_2537.html (8/17/2006).

48. Ion Hazzikostas, "Note: Federal Court Abstention and the Hague Child Abduction Convention," 79 *New York Law Review,* 421 (April 2004).

49. *Declaration of Basic Principles of Justice for Victims of Crime and Abuse of Power,* adopted by General Assembly resolution 40/34 of 29 November, 1985. United Nations, New York. Available online: www.ohchr.org/english/law/victims.htm

50. See Rudolph J. Rummel, "Power, Genocide and Mass Murder," 31/1 *Journal of Peace Research,* 1–10 (1994).

51. *Human Rights in the Administration of Justice: A Manual on Human Rights for Judges, Prosecutors, and Lawyers.* Professional Training Series No. 9. Office of the High Commissioner for Human Rights in cooperation with the International Bar Association. Available online: https://webmcdev.oddl.fsu.edu/human-rights/

52. *Universal Declaration of Human Rights,* adopted and proclaimed by General Assembly Resolution 217 A (III) of 10 December 1948.

53. *Human Rights in the Administration of Justice: A Manual on Human Rights for Judges, Prosecutors, and Lawyers.* Professional Training Series No. 9. Office of the High Commissioner for Human Rights in cooperation with the International Bar Association. Available online: https://webmcdev.oddl.fsu.edu/human-rights/

54. Eur. Court HR, *Case of Mahmut Kaya vs. Turkey,* judgment of 22 September, 2005 para. 85, of the text of the judgment as published at http://echr.coe.int/

55. Peter Dross, *Survivors of Politically Motivated Torture: A Large, Growing, and Invisible Population of Crime Victims,* Office for Victims of Crime, U.S. Department of Justice, Washington, D.C., January 2000.

56. *Declaration on the Protection of All Persons from Being Subjected to Torture and Other Cruel, Inhuman or Degrading Treatment or Punishment,* General Assembly, United Nations, New York, 1975.

57. *The Convention Against Torture and Other Cruel, Inhuman, or Degrading Treatment or Punishment,* General Assembly, United Nations, New York, 1984.

58. Id. at art. 1, para. 1.

59. *Denounce Torture,* Amnesty International USA, available online: http://amnestyusa.org/stoptorture/aboutn.html

60. Peter Dross, *Survivors of Politically Motivated Torture: A Large, Growing, and Invisible Population of Crime Victims,* Office for Victims of Crime, U.S. Department of Justice, Washington, D.C., January 2000.

61. Survivors of Torture, International, San Diego, Calif.; Available online: www.notorture.org/links.html.

62. Peter Dross, *Survivors of Politically Motivated Torture: A Large, Growing, and Invisible Population of Crime Victims,* Office for Victims of Crime, U.S. Department of Justice, Washington, D.C., January 2000 at p. 5.

63. *Denounce Torture,* Amnesty International USA; available online: http://amnestyusa.org/stoptorture/aboutn.html

64. *Manual on the Effective Investigation and Documentation of Torture and Other Cruel, Inhuman or Degrading Treatment or Punishment,* (Istanbul Protocol), submitted to the United Nations High Commissioner for Human Rights, United Nations Publication, New York (August 9, 1999).

65. Dennis Coday, "Pope Prays for Child Soldiers," 40/23 *National Catholic Reporter,* 7 (April 9, 2004).

66. "The Hidden Health Trauma of Child Soldiers," 363/9412 *The Lancet* 831 (March 13, 2004).

67. International Standards [Coalition to Stop the Use of Child Soldiers], available online: www.child-soldiers.org/resources/international-standards (8/17/2006).

68. IRIN Web special on Child Soldiers, available online: http://irinnews.org/webspecials/childsoldiers/print/intro.asp (8/17/2006).

69. *Child Soldiers Global Report 2004,* Coalition to Stop the Use of Child Soldiers, London (2004).

70. Id. @p. 3 www.child-soldiers.org/resources/global-reports

71. Id. @p. 4 www.child-soldiers.org

72. IRIN Web special on Child Soldiers, available online: http://irinnews.org/webspecials/childsoldiers/print/intro.asp

73. Amnesty International USA, available online: www.amnestyusa.org/child_soldiers/index.do (8/17/2006).

74. Child Soldiers: An affir to Humanity, available online: www.un.org/rights/concerns.htm (8/17/2006).

75. "Tens of Thousands of Girls Fighting on the Front Lines," 1 *Women in Action,* 6 (April 2004).

76. The Use of Children as Soldiers in Africa, available online: www.reliefweb.int/library/documents/chilsold.htm (8/17/2006).

77. Daya Somasundaram, "Child Soldiers: Understanding the Context," 324 *British Medical Journal,* 1268–1271 (May 25, 2002).

78. Supra @ fn.76

79. Landmine Monitor Deport 2005: Toward a Mine-Fire world, available online: www.icbi.org/lm2005/

80. Id.

81. Platform for the Promotion of Early Warning, available online: www.unisdr.org/ppew/tsunami/what-is-tsunami:/backinfor-historical.htm

82. Id.

16

CONSTITUTIONAL AND CIVIL RIGHTS OF VICTIMS

Chapter Outline

Learning Objectives

After reading this chapter, you should be able to:

- Distinguish between the various theories upon which liability may be imposed on tortfeasors
- Explain the history and significance of 42 U.S.C. Section 1983
- Discuss the ramifications of the Violence Against Women Act and how it affects the field of victimology
- Understand the use of injunctions
- Distinguish between absolute and qualified immunity

Up to this point, the text deals with situations in which victims have been injured by individuals acting alone or in concert with other perpetrators. In these situations, victims turn to those employed by the criminal justice system to assist them in punishing these persons. However, occasionally there are instances when those who work in the criminal justice system harm or contribute to the harm suffered by persons. These offenders may face criminal penalties as well as civil damages. In addition to pursuing recovery based on theories of negligence and/or intentional torts, the law provides victims with an additional set of rights which should always be considered when evaluating alternatives dealing with monetary recovery or other efforts to make these victims whole.

Section 1983 Actions

Introduction

It must be stressed that the great majority of those who work in the criminal justice system are honest, caring professionals. However, there are those who intentionally or negligently injure citizens. When those in the criminal justice system commit acts that injure others, they may be charged with a violation of either a state or federal criminal statute. If the offender's actions violate a person's federal civil rights, two criminal statutes may offer that individual redress. These statutes require action by the federal prosecutor and do not permit the victim to sue wrongdoers.[1]

Much confusion surrounds the historical evolution of the present-day civil rights acts. This is not a history text; however, understanding the background and evolution of these laws assists professionals in explaining their scope and function to victims. The first law passed by Congress was the Civil Rights Act of 1866.[2] This law declared that all persons born in the United States were citizens regardless of race or prior conditions of servitude. The act made it a crime for any person under color of law to deprive a person of any right secured or protected by the Constitution or the laws of the United States. This law failed to stop the continuing racial strife in the southern states and after race riots in Memphis and New Orleans, Congress enacted the Enforcement Act of 1870.[3] This law was intended to guarantee the right to vote without regard to color, race, or previous conditions of servitude. The Enforcement Act made it a crime for a state official to prohibit a person the right to vote. The historical roots of the present-day federal civil rights criminal codes are found in the Civil Rights Act of 1866 (18 U.S.C 242) and in the Enforcement Act of 1870 (18 U.S.C. 241). In response to continuing violence against Blacks, Congress enacted the Ku Klux Klan Act of 1871.[4] This act is best known for its primary civil enforcement mechanism—the ability to file a federal lawsuit for acts under color of law that violate a person's federal civil rights—and was the forerunner of the present-day law allowing such suits (42 U.S.C. 1983). However, when originally enacted it was viewed as a federal criminal sanction for those who engaged in violence against Blacks, specifically members of the Ku Klux Klan.

Title 18 of the United States Code Section 241 prohibits conspiracies to deprive a person of his or her civil rights.[5] Section 242 prohibits civil rights violations by persons acting under color of law. The government must prove four elements to establish a violation of Section 242: (1) the victim was an inhabitant of a state, district, or territory of the United States; (2) the defendant acted under color of law; (3) the conduct deprived the victim of a right guaranteed by the United States Constitution; and (4) the defendant acted with a specific intent to violate the protected right.[6]

In addition to the criminal sanctions facing those who violate a person's federal civil rights, Congress has provided an additional remedy in the form of civil damages. Title 42 of the United States Code Section 1983 provides in part:

> *Every person who, under color of any statute, ordinance, regulation, custom, or usage of any State or Territory, subjects, or causes to be subjected, any citizen of the United States or any other person within the jurisdiction thereof to the deprivation of any rights, privileges, or immunities secured by the Constitution and laws, shall be liable to the party injured in an action at law, suit in equity, or other proper proceedings for redress. . . .*[7]

This quote has been the basis for thousands of lawsuits against those employed in the criminal justice system. It is an important legal tool for victims who have been injured by police officers and others in positions of authority. As will be discussed, Title 42 has several advantages over the intentional torts already discussed in other chapters.

Requirement of State Action

The United States Supreme Court addressed the scope of the Civil Rights Act of 1871 when it interpreted the phrase "under color of state law" in its decision of *United States v. Classic.*[8] The court reversed the dismissal of criminal charges brought against election officials who had engaged in fraudulent activities during a primary election. The court stated that "misuse of power, possessed by virtue of state law and made possible only because the wrongdoer is clothed with the authority of the state, is action taken 'under color' of state law."[9]

The Supreme Court further expanded this definition four years later in 1945 when it decided *Screws v. United States*. The court held that a sheriff's fatal beating of a Black prisoner was conduct "under color" of law.[10] Therefore, in criminal cases, conduct *under color of law* involves unauthorized, unlawful conduct of an official when the pretense of authority under which the officer acted furthered or assisted that officer in violating a person's constitutional rights in any way. *Screws* and *Classic* established the availability of criminal actions by persons who were victims of law enforcement misconduct. However, from 1945 until 1961, Section 1983 was virtually ignored by those who were wronged by illegal conduct by agents of the government.

Scope of Liability

The gradual expansion of the due process clause incorporating the Bill of Rights and the growth of the equal protection and due process concepts allowed victims of official misconduct greater latitude in filing of lawsuits. In 1961, the Supreme Court decided *Monroe v. Pape* and established the framework for future use of Section 1983 by those who were victims of illegal governmental activity.[11] In *Monroe*, the plaintiff and his family filed a civil lawsuit, instead of criminal action using Section 1983 against thirteen Chicago police officers and the city of Chicago, alleging that the officers broke into their home without a warrant, forced them out of bed, and made them stand naked while the officers searched the house. The police then took the plaintiff to the police station and held him incommunicado for ten hours before releasing him without filing any charges. The plaintiff claimed that the police acted "under color of law" and deprived them of their constitutional protection against unreasonable searches and seizures. The Supreme Court held that color of law had the same meaning in a civil case as it did in a criminal case and concluded that because Section 1983 provided for a civil action, the plaintiffs need not prove that the defendants acted with a specific intent to deprive a person of a federal right. However, the court dismissed the city of Chicago, holding that municipalities were immune from liability under the statute.

In 1978, the law surrounding civil rights violations expanded even further with the Supreme Court decision in *Monell v. Department of Social Services*.[12] In *Monell*, the plaintiffs were a class of female employees who alleged that the board of education of the city of New York and the New York Department of Social Services were forcing pregnant employees to take unpaid leaves of absence before those leaves were medically necessary. The lawsuit sought injunctive relief and back pay for the unlawful forced leaves. The defendants included the mayor, the city of New York, the commissioner of the board of education and the board itself, and the Department of Social Services and its chancellor. In allowing the lawsuit to go forward the court held that Section 1983 was violated whenever:

1. a person was deprived of a right, privilege, or immunity guaranteed under the Constitution and federal laws, and
2. such a deprivation resulted from the official policy or custom of a local governmental entity.

The Supreme Court decision was to have a tremendous impact of the desirability of suing individuals employed by municipalities. Victims of illegal action by agents of municipalities now had a deep pocket that they could reach. It must be stressed that *Monell* addressed the liability of local governmental agencies and not individual states.

Monell also overruled *Monroe* by holding that municipalities were "persons" and therefore not completely immune from suit under Section 1983. However, *Monell* did not address whether local governments, although not entitled to absolute immunity, could claim limited immunity in some situations. This question was answered in *Owens v. City of Independence* which held that the city was entitled to limited immunity from lawsuit based on the good faith of its officials.[13]

These and other decisions have given victims of illegal local governmental activity an option that should always be considered when local government actions injure them. Using either "due process" or "equal protection," almost any intentional tort committed by a state or local official can be converted into a constitutional violation and thereby made the subject of a Section 1983 action. Additionally, if the plaintiff prevails in these actions, that person is entitled to an award of attorney's fees in addition to any equable or money relief.[14] This provision allowing attorney's fees encourages attorneys to take on lawsuits that indicate they have the potential for success.[15]

1983 Theories of Liability

A number of theories of liability under Section 1983 hold individual officials and in many instances their local agency liable for injury to victims. A discussion of these theories is beyond the scope of this text; however, several theories of liability should be discussed because of the nature of the acts committed by agents of municipalities.

Denial of Equal Protection

One famous case in the victim's movement involving a denial of equal protection concerned a police department's response to calls for help by a battered spouse. Starting in October 1982 and continuing until June 1983, Tracey Thurman repeatedly contacted the police department in Torrington, Connecticut, begging for protection from her estranged husband, Buck. Tracey signed several sworn complaints against Buck; however, the police department considered the incidents a family matter and did not respond to them in the same manner as they did to "stranger assaults."

On the day of the final beating, Buck stabbed Tracey repeatedly. A police officer arrived and asked Buck for the knife, but did not arrest or restrain him in any manner. Buck gave the officer the knife and then proceeded to stomp on Tracey's head in front of the officer. He then went inside the house and returned with their son and cursed and kicked Tracey in the head. This series of blows left her partially paralyzed. Other officers arrived and they did not arrest Buck until he tried to assault Tracey as she lay on the ambulance stretcher.

Tracey filed suit in federal court against the city of Torrington, its police department, and all twenty-four officers that she had contacted over the years about Buck's assaultive acts. She alleged that the police department and its officers had been negligent in responding to her and further that they had violated her constitutional rights to equal protection under the law by treating her differently than they would persons who were assaulted by strangers.[16]

The jury awarded Tracey $2.3 million in damages and although the city's insurance company paid the judgment, it indicated that it might not pay any future awards of any police department that refused or failed to educate their officers about domestic violence.[17]

In recent years, victims of family violence have turned to the courts in an attempt to require law enforcement departments to provide effective intervention and protection against spousal assault. *Balistreri v. City of Pacifica* involved a spouse who obtained a restraining order against her husband. He violated this order numerous times and even after serious physical injuries and a firebomb being thrown through her window, the police refused her request to arrest the husband. The federal court dismissed a portion of her complaint, but allowed the allegation that the police had violated her equal protection rights in that she had shown that the officers may have treated her differently from other crime victims because she was a battered woman.[18]

Czachorowski v. Degenhart was a New York Superior Court case in which several battered women sued the police department for failing to comply with a state law requiring officers to advise victims of domestic violence of their rights and available services. The case was settled for a change in policy where the police agreed to hand out informational material, train officers in domestic violence, and institute a complaint procedure for victims of spousal abuse.[19]

In *Watson v. City of Kansas City* a federal court ruled that the victim could proceed with her suit against the police department. Nancy Watson was married to a Kansas City police officer who abused her and her son on numerous occasions. When she requested assistance from the police, they refused to help and threatened to take her child away and arrest her. After being raped and battered by her husband, she escaped and he committed suicide. She sued the police department for a denial of equal protection.[20]

As the discussion illustrates, victims of spousal abuse have turned to the courts in an attempt to force police departments to arrest the perpetrators of this form of family violence. Increasingly, courts have begun to listen and rule in their favor both on constitutional and tort grounds.

Failure to Act

In certain situations, local agencies may be liable for injuries to citizens that have occurred because of the agencies' failure to act. These failures may involve lack of proper training, lack of proper supervision, or lack of protection on the part of law enforcement officers. It should be stressed that many times plaintiffs will allege a violation of their civil rights based on all these theories.

Failure to Train

Billings v. Vernal City involved a rookie police officer who had been on the force for less than two weeks when he broke the plaintiff's arm while trying to arrest him.[21] The arrest was illegal because the officer did not have probable cause to place the plaintiff under arrest. The officer was on duty prior to completing the basic training required of all law enforcement officers in the state of Utah. The city argued that such a procedure was proper in that state law allows a police officer to receive formal training "within eighteen months" after beginning duty. The court held that to allow such a police officer on duty for "one minute" was grossly negligent. The plaintiff was awarded $23,500 in damages, $12,000 in court costs, and $25,000 in attorney's fees.

In 1989, the Supreme Court held that municipalities can be held liable under Section 1983 for failure to train their police officers if such failure amounts to "deliberate indifference."[22] In *City of Canton v. Harris*, the court stated that deliberate indifference occurs when ". . . in light of the duties assigned to specific officers or employees the need for more or different training is so obvious, and the inadequacy so likely to result in [a] violation of constitutional rights, that the policymakers of the city can reasonably be said to have been deliberately indifferent to the need."[23] The Court stated that the failure to train the officer must be closely related to the ultimate injury.

Failure to Supervise

In many private sector situations, supervisors are often sued for actions of their employees based on the common law theory of **respondeat superior**, which is Latin for "let the master answer." Under this doctrine, the master (employer or supervisor) is responsible for the acts or omissions of his servant (employee) toward those to whom the master owes a duty of care. Liability normally attaches if the servant (employee) fails to use due care during the course of employment. This doctrine does not apply to public employment because police chiefs are not the masters of their employees. Both the chief and the officers work for a common master—the city. However, the doctrine applies to sheriffs because under common law deputies serve at the pleasure of the sheriff and therefore act for the sheriff in the course of employment.

However, in certain situations local police supervisors have been held liable for failure to properly supervise their officers. In *Dewell v. Lawson*, the chief of police was held liable for failing to establish procedures for the diagnosis and treatment of jail inmates.[24] The plaintiff was arrested and detained for public intoxication. He experienced a diabetic reaction that resulted in a coma, stroke, and ultimate death when the jailer failed to recognize the medical condition and therefore did not provide proper medical care. In *Grandstaff v. City of Borger*, the police chief was held liable for acts of his officers when they shot an innocent man during an apprehension of a suspect.[25] The officers opened fire on a pickup driven by the victim when he entered the area to offer assistance after seeing police activity near his house.

In *Parrish v. Luckie,* the city was liable for an officer's sexual assault of a woman, because the city had knowledge of the officer's propensity for violence and failed to take any corrective action.[26] The officer was investigated on two prior occasions for child abuse and criminally charged in one of those incidents. The department had also received complaints from other citizens that the officer had solicited sexual favors from several store clerks. However, the police chief failed to take any action and investigators discouraged citizens from filing complaints. The jury awarded damages in the amount of $200,000 against both the officer and the chief of police, and because it was alleged that they acted in their official capacity, the city was responsible for paying the judgment.

Failure to Protect

In other situations, officers will be held liable for failing to follow up on actions they initiated. *Fundiller v. City of Cooper* involved a drug transaction with an undercover officer that resulted in the plaintiff being shot five times.[27] Other officers arrived at the scene and dragged Fundiller from his car and handcuffed him causing further injury. The appellate court stated that the city and its officials may be liable under Section 1983. The court established the standard for determining liability of agencies and their officers for practices that have become a custom or policy, stating that the custom must be created by an individual who represents the official policy of the agency and a causal link must exist between the act and the custom. In the area of liability for failure to protect, the court held that supervisors may be liable if a causal link exists between the employee's acts and the acts of the supervisor. The court further ruled that mere presence at the scene of the incident with a failure to act to protect the victim is sufficient for liability.

In *Raucci v. Town of Rotterdam,* a federal court ruled that the municipality owed a battered woman a special duty to protect her from her estranged husband because of actions by the police department which had assured her of protection. In spite of these assurances, the husband killed their six-year-old son and wounded the wife. The court upheld a jury verdict awarding the wife damages.[28]

Smith v. Wade involved a federal civil rights lawsuit by an inmate against a correctional officer who placed inmates with known dangerous propensities in a cell with the victim.[29] The Supreme Court upheld the award of compensatory and punitive damages against the officer stating that such damages are permitted when the conduct is shown to be motivated by evil intent or when it involves reckless or callous indifference to the federally protected rights of others.

The United States Supreme Court may have weakened a victim's recovery in the area of failure to protect when it decided *Castle Rock vs. Gonzales.*[30] This case concerned a local municipality's failure to enforce a valid restraining order. This case is discussed in more detail in the following section dealing with restraining orders.

Violence Against Women Act

Background

In August 1994, Congress passed and President Clinton signed the controversial Crime Bill.[31] While this act caused much debate and controversy, one act from the Crime Bill received support from both parties: the Violence Against Women Act (VAWA) of 1994.[32] The VAWA contains one of the Crime Bill's largest crime prevention programs that attempts to respond to the national problem of gender-based violence. It makes crimes committed against women similar to those that are motivated by religious, racial, or political bias.

The act was re-authorized in 2000, and in 2006, President Bush signed the new Violence Against Women Act of 2005 into law. This law continues the focus on studying and preventing violence against women that the previous laws started. It provides funding and other tools that cities need to combat domestic violence.[33]

The act addresses gender-based violence in five areas: Title I, Safe Streets for Women, increases sentences for repeat offenders who continue to commit crimes against women; Title II, Safe Homes for Women, focuses on domestic violence; Title III, Civil Rights for Women, creates the first civil rights remedy for gender-based violence; Title IV, Safe Campuses, funds research on problems facing women on college campus; and Title V, Equal Justice for Women in the Courts, provides training for judges to address the problem of gender bias within the legal system. Although all sections of this law are important, of particular significance in this chapter is Title III which establishes civil rights violations for gender-based acts of violence.

Gender-Based Civil Rights

The creation of this federal civil rights law recognizes that gender-based violence against women should be accorded the same dignity as a violation of an individual's constitutional rights. The victim of this type of discrimination may recover compensatory and punitive damages and obtain an injunction to prevent future acts of violence.

The Title III of the act contains three major goals: First, it is intended to demonstrate that violence against women cannot be perceived as only a "family" problem, a "private" matter, or a sexual "miscommunication."[34] Second, the law treats gender-motivated violence the same as other bias-motivated attacks. Third, and perhaps most important, the law provides federal remedy for victims of gender-based violence that is not presently available in state courts.

Title III contains four major sections:

1. Section 302 subsection (b) states that every person has the right to be free from crime of violence motivated by gender.
2. Section 302 subsection (c) states that all persons, including those who act under color of any statute, ordinance, regulation, custom, or usage of any state, who commit a gender-motivated crime of violence are liable for compensatory and

punitive damages as well as injunction, declaratory relief, and other such relief as a court may deem appropriate.

3. Section 302 subsection (d) defines a crime of gender-motivated violence as an act or series of acts that would constitute a felony against the person or that would constitute a felony against property if the conduct presents a serious risk of physical injury to another and that would come within the meaning of state or federal offenses described in Title 18 of the United States Code.[35] Such crime of violence is considered to be motivated by gender if it is committed because of the gender or on the basis of gender and is due at least in part to the animus (prejudice, spiteful or ill will) based on the victim's gender.

4. Section 302 subsection (e) states that nothing in this section entitles a person to relief based on random acts of violence unrelated to gender.

By establishing a civil rights cause of action for gender-based acts of violence, Congress has placed gender at the same level as race and religion. The VAWA and its new civil rights must await interpretation by the courts to determine its full scope and extent; however, there is every reason to believe that it will be accorded the same type of reception that other civil rights laws have received and therefore in the future female victims of violence will have a new legal weapon at their disposal.

Injunctions

Injunctions are restraining orders or protective orders which are court orders that prohibit the offender from having any contact with the victim.[36] They are civil versus criminal in nature and require a judge to rule on sufficient evidence to support the issuance of such an order. These orders are now available in forty-eight states and the District of Columbia. They offer the option of preventing contact such as harassment or threats which might ordinarily lead to an escalation of emotions and future violence.

The state of Massachusetts is one of the leaders in collecting data regarding the effectiveness of restraining orders.[37] In the fall of 1992, efforts by victim services advocacy groups and others resulted in changes to the state justice delivery system. Massachusetts created a Registry of Civil Restraining Orders designed to provide police and the courts with accurate and reliable information necessary to respond appropriately to victims' needs. It was the first statewide database of restraining order information in the nation.

For the program to be effective, a number of criminal justice professionals had to be able to access the database. The Office of the Commissioner of Probation established a statewide users community (see Figure 16.1). In Massachusetts, the agencies shown have access to the registry.

The program was designed for use on computers. Because of the importance of the data stored in the system, the computer program had to be easy to use and simple to learn. Massachusetts developed the program in COBOL on a Unisys

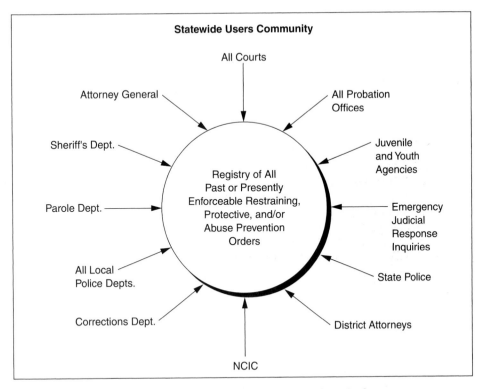

FIGURE 16.1   **State of Massachusetts Accessing Restraining Orders**

mainframe. At the center of the restraining order program was the data entry screen (see Figure 16.2). This screen is used to enter, display, and update restraining order information. Quality control monitoring was utilized to ensure timeliness, accuracy, and completeness of all information. Since 1992, other states have followed Massachusetts lead and have adopted statewide restraining order registries. A computerized database is an important goal in responding to victims of crime and specifically to spousal abuse; however, certain geographical areas in the United States still do not use restraining orders. As the following discussion indicates, the debate continues regarding the effectiveness of this unique tool in preventing spousal abuse.

Background and Use of Restraining Orders

In the past, problems with the use of restraining orders stemmed from lack of clarity in the law and many police officers' unfamiliarity with this civil sanction. In 1983, only seventeen states provided protection against abuse from individuals who were living together but not married. However, by 1988, twenty-two states had added such protection to their statutes authorizing restraining orders.

CIVIL RESTRAINING ORDER SCREEN

DEFENDANT
PRIMARY NAME: DOE, JOHN   **DOB:** 03/09/65   **PROBATION**
                                                                CENTRAL FILE #: 123457CV

                                     P. O. B.: SOMERVILLE, MA

SEX: M   **SS#:** 012–22–2222   **MOTHER:** JANE JONES
                                                  FATHER: JOHN

ALIAS NAME: MOE, JOHN   6/9/65
                DOE, J.W.   3/9/65
                LEO, JOHN   3/9/65

PLAINTIFF
NAME: SMITH, JANE
         2022 MAIN ST.
         ANYTOWN, USA

DOCKET #: _____

TYPE OF
ORDER: MASS GENERAL LAWS: _____ ;   SECTION: _____

ORDER DATE: ___/___/___   **EXPIRATION DATE:** ___/___/___   **STATUS:**
                                                                  [ ] OPEN
                                                                  [ ] CLOSED

COURT ORDERS:
[ ] REFRAIN FROM ABUSE
[ ] NO CONTACT
[ ] VACATE/STAY AWAY (RESIDENCE)
[ ] ADDRESS IMPOUNDED
[ ] STAY AWAY (WORKPLACE)
[ ] SURRENDER CUSTODY
[ ] SUPPORT PAYMENTS
[ ] COMPENSATION
[ ] VISITATION RIGHTS: SEE ORDER
[ ] OTHER: SEE ORDER

FIGURE 16.2   State of Massachusetts Computer Screen

The use and nature of restraining orders vary from state to state. Most states now authorize persons who are married, related by blood, or cohabitants to request the issuance of such an order. The six types of behavior that may be prohibited by a restraining order are:

1. Protection against physical assault
2. Threatened physical abuse

3. Attempted physical abuse
4. Sexual assault of an adult
5. Sexual assault of a child
6. Damage to the personal property of the victim

As the list indicates, restraining orders may be issued for a wide variety of acts committed by the offender. However, simply having the order issued does not solve the problem. Due process requires that the offender be served with a copy of the order for it to be effective.

A majority of states provide for the issuance of temporary or emergency restraining orders. These orders are issued by the judge and usually require the threat of immediate injury to the victim. The United States Supreme Court upheld the issuance of these ex parte type of orders if (1) the request includes specific facts that justify the relief, (2) the notice and opportunity for a full hearing are given as soon as practicable, and (3) the order is issued by a judge.[38]

In most jurisdictions, police officers or process servers are responsible for serving restraining orders. The five basic methods of service of a temporary or emergency restraining order are (1) personal service, (2) informing the offender of the existence of the order, (3) leaving a copy with the victim so that she can serve the offender, (4) posting the notice and order at the residence of the victim, and (5) mailing a copy of the order via certified mail to the offender.

Some police departments have established procedures in which officers can contact judges while they are at the scene of a domestic dispute and have the judge authorize the issuance of such an order via the telephone. The officer then serves the suspect at the scene and requires him to leave the premise. Once a temporary order is issued, it becomes effective immediately and is valid until a formal hearing can be held at which time the abuser has a right to contest the allegations made by the victim. However, the issuance of the temporary order precludes the offender from having any contact with the victim until the formal hearing.

Restraining orders may provide different forms of relief for the victim of spousal assault. The traditional and most common form of relief is a no-contact order that prevents the offender from having any form of contact with the victim either at her residence, work, or anywhere else. This no-contact order includes telephone, written, and physical contacts. Many orders will set forth specific conditions regarding the visitation of any children that may be involved in the situation. Some will designate certain locations for the visit and others will require that the offender not consume any alcohol or drugs prior to the visit. A majority of the statutes authorize the court to require counseling for both parties. Even if the counseling does not solve the immediate problem, it is a visible sign of the authority of the court and should serve as a constant reminder to the offender of the power that the court now has over his existence.

In the event the abuser violates the restraining order, many statutes authorize charging the offender with civil contempt, criminal contempt, or a misdemeanor violation of a court order. Although police officers cannot normally arrest a person charged with civil contempt, the court may order that the offender pay a fine and serve a period of incarceration. Criminal contempt, if authorized by the state statute, would allow officers to arrest the offender if they found him in violation of the order. Criminal contempt in many jurisdictions is treated as a misdemeanor; however, many restraining order statutes allow officers to make warrantless arrests in these situations. If the violation of the order is considered a misdemeanor, many statutes also authorize the warrantless arrest of the offender. As the next section discusses, the use of this form of sanction still poses many problems.

While many statutes provide for civil contempt, criminal contempt, or even violation of criminal statutes, there is no guarantee that the order will be effective. In *Castle Rock vs. Gonzales*, the United States Supreme Court addressed the issue of a municipality's liability for failure to enforce a restraining order.[39] In 1999, Jessica Gonzales obtained a protective order against her husband as part of divorce proceedings. The order listed the requirements of Colorado law, which mandated that officers use every reasonable means to enforce a restraining order, including the requirement that the officer "shall" arrest a person when there is probable cause to believe he or she has violated the order. The order provided for visitation of the children on alternate weekends.

One afternoon, while the kids were playing outside, Mr. Gonzales kidnapped them. Over the next ten hours, Jessica made repeated requests to the Castle Rock Police Department to enforce her protective order, but they failed to do so. At 3:30 on the morning after he kidnapped the children, Mr. Gonzales appeared at the police station and opened fire with his weapon. He was killed by officers who returned his fire. Afterward, the officers found the dead bodies of Jessica's three children inside his truck.

Jessica Gonzales sued the City of Castle Rock for failing to enforce her protective order. However, the Supreme Court ruled that despite the mandatory arrest laws in effect in Colorado at that time, Jessica had no personal entitlement requiring the police to enforce the order. It went on to state that the statute simply required police to enforce the order, and the court refused to assume that the statute was meant to benefit victims of domestic violence.

There was a strong reaction by the victim's movement to the *Castle Rock* decision. In essence, it fails to recognize the dynamics and dangers of domestic violence. Some victim advocates are advising victims and their attorneys to request more specific language in their orders. Others are relying on state tort remedies to hold law enforcement agencies liable. *Castle Rock* has caused us to rethink our traditional responses to restraining orders. Only time will tell what comes from this landmark decision.

Advantages and Disadvantages

Restraining orders provide the victim with another option in lieu of arrest. There are several advantages to the use of restraining orders.[40] Most arrests result in the offender being released in a matter of hours or within a few days at the most. A restraining order can be valid for up to a year in most cases.

Arrests may result in the loss of employment which might increase the tension that already exists in the relationship. Restraining orders do not preclude the offender from continuing with his employment, but at the same time they prevent him from living with the victim.

Restraining orders carry the weight and majesty of a judicial edict and some offenders may think twice before violating a court order. Although some offenders may have had numerous contacts with police and even the judicial system, most have not been involved with a direct order from a judge stating that they will not engage in certain conduct. The specter of facing a judge after violating an order may act as a deterrent for some abusers.

Just as there are advantages in this form of protection, so are there serious potential disadvantages in relying solely on the use of restraining orders in this area of family violence. The most obvious and threatening disadvantage is that the offender may simply ignore the order with the resulting injury to the victim. A restraining order is merely a piece of paper that carries only as much force and effect as the offender attaches to it. If the offender chooses to ignore it, there is no protection for the victim, unless she can contact the police and they can arrive and intercede before the abuser attacks and harms her.

There are additional disadvantages to the use of restraining orders. Many of these weaknesses are written into the very statutes that were enacted to protect the victim. Some statutes require the payment of a filing fee prior to issuance of a restraining order. Although most jurisdictions allow for the waiver of the fee if the victim cannot afford to pay it, some include the income of the abuser in determining if the fee can be waived. The payment of such fees acts as a deterrent to requesting a restraining order.

Some statutes require court or county clerks to assist the victim in filling out the forms requesting the restraining order. However, no state-provided funds or mandated special training is available for these clerks in this sensitive function. A great majority of spousal assault occurs in the evening or on the weekend after the courts are closed. Only twenty-three states provide for the issuance of emergency orders after normal working hours. Thus during the victim's greatest time of need, there is no alternative available to obtain these orders.

Most states require personal service of the order for them to become effective. However, many offenders are difficult to locate and therefore the victim is not protected until the abuser has been served. There is a lack of monitoring of the compliance with restraining orders. If the offender can convince or threaten the victim to remain silent, neither law enforcement officers nor the court will be aware that the offender has violated the order.

In 2006, the *Orange County Register*, a respected Southern California newspaper, conducted an investigation into the use and effectiveness of restraining orders.[41] Key findings from the investigation revealed a system in disarray with conflicting procedures and processes between counties. Even more alarming, one in seven restraining orders issued by a judge were not served on the perpetrator. An order is not effective until served. The *Register* also pointed out that hundreds of restraining orders are not entered in the state database used by law enforcement agencies, and without proof of a valid order, police are powerless to take action.

Although the use of restraining orders presents some serious problems, they do provide some victims of spousal assault with an option that may protect them.

Defenses

Simply establishing that a person has violated the victim's civil rights does not end the inquiry. The law provides a number of defenses for both individuals and agencies accused of violating another's civil rights. There are two types of defenses: substantive and procedural. *Substantive defenses* are those that claim one of the elements of a civil rights action has not been met. For example, the defendant may argue that no constitutional right was violated by the officer. *Procedural defenses* challenge the validity of the lawsuit based on issues such as lack of jurisdiction (federal courts have specific jurisdictional requirements that must be satisfied to sue in federal court), statute of limitations, and other procedural requirements.[42]

Two common forms of defense raised in civil rights cases are *absolute immunity* and *qualified immunity*. Both of these defenses are considered "official immunity." At English common law the concept of sovereign immunity developed based on the assumption that kings were divine and therefore could do no wrong. Thus, the king's subjects could not sue the king. Early American court decisions relied on this rationale to support the position that the United States could not be sued without its permission. As a result, in 1946 Congress passed the Federal Tort Claims Act that allowed citizens under certain circumstances to sue the government and its agents or employees.[43]

The historical rationale for official immunity is based on the concept that a government can only act through its agents or officials and official immunity protects those who carry out these actions. Another justification for official immunity was set forth by the Supreme Court when it held:

> The public interest requires decisions and action to enforce laws for the protection of the public. . . . Implicit in the idea that officials have some immunity—absolute or qualified—for their acts, is a recognition that they may err. The concept of immunity assumes this and goes on to assume that it is better to risk some error and possible injury from such error than not to decide or act at all.[44]

The courts have consistently used the common law doctrine of immunity when dealing with Section 1983 cases. As will be discussed, the distinction between absolute and qualified immunity has on occasion become blurred and confusing.

Absolute Immunity

Absolute immunity is a complete shield in a lawsuit and involves a determination that there is no liability for any damages that the victim may have suffered as a result of the actor's conduct. Therefore, when a defendant has absolute immunity, any civil lawsuit will be dismissed by the court without ever considering the plaintiff's claim for damages. However, this defense is not automatic—it must be pled and proved by the defendant before the court will act to dismiss the lawsuit.

The concept of absolute immunity is to encourage a decision-making process without fear of reprisals no matter how unpopular such a decision may be for a particular person or group of persons. For absolute immunity to apply, persons must be acting within the broad general scope of their duties.[45] Additionally, absolute immunity applies even if it is determined that the person acted with malice or other evil intentions. A grant or absolute immunity prevents any civil lawsuits from going forward.

Society has determined that certain individuals and situations should be accorded the shield of absolute immunity. Judges when acting in their judicial capacity are afforded absolute immunity as are witnesses when they are testifying in court. Prosecutors depending on their role and function in the judicial system may have either absolute or qualified immunity.[46] If a prosecutor is acting as an advocate, his or her actions are absolutely immune; however, if the prosecutor is acting in a nonadvocatory role such as investigating cases or administering the office, he or she is afforded only qualified immunity.

Qualified Immunity

Qualified immunity is also known as the *good faith defense.* It is a defense that has grown and evolved during the last hundred years. The present-day defense of qualified immunity has its basis in the U.S. Supreme Court decision of *Anderson v. Creighton.*[47] In *Anderson,* an FBI agent and several local law enforcement officers conducted a warrantless search of the victim's home under the mistaken belief that a bank robbery suspect was in the home. According to the Creightons, the officers brandished shotguns, assaulted their daughter, and knocked Mr. Creighton to the ground. They arrested him and placed him in jail overnight before releasing him without filing any charges. The Creightons filed a Section 1983 action alleging that the officers violated their Fourth Amendment right to be free from unreasonable searches. The officers claimed they were immune from such lawsuit based on the defense of qualified immunity. The Supreme Court held that individuals would be entitled to qualified immunity if it was determined that the action was the type which a reasonable person could have believed was lawful in light of clearly established law and the information available to that individual at the time of the decision.

The immunity defenses provide those that work in the criminal justice system a shield against meritless lawsuits and at the same time allow a person who has been wronged by those perpetrators to pursue a lawsuit to recover damages for injuries. The laws dealing with the immunity defenses are complex and constantly changing and therefore it is essential that professionals working with victims refer them to attorneys for a complete explanation of their rights in this area.

Summary

This chapter should not be taken as an indictment of law enforcement officers or others who work in the criminal justice system. The overwhelming majority of personnel in this field are caring professionals who obey the law. However, a small percentage of those in the criminal justice system, because of either negligence or intentional acts, injure private citizens. When this occurs, many victims are hesitant to report such injury because of the mistaken belief that they have no recourse against those in power.

Victim services providers need to understand the history and evolution of the present-day laws that hold those in the criminal justice profession liable for injuries to others. Title 42 United States Code Section 1983 is an invaluable tool to use in these situations. It requires that the tortfeasor act under *color of law*. This is a key element in any 1983 action.

The Violence Against Women Act of 1994 has established a new gender-based civil right for women. It provides victims of gender-based crimes with an important legal remedy and states that crimes based on gender will be considered as serious as crimes based on other protected classifications.

Injunctions are a critical aspect of the civil rights of victims of crime. These legal tools are normally used against persons known to the victim, most commonly against former spouses or boyfriends. The effectiveness of injunctions is still being studied. However, some states have automated their records and now law enforcement agencies can access these records from statewide databases.

Simply knowing that the victim has been injured by someone acting under color of law is only the first step in this process. Victim services providers must be aware of the various types of defenses available to those in the criminal justice system. By understanding these defenses, professionals can better advise victims of their constitutional and civil rights.

Key Terms

Under color of law involves unauthorized, unlawful conduct of an official when the pretense of authority under which the officer acted furthered or assisted them in violating a person's constitutional rights in any way.

Respondeat superior is latin for "let the master answer." Under this doctrine, the master (employer or supervisor) is responsible for the acts or omissions of his servant (employee) toward those to whom the master owes a duty of care.

Injunctions are restraining orders or protective orders which are court orders that prohibit the offender from having any contact with the victim.

Discussion Questions

1. Does the potential of civil liability affect how police respond to victims of crime?

2. Should local agencies be held liable for failing to train their officers if the officers acted in good faith?

3. Why is the requirement of state action important in 1983 lawsuits?

4. Is a gender-based civil rights law necessary?

5. Are temporary restraining orders a useful tool in responding to domestic violence? List those situations in which you would recommend issuance of a temporary restraining order and those situations in which it would not be appropriate.

6. Should absolute immunity exist? Why? Why not?

Suggested Readings

Peter Finn & Sarah Colson, *Civil Protection Orders: Legislation, Current Court Practice and Enforcement*, (National Institute of Justice, Washington, D.C.) March 1990.

M. D. Dubber, *Victims on the War on Crime: The Use and Abuse of Victims' Rights*, (New York University Press) 2006.

The Crime Victim's Right to be Present, (U.S. Department of Justice, Office for Victims of Crime, Washington, D.C.) 2001.

Endnotes

1. See *Powers v. Karen* 768 F. Supp. 46 (E.D. N.Y. 1991).
2. Civil Rights Act (Enforcement Act) of 1866, ch. 31, 14 Stat. 27.
3. Enforcement Act of 1870 (Act of May 31, 1870), ch. 114, 16 Stat. 140, amended by Act of Feb. 28, 1871, ch. 99, 16 Stat. 433.
4. Ku Klux Klan (Anti-lynching) Act, ch. 22, 17 Stat. 13 (1971).
5. 18 U.S.C. Section 241 (1988).
6. 18 U.S.C. Section 242 (1988).
7. 42 U.S.C. Section 1983 (1981, West Supp. 1985).
8. 313 U.S. 299 (1941).
9. 313 U.S. at 326.
10. 325 U.S. 91 (1945).
11. 325 U.S. 167 (1961).
12. 436 U.S. 658 (1978).
13. 455 U.S. 622 (1980).
14. See The Civil Rights Attorneys Fees Awards Act of 1976, 42 U.S.C. Section 1988 (1981, West Supp. 1994).
15. *Hensley v. Eckerhart*, 461 U.S. 423 (1983); and *Farrar v. Hobby*, 113 S.Ct. 566 (1992).
16. *Thurman v. City of Torrington*, 595 F. Supp. 1521 (Conn. 1984).
17. M. Buddy & K. Taylor, "Please Somebody Help Me," *20/20 News* (January 23, 1986). The judgment was later reduced to $1.9 million.
18. 855 F. 2d 1421 (1990).
19. New York Superior Court of Erie County, Case Number 07961 (1988).
20. 520 N.Y.S. 2d 352 (1987).
21. U.S. Dist. Utah, C77-0295 (1982).
22. *City of Canton v. Harris*, 489 U.S. 378 (1989).
23. Id.
24. 489 F.2d 877 (10th Cir. 1974).
25. 767 F.2d 161 (5th Cir. 19875).
26. 963 F.2d 201 (8th Cir. 1992).
27. 777 F.2d 1436 (11th Cir. 1985).
28. 902 F.2d 1050 (1990).
29. 103 S. Ct. 1625 (1983).
30. 125 S Ct. 417 (2005).
31. Pub. L. No. 103-322, 108 Stat. 1796. The Crime Bill contains over $30 billion for punishment and prevention programs.
32. Pub. L. No. 103-322, Title IV, 108 Stat. 1902–1955. Codified in various sections of 8 U.S.C. and 42 U.S.C.
33. "Bush Signs Violence Against Women Act into Law," Family Violence Prevention Fund; available online: http://endabuse.org. (April 4, 2006).
34. See S. Rep. No. 197, 102d Cong., 1st Session 41 (1991).
35. 18 U.S.C. contains two possible crimes of violence: The first is an offense that has an element

of use or attempted use or threatened use of physical force against the person or property of another. The second is any other offense that is a felony and by its nature involves a substantial risk that physical force may be used against the person or property of another in the course of committing the offense.

36. This section has been adapted from Peter Finn & Sarah Colson, *Civil Protection Orders: Legislation, Current Court Practice and Enforcement,* (National Institute of Justice, Washington, D.C.) March 1990.

37. Donald Cochran, "Project History of the Massachusetts Statewide Automated Restraining Order Registry," *Office of the Commissioner of Probation, Massachusetts Trial Court,* (Boston) July 1994.

38. *Mitchell v. W.T. Grant Co.,* 416 U.S. 600 (1974).

39. 125 S Ct. 417 (2005).

40. For an excellent discussion of the advantages to using restraining orders, see Elizabeth Topliffe, "Why Civil Protection Orders Are Effective Remedies for Domestic Violence But Mutual Protective Orders Are Not," 67 *Indiana Law Journal* 1039 (Fall 1992).

41. Monica Rhor, "Orders Often Fail to Restrain Violence," *Orange County Register,* available online: http://www.ocregister.com/ocregister/ (March 20, 2006).

42. There are other technical defenses that are of more interest to lawyers instead of Victim services providers. These include collateral estoppel and double jeopardy, laches, and the Younger Doctrine.

43. 28 U.S.C. Section 1346 et al.

44. *Scheuer v. Rhodes,* 416 U.S. 232, 241–242 (1974).

45. See for example *Stump v. Sparkman,* 435 U.S. 349 (1978) where the Supreme Court held that a judge who ordered a fifteen-year-old girl sterilized without notice to her and based on a simple request of her mother was absolutely immune from a civil lawsuit even though the judge had no express statutory authority for the acts he did.

46. Brian P. Barrow, *"Buckley v. Fitzsimmons:* Tradition Pays a Price for the Reduction of Prosecutorial Misconduct" 16 *Whittier L. Rev.* 301 (1995).

47. 483 U.S. 635 (1987).

17

COMPENSATION AND RESTITUTION OF VICTIMS

Chapter Outline

Learning Objectives

After reading this chapter, you should be able to:

- Distinguish between compensation and restitution
- Understand the rationale behind funding of compensation programs

- List the justification for denying benefits to certain types of victims
- Explain the philosophy underlying the concept of restitution
- Distinguish between the various types of restitution available to victims

Compensation

Introduction

Victims often suffer physical injury, emotional and mental trauma, and financial loss as a result of a crime.[1] The financial loss to crime victims can cause additional stress as they worry about hospital and doctor bills being paid, physical recovery from their injuries, and their ability to return to work. Crime victim compensation programs exist to provide financial assistance to crime victims and hopefully reduce some of these stressors. These programs exist in all fifty states, plus the District of Columbia and many will pay for medical care, mental health counseling, lost wages, and in the case of homicides, funeral costs and loss of support.[2] Although no amount of money can replace the use of an arm or the loss of a loved one, it can help victims preserve their financial stability and dignity and thereby assist in the recovery process.

As discussed in Chapter 1, in 1984 Congress enacted the Victims of Crime Act (VOCA) which established a Crime Victims Fund, supported by revenues from federal offenders. This revenue was based on fines, penalty assessments, and forfeited appearance bonds. When VOCA was enacted in 1984, the fund ceiling or amount that could be allocated to the fund was $100 million. Amendments to VOCA occurred in 1986, 1988, 1990, and in 1992 when Congress removed the ceiling. Although deposits fluctuate yearly, the total amount deposited in the fund from its inception to 1994 was over $1.2 billion.[3]

Some of this money is used to improve the investigation and prosecution of child abuse cases including those child abuse acts committed against Native Americans. However, most of the money in the fund is used to support state victim compensation and victim assistance service programs. *Victim compensation* is a direct payment to, or on behalf of, a crime victim for crime-related expenses such as unpaid medical bills, mental health counseling, funeral costs, and lost wages.[4] *Victim assistance* includes

---

FOCUS: Compensation and Restitution

Victim's Perspectives[5]

"The state paid for both the defense and the prosecution. I had to find a way to pay the $12,000 this crime cost us."

—a victim addressing the issue of compensation

"I think if the criminals who do these things are caught they should have to pay for the damage they do, even if takes them years. My family and I will be trying to recover from this for the rest of our lives."

—a victim addressing the issue of restitution

services such as crisis intervention, counseling, emergency transportation to court, temporary housing, advocacy, and criminal justice support.[6]

VOCA also established special assessments for individual crimes which are levied on every conviction. Additionally, VOCA has a "Son of Sam" provision that requires royalties from the sale of literary rights or any other profits derived from a crime, to be deposited in the Crime Victims Fund and held for five years to satisfy any civil judgment a victim may obtain. If no judgments are filed, these funds become part of the general Crime Victims Fund.[7] Most states also have their own "Son of Sam" laws that cover state crimes.

Victim assistance programs and services have been discussed in previous chapters. These include organizations that provide a variety of services to victims of state and federal crimes. There are over 8000 agencies or organizations that provide services to victims and nearly 3000 of those organizations received some VOCA funding.[8]

Program Operation

California established the first compensation program in 1965, and within three years five other states created similar programs. California is still the largest program in the nation, with payout at about one-third the total benefits paid by all programs combined.[9] The median annual payout per state is approximately $2 million. (One-half of the states pay less and one-half pay more.)

Every state administers a crime victim compensation program through a central agency. (In two states, Arizona and Colorado, operation of the program has been delegated to counties and districts.)[10] These agencies are organized and funded on a statewide basis with administration, claims investigation, and decision making handled at that statewide headquarters. Debate continues among those in the field regarding centralization versus decentralization of compensation services.[11]

Most victim compensation programs are small agencies employing only a handful of staff. The lack of personnel creates delays in processing claims, prevents training of groups regarding their right to compensation, and does not allow for specialized services such as bilingual staff. Some agencies are using student interns or volunteers to carry out staff functions.

These programs provide assistance to victims of both federal and state crimes. Although each state compensation program is independently run, most programs have similar eligibility requirements and offer the same types of benefits. The maximum state award generally ranges between $10,000 and $25,000.[12]

Victims applying for compensation must comply with certain requirements including reporting the crime and filing claims by certain deadlines. In most states, the victim service professional provides compensation applications and information to the victim. The victim then contacts the agency. Program staff then mail an application to the victim who fills it out and returns it to the compensation agency. Once the claim form is received, it is processed by an investigator or claims specialist. These employees do not go into the field to obtain their information, rather they collect data using letters, telephone calls, and other techniques. These investigations must verify a variety of information including the fact that the crime was reported to the proper law enforcement agency, that there is appropriate documentation of medical expenses, that they obtain data regarding funds paid by insurance companies, and that they determine the amount, if any, of lost wages.

Once all pertinent information is gathered, the victim compensation agency will decide whether to make an award, and the monetary value of that award to the victim. In most states, victims may appeal a denial of benefits. These appeals are heard by a different panel than the one who made the original determination. Some states require that the appeal be heard by a judge.

The various state compensation programs are represented by the National Association of Crime Victim Compensation Boards (NACVCB). This is a national organization that provides advocacy, training, and communication among the state boards. Occasionally the NACVCB communicates with Congress and federal agencies on all matters affecting the state compensation programs.

Eligibility

Not all victims of every crime are eligible for state compensation. In general, the majority of states limit compensation to victims who suffered injuries as a result of the criminal conduct of another and to survivors of homicides. Additionally, there is a wide disparity between eligibility requirements in these programs with some states mandating that the victim suffer some sort of physical injury and others allowing for physical or mental injuries. Most states allow the parents of deceased victims to collect compensation.

A majority of states disallow some classes of persons from eligibility. Some states preclude firefighters and police officers from victim compensation awards. The rationale for this exclusion is that if their injuries are job related they are eligible for other state program—workers' compensation. Some states exclude convicted prisoners from filing claims while they are in jail or prison, or serving probation or parole. VOCA has required states to provide compensation to nonresidents victimized within a state as well as persons who are subject to federal jurisdiction, such as Native Americans. Additionally, state residents who are victimized in another state are eligible in their home state if the state where the crime occurred does not have a victim compensation program to which they can apply. If the claim is denied, the victim usually has no recourse, because the crime did not occur in the state of residence. Only if the state where the crime occurred has no program—or does not extend eligibility to the non-resident is the victim allowed to file in the state of residence. However, a few states provide that as long as the victim files where the crime occurred, they may also file in their home state.

Historically, drunk driving was not considered a violent crime that entitled the victim to state-funded compensation. In 1983, only five states classified drunk driving crimes as compensable.[13] As a result of a nationwide public awareness program, as well as successful lobbying by MADD, drunk driving cases are now included as compensable offenses in all states that participate in the VOCA program. Dealing with two or more insurance companies and several lawyers who represent the various parties tends to increase the length of time from filing a claim to receiving an award.[14]

Two key issues are common in drunk driving cases: contributory misconduct and subrogation. Contributory misconduct, discussed in more detail later in this chapter, is an eligibility requirement that applies to all crime victim compensation decisions and takes on special significance in drunk driving cases because of the social environment that accompanies many drinking and driving situations.[15] Many people may go to a bar and have a few drinks and then drive home and believe that they are fit to accomplish that task. Additionally, unlike the majority of crimes, some victims of drunk drivers know the perpetrator and may have been in the same car as the drunk driver when the offense occurred. Some states deny awards if the victim was a willing passenger of a known drunk driver driver, other states reduce payments if the victim voluntarily rode with a known drunk and some states do not consider such activity as misconduct. *Subrogation* is the process in which third parties are asked to reimburse the state for compensation payments previously made to the victim. Generally speaking, the state pays any award to which the victim is entitled under the state compensation laws and then attempts to recoup that payment from any insurance companies that are involved in the incident.

In the past, domestic violence victims were summarily denied compensation. Many states denied these claims because of the belief that the victim contributed to her own injuries by staying in the relationship or that any award would benefit the wrongdoer if he was still living with the victim. Similar to the change in attitudes toward victims of drunk driving, our perception of domestic violence victims has resulted in a change in policy in all states. All states now include domestic violence as a compensable crime.

Some state compensation programs have very few domestic violence claims. The staffs of these programs believe it is because victims underreport this form of violence. Additionally, cultural barriers may prevent certain minority groups from reporting because exposing male offenders to public attention violates cultural norms.

Contributory misconduct occurs when victims participate in the crime or otherwise contribute to their injuries by their own conduct. All states have laws or regulations designed to exclude such parties from receiving compensation. This is one of the most frequent issues facing compensation staff today. The concept of victim participation is a complex and emotional subject that does not have a clear bright line delineating innocent victims from those that caused their own injuries.

In deciding the existence of contributory misconduct, many compensation programs rely on police reports, witness statements, the prosecuting attorney's opinion, the results of any trial, and the oral or written statements of the victim. In most states, if there is an issue of misconduct, the victim is given an opportunity to rebut such a conclusion prior to any final decision resulting in a denial of the claim. Many states do not have hard and fast rules regarding contributory misconduct and end up judging each case on its own merits.

Most states require that the victim promptly report the crime to the police. Generally, states require that a police report be filed within seventy-two hours of

---

PRACTICUM: Contributory Misconduct—Who Is at Fault?[16]

Practicum 1:

The victim was shot by her husband after she had a protection order amended to let him visit their children in her apartment. Did the victim contribute to her injuries?

Holding: Absent other facts, most programs would find no contributory misconduct on the part of the victim.

Practicum 2:

The victim was robbed and shot after accepting a ride from a stranger on a city street at 3 A.M.
Holding: Most programs would find no misconduct.

Query: What if the victim was a prostitute and engaged in her work at the time she accepted the ride?

Practicum 3:

The victim was wounded in a drive-by shooting while talking to a third party.
Holding: Most states would find no misconduct. Query: What if the third party was a drug dealer and the defendant was attempting to make a purchase of drugs? What if the shooting was part of an ongoing gang war for control of the city's drug markets?

---

the discovery of the crime. Additionally, all states require that the victim cooperate in any subsequent investigation or court proceedings. Though a number of states can make an exception when the victim's life or safety is at risk. Apprehension or conviction of the perpetrator is not a requirement of receiving compensation.[17]

Eligibility issues pose complex and emotional problems for victims. Victim service professionals should understand the rationale and basis for these requirements so they can explain them to victims. Being unjustly denied a compensation claim can have severe financial and mental consequences for a victim.

Benefits

Once a victim has qualified for compensation, the next step in the process is determining what type of benefits are available. Many factors are involved in determining the type and amount of benefits available to victims. Some states have a small deductible amount ($50–$100) that must be reached before they will pay compensation. All states pay for only nonreimbursed expenses. In other words, if a victim has private health insurance that covers the cost of medical treatment, the state compensation award will not pay for those expenses.

Collateral financial sources are any payments received by the victim for costs reimbursed by other sources such as private insurance, workers' compensation, restitution, or disability payments. This policy prevents victims from recovering losses for the same injury twice and thus enriching themselves. Although most states attempt to use subrogation in an attempt to recoup money paid to victims, program staffs have reported frustration with the low amounts recovered.[18]

A majority of states compensate victims for a variety of crime-related costs including dental care, plastic surgery, vocational rehabilitation (education), home care, and moving expenses. Most states also pay for mental health counseling. However, deciding who is a qualified mental health provider and determining the appropriate forms of treatment are complex issues facing many compensation staff members. Although some states require mental health professionals to be licensed, other states allow "counseling" to be done by a variety of persons including those without advanced degrees. Additionally, the type and extent of the treatment may be difficult to control because some mental health providers may decide to prolong treatment beyond what is necessary to increase the victim's bill.

A majority of states allow payment for a portion of any attorney's fees incurred by the victim in processing the compensation claim. The amount awarded does not decrease the victim's award, rather it is a separate payment to the attorney. Many compensation staff members feel it is in the victim's best interest to be represented by an attorney when appealing a denial of compensation benefits.

In some states, compensation claims dramatically increased during the period between 1895 and 1992. Several factors contributed to this increase including higher visibility of compensation programs, more awareness and advocacy on the part of victim services providers, and new laws mandating greater compensation of victims. This increase in claims and awards reflects the fact that victim's have an increased awareness that they should receive the financial help they need.

Compensation is only one financial remedy available to victims of crime. Another remedy looks to the offender to make the victim whole. The topic of restitution is discussed in the next section.

Restitution

The facts contained in this Focus box are not drawn from some historical account detailing the early days of restitution. They come from a 1995 newspaper article examining the present-day structure of restitution in Los Angeles.[19]

Introduction

The 1982 *Final Report of the President's Task Force on Victims of Crime* included several key points regarding restitution.[20] The report recommended that legislation be enacted requiring judges to order restitution for property loss and personal injury in all cases unless the judge explicitly finds that restitution is not appropriate. However, the report also stated that although restitution is a proper goal to be pursued, it has limitations. The report noted that restitution cannot be ordered unless the perpetrator is caught and convicted. Even if it is ordered, the offender often has no resources with which to make any payments. Finally, those perpetrators who can make payments may take many years to finally pay off the balance. In the interim, the victim is left to bear the cost of the crime.[21]

As a result of this report and other factors influencing the victims' movement over the last decade, a number of laws have been enacted addressing the issue of restitution. Hillenbrand reports that one reason these laws may have been enacted

FOCUS: Compensating the Victims of September 11

On September 11, 2001, the world changed for the United States. Terrorists highjacked four passenger airliners; the first was flown into the north tower of the World Trade Center, and just eighteen minutes later, the second plane crashed into the south tower. The third plane hit its target: the Pentagon. The fourth plane crashed in a field in Pennsylvania. The United States' response to the victims of the September 11 tragedy has been both praised and criticized.

The injuries and death toll suffered in the attacks were staggering. The attacks killed 2,551 and seriously injured 215 more. Four hundred twenty-five of those were killed or seriously injured were emergency responders. Additionally, people suffered emotional trauma, property damage, and loss of business.

Congress responded by establishing the September 11 Victim Compensation Fund of 2001 as part of the Air Transportation Safety and System Stabilization Act. The first part of this act was to protect the financial viability of the airline industry by limiting their liability, and the second portion established a non-faulty method of compensating victims for their loss.

The act established two options for recovery for victims: (1) they might pursue civil litigation against the airlines with a cap on recovery at the airline's liability coverage, or (2) they could utilize the compensation available from the fund in exchange for a relapse of liability of the airlines.

The fund included calculating an award based on the claimant's age, life expectancy income, marital status, and number and ages of dependents. Contrary to traditional tort law, no punitive damages were available.

The Rand Corporation conducted a study regarding the compensation of the victims of September 11 and found that most of the $38.1 billion in total payouts to individuals and businesses came from insurers ($19.6 billion). The second largest payout was from government programs ($15.8 billion), and the remaining amount came from charitable donations ($2.7 billion).

While many people considered the fund a wonderful and compassionate response by our government, others had questions and criticisms. Some victims' families questioned why the family of a victim who made more money should receive more money than those who made less money. They wondered if one person's life was more valuable than another's. Others questioned why victims of September 11 should receive more compensation than those of the 1995 Oklahoma City bombing.

Discussion questions:

1. Should victims of terrorism receive higher compensation awards than those of other crimes? What about victims of natural disasters?
2. How should we pay for the September 11 fund?
3. What other issues are raised by this form of compensation?

"Sources: Josh Romero, "A Victim's Eye View of the September 11th Victim Compensation Fund," 71/1 *Defense Counsel Journal* 64(7) (January 2004); and "Compensating the Victims of 9/11," *Research Brief*, Rand Institute for Civil Justice, Santa Monica, Calif. (2004).

is the change in perception regarding restitution. She states that society began to view restitution not as a way to punish or rehabilitate the offender, but as a method of bringing justice to victims.[22] Other authorities argue that laws mandating restitution have been passed as "politically correct" with little or no thought given to their effect. This has resulted in a system that does not deliver its promise

---

FOCUS: Who Is Responsible for Collecting Restitution?

Each year, the Los Angeles Municipal Court orders hundreds of defendants convicted of crimes to pay hundreds of thousands of dollars in restitution to their victims. Yet, in the majority of these cases, no branch of the criminal justice system is designated as responsible for collecting the restitution and disbursing it to the victims. Collecting restitution is left as the defendant's responsibility.

The city attorney's office is charged with the responsibility of ensuring that the defendant pays the ordered amount to the victim. In the event restitution is not paid, the city attorney's office then asks the court to find the defendant in violation of probation.

---

of making victims whole. Consequently, victims become more disillusioned with the criminal justice system when they learn that the court order mandating the offender to pay restitution carries no weight or authority.[23]

Even the definition of restitution causes conflict. It represents many things to many people. Whereas the victim may view restitution as a way to regain financial loss and to punish the offender, the court may see it as a method of instilling responsibility in the offender. The agency charged with collecting restitution may view it as simply one more task for an already overburdened department. Traditionally, *restitution* is a court-ordered sanction that involves payment of compensation by the defendant to the victim for injuries suffered as a result of the defendant's criminal act.

As the following Practicum illustrates, the definition of restitution, and who should pay, raises troubling issues. What is fair and just to a victim may seem outlandish to a judge or the perpetrator. The following sections will examine how we happened to arrive at this juncture in our development of victims' rights. Also, the problems in collecting restitution and some innovative methods that address these issues will also be examined.

History

The concept of making a victim whole is not new.[24] As indicated in Chapter 1, the Code of Hammurabi in the eighteenth century included provisions for payment of money to the victim or the victim's family.[25] In Saxton, England, a legal system developed which provided for restitution to the victim's family for the injury incurred by the victim and restitution to the king for violating the king's peace. As discussed earlier, this system eventually evolved into one in which the wrong was perpetrated against the state and not the victim. The victim and the victim's rights became secondary to the pursuit of justice.[26]

Modern restitution as we know it today can be traced to the criminal laws that authorized suspended sentences and the use of probation. By the late 1930s, several states had laws that allowed judges to order restitution as a condition of granting probation.[27] This process viewed restitution as part of the correctional process. In the late 1970s and 1980s, the victims' movement began to argue that

---

PRACTICUM: How Much Restitution Should Be Ordered?

The victim is a forty-two-year-old executive who was robbed in New York's Central Park while on a business trip. The offender took the victim's wallet, which contained a picture of his deceased wife, several credit cards, and $400 in cash. The perpetrator also demanded the victim's Rolex watch. The victim explained that the watch was a gift from his deceased wife, but the assailant tore it off his wrist and then proceeded to pistol-whip him.

The perpetrator was caught and convicted, and the court held a hearing to determine the amount of restitution that should be ordered. The defense attorney argued that his client was homeless and had not worked for three years because of a drinking and drug problem. The prosecutor asked for funds to reimburse the victim for the $400 and the value of the lost Rolex, as well as any medical bills that were not covered either by the state compensation program or the victim's health insurance.

The victim stated that his wife bought him the Rolex twenty-one years ago and it cost her $500; however, today the fair market value of the Rolex was $5,000. The victim wants to replace the watch and is asking for $5,000. He also wants $400 for the lost cash and is asking $10,000 for the lost picture of his wife, stating that he has no other pictures of her. How much restitution should the judge order?

---

restitution show be viewed as protecting victims from suffering financial hardship rather than punishing or rehabilitating the offender.

The modern concept of restitution in the criminal justice system serves a variety of purposes in the administration of justice. Restitution attempts to establish a relationship between the perpetrator and the victim in an effort to make the offender aware of the financial consequences suffered by the victim as a result of the offender's acts. Another purpose of restitution is to advance the concept of personal responsibility and accountability to the victim. A third idea regarding restitution holds that although it cannot undo the wrong, it can assist the victim financially and emotionally and at the same time educate the offender. Finally, restitution serves to punish the offender. The funds used to pay restitution must come from the offender's pocketbook and thus have a continuing impact on that offender.[28]

Types of Restitution

Restitution can now be ordered for a variety of criminal acts, including sex crimes, child sexual abuse, telemarketing fraud, and domestic violence.[29] Restitution can also be ordered to pay for lost wages, child care, and other expenses involved in attending court hearings.[30] Additionally, there are several different types of restitution.[31]

The most common form of restitution is financial, which requires the offender to make payments directly to the actual victim of the crime. Financial–community restitution requires the offender to make payments to a community agency such as a restitution center, which then pays the victim. Individual service restitution requires the offender to perform a service for the actual victim. For example, the offender might be required to repair or replace property damaged during the commission of the crime. Community service restitution requires the offender to perform some beneficial service to the community. In this type of restitution, society serves as the symbolic victim and this is sometimes referred to as "symbolic restitution." Finally, some states authorize restitution fines. Restitution fines differ from actual restitution in that they are collected and deposited in the state's crime victim compensation fund. These monies then become part of the fund's operating expenses.

Restitution may be tied to different aspects of a defendant's sentence and is frequently imposed at the earliest possible time in the criminal process. Additionally, many plea agreements call for restitution. Imposing payment as a condition of probation is the most common method of collecting restitution. A court order may also follow the defendant to the correctional institution. Many states are now imposing the requirement that inmates work while incarcerated and while working in prison, they normally only receive a minimal amount of money (usually far less than the minimal wage). Several states have passed laws requiring that a portion of that amount, no matter how small, be set aside for payment as restitution to the victim. More states are implementing policies that require restitution to be established as a condition of any parole. Additionally, states are passing laws that provide that any restitution order in a criminal case will also be considered as a civil order for remuneration from the defendant to the victim and may be processed in civil courts.

Problems with Restitution

Restitution is a complex process that involves a number of different professionals working in the criminal justice system. Unfortunately, these professionals are usually overworked and under budgeted. As indicated in the article featured in the Focus box at the beginning of this section, many of these professionals claim that collecting and disbursing restitution is someone else's job.[32] This leads to poor communication and diminished accountability among agencies inside the criminal justice system. This, in turn, causes poor consultation and communication with victims. Because there may be no agency controlling or coordinating restitution, judges may impose insufficient or excessive restitution orders.

Many victims feel dissatisfied with the restitution process. They may believe that the amount imposed in the court order was insufficient. Other victims feel powerless as they search for answers to their questions only to be directed from one agency to another.[33]

Occasionally, a crime involves multiple perpetrators against a single victim. If the prosecution grants one perpetrator immunity to testify against the others, the victim will not be able to receive a court order of restitution against that defendant. By the same token, in crimes involving single perpetrators and multiple victims, deciding which victim should receive the limited funds of the perpetrator can create great difficulties.

Another obvious problem with restitution is the socioeconomic status of the perpetrator. In a majority of cases, the offenders are poor and unlikely to earn the funds necessary to make full restitution. Additionally, juvenile offenders are often incapable of obtaining or holding onto jobs that might provide them with the funds necessary to pay the court-ordered restitution.

Methods of Collecting Restitution

Control or monitoring of restitution orders is critical. The American Bar Association (ABA) conducted a survey of restitution directors and recommended that higher compliance rates occur when: (1) efforts are made to monitor payments, and (2) consistent action is taken to respond to delinquencies.[34] Respondents in the survey reported that the highest delinquency rates occurred at the time of the first payment and at mid-sentence. They stated that delinquency seldom occurred at the end of the offender's sentence. This study suggests that early and effective responses to delinquency can successfully interrupt a pattern of nonpayment.

The ABA study also suggests that compliance rates were higher in jurisdictions where the judge made an effort to determine if the offender had the ability to pay before the amount of restitution was set. When judges order restitution at a level so high as to be unreachable, it can result in noncompliance because the offender takes the attitude of why even try to meet this impossible goal. This noncompliance frustrates both the victim and the official charged with collecting restitution.[35]

Finally, the ABA study suggests the implementation of a policy within the criminal justice system that establishes a priority of collecting and disbursing fines, forfeitures, fees, and other assessments. This policy is necessary because oftentimes the offender is not only ordered to pay restitution, but also may have fines and other fees imposed such as repaying the court for the services of the public defender. These competing court-ordered financial obligations may affect the offender's ability to pay restitution to the victim.[36] Other recommendations that may make the restitution process more effective include specializing in the collection of restitution, employing automation, and using other nontraditional methods to collect restitution.

The Los Angeles criminal justice system is a large and sprawling bureaucratic system that seems impervious to change and the Los Angeles Probation Department is one of the largest in the nation. The adult probation department in Los Angeles tested a process of assigning specialized restitution caseloads to some of their officers. Their sole duty is to monitor and collect the court-ordered restitution. This procedure has proved to be so successful that the department has assigned probation officers to each of its offices in Los Angeles, whose primary duty is to collect restitution.[37]

Automation of records and bookkeeping can assist in collecting restitution. An investment in computer systems and software dedicated to the collection and disbursement of restitution sends a message to offenders that this is a high priority. Automation frees staff from performing routine repetitive tasks and can result in allowing them to work more closely with victims. Additionally, it can free up time to send letters informing victims of the restitution process by simply typing in their name and address and hitting the print key. Warning letters to offenders who are delinquent can also be generated quickly without much staff time. Finally, computerization gives staff the ability to collect data and develop statistics regarding restitution.[38]

A number of other innovative methods for collecting restitution are in use across the nation. These include filing civil law suits and obtaining judgments based on the restitution order. In states that allow this process, once the default is placed on the judgment, the victim can garnish the offender's wages, file liens on real property, and attach other assets. One department in Phoenix, Arizona, requires offenders to turn over their uncashed paychecks to the department. The department then cashes the check, deducts the amount owed for restitution, and writes the offender another check for the balance. Some states are using restitution centers which house offenders for six months to a year while they work in the community. Their checks are given to the center which deducts its expenses, other fines, and restitution before paying the balance to the perpetrator.[39] The Office for Victims of Crime continues to fund research in this area by calling for promising practices and policies in the field that address the issue of collection of restitution.

Summary

Crime victim compensation funds can pay for unreimbursed expenses suffered by victims of violent crimes. These state programs are funded by federally imposed fines, forfeitures, and other moneys taken from federal offenders. Each state receives a portion of these funds to compensate victims. More victims are filing claims and although some program managers are concerned over the financial drain caused by these increased claims, most see this as a positive development within the victims' rights movement.

In the last twenty years, restitution has reemerged within the criminal justice system as a valuable method of assisting victims of crime. Victim advocates continue to call for more efficient methods of monitoring and collecting restitution. As a result, professionals within the criminal justice system are reevaluating existing programs and policies in an attempt to meet the demand that restitution make the victim whole. Victim services providers need to be aware of the pros and cons of the restitution process and be prepared to offer suggestions to those who have the power to make necessary changes that will benefit victims of crime.

Key Terms

Victim compensation is a direct payment to, or on behalf of, a crime victim for crime-related expenses such as unpaid medical bills, mental health counseling, funeral costs, and lost wages.

Victim assistance includes services such as crisis intervention, counseling, emergency transportation to court, temporary housing, advocacy, and criminal justice support.

Subrogation is the process in which third parties are asked to reimburse the state for compensation payments previously made to the victim.

Contributory misconduct occurs when victims participate in the crime or otherwise contribute to their injuries by their own conduct.

Restitution is a court-ordered sanction that involves payment of compensation by the defendant to the victim for injuries suffered as a result of the defendant's criminal act.

Discussion Questions

1. Explain how a typical compensation program is funded and operated.

2. Understand the various eligibility requirements for receiving compensation.

3. List the various benefits victims of crime may receive under a state compensation program.

4. Explain why the historical perspective of restitution is important in understanding today's models.

5. Can you list reasons why an incarcerated prisoner should not have to make restitution to a victim? Assume you are the prisoner's advocate and must convince a judge of your position.

Suggested Readings

International Terrorism Victim Expense Reimbursement Program, Report to Congress, (U.S. Department of Justice, Office of Justice Programs, Washington, D.C.) 2006.

R. E. Hartley, *Alternative Dispute Resolutions in Civil Justice Systems*, (LFB Scholarly Publishing, New York) 2002.

M. Hook, *Ethics in Human Services*, (Sidran Institute Press, Baltimore, Md.) 2005.

Crime Victim Compensation: A Fact Sheet and Crime Victim Compensation: An Overview, (National Association of Crime Victim Compensation Boards, Alexandria, Va.) July 1, 1994.

Dale G. Parent, Barbara Auerbach & Kenneth E. Carlson, *Compensating Crime Victims: A Summary of Policies and Practices*, Office of Justice Programs, (U.S. Department of Justice, Washington, D.C.) January 1992.

Focus on the Future: A Systems Approach to Prosecution and Victim Assistance, National Victim Center, MADD, and American Prosecutors Research Institute, (U.S. Department of Justice, Washington, D.C.) no date.

Daniel McGillis & Patricia Smith, *Compensating Victims of Crime: An Analysis of American Programs*, (National Institute of Justice, Washington, D.C.) 1983.

A. J. Lurigio, W. G. Skogan & R. C. Davis, (eds.), *Victims of Crime: Problems, Policies, and Programs*, (Sage, Newbury Park, Calif.) 1990.

B. Gateway & J. Hudson, (eds.), *Criminal Justice, Restitution, and Reconciliation*, (Willow Tree Press, Inc., Monsey, N.Y.) 1990.

National Victim Assistance Academy Text, (Office for Victims of Crime, Washington, D.C.) 1996.

A. R. Roberts, *Helping Crime Victims*, (Sage, Newbury Park, Calif.) 1990.

Barbara E. Smith, Robert C. Davis & Susan W. Hillenbrand, *Enforcement of Court-Ordered Restitution: Executive Summary*, (American Bar Association, Chicago) 1989.

D. Beatty, L. Frank, A. J. Lurigio, A. Seymour, M. Paparozzi, B. Macgargle, *A Guide to Enhancing Victim Services Within Probation and Parole*, (American Bar Association, Chicago) 1994.

Endnotes

1. Much of the material that appears in this section has been adapted from various federally funded projects including NACVCB's *Crime Victim Compensation: A Fact Sheet and* *Crime Victim Compensation: An Overview*, (National Association of Crime Victim Compensation Boards, Alexandria, Va.) July 1, 1994; hereinafter *Crime Victim Compensation*, Dale G.

Parent, Barbara Auerbach & Kenneth E. Carlson, *Compensating Crime Victims: A Summary of Policies and Practices,* Office of Justice Programs, (U.S. Department of Justice, January 1992); hereinafter *Compensating Crime Victims* and *Focus on the Future: A Systems Approach to Prosecution and Victim Assistance,* National Victim Center, MADD, and American Prosecutors Research Institute, (U.S. Department of Justice, Washington, D.C.) no date; hereinafter *Focus on the Future.*

2. *Crime Victim Compensation.*
3. "Victims of Crime Act Crime Victims Fund," *OVC Fact Sheet,* (Office for Victims of Crime, Washington, D.C.) no date.
4. Id.
5. *Final Report, President's Task Force on Victims of Crime,* (GPO, Washington, D.C.) December 1982.
6. Id.
7. *Compensating Crime Victims,* p. 2.
8. Id.
9. *Crime Victim Compensation,* p. 2.
10. Id.
11. *Compensating Crime Victims,* p. 7.
12. "Victims of Crime Act Crime Victims Fund," *OVC Fact Sheet,* (Office for Victims of Crime, Washington, D.C.) no date.
13. Daniel McGillis & Patricia Smith, *Compensating Victims of Crime: An Analysis of American Programs,* (National Institute of Justice, Washington, D.C.) 1983.
14. *Compensating Crime Victims,* p. 20.
15. *Compensating Crime Victims,* p. 21.
16. Adapted from scenarios presented in *Compensating Crime Victims,* pp. 24–25.
17. *Crime Victim Compensation,* p. 3.
18. *Compensating Crime Victims,* p. 30.
19. Michael D. Harris, "No One Wants Responsibility for Restitution," *Los Angeles Daily Transcript,* p. A-1 (January 6, 1995).
20. *Final Report, President's Task Force on Victims of Crime,* (GPO, Washington, D.C.) December 1982.
21. Id. at 38.
22. Susan Hillenbrand, "Restitution and Victim Rights in the 1980s," in A. J. Lurigio, W. G. Skogan & R. C. Davis, (eds.), *Victims of Crime: Problems, Policies, and Programs,* (Sage, Newbury Park, Calif.) 1990.

23. Carol Shapiro, "Is Restitution Legislation the Chameleon of the Victims' Movement?" in B. Gateway and J. Hudson, (eds.), *Criminal Justice, Restitution, and Reconciliation,* (Willow Tree Press, Inc., Monsey, N.Y.) 1990.
24. This section has been adapted from Sterling O'Ran, "Restitution," *National Victim Assistance Academy Test,* (Office for Victims of Crime, Washington, D.C.) 1996; hereinafter *National Victim Assistance Academy Test.*
25. See for example, Gordon, *Hammurabi's Code: Quaint or Forward Looking,* (Rinehart, New York) 1957; and S. A. Cook, *The Laws of Moses and the Code of Hammurabi,* (Adam and Charles Black, London) 1903.
26. Cathryn Jo Rosen & Allen T. Harland, "Restitution to Crime Victims as a Presumptive Requirement in Criminal Cases," in A. R. Roberts, *Helping Crime Victims,* (Sage, Newbury Park, Calif.) 1990.
27. L. F. Frank, "The Collection of Restitution: An Overlooked Service to Crime Victims," 8 *St. John's Journal of Legal Commentary,* 107 (1992).
28. *National Victim Assistance Academy Text,* pp. 21–10–5.
29. *Attorney General Guidelines for Victim and Witness Assistance,* (U.S. Department of Justice, Washington, D.C.) 1995.
30. 18 U.S.C. Section 3663(b) as amended by Section 40504 of P. L. 103–322 (1994).
31. *National Victim Assistance Academy Text,* pp. 21–10–8 through 11.
32. Michael D. Harris, "No One Wants Responsibility for Restitution," *Los Angeles Daily Transcript,* p. A-1. (January 6, 1995).
33. *National Victim Assistance Academy Text,* pp. 21–10–7.
34. Barbara E. Smith, Robert C. Davis, & Susan W. Hillenbrand, *Enforcement of Court-Ordered Restitution: Executive Summary,* (American Bar Association, Chicago) 1989.
35. Id.
36. Id.
37. D. Beatty, L. Frank, A. J. Lurigio, A. Seymour, M. Paparozzi & B. Macgargle, *A Guide to Enhancing Victim Services within Probation and Parole,* (American Bar Association, Chicago) 1994.
38. Id.
39. Id.

18

VICTIM IMPACT STATEMENTS

Chapter Outline

History of Victim Impact Statements
    Purpose
    Constitutional Issues

Use of Victim Impact Statements
    Law Enforcement
    Prosecutors
    Judiciary

Effect of Victim Impact Statements
    Victim Satisfaction
    Sentencing

Victim Impact Panels
    Introduction
    Procedure

Summary

Key Terms

Discussion Questions

Suggested Readings

Learning Objectives

After reading this chapter, you should be able to:

- Explain the constitutional evolution of victim impact statements
- Understand fundamental fairness and how it relates to victim impact statements

- Distinguish between law enforcement and prosecutorial-based victim assistance programs
- Explain how victims view the affect of victim impact statements and compare this with how judges view this process
- Distinguish between victim impact statements and victim impact panels

History of Victim Impact Statements

A new series of rights are emerging in our judicial system.[1] These rights confer upon the victim, or the relatives of deceased victims, the opportunity to speak out or be heard during various phases of the criminal justice process. As with many rights that converge on a single point, an actual or potential conflict results. How we handle this conflict is a reflection of the morals and ethics of our society. This section will review the history of these various rights and examine the rationale behind the current status of the law as it relates to victim impact statements.

Purpose

One controversial "right" bestowed upon victims is known as the *victim impact statement*. This statement presents the victim's point of view to the sentencing authority. Providing the sentencing authority with all relevant information is not a new phenomenon in the criminal justice system. For many years courts have accepted information regarding the defendant prior to the imposition of a sentence.

Traditionally, presentence reports have been utilized by judges to determine the proper punishment for criminal defendants. The report, which is normally prepared by a probation officer, details the defendant's background, education, and prior criminal record. Many of these reports also include information concerning the victim of the crime.[2]

Victim impact evidence is now admitted in sentencing for a variety of criminal acts, including those that fall within the realm of family violence. However, the law on admissibility and use of victim impact statements is based on use of this evidence during death penalty cases. To understand the nature of victim impact statements it is necessary to review how this evidence is used in the most serious type of criminal case-those involving capital punishment.

The use of victim impact evidence during the sentencing phase of a criminal crime raises serious constitutional issues. The right to confront witnesses comes head-to-head with the right to have all relevant evidence placed before the sentencing authority. Intense feelings have been aroused in the Supreme Court when it addressed this issue.

Constitutional Issues

In *Booth v. Maryland*, the Supreme Court initially addressed the issue of using victim impact statements in a sentencing jury's determination.[3] In 1983, John Booth and Willie Reed bound and gagged an elderly couple. Believing the couple might be able to identify them, Booth stabbed them numerous times with a kitchen knife. The trial judge in *Booth* allowed the jury to consider a victim impact statement, which detailed the family and community's respect and admiration for the victims as well as the impact of the murders on the victims' family.[4]

The Supreme Court, in reversing the death sentence, held that it was impermissible to allow the jury access to such evidence in the sentencing phase of a death penalty proceeding.[5] The Court listed three factors which precluded the prosecution from introducing evidence of the homicide's impact on the victim's family.

First, in holding that the victim impact statement (VIS) impermissibly allows the jury to focus on the victim rather than the defendant, the Court stated:

> When the full range of foreseeable consequences of a defendant's actions may be relevant in other criminal and civil contexts, we cannot agree that it is relevant in the unique circumstances of a capital sentencing hearing. In such a case, it is the function of the sentencing jury to "express the conscience of the community on the ultimate question of life or death." When carrying out this task the jury is required to focus on the defendant as a "uniquely individual bein[g]." The focus of a VIS, however, is not on the defendant, but on the character and reputation of the victim and the effect on his family. These factors may be wholly unrelated to the blameworthiness of a particular defendant.[6]

The Court was particularly moved by the fact that the capital defendant does not typically choose his victim and, in fixing the punishment, there should be no correlation between the murder and the grief experienced by the victim's family.

Second, the Court held that the sentence of death should not turn on the characteristics of the victim and the victim's family. Specifically, the Court recognized that the imposition of the death penalty should not be determined on the basis of the ability of the victim's family to articulate their anguish and bereavement, regardless if the victim left behind a family, or on the fact that the victim was a stellar member of the community.[7] These factors focus attention on the victim and away from the central inquiry of whether the defendant's characteristics and background are such that the death sentence is warranted.[8]

Finally, the Court stated that because a VIS contains the subjective perceptions and feelings of family members, the defendant has limited rebuttal opportunity.[9] Further, to the extent the defendant is given an opportunity to rebut such information, "[t]he prospects of a 'mini-trial' on the victim's character is more than simply unappealing, it could well direct the sentencing jury from its constitutionally required task—determining whether the death penalty is appropriate in light of . . . the crime."[10]

In summing up the Court's holding that introduction of the VIS violates the Eighth Amendment's prohibition against cruel and unusual punishment, Justice Powell commented:

> One can understand the grief and anger of the family caused by the brutal murders in this case, and there is no doubt that jurors generally are aware of these feelings. But the formal presentation of this information by the State can serve no other

purpose than to inflame the jury and divert it from deciding the case on the relevant evidence concerning the crimes and the defendant. As we have noted, any decision to impose the death sentence must "be, and appear to be, based on reason rather than caprice or emotion." The admission of these emotionally charged opinions as to what conclusions the jury should draw from the evidence clearly is inconsistent with the reasoned decision making we require in capital cases.[11]

It should be apparent that at the time of the decision in *Booth v. Maryland*, the relevant considerations at the sentencing phase of a murder trial were those aspects of a defendant's background, or character, or those circumstances which extenuate or mitigate the defendant's culpability.

South Carolina v. Gathers followed the rationale of *Booth* and held unconstitutional the imposition of a death penalty based on prosecutorial remarks that were considered inflammatory.[12] Demetrius Gather and three companions sexually assaulted and killed Richard Haynes, a man they encountered in a park. During the incident, the perpetrators ransacked a bag the victim was carrying. The bag contained several articles pertaining to religion, including a religious tract entitled, "Game Guy's Prayer." During the sentencing phase of the trial, the prosecutor's argument included references to Haynes's personal qualities and included a reading of the "Game Guy's Prayer." The Supreme Court reversed the sentence stating that such references to the qualities of the victim were similar to the *Booth* holding, which prohibited victim impact statements. The court determined that such evidence was likely to inflame the jury and thus violate the defendant's Eighth Amendment rights. In a well-reasoned and logical dissent, Justice O'Conner stated, "Nothing in the Eighth Amendment precludes the community from considering its loss in assessing punishment nor requires that the victim remain a faceless stranger at the penalty phase of a capital case." The dissent by Justice O'Conner was a signal that the winds of judicial temperament might be changing.

In *Payne v. Tennessee*, the court completely reversed itself and allowed the imposition of a death sentence to stand, based in part on evidence contained in a victim impact statement. In 1987, Pervis Tyrone Payne entered the apartment of Charisse Christopher and her two children. Payne stabbed Charisse and the two children numerous times with a butcher knife. Charisse and her daughter died; however, three-year-old Nicholas survived.

Payne was caught and convicted for the murders. During the penalty phase, four witnesses testified regarding the defendant's background, reputation, and mental state. These witnesses urged the jury to not impose the death penalty. In rebuttal, the prosecution called the maternal grandmother who was caring for Nicholas. She was allowed to testify, over the defendant's objection, that Nicholas continued to cry out calling for his dead mother and sister. The witness was also allowed to testify regarding her personal grief over the loss of her loved ones.

During the closing argument, the prosecutor hammered on the pain and suffering that Nicholas and his deceased family had endured stating:

But we do know that Nicholas was alive. And Nicholas was in the same room. Nicholas was still conscious. His eyes were open. He responded to the paramedics.

He was able to follow their directions. He was able to hold his intestines in as he was carried to the ambulance. So he knew what happened to his mother and baby sister.

There is nothing you can do to ease the pain of any of the families involved in this case. There is nothing you can do to ease the pain of Bernice or Carl Payne, and that's a tragedy. There is nothing you can do basically to ease the pain of Mr. and Mrs. Zvolanek, and that's a tragedy. They will have to live with it for the rest of their lives. There is obviously nothing you can do for Charisse and Lacie Jo. But there is something you can do for Nicholas.

Somewhere down the road Nicholas is going to grow up, hopefully. He's going to want to know what happened. And he is going to know what happened to his baby sister and his mother. He is going to want to know what kind of justice was done. He is going to want to know what happened. With your verdict, you will provide the answer."[13]

The jury sentenced Payne to death and the case was appealed to the U.S. Supreme Court. Payne contended that the trial court erred when it allowed the maternal grandmother to testify. Relying on *Booth* and *Gathers*, Payne argued that such evidence was a violation of his Eighth Amendment rights.

After reviewing the principles that have guided criminal sentencing over the ages, the Court stated that the consideration of the harm caused by the crime has been an important factor in the existence of the exercise of judicial discretion. The majority opinion went on to state that neither *Booth* nor *Gathers* even suggested that a defendant, entitled as he is to individualized consideration, is to receive that consideration wholly apart from the crime which he has committed.

In setting forth the groundwork for overruling *Booth* and *Gathers*, the Court stated:

> *Under our constitutional system, the primary responsibility for defining crimes against state law, fixing punishments for the commission of those crimes, and establishing procedures for criminal trials rests with the States. The state laws respecting crimes, punishments, and criminal procedures are of course subject to the overriding provisions of the United States Constitution. Where the State imposes the death penalty for a particular crime, we have held that the Eight Amendment imposes special limitations upon that process.*
>
> *The States remain free, in capital cases, as well as others, to devise new procedures and new remedies to meet felt needs. Victim impact evidence is simply another form or method of informing the sentencing authority about the specific harm caused by the crime in question, evidence of a general type long considered by sentencing authorities. We think the* Booth *Court was wrong in stating that this kind of evidence leads to the arbitrary imposition of the death penalty. In the majority of cases, and in this case, victim impact evidence serves entirely legitimate purposes.*[14]

Thus the Supreme Court overruled *Booth* and *Gathers* to the extent that they prohibited introduction of evidence or argument regarding the impact of the crime on the victim, families, and the community. In addition, the Court's decision clearly stated that the decision regarding the admission of such evidence was the prerogative of the individual states. The Court ruled it would not intervene unless the evidence introduced was so unduly prejudicial that it renders the trial fundamentally unfair.[15] If this occurred the court reasoned, the due process clause of the Fourteenth Amendment provides a mechanism for relief.

The decision was not without heated dissent. In a dissenting opinion, Justices Marshall and Blackmun uttered a quote that will ring in the halls of justice and law school classrooms forever: "Power, not reason, is the new currency of this Court's decision making."[16] Justices Marshall and Blackmun went on to point out that the court was disregarding the accepted judicial principle of stare decisis. In a well-reasoned, but emotional conclusion, the justices stated:

> *Today's decision charts an unmistakable course. If the majority's radical reconstruction of the rules for overturning this Court's decisions is to be taken at face value—and the majority offers us no reason why it should not—then the overruling of* Booth *and* Gathers *is but a preview of an even broader and more farreaching assault upon this Court's precedents. Cast aside today are those condemned to face society's ultimate penalty. Tomorrow's victims may be minorities, women, or the indigent. Inevitably, this campaign to resurrect yesterday's "spirited dissents" will squander the authority and the legitimacy of this Court as a protector of the powerless.*[17]

The decision also generated controversy in the academic world when a series of articles appeared condemning the court for both allowing victim impact evidence and appearing to repudiate its acceptance of stare decisis.[18] Although the dissent and certain individuals within the academic community may condemn the majority's opinion, it is now clearly the law of the land. In addition, the Supreme Court's decision enhances the victims' rights movement in the United States. It allows individual states to determine what is relevant evidence in the death penalty phase of a capital crime.

Some would argue that the decision in *Payne* leaves prosecutors and defense attorneys scrambling to determine what type of evidence is admissible under the guise of victim impact statements. The answer is simply that evidence which does not result in rendering a trial fundamentally unfair is proper. This concept of fundamental fairness is not a new, untested, or ill-defined doctrine.

There is a long history defining acts by the state that are classified as fundamentally unfair. The doctrine of fundamental fairness has its roots in two early cases. In *Powell v. Alabama* several black youths were accused of repeatedly raping two young white girls. They were caught, tried, and convicted. Their conviction was overturned on the ground that the failure of the trial court to appoint counsel until the day of the trial was a violation of the defendants' due process.[19] In *Brown v. Mississippi,* a sheriff hung the defendant from a tree and whipped him until he confessed to the murder of a white man. The Supreme Court held that such actions are revolting to the sense of justice and the confession was suppressed.[20]

The *doctrine of fundamental fairness* accepts the concept that due process is a generalized command that requires states to provide the defendant with a fair trial. If the admission of the victim impact evidence "revolts the sense of justice" or "shocks the conscience" of the court, such admission would be erroneous under the due process clause.

Victim impact evidence is now an accepted part of the judicial process. The ability of a victim of family violence to inform the court of the impact of the offender's acts on her life can only benefit the victim and continue to educate the public regarding the dynamics of violence.

Use of Victim Impact Statements

Law Enforcement

Law enforcement officers should understand the victim impact process for a number of reasons: (1) many departmental policy manuals require that they inform victims of this right, (2) the officer can demonstrate concern by explaining the process to the victim, and (3) educating victims about their rights ensures that others within the criminal justice system will understand the impact of crime on the victims.[21] Once any crime has been reported, law enforcement officers should inform the victims of their rights early in the investigation process. They should offer assistance and encourage victims to keep a record or diary of their feelings, emotions and hardships. This record should also track expenses so that the impact statements accurately reflect the appropriate amount of restitution. After an offender's arrest, victims should be encouraged to talk with the local victim—witness coordinator and the prosecutor regarding their feelings about the crime and any plea bargain.

Law enforcement officers do not stop participating in the process simply because they have arrested the perpetrator. Nor should they stop their involvement with the victims of crime. They should "share ownership of the case" by working with and keeping victims informed of their rights. The officer should encourage victims to participate in the process and explain that their information may make a

---

FOCUS: Acceptance of Victim Impact Statements

A particular segment of society believes that victims should not be allowed to speak out at a defendant's sentencing. In February 1995, at the sentencing hearing of Long Island Railroad gunman Colin Ferguson, who shot, wounded, and killed several Long Island commuters, victims spoke out about their anguish and feelings. The *Wall Street Journal,* the *New York Times,* and the *Washington Post* all responded by endorsing the use of victim impact statements.

The *New Republic,* however, argued that the use of such statements might inflame the judge or jury.[22] It stated that one of the most basic requirements of the rule of law is that judges and juries be impartial. Further, the editorial stated that victim impact evidence guarantees "that the trials will degenerate into lawless emotionalism."[23]

difference. Officers should inform victims of the procedures and policies regarding victim impact statements in their jurisdiction. Do they send a letter to the judge? Do they fill out a form? Where do they get this form? Can they talk with the probation officer? A number of questions need to be answered and law enforcement officers are in the best position to answer these questions for victims.[24]

The debate continues in the criminal justice profession regarding the extent of law enforcement's role in the victim impact statement process. Supporters of an active role by law enforcement argue that this process provides victims of crime with information about their rights and thus allows them to participate in the justice process almost from the beginning. Supporters also explain that such a process allows victims to begin to document their feelings and financial losses early in the process. Opponents argue that forcing law enforcement officers to give information regarding victims' rights early in the process leads victims to assume that the offender will be identified, arrested, and convicted. Statistically, a number of crimes occur in which the perpetrator is never caught. Opponents also argue that most victims are not familiar with the criminal justice system and officers will have to spend valuable time educating them about the system when, in fact, the perpetrator may never be caught.[25]

In recent years, many law enforcement agencies have established police-based victim assistance programs. These programs have the ability to provide services to crime victims who might otherwise have been excluded from receiving such services because some of these programs focus on those victims whose cases have formally entered the criminal justice system. For example, a police-based victim assistance program might inform victims of their right to state compensation funds.[26] As the previous chapter explained, these funds are available even if the perpetrator is not apprehended. As these programs gain popularity, victim services providers must be ready to assist law enforcement agencies in setting up their own program and working with these agencies to ensure that victims of crime are informed of their rights.

Prosecutors

The duties of prosecutors and law enforcement officers often overlap within the criminal justice process. Police make arrests, conduct investigations, interrogate suspects, and file cases with the district attorney's office. Many times prosecutors accompany police on raids, sit in on interrogations, and conduct their own follow-up investigations. Just as these two principles in the criminal justice system work together to attain a conviction of the perpetrator, so must they coordinate their efforts in working with victims and their interaction with the criminal justice system. In no place is this more important than during the sentencing phase of any trial.

Our criminal justice system is slowly beginning to recognize that its failure to grant victims an active role in the dispensation of justice is shortsighted because the continued successful functioning of the prosecutor's office depends on the cooperation and assistance of victims. Traditionally, prosecutor's offices have been assigned the role of creating and administrating victim assistance programs. This role was viewed as necessary in that prosecutors have a vested interest in facilitating victim participation in the system.[27]

Placing victim assistance programs in prosecutors' offices provide them with a number of advantages: they have instant access to information about the victim's physical, emotional, and financial status which can assist in charging or deposition of cases; they will lessen the chances that an adversarial relationship will develop between the victim and the prosecutor; and they can favorably influence the victim's decision regarding any proposed plea bargain.[28]

Prosecutors should establish policies and procedures that assign agency responsibility for the distribution and collection of victim impact statements. These guidelines should address the issue of coordination between the various agencies in the criminal justice system. This coordination is necessary so that victims are not filling out two, three, or more impact forms and more importantly, so that victims are not overlooked in the system.

Prosecutors should also ensure that victims are informed of the policies and procedures surrounding the victim impact statement including the following: the purpose and use of the impact statement; who is eligible to submit a statement; how it should be submitted (written, oral, video, etc.); how the court will use the statement; and how to request assistance with filling out the statement. This information will not only assist the prosecutor in arguing for an appropriate sentence, but will also make the victim feel part of the system. Working with crime victims and helping them to prepare a victim impact statement offers a prosecutor a chance to become more responsive to the needs of victims, and thereby improve the nature of the criminal justice system.

Some prosecutors may resist this active involvement with victims. Some may argue that this infringes on the discretion vested in prosecutors, whereas others will claim that victims do not understand the system, and they as prosecutors do not have the time to explain it to them. Just as some prosecutors resisted working with the staffs of rape crisis centers, others may resist this participation by victims of crimes. Victim services providers must be the advocates for these types of change. They are knowledgeable, and experienced, and they understand the system and can work with reluctant prosecutors to overcome any fears or concerns about working with victims of crime.

Judiciary

Crime is an extremely personal phenomenon and therefore no two victims will experience the same emotional, physical, or financial impact. It is imperative that judges have access to all pertinent information prior to sentencing so that they can balance society's needs, the defendant's needs, and the victim's needs. One method of balancing these needs is through the use of victim impact statements.

The *President's Task Force on Victims of Crime* addressed the issue of victim participation at sentencing by stating:

> Victims, no less than defendants, are entitled to their day in court. Victims, no less than defendants, are entitled to have their views considered. A judge cannot evaluate the seriousness of a defendant's conduct without knowing how the crime

has burdened the victim. A judge cannot reach an informed determination of the danger posed by a defendant without hearing from the person he has victimized.[29]

Judges should participate in this victim impact process by ensuring that victims are made aware of the opportunity to present their views prior to sentencing. This presentation of their position should be facilitated by judges, and victims should be allowed to present victim impact evidence in a variety of methods including orally, in writing, by video, or via any other method that accurately presents the victim's feelings to the court.

Americans have always believed that the ultimate responsibility for how the judicial system operates rests with judges. Judges should ensure that victims participate at the sentencing hearing which, with the exception of parole hearings, is the last opportunity that they have to influence the fate of the offender. Allowing victims to be part of this hearing can reaffirm their beliefs in the judicial system.

Effect of Victim Impact Statements

Victim Satisfaction

The effect of victim impact statements is still being studied and debated. One area being studied carefully is victim satisfaction with victim impact statements. Some authorities believe impact statements help the victim emotionally deal with the consequences of the crime. Others believe victims are more satisfied with the criminal justice system if they participate by being allowed to express their feelings in a victim impact statement. This section will briefly examine these and other aspects of victim satisfaction and victim impact statements.

In 1981, a National Institute of Justice study revealed that victims' satisfaction with the criminal justice system increased if they believed that they had influenced the process, regardless of whether they really had. For example, victims who had been able to speak to prosecutors and judges were more satisfied with the system than those who believed they were not able to speak.[30] In 1982, another study indicated that a sense of participation was more critical to victims' satisfaction with the criminal justice process than how severely the defendant was punished.[31] In 1984,

---

FOCUS: Feelings Regarding Victim Impact Statements

"My victim impact statement was the last opportunity I had to let anyone know about my daughter."

—a victim

"I want you to go over each victim impact statement. . . . You have to live with the stupidity of your behavior for the rest of your life, but you also have to understand what these families have to live with as well. . . .

—Judge to a defendant at time of sentencing[32]

another study revealed that victims wanted more information about their case and the opportunity to tell the prosecutor and judge how the case affected them.[33]

In 1989, Dean Kilpatrick reported the results of his research which indicated that victim participation not only affected potential cooperation within the criminal justice system, but that it was also critical in promoting victims' recovery from the aftermath of crime by helping them to reassert a sense of control over their lives.[34] Kilpatrick states that a criminal justice system which denies victims a chance to participate fosters a sense of helplessness and lack of control. He points out that there is a great danger in promising victims participation in the system and then failing to follow through with that promise, because it results in further victimization.

Robert Wells, another noted authority, states that victim impact statements may promote the psychological recovery of victims. Just as talking about what happened promotes healing, writing about it may also assist victims to emotionally deal with the crime. Allowing victims to tell how they were affected by the crime sends a supportive message that the criminal justice system cares about what happened.[35]

However, other experts claim the mental and emotional benefits of victim impact statements and victim participation are overrated. In a 1985 study carried out in Brooklyn, Davis compared the outcome of two court experiments in which victims gave impact statements in one court, and where no statements were allowed in another court. He found no evidence that victims in the court that mandated impact statements felt a greater sense of participation or increased satisfaction.[36] Davis followed this research with a 1989 study in the Bronx Supreme Court in New York.[37] The study analyzed 293 victims of robbery, nonsexual assault, and burglary. Each victim was assigned to one of three classifications: (1) some victims were interviewed and a victim impact statement written and distributed, (2) other victims were interviewed, but no impact statement was prepared, and (3) only the name and address of the victim was recorded. A series of interviews was conducted with each victim. The results of this study indicated that victim impact statements are not an effective means of promoting victim satisfaction within the criminal justice system. There were no data to support the theory that victim impact statements led to greater feelings of involvement, greater satisfaction with the criminal justice system, or greater satisfaction with the sentences imposed on the offenders. Davis concluded that more research is necessary regarding the effect of impact statements on victim satisfaction with the system.

As this discussion indicates, controversy continues over the effect of victim impact statements on victim satisfaction. However, there is sufficient individual and anecdotal evidence of victim approval of the use of impact statements that we should continue using them until definitive studies can be conducted. The next section examines whether victim impact statements affect the outcome of sentencing.

Sentencing

There is limited research on the effect that victim impact statements have on judges. Superficially, it would appear that such evidence can only assist the court in rendering its decision and therefore should be readily accepted and consistently used by the judicial system. However, judges, like every other member of the criminal justice system, are understaffed and overworked. Does additional information really help or does the process simply take more time? Are judges swayed by the emotional appeal of a citizen or are they bound to render impartial justice to the defendant?

Early research indicates that state trial court judges found financial information contained in a victim impact statement useful in determining appropriate sentences and restitution orders.[38] Of those judges interviewed, 70 percent found the information useful and another 20 percent found it useful in regard to restitution orders. Although this research indicates victim impact evidence is useful to judges, this "usefulness" appears limited to the area of restitution and financial issues, and not to other aspects of sentencing the defendant.

In 1990, Erez and Tontodonato produced an important study involving five hundred Ohio felony cases and found that the cases in which a victim impact statement was taken were more likely than those without a statement to result in the offender going to prison rather than receiving probation.[39] This research has been cited by a number of victim impact statement proponents as authority for the position that such statements have an effect on sentencing. Although this study was significant, it had several flaws including a wide disparity in offense seriousness between cases that had impact statements. Additionally, the authors acknowledged that further research needed to be conducted in this area.

Davis and Smith also researched the effect of impact statements on sentencing. In the same 1989 study that examined victim satisfaction, Davis and his associate evaluated the significance of impact statements on judicial sentencing.[40] They concluded that victim impact statements did not produce sentences that reflect the effects of crime on the victims. Nor did they find that sentencing decisions were affected by impact statements once the charge and the defendant's prior record were considered by the court. They did find that the severity of the charges is a high predictor of sentences. Whereas judges professed to be interested in impact statements, prosecutors believed that judges only occasionally considered this information when imposing sentences. Conversely, prosecutors claimed that victims should be consulted on a regular basis, but judges stated that prosecutors rarely related impact evidence to them.

Clearly more research is also needed in this area. Additionally, such research must find a way to get around the "political correctness" of advocating the use of victim impact statements. As Davis's study points out, judges claim they endorse impact statements, but prosecutors don't believe them. On the other hand, the same prosecutors claim they use impact statements, but the judges don't see them. Realistically, few elected or appointed officials in today's climate within the criminal justice system will admit to anything less than wholehearted endorsement of victim impact statements. What is needed is an in-depth study to determine the impact of such evidence outside the realm of political correctness. Until such research is done, we can only speculate on its real effect.

Victim Impact Panels

Introduction

Victim impact panels (VIPs) differ significantly from victim impact statements. However, because they involve victims discussing the impact of the offense on their lives, they are included in this chapter rather than elsewhere in this text. MADD established victim impact panels as a method of dealing with the problem of drunk driving.[41] MADD does not believe that victim impact panels should replace traditional criminal sanctions for driving under the influence. They are offered to enhance and supplement such sentencing by placing offenders face to face with victims of drunk driving whose lives have been changed by someone who drank and then got behind the wheel of a car.

Procedure

MADD or other victim groups select a panel of three to four victims to speak briefly about the drunk driving crashes in which they were injured or a loved one was killed, and what the event has meant to them. They do not blame or judge the attendees. A victim impact panel coordinator moderates the panel, and victims are never allowed to speak at groups in which their own offender is present. The attendees are convicted drunk drivers who are required to attend a panel as an element of their sentences. A probation officer or other agent of the court attends each panel to monitor attendance. Any person who fails to appear for a panel is required to return to court for appropriate action.[42]

Victims who have served on these panels find that telling their stories lightens their personal pain and assists in the healing process. Victims also report that they have experienced something positive from a previously devastating event and they believe that by telling their stories they may be preventing some other family from suffering a similar fate.[43]

The goals of the victim impact panel are to enhance the emotional healing of victims by offering them an opportunity to speak out about the incident. These panels also enable attendees to understand drunk driving from the victim's perspective. Hopefully these stories will curtail the attendees' decisions to drink and drive.

Victim impact panels are different than victim impact statements. However, they both serve to allow victims to express their feelings regarding the consequences of a crime. The opportunity to express feelings regarding the event can be a valuable healing process. Although victim impact panels are relatively new within the criminal justice system, they offer another sentencing option to judges.

Summary

Victim impact statements are now accepted as a constitutionally firm mechanism that may be used in criminal cases, whether these cases are simple assaults or death penalty cases. The use of these statements is governed by the principle of fundamental fairness which requires courts to ensure that the defendant receives a fair trial. A properly conducted victim impact statement does not violate this mandate.

To be effective, the victim impact statement must be accepted by all parties within the criminal justice system. Law enforcement officers should be aware of it and be prepared to inform victims of its availability. Prosecutors are the logical choices to coordinate victim impact statements and should take the lead. Judges are looked upon as the final authority within the criminal justice system and they should demand that the victim have an opportunity to speak at sentencing.

Controversy continues regarding the effectiveness of victim impact statements. More research needs to be conducted on both the issue of victim satisfaction and the effect of impact statements on sentencing. However, victim impact statements should continue to be used because some evidence supports the fact that victims believe the statements are an important right to which they should be afforded.

Victim impact panels are a new technique that offer victims of drunk driving the opportunity to express their feelings. They are similar to victim impact statements in that victims believe they serve a useful function. We must continue to explore alternative mechanisms that assist victims of crime in overcoming the consequences of the criminal act.

Key Terms

Victim impact statement presents the victim's point of view to the sentencing authority.
Doctrine of fundamental fairness accepts the concept that due process is a generalized command that requires states to provide the defendant with a fair trial.

Discussion Questions

1. Explain and give concrete examples of fundamental fairness. Can you list ways in which a victim impact statement would violate this constitutional standard?

2. Should law enforcement officers inform the victim of a crime about victim impact statements? Prepare a form that should be given to victims outlining their rights.

3. How are we ever going to determine if victim impact statements serve a valid purpose in the criminal justice system? How would you structure such a study? What are the pitfalls inherent in these types of studies?

4. Should a drunk driver be mandated to attend a victim impact panel? Why? Justify your answer.

Suggested Readings

Robert Wells, "Victim Impact Statements," *Crime Victim and Witness Assistance Training Project*, (Federal Law Enforcement Training Center, Glyno, Georgia) 1990.

Ellen K. Alexander & Janice H. Lord, *Impact Statements: A Victim's Right to Speak-A Nation's Responsibility to Listen*, (National Victims Center, Arlington, Va.) 1992.

Janice H. Lord, *Victim Impact Panels: A Creative Sentencing Opportunity*, (Mothers Against Drunk Driving, Dallas) 1990.

Endnotes

1. This section has been adapted from H. Wallace, *Family Violence: Legal Medical and Social Perspectives*, (Allyn & Bacon, Boston) 1996.
2. See Phillip A. Talbert, "The Relevance of Victim Impact Statements to the Criminal Sentencing Decision," 36 *UCLA L Rev* 199, 202–211 (1988); and Maureen McLeod, "Victim Participation at Sentencing," 22 *Crim L. Bull.* 501, 505–511 (1986).
3. *Booth v. Maryland*, 482 U.S. 496 (1987).
4. Id. at 500–01.
5. Id. at 509. The Court did, however, carefully note that information typically contained in a victim's statement is generally admissible in noncapital cases and may be considered in capital cases if directly related to the circumstances of the crime. Id. at 508 n. 10. For example, the Court noted that the prosecution may produce evidence as to the characteristics of the victim to rebut an argument made by the defendant (e.g., victim's peaceable nature to rebut claim of self-defense.) Id.
6. Id. at 507–07 (citations omitted).
7. Id. at 505–07.
8. Id. at 507–08.
9. Id.
10. Id.
11. Id.
12. 490 U.S. 805 (1989).
13. 115 L.ED. 728–729.
14. 115 L.Ed. 734–735.
15. 115 L.Ed. 2d 735.
16. 115 L.Ed. 748.
17. 115 L.Ed. 756.
18. See Jimmie O. Clements, Jr., *Casenote, Criminal Law—Victim Impact Evidence—The Scope of the Eight Amendment Does Not Include a Per Se Bar to the Use of Victim Impact Evidence in the Sentencing Phase of a Capital Trial Payne v. Tennessee.* 23 St. Mary's L. J. 517 (1991); Aida Alaka, *Note, Victim Impact Evidence, Arbitrariness and the Death Penalty: The Supreme Court Flipflops in Payne v. Tennessee*, 23 Loy. U. Chi. L.J. 581 (1992); K. Elizabeth Whitehead, *Case Note, Mourning Becomes Electric: Payne v. Tennessee's Allowance of Victim Impact Statements During Capital Proceedings*, 45 Ark. L. Rev. 531 (1992).
19. Powell v. Alabama, 287 U.S. 45, 53 S.C. 55, 77 L.Ed. 158(1932).
20. 297 U.S. 278, 56 S.Ct. 461, 80 L.Ed. 682 (1936).
21. This section has been adapted from Robert Wells, "Victim Impact Statements," *Crime Victim and Witness Assistance Training Project*, (Federal Law Enforcement Training Center, Glyno, Georgia) 1990, hereinafter *Crime Victim and Witness Assistance*.
22. *The New Republic*, p. 9 (April 17, 1995).
23. Id.
24. *Crime Victim and Witness Assistance*.
25. Ellen K. Alexander & Janice H. Lord, *Impact Statements: A Victim's Right to Speak—A Nation's Responsibility to Listen*, (National Victim Center, Arlington, Va.) 1992, hereinafter *Impact Statements*.
26. Id. at p. 10.
27. Id. at p. 14.
28. Id.
29. *President's Task Force on Victims of Crime: Final Report*, (GPO, Washington, D.C.) 1982, p. 77.
30. Barbara Smith & Susan Hillanbrand, *Non-Stranger Violence: The Criminal Courts Responses,*

(National Institute of Justice, Washington, D.C.) 1981.

31. Deborah P. Kelly, "Delivering Legal Services to Victims: An Evaluation and Prescription," 9 *Justice System Journal,* 62 (1982).

32. *Impact Statements* pp. 10, 17.

33. J. Hernon & B. Forst, "The Criminal Justice Response to Victim Harm," *Research Report,* (National Institute of Justice, Washington, D.C.) 1984.

34. Dean Kilpatrick & Randy K. Otto, "Constitutionally Guaranteed Participation in Criminal Proceedings for Victims: Potential Effects on Psychological Functioning," 34 *The Wayne State Law Review,* 17 (1989).

35. Robert Wells, "Victim Impact: How Much Consideration Is It Really Given?" *The Police Chief,* p. 44 (February 1991).

36. Robert C. Davis, *First Year Evaluation of the Victim Impact Demonstration Project,* (Victim Services Agency, New York) 1985.

37. Robert C. Davis & Barbara E. Smith, "Victim Impact Statements and Victim Satisfaction: An Unfulfilled Promise," 22 *Journal of Criminal Justice,* 1 (1994).

38. Susan Hillenbrand, *Victim Rights Legislation: An Assessment of Its Impact on the Criminal Justice System,* (American Bar Association, Chicago) 1987.

39. E. Erez & P. Tontodonato, "The Effect of Victim Participation in Sentencing on Sentence Outcomes," 28 *Criminology,* 451 (1990).

40. Robert C. Davis & Barbara E. Smith, "The Effects of Victim Impact Statements on Sentencing Decisions: A Test in an Urban Setting," 11/3 *Justice Quarterly,* 453 (September 1994).

41. This section has been adapted from Janice H. Lord, *Victim Impact Panels: A Creative Sentencing Opportunity,* (Mothers Against Drunk Driving, Dallas) 1990. Used with permission of MADD.

42. Id. at p. 6.

43. Id. at p. 10.

E p i l o g u e

There are many challenges in the field of victimology. In the previous edition, a series of emerging topics was listed: campus crime, stalking, workplace violence, and others. Some, such as gang violence, are looked at a bit more closely in this edition than in the first, but all of them are still are in need of further study. However, rather than list specific areas for study, this epilogue discusses broad themes that need to be researched and acted upon.

Lack of Research

There are so many areas within the discipline of victimology that cry out for research. Some research has already been done and has raised additional questions, while other areas need initial or groundbreaking study. As with any new discipline, areas for new research are limited only by the imagination.

We need to preserve our history. Many of the outstanding leaders in victimology are growing older. Some of the early leaders have already passed away. There are a number of excellent articles dealing with the history of victimology. However, unlike other significant historical events no one has yet established an oral history of victimology. A number of professionals, advocates, and academics have lived through the various phases of the discipline of victimology. All of their recollections, sometimes conflicting in nature, need to be preserved for those who follow after us.

We do not yet understand the causes of either crime or its enduring impact on victims. More research is need in the area of family violence, effectiveness of restraining orders and victim impact statements, and social and psychological effects on victims of crime, just to list a few areas. Simply select a chapter in this text, and review the literature or lack thereof on any academic search engine and you will find noticeable gaps in knowledge and application.

When the first edition of this text was published in 1998, there were very few academic or professional journals that discussed various aspects of victimology.

However, with the passage of time and the increased awareness of this discipline both within the general public and academe, we have seen an increase in journals at both the national and international level. While there are a number of criminal justice, profiling, and cop shows on television, victimology and victim services have not yet captured the public's interest. This is regrettable because the human drama and emotions encountered in victim advocacy are as intense as—and sometimes even more intense than—that in any of the existing crime dramas on television today.

The Continued Change from a Movement to a Discipline

Many persons in victim services still refer to it as a movement. We must progress and change that thinking to embrace the concept that victimology and victim services are a discipline. A movement is defined as an organized effort to promote or attain a specific end. For example, we think of the efforts to bring equality to our society as the Civil Rights Movement. To most people, a movements connotes passionate and zealous attempt to reach a broad goals. A discipline, by contrast, is defined as a subject that is taught or training that corrects, molds, or perfects the mental faculties or moral character.[1] Disciplines are thought of as learned professions. It may be that victimology continues to be both a movement and a discipline. Being a movement that encompasses passion and zeal while relying on education and training is perhaps what victimology should be.

Broadening Horizons to Embrace International Victimology

As discussed in Chapter 15, international victimology continues to gain recognition and respect within the United States. Our world is shrinking and what happens to victims of a tsunami in the Far East affects our thinking and feelings in the United States. We can also learn from other countries' efforts in the field of victimology.

International conferences and organizations continue to gain members from the United States. These memberships allow for the informal and formal transmission of knowledge. More importantly a network of advocates, professionals, and academics is developing that allow for the instantaneous exchange of promising practices and emerging trends.

Professionalism in Victimology and Victim Services

Victimology is a relatively new academic discipline. Increasingly, universities are offering courses in victimology through various departments: criminology or criminal justice, sociology, social work, psychology, and women studies departments, to mention just a few. Only a few universities offer degrees specifically related to victimology. With the passage of time, it is clear that victimology as an academic discipline will gain wider acceptance and academic degrees will become more available to those who wish to study this profession. Victimology degrees involve a combination of disciplines, including victimology, victim services, law, counseling, psychology, and public policy, to name a few. A sample curriculum, which is currently offered by the Criminology Department at California State University—Fresno, is attached as Appendix A.

Similar to many other new occupations, there are barriers to changing victim services status from merely an occupation to a profession. Traditionally, victim advocates were victims who had suffered pain and hardship as the result of the crime or had been revictimized in the criminal justice system. They became advocates to help others and to prevent them from suffering the type of abuse they endured. Many of these advocates relied on word-of-mouth training or utilized their own experiences or learned on the job. A great number of these early advocates provided outstanding support to victims of crime. However, with time, there came an acknowledgement that more training and education was necessary to fully prepare advocates serving victims of crime. It was hoped that this additional training and education would lead toward professionalism within the field of victim advocacy.

There were and are several obstacles that face this move toward professionalism. The first is defining what is a profession, the second deals with the authority or credentials necessary to perform the duties of the position, the third concerns the type of skills required to perform various functions within the field, and the fourth concerns establishing a standard of ethics for service providers.

Victim Advocacy as a Profession

Perhaps one of the earliest calls for professionalism within the field occurred with the publication of Marlene A. Young's 1993 text, *Victim Assistance: Frontiers and Fundamentals*,[2] in which Young sets forth the nature of professions, discusses the process of professionalization in victim services, and proposes a code of ethics. Experts such as Underwood and Hook have also discussed professionalism within the context of victim advocacy. They attempt to define it in the form of certain characteristics. Thomas Underwood states that the concept of professionalism involves a dynamic process that allows for consideration of the extent of professionalization that an occupation has achieved based on various characteristics.[3] Melissa Hook analyzes ethics as they relate to victim service professionals.[4] She uses as a basis for this analysis the research conducted by the OVC-funded National Victim Assistance Standards Consortium, whose goal was to create a model for competency and ethics for victim services providers.

The evolution of victim advocacy as profession in many ways resembles the transformation of law enforcement from an occupation to a profession. The move toward professionalism in law enforcement started in the 1800s and continues today. Law enforcement has moved from the layperson simply pinning on a badge and acting as an officer to one that requires formal training in state or federal academies prior to being sworn in as a peace officer.[5] More and more programs require, or list as a preference some sort of formal training in victim advocacy before allowing individuals the opportunity to work in the field.

Credentials or Authority to Perform the Duties of the Profession

What authority or credentials should a victim advocate possess in order to perform his or her duties? At present, a person may be employed without any formal training in many victim advocate programs. Some of these programs have internal training and others rely on university—based education. Some states have mandatory state training that prospective victim advocates must undergo. Some argue for a national set of standards that all victim advocates should possess. Others feel that state licensure should be required to practice as a victim advocate. However, at this stage of our evolution as a profession, there is not one accepted standard that all agencies adhere to.

Skills Required for Various Functions within the Field

Several prominent researchers, including Dr. Thomas Underwood and Dr. Steven Walker, have addressed the skills required of a victim advocate. A review of their work indicates that victim advocates need at least three types of skills: Legal, management, and personal skills.

1. Legal skills include public policy knowledge. Advocates need knowledge of victim's rights, the criminal and civil justice systems, public policy and implementation, and research ability, to name just a few of the skills any professional working as an advocate should possess.
2. Management includes budgeting and personnel experience. Victim advocacy is more than simply offering services to victims of crime. It requires that budgets be maintained, grants written, and programs administered. The victim advocate of today is by all definitions a corporate executive in everything but name.
3. Personal skills include responding to the needs of victims and their families. This is considered the most important aspect of victim advocacy; however, it cannot be accomplished effectively without the use of legal and management skills. Responding to the needs of victims includes not only offering advice and support but also having a practical knowledge of counseling and intervention skills, death notification protocols, stress management, and so on.

Ethical Standards for Victim Services Providers

Victim advocates deal with persons who are vulnerable, who lack knowledge about the system, and who are in desperate need of assistance. In the past there have been isolated incidents in which advocates have taken advantage of victims or violated their trust. Furthermore, almost all acknowledged professions have a standard of ethical behavior. Hook suggests that ethical issues in this profession include duel relationships and boundaries (friend vs. client), the issue of confidentiality, and legal responsibilities and liabilities. Young sets forth classifications based on relationships with victims, relationships with colleagues other professionals, and public and professional conduct. Both Young's treatise and Hook's text offer detailed analyse of some of the ethical dilemmas faced by victim advocates.

Evolution as a profession continues with each encounter with a victim. The same zeal and passion that motivated early leaders to form what are now national organizations should be focused on attaining professional status for the victim service occupation. Hopefully, within the next few years, our avocation will become a discipline and a profession.

Endnotes

1. *Webster's Ninth New Collegiate Dictionary,* (1981).
2. Marlene Young, *Victim Assistance: Frontiers and Fundamentals,* NOVA, Washington, D.C. (1993).
3. Thomas Underwood, "Professinalizing the Discipline of Victim Services," *National Victim Assistance Text,* Office for Victims of Crime, U.S. Department of Justice, Washington, D.C. (2003).
4. Melissa Hook, *Ethics in Victim Services,* Sidran Institute Press, Baltimore, Md. (2005).
5. H. Wallace, C. Roberson and C. Steckler, *Fundamental of Police Administration,* Prentice Hall, Englewood Cliffs, N.J. (1995).

Appendix

CRITICAL DATES IN THE VICTIMS' RIGHTS MOVEMENT

1972

- The first three victim assistance programs are created:
  - —Aid for Victims of Crime in St. Louis, Missouri;
  - —Bay Area Women Against Rape in San Francisco, California; and
  - —Rape Crisis Center in Washington, D.C.

1974

- The Federal Law Enforcement Assistance Administration (LEAA) funds the first victim–witness programs in the Brooklyn and Milwaukee District Attorneys' offices, plus seven others through a grant to the National District Attorneys Association, to create model programs of assistance for victims, encourage victim cooperation, and improve prosecution.
- The first law enforcement-based victim assistance programs are established in Fort Lauderdale, Florida, and Indianapolis, Indiana.
- The U.S. Congress passes the Child Abuse Prevention and Treatment Act which establishes the National Center on Child Abuse and Neglect (NCCAN). The new Center creates an information clearinghouse and provides technical assistance and model programs.

1975

- The first "Victims' Rights Week" is organized by the Philadelphia District Attorney.

- Citizen activists from across the country unite to expand victim services and increase recognition of victims' rights through the formation of the National Organization for Victim Assistance (NOVA).

1976

- The National Organization for Women forms a task force to examine the problem of battering. It demands research into the problem, along with money for battered women's shelters.
- Nebraska becomes the first state to abolish the marital rape exemption.
- The first national conference on battered women is sponsored by the Milwaukee Task Force on Women in Milwaukee, Wisconsin.
- In Fresno County, California, Chief Probation Officer James Rowland creates the first victim impact statement to provide the judiciary with an objective inventory of victim injuries and losses prior to sentencing.
- Women's advocates in St. Paul, Minnesota starts the first hotline for battered women. Women's Advocates and Haven House in Pasadena, California, establish the first shelters for battered women.
- Victimology: 1st scholarly journal published by Emilio Viano An International Journal.

1977

- Oregon becomes the first state to enact mandatory arrest in domestic violence cases.

1978

- The National Coalition Against Sexual Assault (NCASA) is formed to combat sexual violence and promote services for rape victims.
- The National Coalition Against Domestic Violence (NCADV) is organized as a voice for the battered women's movement on a national level. NCADV initiates the introduction of the Family Violence Prevention and Services Act in the U.S. Congress.
- Parents of Murdered Children (POMC), a self-help support group, is founded in Cincinnati, Ohio.
- Minnesota becomes the first state to allow probable cause (warrantless) arrest in cases of domestic assault, regardless of whether a protection order had been issued.

1979

- Frank G. Carrington, considered by many to be "the father of the victims' rights movement," founds the Crime Victims' Legal Advocacy Institute, Inc., to promote the rights of crime victims in the civil and criminal justice systems. The nonprofit organization was renamed VALOR, the Victims' Assistance Legal Organization, Inc., in 1981.

- The Office on Domestic Violence is established in the U.S. Department of Health and Human Services, but is later closed in 1981.

- The U.S. Congress fails to enact the Federal Law Enforcement Assistance Administration (LEAA) and federal funding for victims' programs is phased out. Many grassroots and "system-based" programs close.

1980

- Mothers Against Drunk Driving (MADD) is founded after the death of thirteen-year-old Cari Lightner, who was killed by a repeat offender drunk driver. The first two MADD chapters are created in Sacramento, California, and Annapolis, Maryland.

- The U.S. Congress passes the Parental Kidnapping Prevention Act of 1980.

- Wisconsin passes the first "Crime Victims' Bill of Rights."

- The First National Day of Unity in October is established by NCADV to mourn battered women who have died, celebrate women who have survived the violence, and honor all who have worked to defeat domestic violence. This Day becomes Domestic Violence Awareness Week and, in 1987, expands to a month of awareness activities each October.

- NCADV holds its first national conference in Washington, D.C., which gains federal recognition of critical issues facing battered women, and sees the birth of several state coalitions.

- The first Victim Impact Panel is sponsored by Remove Intoxicated Drivers (RID) in Oswego County, New York.

1981

- Ronald Reagan becomes the first President to proclaim "Crime Victims' Rights Week" in April.

- The disappearance and murder of missing child Adam Walsh prompts a national campaign to raise public awareness about child abduction and enact laws to better protect children.

- The Attorney General's Task Force on Violent Crime recommends that a separate Task Force be created to consider victims' issues.

1982

- In a Rose Garden ceremony, President Reagan appoints the Task Force on Victims of Crime, which holds public hearings in six cities across the nation to create a greatly needed national focus on the needs of crime victims. The Task

Force *Final Report* offers 68 recommendations that become the framework for the advancement of new programs and policies.

- The Federal Victim and Witness Protection Act of 1982 brings "fair treatment standards" to victims and witnesses in the federal criminal justice system.
- California voters overwhelmingly pass Proposition 8, which guarantees restitution and other statutory reforms to crime victims.
- The passage of the Missing Children's Act of 1982 helps parents guarantee that identifying information of their missing child is promptly entered into the FBI National Crime Information Center (NCIC) computer system.
- The first Victim Impact Panel sponsored by MADD, which educates drunk drivers about the devastating impact of their criminal acts, is organized in Rutland, Massachusetts.

1983

- The Office for Victims of Crime (OVC) is created by the U.S. Department of Justice within the Office of Justice Programs to implement recommendations from the President's Task Force on Victims of Crime.
- The U.S. Attorney General establishes a Task Force on Family Violence, which holds six public hearings across the United States.
- The U.S. Attorney General issues guidelines for federal victim and witness assistance.
- In April, President Reagan honors crime victims in a White House Rose Garden ceremony.
- The First National Conference of the Judiciary on Victims of Crime is held at the National Judicial College in Reno, Nevada.
- President Reagan proclaims the first National Missing Children's Day in observance of the disappearance of missing child Etan Patz.
- The International Association of Chiefs of Police Board of Governors adopts a Crime Victims' Bill of Rights and establishes a victims' rights committee to bring about renewed emphasis on the needs of crime victims by law enforcement officials nationwide.

1984

- The passage of the Victims Of Crime Act (VOCA) establishes the Crime Victims Fund, made up of federal criminal fines, penalties and bond forfeitures, to support state victim compensation and local victim service programs.
- President Reagan signs the Justice Assistance Act, which establishes a financial assistance program for state and local government and funds 200 new victim service programs.

- The National Minimum Drinking Age Act of 1984 is enacted, providing strong incentives to states without "21" laws to raise the minimum age for drinking, saving thousands of young lives in years to come.
- The National Center for Missing and Exploited Children (NCMEC) is created as the national resource for missing children. Passage of the Missing Children's Assistance Act provides a Congressional mandate for the Center.
- The Spiritual Dimension in Victim Services is founded to involve the religious community in violence prevention and victim assistance.
- The U.S. Congress passes the Family Violence Prevention and Services Act, which earmarks federal funding for programs serving victims of domestic violence.
- Concerns of Police Survivors (COPS) is organized at the first police survivors' seminar held in Washington, D.C., by 100 relatives of officers killed in the line of duty.
- The first National Symposium on Sexual Assault is co-sponsored by the Office of Justice Programs and the Federal Bureau of Investigation.
- A victim–witness notification system is established within the Federal Bureau of Prisons.
- The Office for Victims of Crime hosts the first national symposium on child molestation.
- Victim–Witness Coordinator positions are established in the U.S. Attorneys' offices within the U.S. Department of Justice.
- California State University, Fresno, initiates the first Victim Services Certificate Program offered for academic credit by a university.
- Remove Intoxicated Drivers (RID) calls for a comprehensive Sane National Alcohol Policy (SNAP) to curb aggressive promotions aimed at youth.

1985

- The Federal Crime Victims' Fund deposits total $68 million.
- The National Victim Center is founded in honor of Sunny von Bulow to promote the rights and needs of crime victims, and to educate Americans about the devastating effect of crime on our society.
- The United Nations General Assembly passes the International Declaration on the UN Declaration of Basic Principles of Justice for Victims of Crime and the Abusive Power.
- President Reagan announces a Child Safety Partnership with twenty-six members. Its mission is to enhance private sector efforts to promote child safety, to clarify information about child victimization, and to increase public awareness of child abuse.
- The U.S. Surgeon General issues a report identifying domestic violence as a major public health problem.

1986

- The Office for Victims of Crime awards the first grants to support state victim compensation and assistance programs.
- Rhode Island passes a constitutional amendment granting victims the right to restitution, to submit victim impact statements, and to be treated with dignity and respect.
- MADD's "Red Ribbon Campaign" enlists motorists to display a red ribbon on their automobiles, pledging to drive safe and sober during the holidays. This national public awareness effort has since become an annual campaign.

1987

- The Victims' Constitutional Amendment Network (VCAN) and Steering Committee is formed at a meeting hosted by the National Victim Center.
- Security on Campus, Inc. (SOC) is established by Howard and Connie Clery, following the tragic robbery, rape, and murder of their daughter Jeanne at Lehigh University in Pennsylvania. SOC raises national awareness about the hidden epidemic of violence on our nation's campuses.
- The American Correctional Association establishes a Task Force on Victims of Crime.
- NCADV establishes the first national toll-free domestic violence hotline.

1988

- The National Aging Resource Center on Elder Abuse (NARCEA) is established in a cooperative agreement among the American Public Welfare Association, the National Association of State Units on Aging, and the University of Delaware. Renamed the National Center on Elder Abuse, it continues to provide information and statistics.
- *State v. Ciskie* is the first case to allow the use of expert testimony to explain the behavior and mental state of an adult rape victim. The testimony is used to show why a victim of repeated physical and sexual assaults by her intimate partner would not immediately call the police or take action. The jury convicts the defendant on four counts of rape.
- The Federal Drunk Driving Prevention Act is passed, and states raise the minimum drinking age to 21.
- Constitutional amendments are introduced in Arizona, California, Connecticut, Delaware, Michigan, South Carolina and Washington. Florida's amendment is placed on the November ballot where it passes with 90 percent of the vote. Michigan's constitutional amendment passes with over 80 percent of the vote.
- The first "Indian Nations: Justice for Victims of Crime" conference is sponsored by the Office for Victims of Crime in Rapid City, South Dakota.

- VOCA amendments legislatively establish the Office for Victims of Crime, elevate the position of Director by making Senate confirmation necessary for appointment, and induce state compensation programs to cover victims of homicide and drunk driving.

1989

- The legislatures in Texas and Washington pass their respective constitutional amendments, which are both ratified by voters in November.

1990

- The Federal Crime Victims' Fund deposits total over $146 million.
- The U.S. Congress passes the Hate Crime Statistics Act requiring the U.S. Attorney General to collect data of incidence of certain crimes motivated by prejudice based on race, religion, sexual orientation, or ethnicity.
- The Student Right-to-Know and Campus Security Act, requiring institutions of higher education to disclose murder, rape, robbery, and other crimes on campus, is signed into law by President Bush.
- The Child Protection Act of 1990, which features reforms to make the federal criminal justice system less traumatic for child victims and witnesses, is passed by the U.S. Congress.
- The first National Incidence Study on Missing, Abducted, Runaway, and Throwaway Children in America shows that over one million children fall victim to abduction annually.
- The National Child Search Assistance Act requires law enforcement to enter reports of missing children and unidentified persons in the NCIC computer.

1991

- U.S. Representative Ilena Ros-Lehtinen (R-FL) files the first Congressional Joint Resolution to place victims' rights in the U.S. Constitution.
- The Violence Against Women Act of 1991 is considered by the U.S. Congress.
- California State University, Fresno, approves the first Bachelors Degree Program in Victimology in the nation.
- The Campus Sexual Assault Victims' Bill of Rights Act is introduced in the U.S. Congress.
- The results of the first national public opinion poll to examine citizens' attitudes about violence and victimization, *America Speaks Out*, are released by the National Victim Center during National Crime Victims' Rights Week.
- The U.S. Attorney General issues new comprehensive guidelines that establish procedures for the federal criminal justice system to respond to the needs of crime victims.

- The first national conference that addresses crime victims' rights and needs in corrections is sponsored by the Office for Victims of Crime in California.
- The first International Conference on Campus Sexual Assault is held in Orlando, Florida.
- The American Probation and Parole Association (APPA) establishes a Victim Issues Committee to examine victims' issues and concerns related to community corrections.
- The International Parental Child Kidnapping Act makes the act of unlawfully removing a child outside the United States a federal felony.
- The Spiritual Dimension in Victim Services facilitates a conference of leaders of thirteen religious denominations to plan ways in which these large religious bodies can increase awareness of crime victims' needs and provide appropriate services.
- The New Jersey legislature passes victims' rights constitutional amendment, which is ratified by voters in November.
- Colorado legislators introduce a constitutional amendment on the first day of National Crime Victims' Rights Week. Fifteen days later, the bill is unanimously passed by both Houses to be placed on the ballot in 1992.
- In an 8–0 decision, the U.S. Supreme Court ruled in *Simon & Schuster v. New York Crime Victims Board* that New York's notoriety-for-profit statute was overly broad and, in the final analysis, unconstitutional.

1992

- *Rape in America: A Report to the Nation,* clarifies the scope and devastating effect of rape in this nation, including the fact that 683,000 women are raped annually in the United States.
- The Association of Paroling Authorities, International establishes a Victim Issues Committee to examine victims' needs, rights, and services in parole processes.
- The U.S. Congress reauthorizes the Higher Education Bill which includes the Campus Sexual Assault Victims' Bill of Rights.
- The Battered Women's Testimony Act, which urges states to accept expert testimony in criminal cases involving battered women, is passed by Congress and signed into law by President Bush.
- In a unanimous decision, the U.S. Supreme Court—in *R.A.V. vs. City of St. Paul*—struck down a local hate crimes ordinance in Minnesota.
- Five states—Colorado, Kansas, Illinois, Missouri, and New Mexico—ratify constitutional amendments for victims' rights.
- Twenty-eight states pass anti-stalking legislation.
- Massachusetts passes a landmark bill creating a statewide computerized domestic violence registry and requires judges to check the registry when handling such cases.

1993

- Wisconsin ratifies its constitutional amendment for victims' rights, bringing the total number of states with these amendments to fourteen.
- President Clinton signs the "Brady Bill" requiring a waiting period for the purchase of handguns.
- Congress passes the Child Sexual Abuse Registry Act establishing a national repository for information on child sex offenders.
- Twenty-two states pass stalking statutes, bringing the total number of states with stalking laws to fifty, plus the District of Columbia.

1994

- The American Correctional Association Victims Committee publishes the landmark *Report and Recommendations on Victims of Juvenile Crime,* which offers guidelines for improving victims' rights and services when the offender is a juvenile.
- Six additional states pass constitutional amendments for victims' rights—the largest number ever in a single year—bringing the total number of states with amendments to twenty. States with new amendments include: Alabama, Alaska, Idaho, Maryland, Ohio, and Utah.
- President Clinton signs a comprehensive package of federal victims' rights legislation as part of the Violent Crime Control and Law Enforcement Act. The Act includes:
    —Violence Against Women Act, which authorizes more than $1 billion in funding for programs to combat violence against women.
    —Enhanced VOCA funding provisions.
    —Establishment of a National Child Sex Offender Registry.
    —Enhanced sentences for drunk drivers with child passengers.

1995

- The Federal Crime Victims' Fund deposits total $233,907,256.
- The Crime Victims' Rights Act of 1995 is introduced in the U.S. Congress.
- Legislatures in three states—Indiana, Nebraska, and North Carolina—pass constitutional amendments which will be placed on the ballot in 1996.
- The National Victims' Constitutional Amendment Network proposes the first draft of language for a federal constitutional amendment for victims' rights.
- The U.S. Department of Justice convenes a national conference to encourage implementation of the Violence Against Women Act.
- The first class graduates from the National Victim Assistance Academy in Washington, D.C. Supported by the Office for Victims of Crime, the

university-based Academy provides an academically credited 45-hour curriculum on victimology, victims' rights, and a myriad other topics.

1996

- Federal Victims' Rights Constitutional Amendments are introduced in both houses of Congress with bipartisan support.
- Both presidential candidates and the Attorney General endorse the concept of a Victims' Rights Constitutional Amendment.
- The Federal Crime Victims' Fund reaches an historic high with deposits totaling over $500 million.
- Eight states ratify the passage of constitutional amendments for victims' rights—raising the total number of state constitutional amendments to 29 nationwide.
- The Community Notification Act, known as "Megan's Law," provides for notifying communities of the location of convicted sex offenders by amendment to the national Child Sexual Abuse Registry legislation.
- President Clinton signs the Antiterrorism Act providing one million dollars in funding to strengthen antiterrorism efforts, making restitution mandatory in violent crime cases, and expanding the compensation and assistance services for victims of terrorism both at home and abroad, including victims in the military.
- The National Domestic Violence Hotline is established to provide crisis intervention information and referrals to victims of domestic violence and their friends and family.
- To fully recognize the sovereignty of Indian Nations, OVC for the first time provides all grants in Indian Country directly to the tribes.
- OVC launches a number of international crime victim initiatives including working to foster worldwide implementation of a United Nations declaration on victims' rights and working to better assist Americans who are victimized abroad.
- The VOCA definition of "crime victim" is expanded to include victims of financial crime, allowing this group to receive counseling, advocacy, and support services.
- The Church Arson Prevention Act is signed into law in response to an increasing number of acts of arson against religions institutions around the country.

1997

- The Federal Crime Victims Fund deposits total $363 million.
- Congress passes the Victims' Rights Clarification Act of 1997 to clarify existing federal law allowing victims to attend a trial and give Victim Impact Statements during sentencing both in capital and non capital cases.

- Congress enacts a federal anti-stalking law.
- OVC officially launches it web homepage allowing internet access to its comprehensive services.
- *New Directions from the Field: Victims' Rights ad Services for the 21ˢᵗ Century* is published by OVC.

1998

- Congress enacts the Child Protection and Sexual Predator Punishment Act providing for numerous sentencing enhancements and other initative addressing sex crimes against children.
- Congress passes the Crime victims with disabilities Act represent the first effort to gather information about the extent of victimization of individuals with disabilities.
- The Identity theft and Deterrence At is signed into law which outlaws identity theft.
- OVC provides funding to the U.S. Department of State to support a Victim Assistance Specialist to improve the coordination of services provided to U.S. citizens who become victimized abroad.

1999

- The Violence Against Women Act II is introduced in Congress.
- The fifth National victim Assistance Academy (NVAA) is held in June at five university locations across the United States.
- OVC issues the first grants to create State Victim Assistance Academies.
- The National Crime Victim Bar Association if formed to promote justice for victims of crime.

2000

- Congress passes a new national drunk driving limit of 0.08 blood alcohol concentration.
- President Clinton signs into law the Violence Against Women Act of 2000 extending the current law until 2005.
- The Internet Fraud Complaint Center Web site is created by the federal government to combat internet fraud.
- Congress passes the Trafficking Victims Protection Act to combat trafficking in persons.
- In November, the National Victim Assistance Academy (NVAA) launches its Advanced Topic Series.

2001

- There were 3,047 victims killed in the terrorists attacks on American soil on September 11.
- Congress responds to the attacks with a series of laws protecting the financial health of the airline industry, tax relief for victims, a special compensation fund and other protections.
- The USA Patriot Act is passed.

2002

- The National Association of VOCA Assistance Administrators is created to provide technical assistance and training to sate VOCA administrators.
- OVC sponsors a National Public Awareness and Education Campaign in conjunction with Justice Solutions, Parents of Murdered Children and the Victims' Assistance Legal Organization to promote the scope and availability of victims' rights and services nationwide.
- Congress appropriates approximately $20 million to fund services to trafficking victims.
- All 50 states, the District of Columbia, U.S. Virgin Islands Puerto Rico and Guam have established crime victim compensation programs.

2003

- OVC celebrates its twentieth anniversary of service to crime victims and those who assist them.
- Congress passes the PROTECT Act—also known as the "Amber Alert' law— which creates national network of AMBER (America's Missing: Broadcast Emergency Response) to facilitate rapid law enforcement and community response to kidnapped or abducted children.
- The American Society of Victimology (ASV) is established in Kansas City, Kansas.
- Congress passes the Prison Rape Elimination Act designed to track and address the issue of rape in correctional institutions.
- The United States Postal Service releases the Stop Family Violence postage stamp to raise money for domestic violence prevention programs.
- Congress appropriates $22 million to be used for awareness, intervention and prevention of domestic violence in the military.

2004

- Congress passes legislation defining aggravated identity theft and establishing penalty enhancements for the crime.

- October 12 marks the twentieth anniversary of the enactment of the Victims of Crime Act which has collected $6 billion for services to crime victims.
- Congress enacts the Justice for All Act which provides substantive rights for crime victims.

2005

- The U.S. Department of Justice established an online national sex offender registry that provides real time access to public sex offender data nationwide.
- Congress establishes the Victims' Rights Causus whose mission is to elevate crime victim issues in Congress without infringing on the rights of the accused.
- The American Bar Association releases "Elder Abuse Fatality Review Teams: A Replication Manual," whiich provides guidance for communities that want to establish Elder Abuse Fatality Review Teams.

Source: Adapted and modified from material compiled by the National Victim Center and U.S. Department of Justice Office for Victims of Crime, Victims' Assistance Legal Organization, Inc. (VALOR), and the many national, state and local victim services providers who offered documentation of their key victims' rights landmark activities.

VICTIMOLOGY-RELATED WEB SITES

Federal Agencies/Resources

Bureau of Justice Assistance	www.ojp.usdoj.gov/BJA
Bureau of Justice Statistics	www.ojp.usdoj.gov/bjs
Center for Substance Abuse Prevention	http://prevention.samhsa.gov
Center for Substance Abuse Treatment	http://csat.samhsa.gov
Centers for Disease Control and Prevention	www.cdc.gov
Federal Bureau of Investigation	www.fbi.gov
Uniform Crime Reports	www.fbi.gov/ucr/ucr.htm
Federal Judicial Center	www.fjc.gov
FirstGov	www.firstgov.gov
National Archive of Criminal Justice Data	www.icpsr.umich.edu/NACJD/index.html
National Clearinghouse for Alcohol and Drug Information	http://www.ncadi.samhsa.gov
National Criminal Justice Reference Service	www.ncjrs.org
National Highway Traffic Safety Administration	www.nhtsa.dot.gov
National Institute of Corrections	www.nicic.org
National Institute of Justice	www.ojp.usdoj.gov/nij
National Institute on Alcohol Abuse and Alcoholism	www.niaaa.nih.gov
National Institute on Drug Abuse	www.drugabuse.gov
National Sex Offender Registry	http://www.nsopr.gov/
Office for Victims of Crime	www.ovc.gov
Office of Community Oriented Policing Services	www.cops.usdoj.gov
Office for Justice Programs	www.ojp.usdoj.gov
Office of Juvenile Justice and Delinquency Prevention	www.ojjdp.ncjrs.org
Office of National Drug Control Policy	www.whitehousedrugpolicy.gov
Office on Violence Against Women	www.usdoj.gov/ovw/
Supreme Court of the United States	www.supremecourtus.gov
THOMAS: Federal Legislation	http://thomas.loc.gov
U.S. Department of Education, Higher Education Center for Alcohol and Other Drug Prevention	www.edc.org/hec
U.S. Department of Education Office of Safe and Drug-Free Schools	www.ed.gov/about/offices/list/osdfs
U.S. Department of Health and Human Services Grantsnet	www.hhs.gov/grantsnet

U.S. Department of Health and Human Services: Grants Information	www.hhs.gov/grants/index.shtml
U.S. Department of Health and Human Services, HRSA Funding Opportunities	www.hrsa.gov/grants/default.htm
U.S. Department of Justice	www.usdoj.gov
U.S. Department of State Bureau of Consular Affairs, Overseas Citizens Services Victim Assistance	http://travel.state.gov/travel/tips/emergencies/emergencies_1748.html
U.S. Department of Veterans Affairs National Center on PTSD	www.ncptsd.org
U.S. House of Representatives Victim's Rights Caucus	http://www.house.gov/poe/vrc/index.htm
U.S. Parole Commission	www.usdoj.gov/uspc

National Victim-Related Organizations

American Bar Association	
Center on Children and the Law	www.abanet.org/child
Commission on Domestic Violence	www.abanet.org/domviol
Commission on Law and Aging	www.abanet.org/aging
American Humane Association	www.americanhumane.org
American Professional Society on the Abuse of Children	www.apsac.org
Anti-Defamation League	www.adl.org
Asian Task Force Against Domestic Violence	www.atask.org
Battered Women's Justice Project	www.bwjp.org
Child Abuse Prevention Network	http://child-abuse.com
Childhelp USA	www.childhelpusa.org
Child Quest International	www.childquest.org
Child Welfare League of America	www.cwla.org
Concerns of Police Survivors	www.nationalcops.org
Family Violence & Sexual Assault Institute	www.fvsai.org
Family Violence Prevention Fund	http://endabuse.org
Institution on Domestic Violence in the African American Community	www.dvinstitute.org
Justice Solutions	www.justicesolutions.org
Mothers Against Drunk Driving	www.madd.org
National Alliance to End Sexual Violence	www.naesv.org
National Association of Crime Victim Compensation Boards	www.nacvcb.org
National Association of Social Workers	www.naswdc.org
National Association of VOCA Assistance Administrators	www.navaa.org
National Center for Missing & Exploited Children	www.missingkids.com
National Center for Victims of Crime	www.ncvc.org

National Center on Elder Abuse	www.elderabusecenter.org
National Children's Alliance	www.nca-online.org
National Clearinghouse on Child Abuse and Neglect Information	http://nccanch.acf.hhs.gov
National Coalition Against Domestic Violence	www.ncadv.org
National Coalition of Homicide Survivors	www.mivictims.org/nchs
National Court Appointed Special Advocates Association	www.nationalcasa.org
National Crime Victim Law Institute	http://www.lclark.edu/org/ncvli/
National Crime Victims Research and Treatment Center	www.musc.edu/cvc
National Fraud Information Center	www.fraud.org
National Insurance Crime Bureau	www.nicb.org
National MultiCultural Institute	www.nmci.org
National Network to End Domestic Violence	www.nnedv.org
National Organization Against Male Sexual Victimization	www.malesurvivor.org
National Organization for Victim Assisstance	www.trynova.org
National Organization of Parents Of Murdered Children, Inc.	www.pomc.com
National Resource Center on Domestic Violence	www.nrcdv.org
National School Safety Center	www.nssc1.org
National Sexual Violence Resource Center	www.nsvrc.org
National Victim Assistance Academy (OVC)	www.ojp.usdoj.gov/ovc/assist/vaa.htm
National Victim Assistance Academy (VALOR)	www.nvaa.org
National Victims' Rights Constitutional Amendment Network	www.nvcan.org
National Violence Against Women Prevention Research Center	www.vawprevention.org
Parents for Megan's Law	www.parentsformeganslaw.com
Prevent Child Abuse America	www.preventchildabuse.org
Rape, Abuse & Incest National Network	www.rainn.org
Safe Campuses Now	www.safecampusesnow.org
Safe NOW Project, Inc.	http://safenowcproject.org
Security on Campus, Inc.	www.securityoncampus.org
Stalking Resource Center	www.ncvc.org/src
Victims' Assistance Legal Organization (VALOR)	www.valor-national.org
Voices for America's Children	www.childadvocacy.org
Witness Justice	www.witnessjustice.org

National Criminal and Juvenile Justice- and Public Policy-Related Associations

American Center for Law and Justice	www.aclj.org
American Correctional Association	www.aca.org
American Correctional Health Services Association	www.corrections.com/achsa
American Council for Drug Education	www.acde.org

American Jail Association	www.corrections.com/aja
American Judges Association	http://aja.ncsc.dni.us
American Probation and Parole Association	www.appa-net.org
American Youth Policy Forum	www.aypf.org
Association for Conflict Resolution	www.acrnet.org
Association of Paroling Authorities International	www.apaintl.org
Association of State Correctional Administrators	www.asca.net
Balanced and Restorative Justice Project	www.barjproject.org
Center for Restorative Justice & Peacemaking	http://ssw.che.umn.edu/rip
Center for Sex Offender Management	www.csom.org
Center on Juvenile & Criminal Justice	www.cjcj.org
Coalition for Juvenile Justice	www.juvjustice.org
Community Anti-Drug Coalition Institute	http://cadca.org
Community Justice Exchange	www.communityjustice.org
Community Policing Consortium	www.communitypolicing.org
Correctional Educational Association	www.ceanational.org
Council of State Governments	www.csg.org
Governors Highway Safety Association	www.ghsa.org
Higher Education Center for Alcohol and Other Drug Prevention	www.edu.org/hec
Institute for Law and Justice	www.ilj.org
International Association of Campus Law Enforcement Administrators	www.iaclea.org
International Association of Chiefs of Police	www.theiacp.org
International Association of Reentry	http://www.reentry.cc/
Join Together	www.jointogether.org
National Association for Community Mediation	www.nafcm.org
National Association for Native American Children of Alcoholics	www.whitebison.org/nanacoa
National Association of Attorneys General	www.naag.org
National Association of Counties	www.naco.org
National Association of Court Management	www.nacmnet.org
National Association of Drug Court Professionals	www.nadcp.org
National Association of Police Organizations	www.napo.org
National Association of State Alcohol & Drug Abuse Directors	www.nasadad.org
National Association of State Judicial Educators	http://nasje.umn.edu
National Association of Women Judges	www.nawj.org
National Center on Addiction and Substance Abuse	www.casacolumbia.org
National Center for Neighborhood Enterprise	www.ncne.com
National Center for State Courts	www.ncsconline.org
National Conference of State Legislatures	www.ncsl.org
National Consortium for Justice Information and Statistics	www.search.org
National Council of Juvenile and Family Court Judges	www.ncjfcj.org

National Criminal Justice Association	www.ncja.com
National District Attorneys Association	www.ndaa-apri.org
National Governors Association	www.nga.com
National Indian Justice Center	www.nijc.indian.com
National Judicial College	www.judges.com
National Juvenile Detention Association	www.njda.com
National Law Enforcement and Corrections Technology Center	www.nlectc.org
National League of Cities	www.nlc.org
National Mental Health Association	www.nmha.org
National Organization of Black Law Enforcement Executives	www.noblenatl.org
National Sheriffs' Association	www.sheriffs.org
Partnership for a Drug-Free America	www.drugfreeamerica.org
Police Executive Research Forum	www.policeforum.org
Police Foundation	www.policefoundation.org
Restorative Justice Online	www.restorativejustice.org
Restorative Justice Project	www.fresno.edu/pacs/rjp
Southern Poverty Law Center	www.splcenter.org
State Justice Institute	www.statejustice.org
Victim Offender Mediation Association	www.voma.org

Source: OVC Victim Right Week Maternal (2006).

INDEX

National Center on Child Abuse
and Neglect (NCCAN), 186
National Child Abuse and Neglect
Data System (NCANDS),
186, 188
National Coalition Against Sexual
Assault, 17
National College Women Sexual
Victimization Study (NCWSV),
132, 142
National Committee for the
Prevention of Elder Abuse, 210
National Crime Information
Center, 148
National Crime Survey (NCS),
16, 27
National Crime Victimization
Survey (NCVS)
data included, 31
offenses included, 27, 31
questionnaire, 28–30f
sample size, 31
statistics, category-specific, 24
and Uniform Crime Reports,
compared, 31–32, 33
validity problems, 31
victimizations, as basic
measure, 28
National Family Violence Surveys,
34–35, 167
National Gay and Lesbian Task
Force Policy Institute, 251
National Highway Traffic Safety
Administration, 122
National Incidence Study on
Missing, Abducted, Runaway,
and Throwaway Children in
America (NISMART), 297–98
National Incident-Based Reporting
System (NIBRS), 27
National Institute of Justice, 19, 88,
161, 172, 173, 175
National Organization for Victim
Assistance (NOVA), 16, 85, 105
National Stalker and Domestic
Violence Reduction Act, 148
National Victims Center, 135–36
National Violence Against Women
Survey, 161
National White Collar Crime
Center, 92
The National Women's Study, 136
National Youth Gang Suppression
and Intervention, 260–61

Natural/biological sexual
harassment model, 151
Necessity, 279
Negligence
defined, 268, 270
elements of, 270–72
foreseeability, 271
proximate or legal cause of the
injury, 271
Network television, 100
Neutralization theory, 214–15
New Republic, 356
Newspapers
dailies and weeklies, 100
side bar stories, 100
wire services, 100
New York City Gay and Lesbian
AntiViolence Project, 255–56
New York Times, 139, 356
NiCarthy, G., 163
Ninth Circuit Court of
Appeals, 41
Nix v. *Whiteside*, 50
Nolo contendere, 53, 54
Nominal damages, 269
Nonfatal injuries, intangible
losses, 91
Nontraditional families, 252
Nonviolent crime
economic crime, 36
lack of attention to, 35
white-collar crime, 35–36
Norman Conquest of 1066, 5
Not guilty plea, 53, 54

O

Obsessive marital rapes, 145
Office for Victims of Crime (OVC),
18, 230, 289, 301–02
Office of Juvenile Justice and
Delinquency Programs, 187
Office of Overseas Citizens
Services, 289–90
Olweus, D., 259
Omaha Experiment, 174–75
"One-in-four" slogan, 142
Opening statement, 54–55
Opportunity model of
victimization, 13–14
Organizational sexual harassment
model, 151–52
Outing, 254
Owens v. *City of Independence*, 319

P

Pacific Sociological Association, 199
Pagelow, M. D., 182, 199
Painter, S. L., 163–64
Palzer, Lawrence, 201
Pape, Monroe v., 318
Parens patrea, 46
Parental child abductions, 297–99
Parents of Murdered Children
(POMC), 17
Parole, 51
Parricide, 119
Parrish v. *Luckie*, 322
Parties involved, criminal justice
process
correctional system, 50–51
courts, 50
defense attorneys, 49–50
law enforcement, 47–48
perpetrators, 47
prosecutors, 47–48
victims, 47
Patriarchy, 7
Patterns in Forcible Rape (Amir), 14
Paul C. A., Constant A. v., 254–55
Payne, Pervis Tyrone, 353
Payne v. *Tennessee*, 353–55
Pepper, Claude, 211
Peremptory challenges, 54
Pernanem, K., 167
Perpetrators, 47
Personalistic theory of child
neglect, 193
Personal jurisdiction, 63
Physical child abuse, 192
"chance events", 192
character-trait model, 192
child fatalities, 186
defined, 182–83
environmental-sociological-
cultural model, 192–93
environmental stress model, 192
family structure model, 192
historical background, 185
infanticide, 185
interactional model, 192
mental illness model, 192
psychodynamic model, 192
psychopathological model,
191–92
psychosocial systems model, 193
role of the child, 192
social learning model, 193

Victim-offender mediation (VOM), 73–74
Victim-Offender Reconciliation Program (VORP), 73
Victimologia, 285
Victimology, 285
Victimology
as academic discipline, x, 2–3, 367
defined, 3
ethical standards, 369–70
and family violence, ix
historical development, 2
international aspects of. *see* International victimology
Karmen's theory, 12
multidisciplinary perspective, ix, 12
professionalism within, 367–68
related Web sites, listed, 384–88
theories, 9–16. *see also* Theories, victimology
Victim perception concept (Wolfgang and Amir), 14
Victims and Media Program, Michigan State University School of Journalism, 102–03
Victims' Bill of Rights, 17
Victim services, as cost of crime, 90
Victims of Crime Act (VOCA)
Crime Victims Fund, 111–12, 336–37
"Son of Sam" provision, 337
and victims' rights movement, 18
Victims' rights
Code of Hammurabi, 4
conservatism, 1980s and 1990s, 8–9
information, 47
privacy, 47
social forces affecting, 6–9
U.S. Constitution, 15
Victims' Rights Constitutional Amendment, 17, 18, 105
Victims' rights movement
beginnings of, 8–9, 16
critical dates in, 371–83
lack of funding, 16–17
professionalism and training issues, 17, 18–19

public awareness, 17–18, 19
specialized groups, separation into, 17
Victim typologies
Mendelsohn's, 9
von Hentig's, 10–11
Vinson, Meritor Savings Bank v., 151
Violence, defined, 34
Violence Against Women Act (VAWA), 19
background, 323
gender-based civil rights, 323–24
Violence in the media theory for school violence, 258
Violent Crime Control and Law Enforcement Act, 19
Violent crimes
clinical studies, 35
costs of, 89–90
decline in, 31
reporting of, 26
Virginia McMartin Preschool, 201
Visionary type serial murderers, 120
Voir dire examination, 54, 68
von Hentig, Hans, 10–11, 285, 286
von Hentig's theory of victimization
the activating sufferer, 11
general classes of victims, 10
psychological types of victims, 10–11
von Hirsh, Andrew, 56

W

Wade, Baker v., 255
Wade, Smith v., 322
Wainwright, Gideon v., 49
Walkate, S., 14
Walker, Lenore E., 162–63
Walker, Steven, 369
Wall Street Journal, 356
Washington Post, 356
Waterman, C. K., 251
Watson v. *City of Kansas City*, 320
Weapons of mass destruction, 289
Weatherburn, Peter, 251

Web sites, related victimology, 384–88
Weiner, L., 152
Weiner, Neil Alan, 35
White-collar crime
definitions, 35–36
disaster fraud, 92
email fraud, 93
identity theft, 92–93
software piracy, 92
telemarketing fraud, 93
UCR exclusion of, 27
Whiteside, Nix v., 50
Whitman, Charles, 120
Widom, C. S., 191
Wiggins, M. E., 233
Williams, D., 193
William the Conqueror, 5
William v. *Florida*, 54
Wilson, A. Y., 119
Wilson, Mary Ellen, 185
Wire services, 100
Wisconsin v. *Mitchell*, 229–30
Wolf, R. S., 212, 213
Wolfgang, Marvin E., 12
Wolfgang's study of homicide, 12, 14, 118
Women. *see also* Feminist movement; Rape
dependency, 165–66
discrimination and violence against, 6–8, 19
hate crimes against, 229
sexual victimization of, 7–8
shelters for abused, 161
World Society of Victimology (WSV), 285
Writ of Certiorari, 44
Wrongful death, 272–73
Wrongful death statutes, 272

Y

Yllo, Kersti, 144, 145
Young, Marlene, 286

Z

Zona, Michael A., 35